ANTISLAVERY, ABOLITION, AND THE ATLANTIC WORLD
R. J. M. Blackett and James Brewer Stewart, Editors

NO TAINT OF COMPROMISE

Crusaders in Antislavery Politics

FREDERICK J. BLUE

Louisiana State University Press
BATON ROUGE

Designer: Amanda McDonald Scallan
Typeface: Sabon
Typesetter: G & S Typesetters, Inc.
Printer and binder: Thomson-Shore, Inc.

Library of Congress Cataloging-in-Publication Data

Blue, Frederick J.
  No taint of compromise : crusaders in antislavery politics / Frederick J.
Blue.
    p. cm. — (Antislavery, abolition, and the Atlantic world)
  Includes bibliographical references and index.
  ISBN 0-8071-2976-3 (alk. paper)
  1. Antislavery movements—United States—History—19th century.
2. Abolitionists—United States—Political activity.   I. Title.   II. Series.
E449.B67   2004
973.7'114—dc22

                                                              2004011063

Letters from Alvan Stewart are cited by courtesy of the New York State
Historical Association, Cooperstown, New York, and the New-York
Historical Society (Alvan Stewart Papers).

For my four wonderful grandkids,
Claire, Dylan, Alex, and Tiffany

CONTENTS

Contents

PREFACE

IN 1862, INDIANA Republican George Washington Julian narrowly won re-election to the House of Representatives in the face of conservative Republican opposition and a major Democratic challenge. Years later he looked back proudly on that victory and suggested that "my triumph had no taint of compromise." He had refused to back down on his political antislavery principles. Julian's victory came at a time when President Abraham Lincoln had just announced his Preliminary Proclamation of Emancipation, beginning the process of converting a war to save the Union into one to end slavery. For those like Julian, who were committed to destroying slavery through the political process, almost a quarter century of agitation appeared on the verge of a successful climax. The political attack on slavery had begun in the late 1830s with the first challenge to William Lloyd Garrison, who opposed voting, the seeking of public office, or the support of any political party. Political agitation had progressed slowly, first through the abolitionist Liberty party and then, in 1848, to the more moderate Free Soil party, which was committed only to preventing the expansion of slavery beyond the existing slave states. The Republican party of the 1850s had continued the Free Soil approach, but slave state secession and the Civil War led the majority in the party to adopt the original Liberty party goal of abolition. In 1862, the process appeared to be nearing completion, and, for those like Julian, it was a time to celebrate their victory.

The Indiana congressman was one of a group of political antislavery leaders whose numbers had grown dramatically through the 1840s and 1850s.

A few had been idealists who sometimes had naively assumed that achieving emancipation and equal rights for all African Americans might require only a minimal amount of agitation. Most, however, were astute realists who understood that it would be a long struggle in the face of the intransigence of southern slaveholders and their many northern allies. They understood that winning voter support would be a protracted effort in convincing not only their active opponents but also the vast numbers who more passively preferred the status quo to an attack on racial inequities.

By the mid-1840s, a growing number of northerners believed that the campaign against slavery could best achieve its goal by using the political process. On the other hand, the Garrisonian approach to abolition continued to stress nonresistance and opposition to the political route, and its advocates talked increasingly of disunion rather than political debate and ballot. In sharp contrast, politicians like Julian believed that the political arena could best win increasing numbers of converts and an eventual end of slavery. While they, on occasion, had sacrificed some of their antislavery beliefs and adjusted their approach to suit realistic goals, they never compromised on the need for a political attack on slavery. And as the war continued, some (but not all) sought to expand their goal to include the right to military service in Union armies and suffrage for the black population. This is a study of the varieties of American antislavery political leadership—of those men and women who insisted that politics was the best road to abolition and equal rights.

ACKNOWLEDGMENTS

ANTISLAVERY POLITICAL LEADERS were a diverse group, and my choice to study and write about them led me to seek the assistance of an equally diverse group of historians, all of whom willingly lent their time and expertise. Among those who provided invaluable suggestions with the specific subjects of this study were Hugh Davis of Southern Connecticut State University; Michael Pierson of the University of Massachusetts, Lowell; Michael McManus of Madison, Wisconsin; Roland Baumann, Archivist at Oberlin College; Bill and Jane Ann Moore of the Lovejoy Society; Jonathan Earle of the University of Kansas; and Jack Patrick and Diane Barnes of Youngstown State University. Their knowledge of one or more of my subjects provided all-important insight.

Several historians made important suggestions as I formulated the project and decided who were the most appropriate individuals to study. Especially helpful in this regard were Daniel Feller of the University of Tennessee and Stanley Harrold of South Carolina State University. James Stewart of Macalester College and R. J. M. Blackett of Vanderbilt University, the series editors, read the entire manuscript and offered important suggestions on how to tighten the focus and approach. Dominic J. Capeci of Southwest Missouri State University has read and critiqued virtually everything I have written over more than thirty-five years of research; with this study he offered his usual constructive criticisms and encouragement, keeping me on target whatever the obstacle. I am forever grateful for his constant assistance and steady friendship.

Acknowledgments

Youngstown State University provided necessary assistance with a faculty improvement leave and additional released time away from the classroom for research. The university's library staff, especially Amy Kyte, Mary Ann Johnson, Ellen Banks, Brian Brennan, and Debra Beronja, went out of their way to help me track down obscure and elusive sources. Several individuals in the history department offered much-needed help along the way, including Bonnie Harris and graduate assistants David Swader and Joseph DiBlasio. My colleague William Jenkins offered steady encouragement and suggested the book's title.

For their permission to quote from letters of Alvan Stewart in their possession, I am most grateful to the New-York Historical Society, New York City, and the New York State Historical Association, Cooperstown.

Maureen Hewitt, Sylvia Frank Rodrigue, and Lee Sioles of the Louisiana State University Press provided all-important direction and guidance in seeing the project through to completion. Thanks also to John Quist of Shippensburg University, who reviewed the manuscript and offered supportive and constructive comments.

Most of all, my wife, Judy, was always caring and understanding throughout the many months required to complete what at times seemed to both of us to be an endless project. For her support and companionship I will always be grateful.

CAST OF CHARACTERS

ALVAN STEWART (September 1, 1790–May 1, 1849). New York Liberty party leader, among the founders of the party; refused to abandon Liberty party with Free Soil party formation; attorney; argued that the U.S. Constitution was an antislavery document.

JOHN GREENLEAF WHITTIER (December 17, 1807–September 7, 1892). Massachusetts poet, abolitionist, and journalist; among original Massachusetts Liberty party leaders; joined Free Soil and Republican parties; corresponding editor for Free Soil–Republican journal *National Era*.

CHARLES HENRY LANGSTON (1817–December 14, 1892). Born in Virginia to a black mother who had been a slave and a white father; moved to Chillicothe, Ohio, in 1834; attended Oberlin College; supported Free Soil and Republican parties; worked for repeal of Ohio black laws; convicted for role in Oberlin-Wellington slave rescue case, 1858–1859.

OWEN LOVEJOY (January 6, 1811–March 25, 1864). Brother of Elijah Lovejoy, born in Albion, Maine; Congregational minister in Princeton, Illinois; joined Liberty, Free Soil, and Republican parties; served in Congress as Republican from 1857 until death; friend of Lincoln.

SHERMAN M. BOOTH (September 25, 1812–August 10, 1904). Born in New York; Yale graduate, 1841; helped organize Liberty party in Connecticut; moved to Wisconsin in 1848; Free Soiler and Republican; convicted for role in Glover slave rescue case.

JANE GREY SWISSHELM (December 6, 1815–July 22, 1884). Journalist and reformer; published *Saturday Visiter* in Pittsburgh; supported Free Soil party; moved to St. Cloud, Minnesota, in 1857; edited *St. Cloud Democrat* and continued antislavery agitation.

GEORGE WASHINGTON JULIAN (May 5, 1817–July 7, 1899). Indiana Quaker; left Whigs to join Free Soil and then Republican parties; vice presidential candidate of Free Soilers in 1852; member of House of Representatives, 1849–1851; Radical leader in House, 1861–1871.

DAVID WILMOT (January 20, 1814–March 16, 1868). Pennsylvania Democrat; member of Barnburner faction; authored Wilmot Proviso in 1846; worked with New York Free Soilers; helped form Republican party in Pennsylvania; elected to U.S. Senate during Civil War.

BENJAMIN AND EDWARD WADE. Benjamin: (October 27, 1800–1878). Ohio Whig; refused to join Free Soilers; elected to Senate in 1851; joined Republicans; remained in Senate until 1868; chair, Committee on the Conduct of the War. Edward: (November 22, 1802–August 13, 1866). Cleveland attorney and Liberty party leader; elected to Congress as a Free Soiler and Republican, served 1853–1861.

JESSIE BENTON FRÉMONT (May 31, 1824–December 27, 1902). Born in Virginia; at age seventeen, married John C. Frémont; active supporter and organizer of his presidential campaign of 1856; endorsed his order to free Missouri slaves belonging to Confederates; supported his presidential efforts in 1864.

NO TAINT OF COMPROMISE

NO TAINT OF COMPROMISE
Varieties of Antislavery Political Leadership

THE ANTISLAVERY MOVEMENT was never monolithic. Reformers rarely are of a single mind, and abolitionists were especially prone to division. Indeed, there was seldom unity when strong personalities debated the attack on slavery. Perhaps the most divisive issue was the wisdom of working within the political structure to attack slavery. Much has been written of the efforts of William Lloyd Garrison and his legions to work outside of the party system and to resist the efforts of those who disagreed. At first those opposed to the Garrison approach worked within the two-party system to challenge the stance of the major parties, but many reluctantly concluded that Democrats and Whigs, with their strong southern wings, could not be moved and that only a third party could affect change. Yet James G. Birney won a meager seven thousand votes as the Liberty party presidential candidate in 1840, the first third-party effort to attack slavery. That number was a tiny fraction of the abolitionists, most of whom sat out the election, believing participation would compromise antislavery principle. Others, more inclined to politics, stayed within the two-party system and voted for the Whigs and William Henry Harrison. Even when Birney's vote increased to sixty-two thousand in 1844, the vast majority of abolitionists refused to participate or voted Whig.[1] These differences have been described in detail by historians, many of them biographers of abolitionists.[2]

1. Birney's 1840 vote of 7,069 represented roughly 0.3 percent of the 2.4 million votes cast. In 1844, the Liberty party received 2.3 percent of the 2.7 million votes. In both cases most of the approximately 250,000 members of abolition societies rejected any role in politics.

2. The literature dealing with the abolition movement is immense, both biographical and organizational. Among the first to address the issue of Garrison versus the political abolition-

In contrast, this study examines those who believed that the political system was the best means to attack slavery, yet came to that conclusion for different reasons and approached politics from varying perspectives. Some entered politics through the Liberty and Free Soil parties, having first opposed political action completely. Others came out of the two-party structure to bolt either the Democratic or Whig organizations because southern control—or what they called "The Slave Power"[3]—prevented any real movement toward either abolition or stopping the spread of slavery. Not surprisingly, they rarely agreed on the best approach, although most finally coalesced in the Republican party of the mid-1850s.

This inquiry looks at representatives of the full spectrum of opinions and approaches to antislavery politics.[4] It begins with those who formed or later joined the abolitionist Liberty party during its eight-year history from 1840

---

ists was Louis Filler's *The Crusade Against Slavery, 1830–1860* (New York: Harper and Row, 1960), especially pages 137–59. See also Aileen Kraditor, *Means and Ends in American Abolitionism: Garrison and His Critics on Strategy and Tactics, 1834–1850* (New York: Pantheon Books, 1969). Kraditor argues persuasively that Garrison gradually relented in his opposition to political antislavery. Although he could never bring himself to vote, he showed a greater understanding of the Free Soil and Republican parties in the years between 1848 and 1865 than he had of the Liberty party in the early 1840s. See especially pages 170–4.

3. The concept of the Slave Power dated back to the 1780s, especially because of the inclusion in the Constitution of the three-fifths clause granting slave states additional seats in the House of Representatives for their nonvoting slave populations. As widely used before the Civil War, it came to mean the alliance of southerners in Congress with northern Democrats, which gave the South influence beyond its numbers, often in return for patronage rewards. In the 1850s, it included weak northern presidents, Franklin Pierce and James Buchanan, who gave into southern demands. The concept is traced by Leonard L. Richards, *The Slave Power: The Free North and Southern Domination, 1780–1860* (Baton Rouge: Louisiana State Univ. Press, 2000). Larry Gara's "Slavery and the Slave Power: A Crucial Distinction," *Civil War History* 15 (March 1969): 5–18, notes the difference between abolitionists' moral opposition to slavery and the growing northern attack on southern political power resulting from the willingness of significant numbers of northern Democrats to yield to southern demands. Hereafter, the term Slave Power will be used throughout this study without quotation marks.

4. The concept for this study was suggested by the work of Jane and William Pease in *Bound With Them in Chains: A Biographical History of the Antislavery Movement* (Westport, Conn.: Greenwood Press, 1972), which includes examples of both nonpolitical and political abolitionists. The Peases put the emphasis on Garrisonians of the 1830s but provide an important contribution to the overall antislavery movement. A collection of essays edited by Alan M. Kraut, *Crusaders and Compromisers: Essays on the Relationship of the Antislavery Struggle to the Antebellum Party System* (Westport, Conn.: Greenwood Press, 1983), takes a nonbiographical approach yet is valuable in raising issues vital to an understanding of the political antislavery movement.

to 1848. It then examines antislavery advocates who waited until the formation in 1848 of the more moderate Free Soilers, who advocated containing slavery within its present state boundaries and not permitting its expansion to the territories. Finally, this study will focus on reformers who declined to leave the two-party system and waited until the demise of the Whigs in the 1850s to join the Republicans. That party, the newest entry to the two-party system, like the Free Soilers, urged the containment of slavery rather than its immediate abolition. Members believed that the central government must divorce itself from any responsibility to protect slavery, whether it be in the District of Columbia, in federal territories, or through the return of fugitives.

The approach in *No Taint of Compromise* focuses on those who were not necessarily the most prominent political antislavery leaders, but rather individuals who played critical as opposed to central roles in each of the three northern-centered antislavery parties. Rather than looking at much-studied dominant leaders, such as Abraham Lincoln, Frederick Douglass, and Charles Sumner, it will focus on those who undertook the yeoman's work in organizing parties, holding conventions and rallies, editing antislavery newspapers, and, in general, agitating slave-related issues. None of them has been the subject of a modern scholarly biography during the last fifteen years, and several have never received the attention of a biographer.

This history addresses the issues of motivation, antislavery ideology, and commitment to attacking slavery as well as the granting of basic rights to emancipated African Americans, including enfranchisement and service in the Union army. Religious faith, for example, motivated many antislavery advocates who preferred to work within established Protestant denominations, or, feeling those churches to be controlled by proslavery elements, sought more reform-minded independent congregations. They could agree that slavery violated God's moral law and hence required the concerted efforts of people of faith both within and outside of the established churches. They differed in their views of the Constitution and its role in protecting slavery. They rarely agreed with Garrison that it was a proslavery instrument, arguing instead that it offered no protection to slavery beyond the existing slave states. Some even argued it should be construed as an antislavery document. Many also saw other abuses to be attacked. Hence the analysis briefly deals with a host of other reforms—including temperance, women's rights, land reform, and peace—that many advocated.

These reformers shared many traits, and their lives often intersected. A surprising degree of cooperation, communication, and interaction occurred between and among them, sometimes connecting several individuals whom one might assume had little or no contact with one another. This was especially true, but not limited to, those who served together in Congress. At times they clashed even as they struggled with Garrisonians to convince northern voters that the political approach was the best way to address the Slave Power. Yet despite differences, they often displayed a remarkable unity and commonality of purpose and formed close relationships. The varieties of antislavery politics were numerous and ranged in intensity and degree of commitment. Virtually all believed that slavery was a moral evil. Although dedicated to the goal of ending the South's peculiar institution, they occasionally revealed economic self-interests or concern for status.

Despite their differences, diverse styles and motivations seldom prevented them from focusing on the need to convince northern voters that slavery's end could best be accomplished through the political process. Only rarely did they alter their political tactics as they faced the scorn of both Garrisonians on the one hand, and those opposed to any form of antislavery activity on the other. It is true that on occasion they moderated previously held principles to accommodate a less advanced stance, as when Liberty members became Free Soilers and had to abandon immediate abolitionism in favor of the containment of slavery; but never did they abandon their commitment to the political approach. There was, in the words of George Washington Julian, "no taint of compromise" in their dedication to ending slavery and resisting the Slave Power.[5]

The first to act on their antislavery convictions were those who helped form the Liberty party in 1840. Alvan Stewart and John Greenleaf Whittier represent the small group which defied Garrison's belief in the immorality of politics and the futility of working within the political system. In helping to form the third party, dedicated exclusively to abolitionism, they also faced first the silence and then the scorn of Democrats and Whigs who sought to maintain their national constituencies by avoiding a definitive stand on slavery. Stewart, perhaps the most obscure of the eleven individuals under study, was an attorney and abolitionist, born on a farm near South Granville, New York, in 1790. Deeply affected by the religious revivals of Charles G. Finney, he came to abolitionism in part through his evangelical convictions. In 1835 he helped to form the New York State Anti-Slavery Society, and at the end of the decade he broke with the Garrisonians in helping to organize the Al-

5. George W. Julian, *Political Recollections, 1840–1872* (Chicago: Jansen, McClurg, and Co., 1884), 216.

4

bany convention of April 1, 1840, which brought forth the Liberty party. Twice he accepted the largely symbolic third-party candidacy for governor. Unusual among abolitionists, he argued that the Constitution should be interpreted as an antislavery document, rather than one which sanctioned slavery in the states. Unlike most Liberty partisans, Stewart stood by Liberty abolitionist principles in 1847 and 1848 and resisted joining the more moderate Free Soil party. He died in 1849, still professing his political abolitionist beliefs.

Like Stewart, John Greenleaf Whittier came to abolition politics through his religious faith, in his case Quaker beliefs and moral conviction of slavery's evil which he expressed in poetry and essays. Born on a farm near Haverhill, Massachusetts, he emerged as an abolitionist poet through the assistance of William Lloyd Garrison, who published Whittier's first poem in 1826. Initially a Whig, Whittier served briefly in the Massachusetts legislature, but soon broke with that party over its temporizing on slavery. Editing a series of antislavery journals, he used his literary abilities along with his belief in the antislavery legislative approach to become a founding member of the Massachusetts Liberty party in 1840. Whittier's poetic and political careers continued to compliment each other through the 1840s, as he moved with most Massachusetts Liberty people to the Free Soil party in 1848. During that party's six-year history, his chief political contribution was as a corresponding editor of the Free Soil and later Republican journal *The National Era,* advocating a strong political response to what he regarded as the proslavery policies of Democrats and Whigs. By the late 1850s Whittier's active role in antislavery politics declined, even as his written attacks on slavery increased. During the Civil War he overcame his Quaker pacifism to support what he deemed the war to end slavery.

Because of their race, African Americans typically had little opportunity to participate in pre–Civil War American politics. Denied the right to vote or to hold elective office in virtually all states in the North, they found themselves limited to work in black communities and, peripherally, in antislavery political parties. One of those who used his opportunities to their fullest was Charles Henry Langston. The son of a black mother and white plantation owner, he was born in Virginia in 1817; following his parents' death in 1834 he moved with his brothers to Chillicothe, Ohio. Langston was educated in the segregated schools of Ohio, and he entered Oberlin in 1841. Deeply motivated by Christian convictions, he and his brother John Mercer Langston played an active role in Ohio's Negro Convention Movement of the 1840s and 1850s, which consistently sought political rights for black Ohioans and urged voters to support the Liberty, Free Soil, and Republican parties. Charles Langston was perhaps best known for violating the Fugitive Slave Act of 1850 to aid the escape of fugitive John Price. Following his conviction in the Oberlin-Wellington slave rescue case of 1858, he delivered an impassioned courtroom speech deploring the lack of equality endured by northern blacks. During the Civil War he actively recruited black troops for the Union and opened a school for the freed population in Leavenworth, Kansas, while his better-known brother John went on to a career in Congress. Charles spent his remaining years in Lawrence, Kansas, as a farmer and grocer, playing an integral part in the postwar efforts to gain equality for African Americans.

Owen Lovejoy, too, was overshadowed by his better-known brother, the martyred abolitionist Elijah. Owen, born in 1811 in Albion, Maine, moved to Illinois to be with Elijah just prior to his murder by an antiabolition mob in Alton in 1837. Long committed to a career in the ministry, Lovejoy became the pastor of the Princeton, Illinois, Congregational Church in 1843. His religious convictions reinforced his devotion to an active role in the Underground Railroad of northern Illinois. Like Stewart, he believed that the Constitution did not sanction slavery. He joined the Liberty party as its unsuccessful candidate for Congress in 1846. In 1848, he attended the Free Soil convention in Buffalo and again ran for Congress as a third-party candidate. Reluctantly abandoning his abolition stance in favor of containment, he opposed Stephan A. Douglas's Kansas-Nebraska Act in 1854 and was a founder of the Illinois Republican party in the mid-1850s. A close friend and associate of Abraham Lincoln, he was finally elected to Congress as a Republican in 1856, serving until his death in 1864. Before and during the Civil War Lovejoy engaged in numerous heated exchanges with proslavery members of the House. He urged President Lincoln to move beyond the goal of saving the Union to include abolition and equality for African Americans even as he defended the president for moving slowly on these issues. His efforts included urging the use of black troops in Union armies and greater equality for free blacks.

Another early participant in the Liberty party politics, albeit more representative of the Free Soil–Republican position of containment, was Sherman M. Booth of Wisconsin. Booth represents the transition in the political spectrum to a more limited approach to antislavery, yet within the sphere of this form of antislavery politics his devotion to principle was just as deep as that of other Liberty members. Especially was this true regarding runaway slaves, for Booth (like Langston) became the center of a court case involving the federal Fugitive Slave Act and went to remarkable extremes to resist the law's enforcement. Born in 1812 in Davenport, New York, Booth became a temperance lecturer before graduating from Yale in 1841. While in college he helped organize New Haven's small Liberty party and after graduation became its Connecticut agent. In May 1848 he moved to Wisconsin and took charge of the party's journal, *The American Freeman.* With other Wisconsin Liberty men he gladly accepted the fusion of the party into the Free Soil movement and attended the new party's Buffalo convention in August 1848. More comfortable in a party which rejected abolition for containment, Booth quickly emerged as an influential and controversial Free Soil and then Republican leader. A forceful speaker and writer, he led the state's defiance of the Fugitive Slave Act of 1850 as well as spearheaded efforts to prevent Free Soilers from returning to their old parties, as many did in the atmosphere of compromise between 1849 and 1853. When fugitive slave Joshua Glover was arrested in 1854, Booth was a key participant in forcing his release and aiding in his escape to Canada. Using that incident and the passage of the Kansas-Nebraska Act, Booth led the drive to form the state's Republican party in 1854. Tried, convicted, and jailed for his role in the Glover case, Booth benefitted from the state supreme court's declaring of the federal fugitive law to be unconstitutional in 1855. In part due to Booth's influence, the state's Republican party was perhaps as radical on slave and race-related issues during the 1850s as any in the North. Booth's final success on racial issues was in helping to secure the right of black men to vote in Wisconsin in 1866.

The conventional means of measuring political influence would eliminate both black and white women from consideration since women could not vote or hold office in any state before the Civil War. Yet such a measure is clearly insufficient, for women did have an impact on the political world through various forms of agitation, including editorials, oratory, and behind-the-scenes pressure. Women had long been members of the abolition movement, beginning in New England and spreading to the states of the Old Northwest. Yet through the 1830s and 1840s most women who took up the cause of slaves did so as Garrisonians, opposing the direct political party approach to antislavery. Active participants in the petition campaigns of the 1830s, they also assisted fugitive slaves, played a significant role in fundraising efforts, such as antislavery fairs conducted to support abolition, and were constant moral voices in their churches, challenging ministers and members alike to stand up against slavery and the Slave Power. Reform-minded women also took up their own cause and frequently put economic, social, legal, and political equality with men ahead of the cause of antislavery. Seeking the right to vote, however, usually did not mean using the vote to support an antislavery party. Thus the women's rights movement could detract from rather than augment the political antislavery movement. Black women, especially, were rarely political activists, preferring to concentrate on the more pressing need of direct aid to fugitives and those still in bondage. Yet for a significant number of women, political activism, if not direct political participation, was a realistic alternative to the Garrisonian approach to antislavery. Many became involved through their churches, pressuring ministers and all-male governing boards to take a more pronounced stand against slavery. Especially in the 1850s after the passage of the Fugitive Slave and Kansas-Nebraska acts, along with growing southern insistence on the positive good argument in defense of slavery, women championed the cause of the Republican party and campaigned actively or behind the scenes for its candidates. Especially did women respond to the candidacy of John C. Frémont, due in part to the appeal of his ambitious wife, Jessie.[6]

One woman who reached thousands of northerners with her attacks on slavery through the Free Soil and Republican parties was Jane Grey Swisshelm. Born near Pittsburgh in 1815, she was raised in the strict Covenanter tradition of the Presbyterian Church and embraced the belief that slavery was incompatible with Christianity. Before her stormy marriage to James Swisshelm ended in divorce, his business had brought the couple to Louisville for two years, providing her with what few abolitionists could claim, direct contact with slavery. She was especially horrified by slavery's impact on female slaves and the tragedy it brought to black families. Returning to Pittsburgh, she became a journalist, first writing for an abolitionist newspaper and then beginning her *Saturday Visiter,* which she published for the next six years. She enthusiastically endorsed Free Soil candidates Martin Van Buren and John P. Hale in 1848 and 1852 and built up a substantial circulation for the *Visiter.* She was a vehement opponent of the Fugitive Slave Act, and also supported women's equality, especially property and political rights. Yet she insisted that the cause of women and antislavery should be

6. The role of women in all aspects of the antislavery movement is described in Julie Roy Jeffrey, *The Great Silent Army of Abolitionism: Ordinary Women in the Antislavery Movement* (Chapel Hill: Univ. of North Carolina Press, 1998).

kept as separate issues, believing that if sought together one might detract from the other. When her paper failed financially, she moved to St. Cloud, Minnesota, where she battled with local proslavery politicians and began the *St. Cloud Democrat,* using it to support the Republican party, Lincoln's presidency, emancipation, and the Union war effort. During these years she lectured on both women's rights and abolition. After the war she published yet another paper, the *Reconstructionist,* to support the Republican program of Reconstruction and attack that of President Andrew Johnson. Throughout her colorful life she was a constant champion of the separate issues of antislavery and racial equality on the one hand, and women's rights on the other.

As the spectrum of political antislavery moves to more traditional party interests, it includes those who began in the two-party system but left it to become Free Soilers. The party formed in 1848 included not only most Liberty activists (with the exception of those like Alvan Stewart who refused to give up abolitionism), but others who abandoned either the Whig or Democratic parties to come to Buffalo to challenge the major parties' refusal to oppose the spread of slavery. Key among this group was a Massachusetts faction known as the Conscience Whigs, which included Charles Sumner and Charles Francis Adams. A less visible group of antislavery Whigs from the Old Northwest, led by Joshua Giddings of Ohio, also included an Indiana Quaker soon to be prominent as both a Free Soiler and a Republican, George Washington Julian. Born in the eastern Indiana town of Centerville in 1817, Julian studied law and was elected to the state legislature in 1845 as a Whig. Motivated by his Quaker upbringing and the teachings of the Unitarian theologian William Ellery Channing, he saw slavery as a moral evil. Thus, his logical break with the Whigs in 1848 to join the new Free Soil party. Elected to Congress in 1849, Julian resisted the atmosphere of compromise and maintained his third-party loyalties, being rewarded with the Free Soil vice presidential nomination in 1852. In the mid-1850s he assumed a prominent role in the movement for homestead legislation, which he saw as another means to halt the spread of slavery, for if small farmers took land in the territories, then slaveholders could not. In 1860, he won the first of five consecutive terms in Congress as a Republican, dedicated to the destruction of slavery. A member of the Committee on the Conduct of the War, Julian was among those who constantly prodded Abraham Lincoln to move more quickly on emancipation and rights for free blacks. In 1872, he joined the Liberal Republican movement when he concluded that the Republican party had deserted its Reconstruction policies and its commitment to equal rights for African Americans. For Julian, party labels were far less important than reform in behalf of slaves, free blacks, and the landless.

The largest group in the Free Soil coalition of 1848 was antislavery Democrats, the majority being New Yorkers. When the national party rejected their demand that slavery be denied the right to expand, they bolted to lead the new third party. In this decision they had endorsed the Wilmot Proviso introduced in Congress in 1846 by Democratic representative David Wilmot to prevent the spread of slavery into territories that might be acquired from Mexico. Born in Bethany, Pennsylvania, in 1814, Wilmot rose in politics as a Jacksonian Democrat and was elected to Congress in 1844. With his Proviso still pending in Congress, he joined the New York antislavery Democrats in supporting the new Free Soil organization committed to preventing the spread of slavery. For Wilmot, the containment concept was primarily a means to the Jacksonian goal of equality of opportunity to protect the interests of his own constituents, the small white farmers who might seek land in new territories; it was also a way to bring an eventual end to slavery. It was clear to Wilmot that the evil of slavery could affect whites as well as blacks, Pennsylvanians as well as Virginians. Unlike others in this study, he was only secondarily concerned with the inhumanity of slavery and the plight of slaves themselves; his small farming constituents received most of his attention. Because Free Soil strength in Pennsylvania was limited, he never officially left the Democratic party, and thus proslavery Democrats led by James Buchanan were able to prevent his renomination for Congress in 1850. Needing a place in the two-party system to have any hope of building an antislavery constituency for his own political advancement, Wilmot faithfully supported Democrat Franklin Pierce for president in 1852. Passage of the Kansas-Nebraska Act in 1854 led him finally to leave the party and assume a leading role in formation of the new Republican party. Wilmot campaigned enthusiastically for John C. Frémont in 1856 and Abraham Lincoln in 1860, and he served in the Senate during the early years of the Civil War. There he took special pleasure in the 1862 act that adopted his Proviso's principle and banned slavery in all Federal territories. Wilmot had approached the antislavery movement from a traditional two-party position, worked with the Free Soilers briefly, and reentered the two-party system as a Republican committed to containment and finally wartime abolition. His was thus a genuine and consistent concern for slavery's impact on small farmers and workers more than it was about African Americans.

Some dedicated antislavery advocates refused to cooperate with third-party antislavery movements, believing that the best way to forward the cause was from within the two-party system. Benjamin Franklin Wade was such a man, spending his entire political life as a Whig and then a Republican. In so doing, he broke with his less prominent brother Edward, who approached antislavery from within the Liberty and Free Soil parties before becoming a Republican. The Wade brothers thus offer a sharp contrast in political antislavery methods. In the political antislavery spectrum, Benjamin represents a unique approach compared to the others in this study: while his ideological position was similar to that of Lovejoy, Julian, and several others, including his brother Edward, his political strategy was to work within the two-party system. Both Wade brothers were born in rural Massachusetts, Benjamin in 1800 and Edward in 1802. When the family migrated to Ohio in 1821, they lived first in Andover in the Western Reserve before both studied law under the direction of the prominent Canfield attorney Elisha Whittlesey. Both practiced law for a time in Jefferson, Benjamin as a partner of fellow Whig and antislavery advocate Joshua Giddings. When the firm dissolved in the depression conditions of the late 1830s, the Wade brothers and Giddings went their separate ways. Giddings won election to Congress and Benjamin to the state senate, while Edward pursued his legal practice.

For Benjamin Wade the two-party system was the most effective way to attack slavery. Given the strong antislavery beliefs in northeastern Ohio, he might have advanced as rapidly within the Liberty and Free Soil parties as he did with the Whigs. But if third parties were strong on the Western Reserve, they were not in the state legislature or in Congress, where he felt little could be accomplished as a member of a tiny, despised minority. Wade worked in the legislature for repeal of Ohio's discriminatory black laws, yet rationalized voting for slaveholders Henry Clay and Zachary Taylor for president in 1844 and 1848, believing that the Whig party could still move against slavery in Congress. Wade took an active role in resistance to the Fugitive Slave Act of 1850, which contributed to his election to the U.S. Senate in 1851. There he would remain for the next eighteen years. Opposition to the Kansas-Nebraska Act and the decline of the Whig party led him to a central role in the founding of Ohio's new Republican party, but still within the two-party system. During the Civil War he chaired the Committee on the Conduct of the War, using it as a forum to advance the agenda of Radical Republicans in regard to military, emancipation, and reconstruction policies. A consistent critic of the Lincoln policies, he was even more vehement in his attacks on the policies of Andrew Johnson toward the former Confederate states. As president pro tem of the Senate, he would have become president had Johnson been convicted in the impeachment trial of 1868. Denied reelection to the Senate in 1868 in part because of his advocacy of black suffrage, he never wavered in his support of the Whig and Republican parties. Benjamin Wade consistently fought for the end of slavery, the granting of civil rights for African Americans, and the punishment of rebel leaders, even as he worked within the two-party system.

Edward Wade, in contrast, broke with the Whig party in 1841 after backing William Henry Harrison for the presidency the previous year. While concentrating on his law practice, he moved with other Liberty members to the new Free Soil party in 1848. In 1852 he was elected to Congress from a Cleveland district and served four terms. The formation of the Republican party brought a reconciliation with brother Benjamin. Although never prominent in the House of Representatives, Edward signed the call for a new antislavery party in 1854 and maintained a steady devotion to antislavery and the rights of free blacks. With beliefs similar to those of his brother, Edward presents a significant contrast in approach to antislavery politics, arguing consistently that Democrats and Whigs could not be depended on when it came to the welfare of African Americans.

Political influence was not confined to men, and like their male counterparts, women acted out of a variety of motives. Some, such as Jane Swisshelm, were motivated by their own or women's interests, while others became involved politically more to forward their husband's or father's careers. These women typically believed strongly in the antislavery convictions of male family members but also came to embrace antislavery goals on their own. Thus Jessie Benton Frémont, who publicly and privately championed the causes and actions of her husband: explorer, politician, and soldier John Charles Frémont. Jessie was born in 1824 in Virginia, the daughter of prominent Missouri Democratic senator Thomas Hart Benton. In 1841, she defied her father with her secret marriage to the young army officer, and for close to fifty years she served as Frémont's adviser and collaborator, often defending him against numerous critics. She strongly supported his moderate antislavery stance during his brief tenure in the Senate in the early 1850s. She played a significant, albeit a largely unseen role in John's presidential campaign in 1856 as the Republican candidate against Democrat James Buchanan. She took charge of much of the campaign activity (including helping to prepare a campaign biography of her husband), an effort which some referred to as the "Frémont and Jessie" campaign. Early in the Civil War she urged and then supported John's efforts to free the slaves belonging to rebels in his Missouri command. Lincoln then removed Frémont, later derisively labeling Jessie a "female politician" following a heated White House meeting in which she had defended her husband's actions. She opposed what she regarded as the president's overly lenient stance against slavery and urged her husband to challenge Lincoln for the 1864 Republican presidential nomination. Never an active abolitionist, nor a member of the women's rights movement, she nonetheless consistently opposed slavery from a stance of containment before the war and abolition during the conflict. Restrained by her gender, she managed to play a more active political role than any American woman before her. Not politically involved when third parties were the usual way to express antislavery support, she worked within the two-party system in California politics and then quickly embraced the Republican party when it formed in 1854. Jessie Benton Frémont thus falls within the conservative tradition of political antislavery activists.

Placing individuals within the political spectrum is made more difficult because some began their efforts in antislavery politics with what appeared to be a more traditional approach than that which they espoused by the time of the war. Yet in each case there is a definite date when each individual made a commitment. Degree of commitment, on the other hand, is a much more elusive and subjective measuring rod and thus a less satisfactory standard. In this study the starting point of each career will be used rather than its climax in determining placement. Thus for example, George W. Julian, who began his career as an Indiana Whig, rejected the Liberty appeal and did not become a part of the antislavery movement until the Free Soilers were formed. Yet as a Republican he became one of the most vehement advocates of abolition and civil rights during the Civil War. So also did Benjamin Wade, who rejected even the moderate Free Soil party yet became, with Julian, the harshest of Lincoln's wartime critics in his advocacy of emancipation and racial equality.

The politicians in this study range from Liberty activists, including Stewart, Whittier, Langston, Lovejoy, Booth, and Edward Wade, to those who were not Liberty members but became Free Soilers, including Julian, Swisshelm, and Wilmot, and finally to those who eschewed third parties entirely and instead became active Republicans, including Benjamin Wade and Frémont. Reviled by the Garrisonians for their alleged willingness to compromise antislavery principle, all but Stewart eventually found a home in the Republican party of the 1850s. During the Civil War most were unhappy with the slow pace of abolitionism pursued by Abraham Lincoln and urged a more immediate attack, rarely appreciating the pressures the president faced from all directions in his war policies. Most crusaders in antislavery politics were interested in extending civil and political rights to free blacks. These leaders were typically involved in a variety of other reform movements of the era, but all believed, consistently and without compromise, that the ending of slavery should be the primary goal of the political process. This study will show the variety of approaches to political antislavery by looking at the political philosophy and activities of each of the eleven individually and then comparing them as a group. It thus seeks to provide greater understanding of and insight into a vital element in nineteenth-century politics.

TWO

A SELF-SHARPENING PLOUGH
Alvan Stewart's Challenge to Slavery

THERE WAS LITTLE in Alvan Stewart's early years to suggest a lifetime crusade in behalf of the slave or a decade of Liberty party organizing and campaigning. Born near South Granville, New York, in 1790, he grew up in a traditional Protestant farming family doing the chores expected of most young boys in rural America. We know little of the Stewart family's politics during the Federalist Era of George Washington and John Adams. When Alvan was five he moved with his parents to Westford in the new state of Vermont. There he attended school and later taught in the common schools while enrolled at Burlington College, where he excelled in languages and public speaking. After a brief stay in Montreal, where he studied French, Alvan settled in Cherry Valley, New York, and completed the study of law which he had begun in Vermont. He married Keziah Holt of Cherry Valley, and together they had five children. An eminently successful attorney, he quickly emerged from obscurity and began to amass a sizeable income and property holdings, using his "wit, irony and sarcasm" to augment his vast knowledge of the law to convince judges and juries to rule in behalf of his clients.[1] Elected mayor of Cherry Valley in 1821, he initially aligned himself with the Van Buren Democrats, perhaps in response to their apparent

1. *Utica Observer Dispatch,* December 1, 1929.

commitment to racial equality in New York. Within a decade, however, he had left the Democrats and joined the National Republicans as an advocate of protective tariffs and internal improvements, reflecting his increased wealth and improved status. For many young men hoping to rise on the economic ladder, the party of Henry Clay better represented their aspirations— and in Stewart's case those of his potential clients. Having shown little interest in reform in his first forty years, he appeared destined to remain a prominent attorney with a deep interest in two-party politics.[2]

Within the emerging antislavery philosophies and strategies of the 1830s, Alvan Stewart's approach represents the most radical of those in this study. Early in the decade he moved from a career as an attorney representing traditional economic interests to that of a reformer committed to the destruction of slavery. Affected by the evangelistic atmosphere of central New York, he, like so many other reformers, experienced mob retaliation; unlike most others, he adopted the view that the Constitution was not the proslavery document that the Garrisonians and other abolitionists insisted it was, but rather should be interpreted as a weapon to use against slavery. He was among the original founders of the Liberty party in 1840, the tiny advance group of political abolitionists who believed that slavery was vulnerable to an attack from within the political system rather than from the prevailing Garrisonian approach, which rejected politics. Developing his constitutional argument, by the mid-1840s he spearheaded a small Liberty faction which refused any compromise with those arguing for the containment rather than the abolition of slavery. As the Liberty party prepared to become a part of the more moderate Free Soil party in 1848, Stewart, in failing health, was forced to drop out of politics. Despite his tepid endorsement of the Free Soilers, he never relented in his demands for total and immediate abolition. He would die in 1849, still clinging to his belief that the original Liberty stance was the only way to deal with the moral evil of slavery.

As the 1830s opened, northern states in general—and central New York in particular—proved ripe for a rash of unsettling religious and secular reform movements which would have a major impact on Stewart's life. For decades since the Revolution many northerners had acquiesced in southern slavery. The small abolitionist movement had been dominated by Quakers

2. There is no full-length biography of Stewart. A brief analysis is included in Gerald Sorin, *The New York Abolitionists: A Case Study of Political Radicalism* (Westport, Conn.: Greenwood, 1971), 47–52. See also the entry by Milton C. Sernett in *American National Biography,* ed. John Garraty and Mark Carnes (New York: Oxford Univ. Press, 1999), 20:742–3.

and elitist leaders in Pennsylvania and, to a lesser degree, New York, as well as limited agitation from within the small free black community of the North. The Pennsylvania Abolition Society and the New York Manumission Society had frequently urged a gradualistic and compensated form of abolition and had created controversy whenever slave issues were debated.[3] Now, however, with William Lloyd Garrison and the Massachusetts Anti-Slavery Society leading the way with more radical tactics and abolition philosophy, many northerners supported with emotion these new attacks on slaveholders. Their feelings were intensified by religious revivals, most strongly felt in central New York. Revivalist preachers led by Charles G. Finney helped spawn an interest in a variety of reforms, especially abolition and temperance. Stewart's initial response showed more of an inward and personal need to reform himself than a concern over the plight of southern slaves. He indicated a desire to "search after the everlasting Riches of Christ" by "speaking and performing what I consider the Rules of Christianity impose on a humble suppliant." We know little of Stewart's religious beliefs and theology beyond such statements, but we can assume that, given his background and residence in an area so affected by evangelical revivals, he became an active church member. In 1830, regretting that "so many of my days have run to waste," he pledged to his mother total abstinence, realizing, in the words of one contemporary, that he "could not rely on any half-way measures" to overcome his earlier dependence on alcohol.[4]

By 1832, Stewart was devoting more time to temperance and antislavery lecturing and less to his legal practice. The next year he moved to Utica to continue his practice and reform interests and to be closer to the Oneida Institute, which under Beriah Green had become a center of reform, especially abolitionism.[5] Joining the Garrisonian American Anti-Slavery Society, he was soon lecturing throughout central and western New York, the region

3. For a study of the years before 1830, the neglected period of American abolitionism, see Richard S. Newman, *The Transformation of American Abolitionism: Fighting Slavery in the Early Republic* (Chapel Hill: Univ. of North Carolina Press, 2002).

4. Stewart to Uriel Stewart, July 12, 1830, Stewart Papers, New-York Historical Society, New York (hereafter cited as Stewart Papers); Sorin, *New York Abolitionists*, 49; Levi Beardsley, *Reminiscences; Personal and Other Incidents; Early Settlement of Otsego County, etc.* (New York: C. Vinten, 1852), 168–9; Milton C. Sernett, *North Star Country: Upstate New York and the Crusade for African American Freedom* (Syracuse, N.Y.: Syracuse Univ. Press, 2002), 16–23.

5. See Milton C. Sernett, *Abolition's Axe: Beriah Green, Oneida Institute and the Black Freedom Struggle* (Syracuse, N.Y.: Syracuse Univ. Press, 1986).

called the burned-over district due to its emphasis on evangelicalism and social reform. Fund-raising, lecturing, and organizing soon replaced his legal work entirely. By the fall of 1835, he had found his life's work and joined with fellow reformers to found the New York State Anti-Slavery Society (NYSASS). Neither two-party politics nor a career within the legal establishment held the kind of attraction for him that it had only a few years earlier. He was an impressive and powerful speaker, effectively using his tall and well-built body, deep learning, and intense humor to win over his audiences as he had earlier convinced juries in behalf of his clients. Unlike most abolitionists, he even found bloody slave insurrection justifiable in the face of continued southern intransigence.[6] He appeared consumed with an anti-slavery zeal.

Stewart wrote the call for the organizing meeting of the abolition society to be held in Utica on October 21, 1835. In an era of mob violence against abolitionists throughout the free states, the gathering raised a storm of protest after more than four hundred signed Stewart's call for the convention. Utica's common council had narrowly approved the meeting after a stormy session.[7] The more than six hundred who gathered hoping for a peaceful meeting instead found the Second Presbyterian Church on Bleecker Street stormed by antiabolitionists shouting "Break down the doors! Damn the fanatics!" The mob forced the members to suspend their proceedings shortly after Stewart had completed his introductory remarks. He had opened with an address describing how slavery challenged the "liberty of discussion, of conscience and the press." Behind the mob were men of wealth and social standing led by the mayor, Joseph Kirkland, and Jacksonian congressman Democrat Samuel Beardsley, the latter of whom was the most outspoken in his attacks on abolitionists. Stewart, who had earlier joined the American Peace Society, believed that he could not sit passively in the face of mob violence. He thus asked Utica officials to protect the abolitionist meeting and was prepared to defend his own home if necessary.[8] To the fiery, often-emotional New Yorker, self-defense was a higher priority than the pacifism

6. Luther R. Marsh, "Sketch of Alvan Stewart," Alvan Stewart Correspondence, New York State Historical Association Library, Cooperstown, N.Y. (hereafter cited as Stewart Correspondence); Beardsley, *Reminiscences,* 168–70. See also Stewart to Samuel Webb, June 25, September 30, 1840, Stewart Papers.

7. Leonard Richards, *Gentlemen of Property and Standing: Anti-Abolition Mobs in Jacksonian America* (New York: Oxford Univ. Press, 1970), 85–9.

8. Luther R. Marsh, ed., *Writings and Speeches of Alvan Stewart on Slavery* (New York: A. B. Burdick, 1860), 13–8; Sernett, *North Star Country,* 49–50.

associated with the peace movement. Like so many abolitionists forced to defend their views, he believed that the right to protest against an immoral institution might require a sacrifice of other principles.

The mob spared Stewart's home, although it later attacked the office of the *Oneida Standard and Democrat,* which had defended the right of the abolitionists to meet.[9] Stewart and his colleagues then reassembled forty miles away at the home of Gerrit Smith in Peterboro. The wealthy landowner and philanthropist Smith, like many others, was himself initially convinced of the legitimacy of the meeting as much by the threat to civil liberties of whites as by antislavery principle. It was the denial of First Amendment guarantees of freedom of speech and press and the right to assemble peaceably that moved many to protest in behalf of the slave. John Quincy Adams, James G. Birney, and Salmon P. Chase were among others who first embraced political antislavery when their own rights appeared threatened. At Smith's home abolitionists formed the New York State Anti-Slavery Society and elected William Jay as its president. In response to his forceful leadership and eloquence, they chose Stewart to preside over the executive committee which would manage the society's activities. Following his lead, the meeting approved resolutions rejecting the colonization of African Americans outside of the country and endorsing an all-out attack on slavery. When Democratic governor William Marcy attacked the organization as a group of dangerous agitators in his address to the legislature in 1836, Stewart responded by suggesting that "the crime of these abolitionists" was their "belief that slavery is wrong, and ought immediately to come to an end." Rather than crushing the movement, the events of 1836 had "been the direct means of adding thousands to the Abolitionists."[10]

Stewart would soon be in correspondence with abolitionists in other states concerning the appropriate response in the face of accelerating mob violence. In 1836, his close ally William Goodell initiated a weekly newspaper, the *Friend of Man,* in Utica which helped to spread their ideals. In May 1838, when angry antiabolitionists destroyed the recently completed Freedom Hall in Philadelphia, Stewart urged his close friend there, the Quaker leader Samuel Webb, to "go on," for "the Slave and freeman all look to you to build a second temple of liberty." He concluded: "You are engaged

9. Richards, *Gentlemen of Property and Standing,* 91–2.

10. Stewart, "Response to the Message of Gov. Marcy, Feb., 1836," in Marsh, ed., *Writings and Speeches,* 15–8, 58–85; Ralph Harlow, *Gerrit Smith: Philanthropist and Reformer* (New York: Holt, 1939), 122–3.

in a mighty work." Earlier in 1838, Stewart participated in a Rochester abolition meeting which approved a resolution condemning the recent murder of Elijah P. Lovejoy by an angry mob in Alton, Illinois, as he defended his abolition press. Stewart noted that Lovejoy had fallen "in the cause of liberty, and the true sons of liberty are aroused in his behalf." But Lovejoy was not the only one to be remembered: "Let us not forget that the life of the slave is one continued scene of martyrdom equal in anguish and horrour to that of Lovejoy." Finally, he reminded his listeners that action was needed to prevent future violence, for "the blind and perverse mob at Alton were only acting out public sentiment. They knew that the mobs at Boston and New York, and Utica were never called to account and the sufferers never received redress."[11] The events of the late 1830s had accelerated Stewart's move— with a small group of like-minded abolitionists led by Smith and Goodell— to an entirely new phase of antislavery agitation. It would be seen in their break with Garrison in a two-pronged challenge to the New Englander's approach. The issues Stewart would raise involved the nature of the Constitution and the wisdom of political action.

As he labored in behalf of the NYSASS, giving extensively of his time and income, Stewart first took the highly controversial stance that the Fifth Amendment, rather than protecting the property of slaveholders, deprived slaves of their freedom without the due process of law. Even though virtually all politicians and most abolitionists could agree that the Constitution was a proslavery document, Stewart urged the position that the federal government could and should legally attack slavery wherever it existed. It would be 1838 before he could convince his circle of friends in New York to approve his stance, and his efforts to convince New England leaders would be an ongoing struggle. One of his New York colleagues, William Goodell, noted that Stewart was responsible for persuading him and fellow abolitionist Myron Holley of Rochester to adopt this position. At the annual meeting of the American Anti-Slavery Society in New York, in May 1838, Stewart offered a resolution "that the Federal Government had constitutional power to abolish slavery in the slave States." Stewart's impassioned speech in defense of his motion convinced a majority of the delegates, many of whom were attorneys. As he explained to his wife: "I have argued my constitutional argument for two days. Mr. William Jay, Mr. Birney, Mr. Leavitt, Mr. Eleazer Wright,

---

11. Stewart to Samuel Webb, May 20, June 16, 1838, Stewart Papers; Stewart, January 10, 1838, in Joseph C. Lovejoy and Owen Lovejoy, *Memoir of the Rev. Elijah P. Lovejoy,* with an introduction by John Quincy Adams (New York: J. S. Taylor, 1838), 362–6.

Mr. Loring of Boston, Mr. Phillips of same place came down upon me like a thunder shower, about ten of them and I was almost alone in my argument. The vote was finally taken and there were 47 for me and 37 against me," a vote which was not representative of abolitionist sentiment, and his resolution failed to achieve the necessary two-thirds vote for adoption. Still, he believed it an "immense victory" in convincing so many.[12]

Many were not nearly as receptive to Stewart's approach. William Jay suggested that his "vile heresy" regarding the Constitution and slavery should bring his expulsion from the New York abolition society. In the Old Northwest, Cincinnati editor Gamaliel Bailey, although not a Garrisonian, reflected the thinking of many abolitionists by referring to Stewart's "unfounded assumption." Said Bailey: "I am no lawyer and may have committed some technical blunders, but I could not refrain from attacking what I considered so dangerous a heresy." He concluded that the adoption of Stewart's views would be "most disastrous to our cause," for it might expose them to ridicule. James G. Birney agreed and argued that "Unless something be done during the present year to convince the community, that his movement is repudiated by the great body of Abolitionists, our case will be a bad one." Nonetheless, the New Yorker persisted in his arguments and soon published his views as "A Constitutional Argument on the Subject of Slavery."[13]

As Stewart urged his argument of slavery's unconstitutionality and began to move toward advocating political action, he did so in the belief that an even stronger enemy than the slaveholder of the South was his northern proslavery ally, who Stewart believed controlled the two parties in so many states and in Congress. Addressing the New England Anti-Slavery Society convention in Boston in late May 1838, Stewart asked: "Is there a *meaner* man on earth than the slaveholder—more morally loathsome—more mis-

12. Goodell, in Marsh, ed., *Writings and Speeches,* 27–8; Stewart to Kesiah Stewart, May 7, 1838, Stewart Correspondence; Sorin, *New York Abolitionists,* 50; John Greenleaf Whittier to *Pennsylvania Freeman,* May 6, 1838, in John B. Pickard, ed., *The Letters of John Greenleaf Whittier* (Cambridge, Mass.: Harvard Univ. Press, 1975), 1:292–4; Jacobus Ten Broek, *Equal Justice Under the Law* (New York: Collier, 1965), 281–95; William M. Wiecek, *The Sources of Antislavery Constitutionalism in America, 1760–1848* (Ithaca, N.Y.: Cornell Univ. Press, 1977), 255–7.

13. Jay to Elizur Wright, April 13, 1838, Wright Papers, Boston Public Library; Bailey to Birney, May 24, 1838, Birney to George W. Benson, June 13, 1838, Dwight Dumond, ed., *Letters of James Gillespie Birney, 1831–1857* (1938; reprint, Gloucester, Mass: Peter Smith, 1966), 1:455–9; *The Philanthropist* (Cincinnati), April 30, 1839.

erably vile? . . . He was the Northern apologist—the paid pander and pimp of the slaveholder. . . . Whether a Governor, a Judge or an Attorney general, sir, he is the meanest wretch that crawls upon God's earth." With northern two-party politics dominated by "the instigator and defender of mobs," only "an independent political party dedicated to abolition could stand up to him."[14] In Stewart's eyes, neither the Democratic nor the Whig party would ever resist southern demands in behalf of slavery for fear of alienating a major block of voters. Only through a third party of truly dedicated abolitionists could the interests of the slave be protected.

Knowing that Democrats and Whigs would reject an attack on slaveholders and their northern allies out of hand, Stewart reached the obvious conclusion that an abolitionist third party was the only recourse. Again, such a stance would need to reckon with the intense Garrisonian resistance that had evolved during the 1830s. Garrison had initially appeared open to a political approach, endorsing "a Christian party in politics" in 1835, and had spoken of the need for a no-compromise approach "to remove slavery by moral and political action." But by the late 1830s the moral, nonpolitical approach, moral suasion as Garrison labeled it, had won out. In his mind, political action of any kind could lead only to a compromising of antislavery principle. Garrison argued that a third party could get little accomplished because the major parties, so thoroughly dominated by the Slave Power, would block their feeble efforts. Legislative and political efforts would be futile until the people were won over by moral suasion. He thus rejected the initial practice of some abolitionists of questioning Democratic and Whig candidates on slave-related issues and supporting those found to be least objectionable. Nor was the abolitionist tactic of petitioning Congress on slave-related issues of any value. Said Stewart: "We might as well send the lamb as an ambassador to a community of wolves. I would not lift my hand to sign a petition to Congress to be insulted by that body." On the latter point Stewart could agree that with the approval of the Gag Rule in the House of Representatives in 1836, petitioning had actually backfired. Not only were they "a waste of labor," but they had actually curtailed abolitionists' liberties without giving any help to the slave.[15]

By 1838, Garrison had repudiated "all human politics" and concluded that, at least for himself, voting was a sin. He as well as most non-

14. *Pennsylvania Freeman,* May 31, 1838; Pickard, ed., *Letters of Whittier,* 1:298.

15. Stewart to Myron Holley, December 16, 1839, Stewart to Edwin W. Clarke, September 14, 1839, Stewart Papers.

Garrisonians found that questioning Democrats and Whigs had little effect.[16] Stewart argued that opponents of slavery were foolish to believe that either major party could be persuaded to nominate even moderately antislavery candidates. To believe otherwise ignored the obvious, for they "hate us more than they do each other." Nor would they "come out and forsake their pro-slavery candidates and nominate Abolitionists and elect them. Elect them for what? To do the very thing both of the great parties hate—to wit to abolish Slavery its roots and prongs." It was an "infinite absurdity" to expect the impossible. Instead, at best they might nominate some "milk and water or a vainglorious abolitionist." Nor would the Garrisonian tactic of moral suasion bring the desired results. As he reminded his friends Holley and Webb: "We can never bring the immorality and wickedness of slavery as an argument for the abolition to a people whose Priesthood hold Slavery a bible institution." The only way to "behead the monster" slavery was through the political pressure of a third party.[17]

For a growing number of New York and Massachusetts dissidents, third-party activity appeared to be the only avenue available to challenge slavery effectively, although it was Stewart and his New York circle who led the way. In their state both the Van Buren Democrats and the Whigs of William H. Seward and Thurlow Weed ignored the abolitionist challenge, feeling it unnecessary to respond to a dissident group they felt represented so few voters. In Stewart's eyes, neither the Democratic nor the Whig party would ever stand up to southern demands for fear of alienating a major faction of voters. He must help form a third party to resist the Slave Power. Following a month of travel in New York and Vermont in late 1838, Stewart was convinced that "we must form a 3d party or we shall be overwhelmed" by Whigs and Democrats. In early 1839, the NYSASS executive committee approved a Myron Holley resolution endorsing a distinct party, but again, as Goodell recognized, it was Stewart who "had previously done much to prepare abolitionists for that movement." The New York organization agreed with Stewart that "if we ever strike a political blow for the slave, we must go deep." Since questioning the major party candidates had brought no results,

16. Garrison to Thomas Shipley, December 17, 1835, in Richard H. Sewell, *Ballots for Freedom: Antislavery Politics in the United States, 1837–1860* (New York: Oxford Univ. Press, 1976), 8, 20; *The Liberator*, December 14, 1833, December 20, 1834. For the Garrisonian approach on both political abolitionism and the Constitution, see Kraditor, *Means and Ends*, 158–68, 195–212.

17. Stewart to Webb, August 5, 1839, Stewart to Holley, December 16, 1839, Stewart to Edwin M. Clarke, September 14, 1839, Stewart Papers; Sewell, *Ballots for Freedom*, 51.

they concluded that only a separate party which could draw enough voters away to affect the outcome would cause a major party shift in position. With Garrisonians in firm control among New England abolitionists, a political challenge was more likely to begin in New York, a state so affected by evangelical reform movements. The Garrisonian moral suasion stance could not "protect the weak from the power of the strong," said Stewart.[18] In the spring he and his abolitionist colleagues would take concrete steps to establish such a party.

Stewart and his allies felt they had been left no choice but to organize a separate party when, in early 1839, Senator Henry Clay condemned those contemplating a third party. In a blatant bid for southern Whig support for his party's 1840 presidential nomination and fearing the emergence of political abolitionism, Clay charged in a Senate speech that its advocates "have ceased to employ the instruments of reason and persuasion [and] have made their cause political" by appealing "to the ballot box." He continued by attacking the goal "of liberty to the descendants of Africa in the United States." Preferring "the liberty of my own race to that of any other race," he concluded that emancipation would trample the rights of states and bring on a bloody civil war. Abolitionists, he concluded must "pause in their mad and fatal course."[19] Many abolitionists like Stewart who had earlier held out hope that Clay as president might at least permit open debate now felt betrayed and became more convinced of the need for a third-party attack on slavery.

The decision to form an abolitionist party was a deliberate one which won adherents gradually and sometimes reluctantly in Stewart's Mohawk Valley region of New York. Many of the early supporters were members of evangelical Protestant churches that emphasized local reform questions and local authority over the centralized direction that a political party might bring. Many belonged to the Presbyterian, Congregational, and Methodist churches. Such congregations had little tradition of working together in a common effort and had rarely been part of a common reform movement. Few in New York had responded to Garrison's moral suasion campaign, and the Presbyterians and Methodists were part of denominations with southern affiliations. Although many felt strongly against slavery and its immorality,

18. Stewart to Webb, November 21, 1838, Stewart to E. W. Clarke, September 14, 1839, Stewart Papers; Sorin, *New York Abolitionists*, 52.

19. *Congressional Globe,* 25th Cong., 3rd sess., Appendix, 354–9; Sewell, *Ballots for Freedom*, 48.

few were inclined at first to independent antislavery politics. Only by the mid-1840s were Stewart and other leaders able to convince many "to vote as they pray," to see slavery as sinful, and to regard voting "as a moral and religious duty." Beginning in the mid-1830s, several of these denominations faced challenges from within by those demanding a more vigorous devotion to abolitionism as well as a more evangelistic approach on religious issues. Increasing numbers of these "comeouter" groups in the Mohawk Valley separated from their parent bodies and formed separate congregations. It was in those communities where such evangelical, comeouter congregations were most prevalent that the New York Liberty vote would be strongest.[20]

Initial steps in the direction of an abolitionist party came in 1839, through NYSASS-dominated meetings such as that in Albany on July 31, where delegates approved a resolution to support none but antislavery candidates. Stewart pushed for the next logical step, that of a separate third-party effort, but at this point only Holley of his New York colleagues was convinced while Goodell and Smith remained reluctant. Stewart was by now convinced "that a third party or an abolition party is the only real available mode to prosecute our great undertaking politically." Outside of their group, Elizur Wright and Joshua Leavitt joined in support, with the latter using the columns of the *Emancipator* to endorse the idea. Holley's efforts to sway a Cleveland, Ohio, meeting of four hundred toward a political approach were narrowly rejected in October. But during the next month a Genesee County, New York, convention in Warsaw called for independent nominations. Despite the selection of James G. Birney of Ohio and Francis P. Lemoyne of Pennsylvania, no party had yet been formed and the candidates declined to run.[21] Still, the movement appeared to be gaining when Gerrit Smith joined the Stewart group seeking a direct challenge to the two parties. Whigs especially were alarmed, fearing inroads among their antislavery voters who had appeared united behind the election of their presidential candidate, William Henry Harrison. Potential converts, such as John Greenleaf Whittier of Massachusetts and Gamaliel Bailey of Ohio, urged waiting until Harrison

20. John R. McKivigan, "Vote as You Pray and Pray as You Vote: Church-Oriented Abolitionism and Antislavery Politics," in Kraut, ed., *Crusaders and Compromisers*, 179–83; Douglas M. Strong, *Perfectionist Politics: Abolitionism and the Religious Tensions of American Democracy* (Syracuse, N.Y.: Syracuse Univ. Press, 1999), 86–90; Sernett, *North Star Country*, 89–92.

21. Dumond, ed., *Letters of Birney*, 1:512 n. 2; Stewart to Webb, August 5, 1839, Stewart Papers; Hugh Davis, *Joshua Leavitt, Evangelical Abolitionist* (Baton Rouge: Louisiana State Univ. Press, 1990), 150–2; Harlow, *Smith*, 145.

clarified his ambiguous position on slave-related issues before bolting the Whigs.[22]

Stewart's efforts were not to be denied, however, and Holley and Smith wrote a call for a nominating convention to convene in Albany on April 1, 1840. At a large preliminary meeting in Arcade, New York, in late January, delegates rejected the major party candidates and endorsed the Albany convention. Abolitionists, said Stewart, were left with no choice, for "we cannot vote for either of the major parties without voting for a slave-holder." In his eyes, the Slave Power controlled Democrats and Whigs.[23] Clearly the party would draw most heavily from the Whigs, and many hoped that a third-party effort would be nothing more than a temporary expedient to be abandoned as soon as the Whigs adopted antislavery grounds. Few other than Stewart would admit, however, that the hopes for such a Whig conversion appeared unlikely, and many must have known that a third-party appeal would not be a temporary one.

The Albany convention was dominated by New Yorkers, although six states were represented in the disappointingly small gathering. With Stewart presiding, a Holley motion to nominate passed narrowly, as many abstained. The delegates chose Birney and Thomas Earle, a Pennsylvania Quaker, and Stewart urged support "of men who would employ all just and constitutional means to elevate the chatteled slave to a fellow sovereign—a freeman."[24] Said Stewart, old methods of questioning were of as little value "as it would be for a man to stand on an iceberg and whistle to the northwest wind to warm the atmosphere." The party remained unnamed until the following year, but the correspondence committee of Stewart, Goodell, and Smith urged nominations of candidates for Congress and state offices as well. Stewart accepted the New York gubernatorial nomination, but he did little campaigning and received only a few hundred votes. It was a meaningless nomination if election were the realistic goal, but important symbolically if Liberty leaders were to begin the arduous task of increasing their party's visibility. Not surprisingly, silence greeted the third party during the 1840 campaign, while Garrisonians dubbed the April 1 meeting the "April Fool's Convention." To Stewart "one thing is certain, if we ever abolish it, [slavery] in

22. Stanley Harrold, *Gamaliel Bailey and Antislavery Union* (Kent, Ohio: Kent State Univ. Press, 1986), 34–7.

23. *Friend of Man* (Utica, N.Y.), April 8, 1840; Sewell, *Ballots for Freedom*, 71; Harlow, *Smith*, 146–8.

24. Harlow, *Smith*, 146–8; Stewart, "Address by the National Committee of Correspondence," in Marsh, ed., *Writings and Speeches*, 234–5.

this world, it must be done by political action, or else it will be accomplished by the slaves rising." He continued, "Our duty is plain never to give either of those parties called Whig or Democratic a vote for hog-constable or President of the U. S. until they nominate thorough abolitionists." If he realized at this early date that the Liberty party might eventually have to abandon its goal of immediate abolitionism in order to add to its meager numbers as Garrison had argued, he never publicly admitted it. He believed instead that "in the act of voting," the abolitionist "acts not for himself alone, but for . . . his neighbors, his country—and indirectly for the world."[25] He optimistically believed that the election would begin the process of a moral transformation which he and other Liberty leaders hoped would ultimately bring emancipation.

Such moral transformation would not come easily or quickly, for the Birney ticket won only seventy-one hundred votes of the close to 2.5 million cast. This was true even though Liberty campaigners adopted many of the moral suasion techniques of the Garrisonians, appealing to the consciences of northern voters at public rallies and in the columns of countless small abolition newspapers. To the credit of the hard-working Stewart and his colleagues, of that meager total, 40 percent of the Liberty vote was cast in New York. Still, Birney's vote was less than 10 percent of the estimated number of male members of antislavery societies. Garrison's antipolitical views as well as those of other abolitionists dissuaded many from voting, while countless others remained loyal to the Harrison-Tyler ticket and the Whigs. Yet Stewart had no difficulty defending his campaigning for Birney, explaining to a critic after Harrison's death that he "could not vote for 'Tyler too,' the man whose life had been spent in petit Larcenies from the helpless." He had no doubt that slaveholder Tyler's "crime is vastly greater than all the horse stealing and sheep stealing in the Nation." He continued: "Am I and that portion of the abolitionists who agreed with me mistaken in refusing to vote for such a man as long as we hold Slavery to be a crime of the greatest magnitude?" He professed to believe that "a great many gentlemen who voted for Harrison and Tyler too, are coming back to us." More would join, for "the Whig slaveholding leader Henry Clay in Congress and John Tyler, the slaveholding Whig President have utterly destroyed the Whig party never to rise again."[26]

25. Stewart to Webb, June 25, 1840, Stewart Papers; Strong, *Perfectionist Politics,* 85–6; Sewell, *Ballots for Freedom,* 70.

26. James B. Stewart, "Abolitionists, Insurgents, and Third Parties: Sectionalism and Partisan Politics in Northern Whiggery, 1836–1844," in Kraut, ed., *Crusaders and Compro-*

In response to the Garrison injunction against political involvement, Stewart argued that the only way to challenge Slave Power control of the federal government was through an aggressive third-party appeal to voters' consciences. Yet if he was optimistic early in the Tyler administration, a year later gloominess enveloped Stewart and many of his colleagues, as Congress seemed bent on legislating the southern agenda, and northerners watched with apparent apathy. "Slavery has undone us. She has crawled into the Constitution, has paralyzed the church, broken the compact, silenced petition, overthrown morality, blotted out humanity, really dissolved the Confederacy and left the Nation undone." A more concerted Liberty effort was needed. Rather than "addressing 50 or 60 already converted A.S. men" and then "go home, do nothing and call this carrying forward the cause," abolitionists must organize locally and nationally, agitate between elections, and make the party "something like a self-sharpening plough." Stewart was ready to put his words into action, and in 1842 he was the Liberty candidate for governor. He received more than seven thousand votes, three times Birney's New York vote for president in 1840.[27]

Nor did he confine his role to his home state, as he continued to urge his view of the power of Congress on slave-related issues even as he expanded his communication with New England and Ohio Liberty leaders. John Greenleaf Whittier urged him to address a Liberty mass meeting in early 1842 in Worcester. Unable to attend, Stewart nonetheless was in regular contact with Whittier as the two compared strategies. He did make several trips to Massachusetts later in the 1840s to confer with Liberty leaders and address abolitionist meetings. Gamaliel Bailey, the Ohio abolitionist editor, was a last-minute convert to Birney in 1840, and Stewart carefully outlined for him those areas where Congress could act against slavery, noting "we can abolish slavery in the District of Columbia and between the slave States because these two kinds of slavery derive their power from the Constitution." In addition, "the fugitive slave act of 1793 by which the free States have become the hunter's great forest of human game, can be abolished by Congress." In these less controversial positions regarding the federal government's jurisdiction over slavery, Stewart found more widespread agreement among abolitionists, and for a time he downplayed his more contro-

misers, 79; Stewart to John Fry, September 3, 1841, Stewart to Webb, November 13, 1841, Stewart Papers.

27. Stewart to Webb, October 10, 1842, November 13, 1841, Stewart Papers; Sernett, *Abolition's Axe,* 114–6; Harlow, *Smith,* 163–4.

versial constitutional arguments. He explained why political action alone remained: "We have appealed to the Church and she has declined the honor. We appealed to Congress and she threw back our petitions, mixed with broken fragments of the Constitution. We have appealed to the slaveholder! He points to the fagot and the flames. . . . We have tried the inapplicable system of questioning the political candidates in this land; hoping by that lever to pry open the prison doors."[28] Throughout the Tyler presidency repeal of the Fugitive Slave Act remained Stewart's focus, for if it were gone "the moment the slaves passed into Pennsylvania, Ohio, Indiana, Illinois, or Iowa from a slave State they would be *free.*" Border state slavery could not last "five years, if we take away the power of *reclamation.*" Only by repeal would the process end whereby "Congress sends the prowling slaveholder, armed with bowie knives, pistols, halters, fetters, and bloodhounds in full cry, through the free States pursuing the fugitive slave."[29] Here was an issue on which most of those inclined toward antislavery could agree.

Throughout the early 1840s, Stewart and his Liberty party colleagues had also to continue their struggle with Garrison and his supporters, who labored to undermine third-party efforts. In 1843, former slave Frederick Douglass and others toured central New York to urge the Garrisonian tenants of disunionism and antipartyism. To Stewart, such a "no government" approach "actually prolonged the slave's bondage," for to separate from the southern states would leave slaves no one to advocate their cause in the national government. Before Douglass arrived in Utica in late July, Stewart and his allies had convinced most of the town's abolitionists to boycott his meeting. What had been planned as a three-day event was reduced to one due to poor attendance. Douglass later complained that the Stewart faction had thwarted his efforts in behalf of political abolitionism.[30] If beating back the Garrisonian challenge had been difficult, increasing support for the Liberty party would be an even more daunting task.

The Liberty party again chose James G. Birney as its candidate in 1844 and, with Stewart's full support, increased its vote to sixty-two thousand in the narrow victory of Democrat James K. Polk over Clay. Of that total, one-

28. Whittier to Stewart, January 1, 1842, Stewart to Bailey, April 1842, in Marsh, ed., *Writings and Speeches,* 25–6, 250–71.

29. Stewart, reply to Rev. Calvin Colton, 1843, in Stewart, "The Act of 1793," in Marsh, ed., *Writings and Speeches,* 389, 377.

30. Sernett, *North Star Country,* 75–6; Frederick Douglass, *The Life and Times of Frederick Douglass* (1892; rev. ed., New York: Collier Books, 1962), 227–8.

fourth were cast in New York, although the Liberty percentage of the total vote was higher in several other northern states. As the two parties stepped up their criticism of the third-party abolitionists, Stewart defended their "unchangeable position, taken on the first of April, 1840," by which Liberty men "refused to give a vote for a slaveholder or his apologist, from constable to President." Against those who charged that Birney's votes had helped elect Polk, Stewart praised those who were "inscribed on the muster roll of human freedom," for they were "the moral army of liberation," seeking "to deliver three millions of slaves to self-ownership."[31]

Stewart had been a prime mover in the 1844 Liberty campaign and had chaired the party's convention in Buffalo. The delegates resisted the Ohio efforts led by Bailey and Salmon P. Chase to adopt a more moderate platform by toning down its abolitionist planks and naming a more prominent candidate who would appeal more effectively to antislavery Whigs and Democrats. To Stewart, the strategy of moderates would only compromise abolitionist principles. Much to his satisfaction, Chase and his faction were unable to find such a candidate and the platform came close to approving Stewart's constitutional position on slavery. Not only would the party "demand the absolute and unqualified divorce of the general Government from Slavery and the restoration of equality of rights, among men," but it affirmed "that amendment of the constitution which declares that no person shall be deprived of life, liberty or property without due process of law." Slavery, it said, depended "on no other support than State legislation, and not on any authority of Congress." It stopped short of a demand that Congress abolish slavery everywhere but indicated that the Liberty party "had not been organized for any temporary purpose" and claimed that no other party represented "the true spirit of the Constitution of the United States."[32] Nor was Garrison's appeal to disunionism the right approach, for to accept a breakup of the Union over slavery would mean acquiescence in the permanent enslavement of millions of African Americans. Stewart would continue to urge his position even though its appeal failed to attract more than a hard core of third-party advocates. Dedication to his abolitionist principles was more critical to him than attracting two-party voters or nonvoting Garrisonians.

During the 1840s, Stewart developed his argument concerning slavery's unconstitutionality which he had initially presented in 1837; in the pro-

31. Stewart to *Democratic Review*, February 1845, Stewart to Liberty party, 1846, in Marsh, ed., *Writings and Speeches*, 409–20, 40–9.

32. Donald Bruce Johnson and Kirk H. Porter, eds., *National Party Platforms, 1840–1972*, 5th ed. (Urbana: Univ. of Illinois Press, 1973), 4–8.

cess he gradually won over other members of his Liberty circle. He first had developed his argument at a NYSASS meeting in Utica, arguing that Congress possessed the constitutional "right to abolish slavery in every state and territory in the Union." In so doing, he challenged the view of many abolitionists—especially Garrison and the American Anti-Slavery Society— that "Congress did not possess the power over the slave states." That group had conceded "we fully and unanimously recognize the sovereignty of each state to legislate exclusively on the subject of slavery . . . we consider that Congress . . . has no right to interfere with any of the slave states" on this subject.[33] Stewart's constitutional challenge was thus directed against both Garrisonian abolitionists and many political abolitionists, as well as virtually all Democrats and Whigs.

Stewart began his argument by pointing out that whenever the Constitution referred to the slave, it consistently used the word person rather than slave. This was true in relation to fugitive slaves and the three-fifths clause. Thus when the Fifth Amendment noted "nor shall any person be deprived of life, liberty, or property without due process of law," it must necessarily include slaves, for "if it did not intend to embrace the slave there would have been exception in relation to the slave." As a result, Stewart reasoned that Congress could pass a law "carrying into effect the spirit and intention" of the Amendment. Such an act would not depend on converting the slave-holding states, for "Congress has ample and complete power over the question."[34]

In advancing his argument, Stewart challenged contemporary views of the Constitution and initially convinced few. In so doing, he had to ignore the sentiments of the Founding Fathers, which claimed that the Constitution legitimized slavery in the states. Further, he believed that the Bill of Rights was binding on states as well as the federal government; in this he was in advance of nineteenth-century thinking and in accord with twentieth-century Supreme Court rulings. To argue for federal supremacy, he had also to ignore James Madison's views recently published following Madison's death in 1836. Madison had made it clear that he and others at the Philadelphia convention and in the First Congress endorsed a federal theory of Union in which the states retained a degree of sovereignty including control over slavery within their borders. Not surprisingly, Stewart's views were rejected or

33. Stewart, "A Constitutional Argument on the Subject of Slavery," September 20, 1837, in Ten Broek, *Equal Justice Under the Law,* 281–95, originally published in *The Friend of Man* (Utica, N.Y., October 1837).

34. Ibid., 288, 295.

ignored by most and held suspect even by his friends when first made public in 1837. But, while many Liberty leaders remained unconvinced, some of his Liberty party friends, including Gerrit Smith and William Goodell, eventually endorsed it, and in the 1840s abolitionists Lysander Spooner and James G. Birney even expanded on it. Spooner, a Massachusetts attorney, published his *The Unconstitutionality of Slavery* in 1845, the most thorough treatise on the subject. In 1847, Stewart found additional constitutional justification for his antislavery views in the general welfare clause and the republican form of government guarantee, and together, Spooner and Stewart became the leading defenders of the unconstitutionality of slavery thesis.[35]

Two years earlier Stewart had argued his views forcefully but unsuccessfully before the New Jersey Supreme Court. New Jersey, in 1804, had been the last northern state to enact a gradual emancipation law. It provided that children born of slaves after July 4, 1804, would remain slaves until age twenty-five if male or twenty-one if female. Slaves born before then remained slaves unless individually freed. The 1840 census showed there to be 674 men and women (or 0.2 percent of the state's population) still in bondage, most of them agricultural workers. A revised state constitution approved in 1844 included an article which stated: "All men are by nature free and independent." The small New Jersey State Anti-Slavery Society (NJSASS) quickly agreed that continued slavery was in violation of the new state constitution. In 1845, the society hired Stewart to present a legal challenge in the state supreme court. A state which had given Birney only sixty-nine votes in 1840 and only slightly more than that in 1844 clearly needed outside assistance in such a legal challenge, and in seeking Stewart's services the NJSASS also endorsed his view that the U.S. Constitution prohibited slavery.[36] As unlikely as that possibility appeared, should the view that the federal constitution was an antislavery document prevail, state action against slavery would be unnecessary.

No such federal ruling was forthcoming, and Stewart sought the overthrow of the remaining vestiges of slavery in New Jersey with an eleven-hour presentation. Although stressing the inherent conflict of New Jersey law with its new constitution, he also resorted to moral and natural law arguments

35. Ibid., 72 n.; see Lysander Spooner, *The Unconstitutionality of Slavery* (Boston: B. Marsh, 1860). For a full analysis of Spooner's theory and Garrison's reaction to it, see Kraditor, *Means and Ends*, 191–5; Wiecek, *Sources of Antislavery Constitutionalism*, 258.

36. Daniel R. Ernst, "Legal Positivism, Abolitionist Litigation, and the New Jersey Slave Case of 1845," *Law and History Review* 4 (1986): 339–40, 342–4.

against slavery as found in the Old Testament book of Exodus. Slavery, said Stewart, violated natural law by denying man's right to life, liberty, and property. He pointed to the Liberty party platform of 1844, which held that the U.S. Constitution was, "when properly interpreted, an anti-slavery document." Most important, slavery was "the exact converse of every proposition contained in the first article" of the state's 1844 constitution, which labeled all men free. In addition, he reviewed and expanded on his views concerning the federal Constitution, adding that slavery deprived New Jersey of "a Republican form of Government."[37]

Defense counsel Abraham O. Zabriskie and Joseph P. Bradley effectively countered Stewart's arguments, rejecting his assertion that no positive law protected slavery in the state and that the constitutional article protecting all men as "free and independent" did not refer to slavery. While presenting able arguments, Stewart was unable to counter effectively their views, and the views of the business community protecting slave property prevailed. The latter feared any challenge to property rights which might later be expanded to regulate business interests in general. By a three-to-one vote the court, on July 17, 1845, upheld the state law of 1804, the one dissenting judge finding Stewart's constitutional views convincing. Three years later the New Jersey Court of Errors and Appeals affirmed the decision. By then, few if any slaves remained alive in the state. Yet Stewart's arguments, while convincing only a few, nonetheless represented a growing minority of political abolitionists.[38]

The remaining years of Stewart's life were not happy ones, as he fought to sustain his antislavery principles against efforts of those which he felt to be compromising. In maintaining his steadfast adherence to abolitionism, he broke with his New York Liberty colleagues when they sought to expand the party platform to include other reforms. His firm adherence to immediate abolition as the only worthy goal of the movement meant that for him other reforms must wait, and any effort to replace abolition with the containment of slavery must be rejected. Stewart, alone among those in this study, would accept nothing other than an immediate end of the peculiar institution. When declining health forced him to move to New York City to live with his

37. Alvan Stewart, *A Legal Argument Before the Supreme Court of the State of New Jersey at the May Term, 1845 at Trenton for the Deliverance of Four Thousand Persons from Bondage* (New York: Finch and Weed, 1845), 23, 46, 38; Wiecek, *Sources of Antislavery Constitutionalism,* 255–7.

38. Ernst, "New Jersey Slave Case," 352–65.

daughter, he gradually broke off contact with the Smith-Goodell faction. During the early months of the Polk presidency, Stewart found fault with southern Democrats on economic issues as well as on questions directly related to slavery. He contended that the reduction of tariff rates would "destroy our laboring men and women of the North and place them on a par with their slaves and miserable whites." So too, the president's veto of an internal improvements bill would mean that "1000 lives on our coasts, rivers and inland seas and from 2 to 5 millions of property will annually be lost." Worst of all, as the Mexican War raged: "The South will spend two millions to be earned by the free states in pursuit of more slave empire." He was hopeful, however, that passage of the Wilmot Proviso banning slavery in any territory acquired from Mexico during that war would mean that "southern zeal for Mexican conquests will suddenly subside."[39] Although the Proviso fell far short of an abolition stance, he believed that all efforts of the Slave Power and its northern allies must be blocked. Passage of the Proviso was one such necessary step.

All Liberty men could agree on the need to prevent the expansion of slavery. Some, however, like the Chase-Bailey faction, wished to make containment the basis of coalition with antislavery Whigs and Democrats, thus abandoning the Liberty goal of attacking slavery wherever it existed. Others, such as Joshua Leavitt, believed both goals to still be attainable but thought preventing its expansion would be acceptable. On the broad principle of rejecting a coalition based on containment, Stewart and the Smith-Goodell group were in accord. So too did they agree on the efforts to amend the New York Constitution to give equal voting rights to black men, an effort that Stewart noted would be "a great struggle."[40] But when the latter sought to expand into a more general reform movement and go beyond Stewart's "one-ideaism" or abolitionist emphasis to include such issues as temperance and world peace, Stewart could not agree and in so doing isolated himself from his former allies. He could support such causes separately, but felt their inclusion in the Liberty platform would only detract from abolition. By late 1846, he rejected insistence on a more general reform party and broke off further contact. Earlier he had a falling out with his old friend Beriah Green when, as a member of the board of trustees of Green's Oneida

---

39. Stewart to Webb, August 11, 1846, in Stewart Correspondence; Stewart to Webb, December 11, 1846, Stewart Papers.

40. Stewart to Webb, January 14, 1846, Stewart Correspondence.

Institute, he had failed to support the school financially to the degree Green felt he could. Stewart had resigned in 1843, and the two were further estranged when, in 1846, Green insisted on expanding the Liberty platform to include reforms not directly related to abolition.[41]

When the Liberty party assembled in Buffalo in 1847, the ailing Stewart was not present as his former associates, now calling themselves the Liberty League, fought unsuccessfully to nominate Smith for president on a more general reform platform. The party instead nominated John P. Hale of New Hampshire for president, but many stood ready to join a broader, if watered-down, antislavery movement led by a more prominent candidate.[42] As events moved toward the creation of the Free Soil party in 1848, the Liberty League persisted with its nomination of Gerrit Smith on an abolition-reform platform. As these events evolved, Stewart remained largely forgotten, isolated, and with few friends. Ironically, Garrison had been correct; political involvement had led to a partial surrender of antislavery principle— but not for Alvan Stewart. He had persuaded some to endorse his abolitionist views, but his former friends were finding other means of challenging slavery. John Greenleaf Whittier, having joined the Free Soil party himself, nonetheless came to his defense as one the most effective antislavery speakers. Few others even remembered him.[43]

On the eve of the presidential election of 1848, with the Free Soil party challenging Democrats and Whigs on a containment-of-slavery rather than abolition platform, led by former president and Liberty party nemesis New Yorker Martin Van Buren, Stewart surprisingly could conclude: "I am a free soil man." Yet for him, Free Soil was little more than a timid, first step toward abolition. Until he died on May 1, 1849, at fifty-eight, he remained far more radical than the Free Soilers on slave-related issues. No one understood this more than William Goodell, who noted in tribute how Stewart had led New York antislavery leaders to promote "a distinct political party to promote the abolition of slavery" and "a national policy directly and positively *against* slavery. . . . Mr. Stewart has laid a foundation for a reputation as enduring as the cause of freedom in America." He was never easy to work with because of his firm refusal to compromise his abolition principles. Said Gerrit Smith, Stewart "was emphatically a man of genius. I never knew one

41. Sernett, *Abolition's Axe*, 114–6; Green to Birney, September 23, 1846, Dumond, ed., *Letters of Birney*, 2:1027–29.

42. Kraditor, *Means and Ends*, 152–7.

43. Harlow, *Smith*, 178–80; *National Era*, September 9, 1847.

more so. He was a man of great thoughts. I never knew one greater. He was a man, too, of tender heart. His pity for the poor and oppressed was very deep."[44] Among those who advocated a political attack on slavery, no one was more committed to immediate abolition than Alvan Stewart.

44. Stewart to Webb, October 19, 1848, Stewart Papers; Goodell, in Marsh, ed., *Writings and Speeches,* 27–33; Smith, May 2, 1857, in Marsh, ed., *Writings and Speeches,* 33. Others paying him tribute at the time of his death included Horace Greeley. See *New York Tribune,* May 10, 1849.

THREE

TO MITIGATE THE SUFFERING
OF OUR COUNTRYMEN

John Greenleaf Whittier, Abolitionist Poet

BIOGRAPHERS OF John Greenleaf Whittier have frequently interpreted his early life with the cliché "a typical New England childhood." Surely little of his formative years suggested a lifelong commitment to reform and antislavery politics. He was born of Quaker parents at the family homestead in December 1807 near Haverhill, Massachusetts, and grew up in the home built by his great grandfather in 1688. His childhood was characterized by strenuous farm labor, which his frail body tolerated with difficulty. Chronic headaches and fatigue were relieved only infrequently by Quaker meetings and sporadic schooling at district schools, for his father's struggling farm efforts could ill afford his absence for extended periods. There was little of the idyllic childhood which he later described in his poem "The Barefoot Boy," for the constant rounds of milking, planting, and harvesting kept him near exhaustion. His father believed that he needed little learning beyond the basics. Yet the young Whittier had a passion for reading, which his family's meager library limited to the Bible and the writings of Quaker leaders. His discovery of the poems of Robert Burns helped open new horizons, and by the time he was a teen he was writing his own poetry which reflected the rich folklore of his heritage. With the family farm usually near the brink of failure, he was largely

self-taught but with a deep appreciation of the New England of his formative years.[1]

Several factors set John Greenleaf Whittier apart from most others within
the political antislavery movement. He was among the initial members of the
Liberty party and joined the mostly New York leadership at Albany in 1840
despite a close personal friendship with William Lloyd Garrison and a realization that joining an antislavery party would jeopardize that relationship. Like so many abolitionists, including Alvan Stewart, he personally experienced the fury of an antiabolition mob in the mid-1830s. Whittier was
unique among abolitionists in his poetry and essays, which he often directed
against slavery. It was his poetry that first caught Garrison's attention, even
before abolitionism drew the two together, and it was his poetry that helped
persuade countless northerners to join the political attack on slavery in the
1840s. As a poet and essayist, he showed minimal interest in holding office,
and, after initial aid to Liberty organizers, he preferred a behind-the-scenes
role and remained most effective as a literary voice for emancipation. In basic agreement with Stewart in 1840, he nonetheless refused to endorse the
constitutional views of the New Yorker. Although supportive of Stewart
even when the latter isolated himself by rejecting the moderate Free Soil
approach to slavery, Whittier found the new third party an effective step
toward eventual emancipation. He filled the columns of the Free Soil organ,
the *National Era*, with attacks on the Slave Power, the Fugitive Slave Act,
and those northerners such as Daniel Webster who accepted it. As civil war
approached, Whittier reconciled his Quaker pacifism with the need to use
force to end slavery. Yet even before the war's inception, he retreated from his
activist role of the 1835–1855 years and found contentment in the poetry of
the New England past. As an early advocate of the political approach to
emancipation, he stands in close harmony with Alvan Stewart's radicalism.

Whittier was the second of four children. It was his younger sister Eliza-

1. There are numerous biographies of Whittier, although none written since the 1980s and
none exclusively from the perspective of the antislavery movement. Several combine his role as
a poet with his interest in reform. Among the best are: Albert Mordell, *Quaker Militant: John
Greenleaf Whittier* (1933; reprint, Port Washington, N.Y.: Kennikat, 1969); John A. Pollard,
John Greenleaf Whittier: Friend of Man (Boston, Houghton Mifflin, 1949); Lewis Leary, *John
Greenleaf Whittier* (New York: Twayne, 1961); Roland Woodwell, *John Greenleaf Whittier: A
Biography* (Haverhill, Mass.: The Trustees of the John Greenleaf Whittier Homestead, 1985);
and Edward Wagenknecht, *John Greenleaf Whittier: A Portrait in Paradox* (New York: Oxford
Univ. Press, 1967). A brief overview of his life is Randall Cluff's entry in *American National Bi-
ography*, 23:320–2.

beth who shared and supported his poetic gifts and artistic ability, and it was she and their mother, Abigail, who sustained his literary efforts even as his father, John, the kindly but plain, practical, and economy-minded Quaker, insisted that farm duties took priority over education and writing. During the winter months the elder Whittier sometimes relented and permitted his son to attend the local school, where he fell under the genial influence of the eccentric young schoolmaster, Joshua Coffin. Coffin introduced him to the poetry of Burns's rural Scotland and the writings of Milton, especially those which emphasized human liberty and may have set Whittier on the path to abolition poems and essays. Quaker principles emphasizing pacifism, social justice, and a God of love were thus ingrained in the boy from an early age.

Whittier wrote his first poetry in 1824 at the age of sixteen. His initial success in publishing came as a result of his father subscribing to the *Newburyport Free Press,* edited by William Lloyd Garrison. It was Whittier's older sister Mary who, unbeknownst to him, submitted his poem "The Exile's Departure" to Garrison in 1826. When he published it in the June 8 issue Whittier was overjoyed; so began a lifelong relationship between the editor and the poet. Garrison published sixteen more of Whittier's poems in 1826. After receiving the first poem, the twenty-year old Garrison paid a surprise visit on him in the midst of his farm chores and then urged the senior Whittier to permit his son to seek further education. The father denied the request due to the press of farm labor, but the next year relented and permitted him to attend the newly opened Haverhill Academy. The young poet worked as a shoemaker and teacher to pay his tuition and, during his two years at the academy, had 150 of his poems published in area newspapers. Among those poems was "The Drunkard to His Bottle," which reflected Quaker temperance and similar influences at the academy in a village where there was easy access to liquor.[2] At this early date, there was no general theme in his poems of 1827 and 1828; his concern for slavery had not yet emerged. He appeared not yet aware even of the mild, gradualistic Quaker tradition of antislavery with its support of colonization.

With encouragement and support from Garrison and others, Whittier began the first of several editorships in 1829, that of *The American Manufac-*

2. Pollard, *Whittier,* 54–5. See also Whittier's letter of May 1882—his "Autobiography"—written "to meet the many demands on him for biographical information." In it the poet provides a brief account of his early years but says little about his later role in antislavery politics. The letter was published by the Trustees of the John Greenleaf Whittier Homestead in 1957.

turer, a political weekly in Boston. There he combined his poetry with politics in a journal that supported Henry Clay in its advocacy of protective tariffs and was equally vehement in its denunciation of the Jacksonian Democrats. Only rarely did he mention in his columns the social and cultural issues of the day, even those of temperance and world peace. His father's declining health forced him to resign this position in the summer of 1829 to return to Haverhill. When the elder Whittier died the following year, the young poet-editor was forced to resume his farm labors despite his own weak physical condition and distaste for farming. Despite the need to provide for his mother, aunt, and younger sister Lizzie, he soon became the editor of the *New England Weekly Review* in Hartford, Connecticut, after having served briefly as the editor of the *Haverhill Gazette.* The next several years were tumultuous ones for Whittier. During his eighteen months in Hartford he intensified his political interests and became an ardent supporter of Clay's nomination for president, using the *Review* to attack Andrew Jackson and Martin Van Buren. His political views conformed with those of most New Englanders of his class and way of life. Whittier's private life was complicated by a rejected courtship and physical exhaustion caused by overwork. His health finally forced his resignation as editor in late 1831 and his return to Haverhill in an attempt to regain strength. By 1832, he had published a short volume of poems and prose, *Legends of New England,* and had become a veteran writer at twenty-three, but his future appeared boxed in by poverty, family responsibility, and broken health.[3] He had published few antislavery poems, but numerous antislavery editorials, always adopting Quaker themes, especially their distaste for the slave trade. Reform concerns included temperance, world peace, and opposition to imprisonment for debt. If he could regain his strength, a future in writing and political journalism and reform perhaps beckoned.

On leaving Hartford, Whittier had hoped to return to his post at the *New England Weekly Review* or at a comparable journal in Cincinnati, but illhealth again prevented it, and meant he could not continue any sustained poetic efforts. Chosen by Massachusetts political leaders as a delegate to the National Republican convention in Baltimore pledged to support Clay's nomination for president, he lamented his inability to attend: "I have been quite ill and still am an invalid." At this point his first love was poetry: "The truth is, I love poetry, with a love as warm, as fervent, as sincere, as any of the more gifted worshipers at the temple of the Muses." But the need for a

---

3. Cluff, "Whittier," 320–1.

steady income meant "I have been compelled to trust to other and less pleasant pursuits for distinction and profit." A future in political journalism was "the only field now open for me, and there is something inconsistent in the character of a poet and a modern politician."[4] Whittier had not yet concluded that his poetry might include support of reform causes as well as historical tributes to his native New England and its traditions.

For a time, Whittier was torn between the incompatible goals of commitment to Clay and his National Republicans and to an emerging interest in abolition. As much as he might have preferred to ignore it, there was no evading the contradiction between Henry Clay the Kentucky slaveholder and Clay the leader of the party of his choice. Throughout the year he worked for the election of Caleb Cushing to the House of Representatives. Cushing's candidacy was bogged down in endless ballots due to the Massachusetts law requiring an absolute majority. Late in the year Whittier made himself available as a compromise choice even though he was several weeks short of the required age of twenty-five. Although National Republicans did not rise to the bait, this temporary lapse from his usual desire to remain behind the scenes reflected both an urge for success in politics and his need to escape his overwhelming poverty. He continued his poetic efforts by completing "Moll Pitcher," an eight hundred–line narrative account of New England spiritualism and witchcraft. And in March 1833 he wrote one last defense of Henry Clay and his tariff policy. But there were signs, too, of an awakening to a role in the developing antislavery crusade.

Throughout 1832, Whittier remained in communication with Garrison, who had led the formation of the New England Anti-Slavery Society early in the year. Whittier's full commitment came early in 1833, although he had earlier praised Garrison in print for his abolition work. Garrison urged him to take a stand: "Whittier, enlist!—Your talents, zeal, influence—all are needed." Several weeks later Garrison lectured in Haverhill, urging "the *immediate* abolition of slavery."[5] Whittier was finally ready to commit himself in keeping with his Quaker faith's dedication to social justice. In May, he wrote a brief, widely circulated pamphlet, "Justice and Expediency," which was an appeal for immediate abolition. After attacking colonization he urged emancipation to begin "in the District of Columbia and the Territories of Arkansas and Florida—which are under Federal jurisdiction." He

---

4. Whittier to Jonathan Law, February 4, 1832, John B. Pickard, ed., *The Letters of John Greenleaf Whittier* (Cambridge, Mass.: Harvard Univ. Press, 1975), 1:74–5

5. Garrison, quoted in Pollard, *Whittier*, 116; *Haverhill (Mass.) Gazette*, April 6, 1833.

concluded that "Nothing unconstitutional, nothing violent should be attempted . . . and the opposition to slavery should be inflexible and constantly maintained." He naively suggested that, in contrast to the southern slave, a worker in New England "may acquire by his labor on the farms of others, in a few years, a farm of his own." Garrison and most other abolitionists were more realistic in their awareness of the plight of northern workers. Later in the year Whittier protested Connecticut's treatment of Prudence Crandall in a ringing defense of free speech and her failed effort to establish a school for black girls; he appeared ready to join the New England abolition efforts with enthusiasm. As he explained years later, Garrison "instrumentality turned me away from . . . 'pleasure, profit and honor' to take sides with the poor and oppressed."[6]

To augment his meager farm income, Whittier published his poem "Touissant L'Ouverture" in the November issue of the *New England Magazine,* describing the heroic slave's efforts to overthrow French rule in Haiti in the 1790s.[7] Still not ready to abandon elective politics, Whittier accepted a National Republican nomination for the state legislature only to be defeated by a Jacksonian. Yet less than a month later he attended the founding meeting of the American Anti-Slavery Society in Philadelphia, telling Garrison beforehand of his desire "to urge upon the members of my Religious Society, the duty of putting their shoulders to the work,—to make their solemn testimony against Slavery visible over the land."[8] The meeting of sixty-two delegates, controlled by Garrison, adopted a Declaration of Sentiments, signed by Whittier and approximately half of the delegates, pledging themselves to oppose colonization and to work "to remove slavery by moral and political action as prescribed by the Constitution of the United States." Years later, during the Civil War, Whittier wrote to Garrison in recollection: "I am not insensible to literary reputation. I love, perhaps too well, the praise and

6. "Justice and Expediency," in John Greenleaf Whittier, *The Writings of John Greenleaf Whittier,* Riverside Edition (Boston: Houghton Mifflin, 1900), 7:27, 53–4; *Haverhill Gazette,* July 23, 1833; Whittier to Garrison, November 24, 1863, in Pickard, *Letters,* 3:52. For a psychological interpretation of Whittier's "conversion" to abolitionism, see Charles A. Jarvis, "Admission to Abolition: The Case of John Greenleaf Whittier," *Journal of the Early Republic* 4 (summer 1984): 161–76. Jarvis argues that joining the movement in 1833 "gave him an identity and mechanism whereby his roles found unity and significance" (175). Rather than a sudden change, however, Whittier's interest in abolitionism appears to have been a gradual and natural evolution of an interest that had been developing over the last decade.

7. Whittier, *Writings,* 3:11–9.

8. Whittier to Garrison, November 12, 1833, in Pickard, ed., *Letters,* 1:133.

good-will of my fellow-men; but I set a higher value on my name as appended to the Anti Slavery Declaration of 1833 than on the title page of any book."9

The next year, 1834, found Whittier hard at work organizing and writing in behalf of abolition. As he told fellow reformer Elizur Wright Jr., he had neglected no "opportunity for the dissemination of truth on the great subject of slavery."10 While maintaining his gentle Quaker disposition and approach, he did not shrink from confrontation, as when he criticized the New Haven clergyman Leonard Bacon for his continued support of colonization. Still, he would not abandon his defense of the Constitution and the right to oppose slavery within its framework. In a lengthy letter in the *Haverhill Gazette* in September, "The Constitution and Slavery," he argued that Congress could "abolish slavery in the District and the Territories" and it could "abolish the domestic slave trade," for "when these *constitutional* and necessary measures shall be carried into effect, the power of slavery will be prostrated forever." Whittier's view of the Constitution was thus in line with many abolitionists who, unlike Alvan Stewart, recognized it sanctioned slavery in the states but permitted an attack in areas outside of state jurisdiction. Political means were the best route, for this could be achieved "by sending our strong and honest men into Congress, and leaving our 'dough-faces,' of all parties at home." In this approach Whittier was anticipating the policy of some abolitionists who later adopted the tactic of questioning major party candidates and supporting those most in line with their position. He urged his friend Caleb Cushing that if he would endorse abolition in the District of Columbia, he could gain two to three hundred votes and secure victory, a pledge Cushing rejected. (Cushing still managed to win election.)11

Throughout the year Garrison published several of Whittier's antislavery poems, including "Plead for the Slave," "Stanzas for the Times" (which concluded: "One voice shall thunder, We are free!"), and "The Slave Ships."12 His 1834 "Hymn" concluded:

9. Whittier, *Writings*, 7:182; Whittier to Garrison, November 24, 1863, in Pickard, ed., *Letters*, 3:52; Woodwell, *Whittier*, 67–8.

10. Whittier to Wright, February 25, 1834, in Whittier, *Letters*, 1:142.

11. *Haverhill Gazette*, September 20, 1834; Whittier to Cushing, October 25, 1834, in Pickard, ed., *Letters*, 1:157–8.

12. Whittier, *Writings*, 3:19–24, 35–8. The poems can also be found in the *Liberator*, April 26, September 20, October 11, 1834.

When smitten as with fire from heaven,
The captive's chain shall sink in dust,
And to his fettered soul be given
The glorious freedom of the just!

He appeared especially concerned with the brutality of the slave trade and the inhumanity of the peculiar institution in general. Whittier attended abolition meetings throughout the region, now attacking Henry Clay "as the enemy of freedom."[13] The young Whittier had thus matured, revealing his combined potential as writer, poet, and antislavery politician.

By the end of 1834, Whittier had fully committed himself to abolitionism, although he did make a brief entry into elective two-party politics. Running as a Whig, he was elected to the state legislature as the representative from Haverhill. But he made little impact and was clearly not comfortable in the body of more than six hundred legislators. He made no speeches during his brief tenure and did not seek a second term. Law-making was clearly not his forte, and his only recorded action in behalf of reform was the introduction of a petition demanding the end of capital punishment. There were no bills relating to slavery, making his decision to retire from the legislature easier.[14]

Before his term ended, however, he became actively embroiled in antislavery activity and found himself among those pursued by antiabolition mobs. After befriending the controversial, flamboyant abolitionist George Thompson, he accompanied the Englishman on a lecture tour into New Hampshire. On September 4, 1835, the pair was pelted with rotten eggs and rocks by a mob which, in Whittier's words, "had drunk themselves into a state of remarkable patriotism." To escape their wrath, the reformers hid in the home of a friend and then beat a hasty retreat out of town. Whittier later recalled: "I kept Thompson, whose life was hunted for, concealed in our lonely farm-house for two weeks." Later in the year, Whittier witnessed Garrison being dragged through the streets of Boston with a rope around him. As pressure on the abolitionists to cease their agitation intensified from both mobs and elected officials, including Governor Edward Everett, the U.S. House of Representatives reacted with the infamous Gag Rule, tabling all antislavery petitions. Whittier responded with a defense of constitutional rights. Writing in the *Essex Gazette,* he answered: "We can neither permit

13. Whittier, *Writings,* 3:29–30; Pollard, *Whittier,* 132.
14. Pollard, *Whittier,* 134; Woodwell, *Whittier,* 73–4, 77–8.

the GAG to be thrust in our mouths by others, nor deem it part of 'patriotism' to place it there ourselves. The more fiercely our rights are assailed, the closer we will hold them to our hearts."[15] By the end of 1836, he was forced to resign his position as editor of the *Haverhill Gazette,* for his antislavery views had become too controversial for the journal's Whig owner to tolerate. Frustrated by the hostility of some New Englanders and the apathy of others, he told Garrison that appealing to the voters and petitioning the legislature would yield more positive results than opposing a political role for abolitionists. Whittier was among the first to advocate political pressure, and at this point Garrison was more receptive to such an approach than he would soon be when political abolitionists began to talk of the need for a third party. Willing to advocate such action for others, Whittier himself continued to prefer writing newspaper editorials and antislavery poetry to reach the consciences of Americans, North and South. During the summer of 1837, he worked as an agent of the American Anti-Slavery Society in New York, sending out petitions. There he associated with such abolitionists as Theodore Weld, Joshua Leavitt, and Henry B. Stanton. Although an able writer, Whittier, complained Stanton, had "no power of originating . . . is a Quaker from head to foot—is rather careless in his business habits." Unsuited for such work, Whittier became tired of the regimented duties and soon resumed his writing in Massachusetts.[16]

By the end of 1837, Whittier had given up any pretense of farming, selling the family homestead in Haverhill and moving with his mother and sister to nearby Amesbury. He bought a cottage house on Friend Street near the Quaker meeting house and lived there the rest of his life. There he wrote most of his poetry and essays, greeted guests attired in his long black Quaker coat, usually using the Quaker dialect in his conversation. By the late 1830s he earned what meager income he could from his role as an antislavery editor and poet. In 1838 he moved briefly to Philadelphia to work on the editorial staff of fellow Quaker Benjamin Lundy's *National Enquirer.* As Lundy's health deteriorated, Whittier replaced him as editor and the Pennsylvania Anti-Slavery Society changed the weekly's name to the *Pennsylvania Freeman.*

15. Whittier to Erastus Brooks, September 9, 1835, in Pickard, ed., *Letters,* 1:173; *Essex Gazette,* February 13, 1836; Whittier, "Autobiography," May 1882; Woodwell, *Whittier,* 88–9.

16. Whittier to Garrison, December 1, 1836, Boston Public Library, in Pollard, *Whittier,* 157; Whittier to Elizabeth Whittier, July 4, 1837, in Pickard, ed., *Letters,* 1:240; Dumond, ed., *Letters of James Gillespie Birney, 1831–1857,* 1:408; Woodwell, *Whittier,* 98–100; Davis, *Leavitt,* 135.

Philadelphia would be the scene of further mob action directed against abolitionists in general and Whittier and his paper in particular, this coming shortly after Pennsylvania had taken away the right to vote from blacks and denied a trial by jury to escaped slaves. When abolitionists opened their Pennsylvania Hall in May 1838, trouble began immediately. With the paper's offices located in the building, Whittier had composed an ode as part of the dedication ceremonies.[17] Antiblack and antiabolitionist sentiment reached a peak on May 17, and with the mayor and city officials refusing intervention, a mob of fifteen thousand, many of whom were drunk, ransacked the building and burned it to the ground. During the conflagration, Whittier courageously disguised himself and entered the building to rescue important papers from his office. Still managing to publish his paper, Whittier described how "the doors were broken open with axes—the Anti Slavery office in the lower story was entered and the books and pamphlets scattered among the crowd." He bitterly concluded: "Pennsylvania Hall is in ashes! The beautiful temple consecrated to Liberty, has been offered a smoking sacrifice to the Demon of Slavery."[18]

Whittier remained with the *Freeman* for two years, although poor health forced him to return to Amesbury for much of that time. Struggling to maintain his tiny income, he composed many of the paper's editorials from his home. He urged the beleaguered Pennsylvania abolitionists on, noting that the forces aligned against them included "mercenary merchants,—selfish and heartless politicians,—time serving priests and their deluded followers,—hypocrites in church and State,—bloated aristocrats and counterfeit democrats." The atmosphere was further "corrupted by the proximity of slavery. Every breeze blows over you from Maryland and Virginia comes loaded with the moral pestilence." More concerned than most white abolitionists about racial equality, he found little support in the struggle against discrimination except within the black community, as the forces of bigotry appeared dominant. With fugitives hunted mercilessly on their escape to Canada, "the rights of the colored citizens of Pennsylvania have been immolated on the Altar of Southern Slavery"; all basic rights of citizens were denied to them.[19] Early in 1839, a Whittier poem attacked newly elected governor David Rittenhouse Porter for his open opposition to antislavery.[20]

17. "Pennsylvania Hall," Whittier, *Writings*, 3:58–63.
18. *Pennsylvania Freeman* (Philadelphia), May 18, 1838; Pollard, *Whittier*, 165.
19. *Pennsylvania Freeman*, October 26, 1838; Mordell, *Whittier*, 100–1.
20. "The New Year," Whittier, *Writings*, 3:63–9.

Finally in early 1840, Whittier announced his resignation from the paper due to personal issues including his many infirmities, especially chronic headaches and stomach troubles. A desire to return to what he believed to be the less repressive society of Boston made his decision easier. His health and poverty were also factors in preventing him from marrying despite a warm interest in several female friends. His Quaker beliefs along with his mother's insistence led him to consider only women of his own faith for a partner, and this, along with his continuing need to support his mother and sister, kept him a bachelor. In early 1840, doctors ordered him to remain in Massachusetts rather than attend a London abolition convention. Henceforth, while he frequently traveled in the East to attend antislavery meetings, Whittier remained in Amesbury, where he wrote editorials and poems and turned increasingly to political action to attack slavery.

Whittier had always been interested in politics and had been active in Whig campaigns throughout mid-1830s. Now, in committing himself to abolition he forsook the Whigs and his favorite Henry Clay, but continued to believe political action was the best means to abolish slavery. He believed that the Constitution provided no protection for slavery and that Congress had the authority to abolish it in the District of Columbia and prevent its spread to areas not yet states. He strongly endorsed the petition movement and thus rallied to John Quincy Adams's efforts to fight the House of Representatives Gag Rule. In 1837, Garrisonians, by then moving more toward immediatism and perfectionism and a rejection of a role for government, watered down his efforts for political antislavery resolutions at the annual meeting of the American Anti-Slavery Society. He later explained: "I looked to the ballot-box, as under God, the chief instrumentality for averting the progress of slavery, differing in this respect from some of my esteemed associates in the antislavery cause."[21] Whittier also fought Garrison in the latter's efforts to broaden the platform and introduce other reform issues, such as women's rights, into the movement, noting in the *Freeman,* "As abolitionists we have a single object; let us keep our eyes single toward it." He urged Garrison to "let the SLAVE have the Liberator as his own."[22]

The major issue between Whittier and Garrison was the political role of abolitionists, but the two were also at odds over Garrison's persistent attack on what he believed were the proslavery views of the churches and the clergy's refusal to repudiate their denominations' southern ties. Like many

21. To Unidentified Correspondent, September 13, 1879, in Pickard, ed., *Letters,* 3:411.
22. *Pennsylvania Freeman,* April 11, June 6, 1839.

abolitionists, Whittier preferred to work to reform these churches rather than to harshly criticize them. Most importantly, Garrison now insisted that it was "the duty of abolitionists to abandon the ballot box and rely only upon moral suasion," while Whittier agreed with those who believed it was "the duty of abolitionists to use their elective franchise for the abrogation of the unholy slave laws." Many abolitionists stood in between these polarized positions, hesitant to enter politics, yet resistant to what they regarded as Garrison's extremism. Despite their strong differences, it was important to Whittier not to "quarrel with the friend of twelve years . . . who first stimulated me to active exertion in the cause of the slave." Nor did he wish to gratify "the enemy by the spectacle of a 'passage of arms' between a Quaker and a Non Resistant." But Garrison's response indicated that the break between the two was more serious. Said Garrison: "Is the difference then, friend Whittier, a 'trifling' one? Is it polemical or political? *You* see nothing ominous of evil to the integrity of our cause; others do."[23]

At the Albany meeting of the American Anti-Slavery Society in August 1839, Whittier and Henry B. Stanton proposed supporting independent candidates for president and vice president, a motion approved over Garrison's opposition. Whittier's motion that voting "so as to promote the abolition of slavery, is of high obligation—a duty which as abolitionists, we owe to our enslaved fellow countrymen," passed 84–77. Garrison's influence meant that Massachusetts delegates opposed by a three-to-one margin while New York's approved by four-to-one.[24] Garrison and his followers had suffered a severe defeat, and it was clear that his organization could not be the vehicle to form a third party.

Whittier himself was still somewhat reluctant to make the break with his former friend, and he did not attend the April 1840 meeting in Albany which nominated James G. Birney for president. Until that nomination, Whittier had still hoped for reconciliation with Garrison and his supporters, noting privately, "I cannot see eye to eye with Garrison and Mrs. (Maria Weston) Chapman. They do injustice as I think to those who dissent from them. There is a dictatorial, censorious intolerant spirit about them which I cannot fellowship. I loathe this whole quarrel—it is not *christian*."[25] He explained that had he been in Albany, "I should vote against a nomination, on

23. Whittier to Garrison, February 24, 1839, in Pickard, ed., *Letters*, 1:331–2. Garrison's response was appended to Whittier's letter (Pickard, ed., *Letters*, 1:333).

24. Sewell, *Ballots for Freedom*, 39–40.

25. Whittier to Samuel J. May, March 27, 1840, in Pickard, ed., *Letters*, 1:402.

the grounds of expediency," for "it would only furnish occasion for increased bitterness and evil speaking among us." He feared that Garrison and his friends would "embarrass, ridicule . . . cover the friends of *practical* abolition with ignominy and defeat." He later urged Birney to decline the nomination because "I do not believe that five hundred voters can be found in this state who will go for the Albany nomination. I do not know of *one* in Essex County." But by the fall, as the campaign heated up, he had moderated his views and now supported Birney's candidacy, lamenting that "the evil spirit" of party politics would keep the New England Liberty vote small.[26] His earlier reluctance had been conditioned by his friendship with Garrison and the lack of enthusiasm for political abolitionism in Massachusetts. In contrast, Alvan Stewart had passionately and consistently embraced the third-party movement from the time of Liberty's inception.

Whittier continued to regret the lack of solidarity among abolitionists, especially in light of what he perceived to be the unity of slaveholders. Estimating that there were roughly the same number of slaveholders as abolitionists (250,000), he decried the control over politics exerted by the former in upholding slavery while the latter seemed bent on apologizing for and defending their right to exist in the face of northern opposition or apathy. Said Whittier, the slaveholder makes his feelings "subordinate to the interests of slavery; the abolitionist waves his abolitionism" to be allowed to stand "on equal terms with incorrigible slaveholders." Even worse, "the slaveholder makes his allegiance to his political party altogether dependent upon *its* allegiance to slavery," while "the abolitionist makes party paramount to principle." He allows issues relating to slavery to be set aside for party unity and lesser issues. Abolitionists must instead unite, putting aside the bitter "dissensions of the past two years." He appealed "to the old spirit of '33," when abolitionists met as one.[27]

Abolitionist divisions would not be easily healed, for neither Garrisonians nor Liberty advocates could compromise and Whittier himself became more committed to the third-party approach. Most of his correspondence dealt with Liberty party matters; he was an officer in various Liberty groups, attended local conventions, helped edit the *Emancipator,* and worked for the election of Liberty candidates. In 1842, he even agreed to be the Liberty party candidate for Congress in his district. In accepting the nomination he

26. Whittier to Birney, March 8, August 12, 1840, Whittier to the Anti-Slavery Convention at Albany, March 22, 1840, in Pickard, ed., *Letters,* 1:388–9, 398–9, 432–3.

27. Whittier to Charles C. Burleigh, October 8, 1840, in Pickard, ed., *Letters,* 1:449–53.

proudly proclaimed: "I am an abolitionist . . . I hate slavery in all its forms, degrees and influences."[28] Although he had no chance of victory, the majority rule in Massachusetts prevented the choosing of a congressman through several ballots. Whittier withdrew in December 1843 due to poor health, having done little campaigning through the long ordeal. For the most part, however, he preferred his role as adviser and publicist for the third party, a role he would execute with competence through the 1840s. Nor did he neglect his antislavery poetry. With renewed vigor he composed "The Relic" and "Massachusetts to Virginia" in 1843, the latter of which included:

> But for us and for our children, the vow which we have given
> For Freedom and humanity is registered in Heaven;
> No slave-hunt in our borders, no pirate on our stand!
> No fetters in the Bay State—no slave upon our land![29]

His publication of a volume of poetry, *Lays of My Home,* in 1843, much of which nostalgically recalled the simple pleasures of his rural boyhood, also established him as an accomplished poet as well as an abolitionist-editor who wrote verse. Liberty editors eagerly used his antislavery poems in their journals as an effective voice in their political crusade.

Although Liberty party strength was greater in New York due to the leadership of Gerrit Smith, William Goodell, Alvan Stewart, and their colleagues, the Massachusetts party maintained a vigorous organization through editorials, conventions, and speeches, and by the mid-1840s had weakened Garrison and his supporters by winning over significant numbers of converts.[30] Liberty editors included Joshua Leavitt (*Emancipator*), Elizur Wright (*Massachusetts Abolitionist*), and Whittier, who edited the *Middlesex Standard* of Lowell, Massachusetts, during the critical 1844 presidential election and Texas crisis. Whittier had long since abandoned his support of Henry Clay, who had treated him as a traitor to Whig causes when he met him in Washington in 1841. He was in full support of James G. Birney's campaign in 1844 and with the Liberty effort to block annexation and statehood for the slave republic of Texas. Regarding Clay's nomination as the Whig

---

28. Whittier to John Hayes et al., October 10, 1842, in Pickard, ed., *Letters,* 1:574. See also Pickard, ed., *Letters,* 1:478; Woodwell, *Whittier,* 146–7.

29. Whittier, *Writings,* 3:80–6.

30. See Reinhard O. Johnson, "The Liberty Party in Massachusetts, 1840–1848: Antislavery Third Party Politics in the Bay State," *Civil War History* 28 (September 1982): 237–65.

candidate, Whittier believed that no one who loved liberty could support the Kentuckian, who had debased "his noble intellect to the service of Slavery." In a reference to the effect of slavery, he described Clay as "a deliberate robber of the poor." Nor did he neglect discrimination at home, as when he condemned a Lowell museum for excluding black children from an exhibit. Two anti-Texas poems, "Texas" and "To Faneuil Hall," along with one attacking John C. Calhoun for urging Texas annexation and opposing adding the free territory of Oregon, added to his Liberty efforts. When a friend, poet Henry Wadsworth Longfellow, published some antislavery poems, Whittier joined other Liberty leaders in urging him to run for Congress. The gentle Longfellow responded that he could not enter "the political arena," for partisan warfare was "too violent, too vindictive for my taste."[31]

Birney's showing in 1844 was a tenfold increase over 1840, but Democrat James K. Polk's victory gave Liberty leaders little consolation. Polk, said Whittier, was "a practical slaveholder, living down in his daily conduct the doctrines of the great Declaration." Undaunted, abolition leaders prepared to press ahead in the third-party effort. New issues surfaced following the election and the addition of Texas as a slave state in late 1845. Whittier could rejoice in the repeal of the Gag Rule in 1844, and on the eve of Texas admission he was present in Washington to present a petition signed by sixty thousand demanding rejection of statehood. He found members of Congress willing to assure him they would oppose admission, only to vote for it, "for they dare not stand up like men against it." He could only sadly conclude that as far as most northern Democrats and Whigs were concerned, "The Slave Power rules Congress, completely, absolutely."[32]

When a boundary dispute between Texas and Mexico fueled by Polk's thirst for California and the entire Southwest led to war between the United States and Mexico in May 1846, Liberty leaders, including Whittier, pictured the war as one to expand slave territory. In addition, a growing number of northern antislavery Whigs and Democrats were finally ready to attack the Polk administration and the Slave Power for its proslave aggressiveness. The election to the Senate of John P. Hale in 1846 by a New Hampshire

31. Whittier to *Essex Transcript,* May 20, 1844, Whittier to Longfellow, September 9, 1844, in Pickard, ed., *Letters,* 1:641, 646–7; *Middlesex Standard* (Lowell, Mass.), July 25, August 15, 1844; Longfellow's response is quoted in Mordell, *Whittier,* 138–9; Woodwell, *Whittier,* 164–5.

32. *Middlesex Standard,* November 14, 1844; Whittier to Elizur Wright, December 15, 1845, in Pickard, ed., *Letters,* 1:681, 683; Pollard, *Whittier,* 220.

Democratic-Liberty coalition gave third-party leaders a stronger candidate than Birney for the next presidential election, and Whittier rejoiced that Hale had "broken the spell which has hither to held the reluctant Democracy in the embraces of slavery." The break between Massachusetts Whig factions over the slavery issue offered Whittier further encouragement, for the antislavery Conscience Whig group included many with whom he was acquainted and with whom he was eager to work. He was especially pleased that Charles Sumner appeared ready to cooperate with Liberty leaders.[33] Whittier had begun a warm correspondence with Sumner a year earlier after the young orator had outraged the Massachusetts Whig old guard with an attack on war in general and on the pending Mexican conflict in particular. It was, said Whittier, "a noble address." In an 1846 speech Sumner had tied slavery with the Mexican War, and Whittier responded by urging him to run for office. The introduction in the House by Pennsylvania Democrat David Wilmot of his proposal banning slavery in all territory acquired in the war against Mexico provided an issue around which all northern antislavery elements could rally.

The political antislavery movement now entered a new phase, albeit one which stressed containing slavery rather than abolishing it. Breaking with the Stewart faction and its insistence on abolition, Whittier and most Liberty men modified their approach. Whittier knew that a larger coalition that included antislavery Whigs and Democrats could more effectively be heard; in this the poet took on a new and more prominent role. As debate over the Wilmot Proviso swirled in Congress and the press, antislavery leaders moved to create a voice in Washington in 1847 with the establishment of the *National Era* and chose Ohio Liberty leader Gamaliel Bailey as its editor. Although Whittier had been considered for the post due to his vast journalistic experience, poor health again precluded such a role. But next to Bailey, he did the most for the new paper's antislavery efforts when he assumed the role of a corresponding editor. Over the next decade, with the comfort of

33. Whittier on Hale, in Mordell, *Whittier,* 147. For Whittier's friendship with Sumner, see J. Welfred Holmes, "Whittier and Sumner: A Political Friendship," *New England Quarterly* 30 (1957): 58–72. See also Anne-Marie Taylor, *Young Charles Sumner and the Legacy of the American Enlightenment, 1811–1851* (Amherst: Univ. of Massachusetts Press, 2001), 221, 230. For a recent interpretation of the northern reaction to the Slave Power and its northern allies, especially Democrats, see Richards, *The Slave Power,* 22. The Conscience Whigs were so named because of their belief in the immorality of slavery. Their opponents who controlled the party received the name Cotton Whigs, due to their economic ties with the South and their dependence, as textile manufacturers, on southern cotton and thus slavery.

home and closeness of family and friends, he contributed 109 poems and 275 essays championing human freedom.[34] Together they represented Whittier's most effective attack on slavery. These writings also served to make him financially secure for the first time.

Whittier and Bailey had long agreed on sectional issues and on Liberty party strategy, and together they championed Hale's candidacy for the Liberty ticket in 1848. As the war continued, Liberty and antislavery Whig protest meetings increased in number and intensity even as Liberty showings in elections of state and national office improved. Whittier continued to urge Charles Sumner and other Conscience Whigs to join them in a common antislavery party. He pleaded with Sumner: "Let me implore you to act."[35] As pressure mounted for a more prominent antislavery Whig or Democrat to replace Hale, Whittier insisted that Hale was the only one that all antislavery elements could rally around "without any compromise of principle." Only Hale could "combine all the scattered fragments of anti Slavery in the country." Whittier argued that proslavery interpretations of the Constitution should not prevent the attack on slavery, for "it has been a mere ruse of war in the hands of Slavery for half a century. It has been made to say and be just what the South wished." Instead, the Constitution should be construed "in the light of Liberty—as we understand it." When the party nominated Hale in its October 1847 convention in Buffalo, Whittier rejoiced. Delegates rejected efforts of Gerrit Smith and William Goodell of New York to use the Alvan Stewart doctrine to have slavery everywhere labeled unconstitutional. They also rejected their attempts to expand the platform to include other reforms. Instead the party settled for planks urging abolition of District of Columbia slavery, the repeal of the 1793 Fugitive Slave Act, and support of the Wilmot Proviso.[36] The convention, led by Salmon P. Chase, had modified its position to leave open the possibility of union with antislavery Whigs and Democrats. For Whittier, the prospect was indeed a promising one, although he did not yet realize that it could mean sacrificing Hale's candidacy to a broader antislavery coalition.

34. Harrold, *Gamaliel Bailey and Antislavery Union,* 84–90.

35. See, for example, Whittier to *National Era,* February 5, 1847, Whittier to Sumner, June 20, 1848, in Pickard, ed., *Letters,* 2:69–71, 103–4; Holmes, "Whittier and Sumner," 59–60.

36. *National Era,* September 2, November 10, 1847; Whittier to Samuel Fessenden, July 21, 1847, in Pickard, ed., *Letters,* 2:93; Johnson and Porter, eds., *National Party Platforms,* 13–4.

The third-party effort coalesced into the Free Soil movement at an enthusiastic convention in Buffalo in August 1848. But before that meeting, preliminary gatherings in Worcester, Utica, and Columbus made it clear that antislavery Whigs and Democrats in key northern states would not accept Hale as their candidate. Even more disheartening to Whittier and his colleagues was the realization that the largest element in the forming coalition, the New York faction known as the Barnburners, would insist on Martin Van Buren as the presidential candidate. While Whittier explained to Sumner his willingness to be part of the movement and to "fall into the ranks of the common soldiers of freedom," he found the former president to be "too old a sinner to hope for his conversion." By the end of July he realized that the Barnburners would insist on Van Buren and admitted he could accept him "if he would commit in favor of abolition in the District of Columbia."[37] Still, he feared that the convention would bring only "a shallow unity," for the Proviso was too narrow a basis for an effective attack on slavery.

Chosen a delegate to Buffalo, Whittier was unable to attend due to illness. In the end he, like most Massachusetts Liberty leaders, swallowed his distrust of Van Buren and campaigned enthusiastically for the Free Soil ticket of Van Buren and Charles Francis Adams, and its containment platform, for he now believed that "the convention has nobly performed its great mission." Only a small New York faction led by Smith and Goodell held out for an abolitionist, and they formed the Liberty League with Smith as its candidate. Whittier agreed instead with delegate Joshua Leavitt that, with the adoption of a satisfactory platform by the Free Soilers, "The Liberty party is not dead but translated."[38] Throughout the campaign Whittier used the columns of the *National Era* to urge readers to back Van Buren and Free Soil, clearly signaling that a prominent candidate with broader appeal was more critical than maintaining Liberty principles uncompromised. Whittier also contributed a volume of antislavery poetry, which Sumner welcomed with praise: "How much more powerful is a song than a bullet." The deliberate omission of a plank calling for equal rights for blacks reflected the thinking of the time, even of those dedicated to eliminating slavery. The leaders of the party feared its inclusion might alienate

37. Whittier to Sumner, June 23, 1848, Whittier to William Channing, July 1, 1848, Whittier to Moses Cartland, July 27, 1848, in Pickard, ed., *Letters*, 2:105, 108, 110.

38. For Leavitt's role at the convention, see Davis, *Leavitt*, 244–9.

far more voters than it would attract. Still, Whittier optimistically hailed the party's commitment to "absolute and universal equality of human rights."[39]

Despite the Free Soil vote's improving to 291,263, compared to Birney's 62,000 in 1844, and the party's 28 percent showing in Massachusetts, where it out-polled Democrats to become the second party, third-party enthusiasm and independence would prove elusive in the months ahead. Bailey and Whittier used the *National Era* unsuccessfully to combat New York and Wisconsin Free Soil reunion with Democrats in 1849 and the Clay efforts to push his compromise proposals through Congress in 1850. The two major parties were equally evil in his eyes, for each served the South as "protectors" of slavery. Free State representatives must use their majority in the House to exercise the constitutional right "to abolish, limit, and restrain slavery."[40] Although Massachusetts Free Soilers held firm to their separate organization, talk of a coalition with Democrats against the dominant Whigs was widespread. For Whittier, most disheartening was Whig senator Daniel Webster's support of Clay's compromise proposals, especially the notorious fugitive slave bill, which he endorsed in his famous Seventh of March speech. Others compared Webster to Judas Iscariot, while Whittier attacked the senator in a famous poem, "Ichabod," published in May in the *National Era*. Rather than a personal attack, the poem was a lament "for one who had deserted a noble cause":

> So fallen, so lost! The light withdrawn
>   Which once he wore!
> The glory from his gray hairs gone
>   Forevermore! . . .
>
> All else is gone; from those great eyes
>   The soul has fled;
> When faith is lost, when honor dies,
>   The man is dead!

39. *National Era,* November 10, 1847, July 20, August 31, October 11, 1848; O. C. Gardiner, *The Great Issue; or, the Three Presidential Candidates* (New York: W. C. Bryant and Co., 1848), 140–1; Sumner to Whittier, December 6, 1848, Sumner Papers, Harvard University; Frederick J. Blue, *The Free Soilers: Third Party Politics, 1848–54* (Urbana: Univ. of Illinois Press, 1973), 77–8.

40. *National Era,* September 13, 1849, March 28, 1850.

> Then, pay the reverence of old days
>> To his dead fame;
> Walk backward with averted gaze,
>> And hide the shame!

Northerners, said Whittier, were "more pained than surprised therefore to find the great Massachusetts senator taking another step downward."[41]

Equally effective was the poet's "A Sabbath Scene," which portrayed a fugitive woman seized by slavehunters during a church service and mocked the clergy's use of the Bible to justify the Fugitive Slave Act under which she was seized:

> I saw the parson tie the knots,
>> The while his flock addressing,
> The Scriptural claims of slavery
>> With text on text impressing.
>
> "Although," said he, "on Sabbath day,
>> All secular occupations
> Are deadly sins, we must fulfill
>> Our moral obligations"[42]

Whittier kept up a steady attack on the Clay proposals throughout the spring and summer in essays in the *National Era* and lamented their becoming law in the fall of 1850. For the next decade, repeal of the Fugitive Slave Act became a rallying cry for virtually all who were part of the antislavery movement.

When Webster became Millard Fillmore's secretary of state in 1850, Democrats and Free Soilers in the Massachusetts legislature worked together to elect his successor. Whittier himself had declined to run for the legislature, arguing that he could not be part of any enforcement of the Fugitive Slave Act. He added, "so far as that is law *I am a nullifier.* By no act or countenance or consent of mine shall that law be enforced in Massachusetts."[43] In exchange for George Boutwell's selection as governor, Free Soilers insisted on Charles Sumner for Webster's Senate seat. Some Democrats, led by Whit-

41. Whittier, *Writings*, 3:159–63; *National Era*, May 2, June 6, 1850; Mordell, *Whittier*, 157.

42. *National Era*, June 27, 1850; Whittier, *Writings*, 3:159–63.

43. Whittier to the Editors of the *Bay State*, in Pickard, ed., *Letters*, 2:164.

tier's former friend Caleb Cushing, balked at the outspoken Sumner, and the legislature remained deadlocked through more than three months of balloting in early 1851. Throughout the stalemate, Whittier, who claimed to have been the first to have urged Sumner to enter the race, now implored him to remain a candidate despite his earnest desire to withdraw. During the long legislative stalemate Sumner visited his longtime friend in Amesbury for further encouragement. With Sumner's ultimate victory on April 21, 1851, the poet wrote joyfully, "Sick abed I heard the guns—Quaker as I am—with real satisfaction."[44] In the decade ahead Sumner would have no firmer friend and editorial ally than John Greenleaf Whittier.

As events of the 1850s moved the nation to the brink of civil war, Whittier remained active in antislavery politics, although he did begin to scale back his activities, in part the result of the escalating violence. He rejoiced in the impressive interest in Harriet Beecher Stowe's *Uncle Tom's Cabin*, first published in serial form in the *National Era*, noting that "the heaviest blow which Slavery has received for the last half century has just been struck by a woman." Despite his intense opposition to the Fugitive Slave Act of 1850, he, like most other Quakers, opposed using force to prevent its enforcement. As fugitive slave Anthony Burns awaited extradition to Virginia in Boston in May 1854, Whittier argued that "that man *must* not be sent out of Boston as a slave. Anything but that." Yet Whittier wrote Burns's attorney of his dread of violence: "I do earnestly hope and pray that no violence or brute force may be resorted to by the friends of freedom. I would die rather than *aid* that wicked law; but I deplore all forcible resistance to it. . . . May God in his mercy keep us from evil in opposing evil." He also wrote "The Rendition" as a further attack on the infamous law.[45] Bloodshed in Kansas following passage of the Kansas-Nebraska Act in May 1854 did not prevent him from supporting the New England Emigrant Aid Company and its efforts to send antislavery settlers to the territory. Families on their way to Kansas sang his poem "The Kansas Emigrants" as they joined in the efforts to keep the region free:

44. Taylor, *Young Charles Sumner*, 320–34; Whitman Bennett, *Whittier, Bard of Freedom* (1941; reprint, Port Washington, N.Y.: Kennikat Press, 1972), 230; Mordell, *Whittier*, 162; Whittier to Sumner, November 3, 1846, Sumner Papers; Whittier to Grace Greenwood, May 18, 1851, Whittier to Sumner, April 24, 1851, in Pickard, ed., *Letters*, 2:177, 176; Holmes, "Whittier and Sumner," 59–62.

45. *National Era*, January 27, 1853; Whittier to Henry Bowditch, May 26, 1854, Whittier to Samuel Sewall, May 29, 1854, in Pickard, ed., *Letters*, 2:257, 260; Whittier, *Writings*, 3: 170–1.

We cross the prairie as of old
The pilgrims crossed the sea,
And make the West, as they the east
The homestead of the free! . . .

When the Act led to the formation of the Republican party, joining Whittier's Free Soilers with antislavery Whigs and Democrats, the poet was in full support, caring little for old party labels: "Show me a party cutting itself loose from slavery, repudiating its treacherous professed allies of the South and making the *protection of Man* its paramount object and I am ready to go with it heart and soul."[46]

Events in 1856 increased Whittier's resolve as well as his fear of violence. In response to the caning of Charles Sumner on the floor of the Senate by South Carolina representative Preston Brooks in May, Whittier called for political unity, lamenting that "the North is not united for freedom as the South is for slavery." Northern division allowed the Slave Power to take "advantage of our folly." He told Sumner that his speech, "The Crime Against Kansas," which had precipitated Brooks's attack, was "a grand and terrible Philippic, worthy of the great occasion—the severe and *awful* Truth which the sharp agony of the national crisis demanded."[47] His poems and essays filled the columns of the *National Era* in behalf of Republican candidate John C. Frémont, and he took heart that southern-backed James Buchanan's victory was won over solid New England support of Frémont. He lamented the violence provoked by John Brown's raid at Harpers Ferry in 1859: "We feel deeply (who does not?) for the noble hearted, self-sacrificing old man. But friends of peace, as well as believers in the Sermon on the Mount, we dare not lend *any* countenance to such attempts as that at Harper's Ferry."[48]

By this time Whittier was concluding his role with the *National Era* and increasingly submitting his poetry to the new *Atlantic Monthly,* due to its greater emphasis on literary works and higher fees, reflecting Whittier's gradual turn from reform to his increasing renown as a poet. Nor was he exclusively an abolition poet, and in fact even as he campaigned for Frémont an increasing number of his works looked back at his own boyhood ("The

46. Whittier, *Writings,* 3:176–7; Whittier to Ralph Waldo Emerson, July 3, 1854, in Pickard, ed., *Letters,* 2:266–7.
47. *Amesbury Villager,* June 5, 1856, in Pollard, *Whittier,* 234–5; Whittier to Sumner, June 13, 1856, in Pickard, ed., *Letters,* 2:297; Holmes, "Whittier and Sumner," 65–6.
48. Whittier to Lydia Maria Child, October 21, 1859, in Pickard, ed., *Letters,* 2:435–6.

Barefoot Boy," 1858) and the New England past ("Maud Miller," 1856). Two volumes of his works were published in 1857. But in 1860 he could rejoice in the election of Abraham Lincoln, having served as a Republican elector, even as he feared the coming of bloody civil war, albeit one which he believed would destroy slavery. He especially celebrated Pennsylvania's support of Lincoln in "To Pennsylvania"—the state whose mobs had destroyed Pennsylvania Hall in 1838 and whose voters had endorsed Buchanan in 1856. The situation left him in a quandary, for he opposed coercion or war against the seceded states ("A Word for the Hour," 1861) but resisted appeasing the South. Concessions to slaveholders "could only strengthen and confirm" the "gigantic conspiracy against the rights and liberties, the Union and life, of the nations." When compromise proposals were debated in early 1861, he told Sumner: "We have done no wrong, unless in submitting to wrong too long; we have nothing to concede that will satisfy the secessionist of the Border States."[49]

Despite his dilemma, Whittier could not resist the Union war effort and instead encouraged fellow Quakers to give support in indirect ways: "Our mission is at this time to mitigate the sufferings of our countrymen, to visit and aid the sick and the wounded, to relieve the necessities of the widow and orphan, and to practice economy for the sake of charity."[50] He believed that the war was just and that northern suffering would bring victory and emancipation. He wrote no battle songs, but his words of encouragement played a role in bolstering Union troop morale. In "Ein Feste Burg ist Unser Gott," he described the war against slavery and his belief that it could not end without abolition:

> In vain the bells of war shall ring
>   Of triumphs and revenges
> While still is spared the evil thing
>   That severest ranges
> But best the ear that yet shall hear
>   The jubilant bell
> That rings the knell of Slavery forever.

49. Whittier to Salmon P. Chase, October 30, 1860, Whittier to Hannah Lloyd Neall, November 8, 1860, Whittier to Sumner, February 6, 1861, in Pickard, ed., *Letters*, 2:474, 475–6, 3:11; Whittier, *Writings*, 3:184–5, 218–9; Mordell, *Whittier*, 149.

50. Whittier, To Members of the Society of Friends, June 18, 1861, in Pickard, ed., *Writings*, 3:21.

Lincoln read the poem and, later evidence suggests, wanted Union solders to hear it, for it was a factor in his eventual decision for emancipation.[51] As the fighting raged, Whittier was no longer active in antislavery politics, but his voice was just as strong and effective in urging and then celebrating the long-sought emancipation. Privately he anguished after only seven months of bloodshed: "The sad war drags along. I long to see some compensation for its horrors, in the deliverance of the Slaves. Without this it is the wickedest war of the nineteenth century."[52] Publicly he maintained a positive and optimistic belief that slavery would shortly die.

For Whittier, Lincoln's Emancipation Proclamation was too long in coming; he had waited impatiently with others for the president's policy to catch up with abolitionists' demands. When the president, in September 1861, revoked John C. Frémont's order freeing slaves belonging to Confederates in his Missouri command, the poet rushed to the general's defense. While recognizing Frémont's act to be premature, in his poem "To John C. Frémont," Whittier responded:

> Thy error, Frémont simply was to act
> A brave man's part without the statesman's tact
> And, taking counsel but of common sense,
> To strike at cause as well as consequence.[53]

Yet as Congress and the president moved slowly toward eventual freedom, Whittier celebrated each step. In April 1862, when the Senate approved a bill ending slavery in the capital, he wrote to Sumner, "Glory to God! Nothing but the hearty old Methodist response will express my joy," and in June he celebrated it in verse:

> Not as we hoped; but what are we?
> Above our broken dreams and plans
> God lays with wiser hands than man's,
> The corner-stones of liberty.[54]

---

51. The poem was published on June 13, 1861, in the *Independent*; Whittier, *Writings*, 3: 219–22; Mordell, *Whittier*, 211.

52. Whittier to Hannah J. Newhall, November 22, 1861, in Pickard, ed., *Writings*, 3:25.

53. *Boston Evening Transcript*, September 28, 1861; Whittier, *Writings*, 3:222–3.

54. Whittier to Sumner, April 11, 1862, in Pickard, ed., *Letters*, 3:30; Whittier, "Astraea at the Capitol," in Whittier, *Writings*, 3:234–6.

When Congress repealed the Fugitive Slave Act in 1864, Whittier rejoiced with Sumner: "Thank God! For the repeal of the accursed law." But he reserved his greatest praise for the Emancipation Proclamation of January 1, 1863, and the passage by Congress of the Thirteenth Amendment in early 1865 in "Laus Deo":

> Send the song of praise abroad!
> With the sound of broken chains
> Tell the nation that, He reigns
> Who alone is Lord and God!

Whittier's Civil War poems were published in a volume called *In War Time and Other Poems,* and included "Barbara Frietchie," describing the patriotic fervor of a ninety-year-old Maryland widow who dramatically defended her country's flag in the face of Stonewall Jackson's efforts to destroy it. The poem included the famous line " 'Shoot if you must, this old gray head, / But spare your country's flag,' she said." Even as emancipation progressed, Whittier, who had long since reconciled his differences with Garrison, recalled the beginnings of the American Anti-Slavery Society in 1833 and reminded its founder that now they must work together "and lift ourselves to the true Christian attitude where all distinctions of black and white are overlooked in the heartfelt recognition of the brotherhood of man."[55]

As the war dragged on into 1864, war-weary Republicans considered for a brief moment shelving the president in favor of Salmon P. Chase or Whittier's friend Frémont. But by that time the poet had come to appreciate the complexity of Lincoln's task as commander-in-chief and the process of emancipation was well under way. He thus visited the Frémonts at their cottage in Nahant, urging the general not to aid the Democratic challenge then mounting under George B. McClellan. As Jessie Frémont later recalled, Whittier had noted, "There is a time to do and a time to stand aside . . . and to renounce self for the good of the greater number." She concluded that "it was a deciding word, coming from you," and in August 1864 Frémont withdrew. At the same time Whittier defended the general against those Republicans who attacked his candidacy as divisive in their efforts to reelect the

---

55. Whittier to Sumner, June 1864, Whittier to Garrison, November 24, 1863, in Pickard, ed., *Letters,* 3:73; "Laus Deo," Whittier, *Writings,* 3:254.

president.[56] True to his forgiving nature, Whittier urged no unnecessary harshness on the defeated Confederacy following the president's assassination, instead preferring to hope that Andrew Johnson would support his goal of "suffrage for the freemen on high moral and Christian ground." Unable, or perhaps unwilling, to visit the troops while the war raged, Whittier revealed in 1876 that he had seen only one regiment during the war—the 54th Colored, under command of Colonel Robert Gould Shaw, when it left Boston for the South in 1863. With the war over, Whittier's work as a reformer and abolitionist appeared finished. In 1866, at fifty-eight, he published his masterpiece, "Snow Bound," a story of nineteenth-century domestic New England life which celebrated his own childhood. The $10,000 fee he received for his longest effort finally relieved him of the financial pressures that had plagued him for so long.[57]

As the nation struggled through the tumult of Reconstruction, Whittier withdrew from the issues that had motivated him so totally since the 1830s. Coincidentally, Garrison also ceased publication of his *Liberator* in 1865 and, over the protests of abolition allies, withdrew from public life. The poet remained a loyal Republican even as his friend Charles Sumner, disillusioned with the Grant administration, bolted in 1872 to support Horace Greeley and the Liberal Republican movement. Always loyal to his friend Sumner, Whittier could not desert the party of Lincoln and emancipation. When a group of black voters, perplexed over Sumner's decision to leave the party which had freed the slaves, sought Whittier's advice, he noted his "respect for your intelligence and capacity for judging wisely for yourselves," even as he urged them to respect their "benefactors."[58] At the same time he declared himself unwilling to be an active part of any political organization, Republican or otherwise. With the full restoration of the Union in 1877 he explained that "the issues seem small and poor," and that he had "had enough of fighting in the old days." Prior to the war Whittier had always insisted that other reforms remain peripheral to abolition despite his sympathy for pacifism, temperance, and workers' and women's rights. Now with slavery

56. Jessie Benton Frémont to Whittier, 1889, in Allan Nevins, *Frémont in the Civil War,* vol. 2 of *John C. Frémont, Pathmarker of the West.* (New York: Frederick Ungar, 1962), 582; Whittier to Garrison, August 29, 1864, in Pickard, ed., *Writings,* 3:75.

57. Whittier to Richard Henry Dana, June 20, 1865, Whittier to Lydia Maria Child, 1876, in Pickard, ed., *Letters,* 3:95–6, 362; Pollard, *Whittier,* 266.

58. Woodwell, *Whittier,* 380–1; Whittier to Colored Citizens, August 3, 1872, in Whittier, *Writings,* 7:16–66; Holmes, "Whittier and Sumner," 68–70.

gone, he still believed that racial equality must remain a priority, but he also endorsed women's suffrage, as he could see no reason why "mothers, wives, and daughters should not have the same right to person, which fathers, brothers, and husbands have." In 1879 he received the Jubilee Singers in his Amesbury home following their tour of Europe and wrote a poem in their honor which included: "Till Freedom's every right is won, / And Slavery's every wrong undone!" On the occasion of his eightieth birthday in 1888, he responded to congratulations from a group of Washington blacks, telling them that he was amazed "at the rapid strides which your people have made since emancipation," and praising them for "their unresentful attitude toward those who formerly claimed to be your masters." As race relations deteriorated in North and South, he unrealistically predicted that the time was approaching when "you will have the free undisputed rights of citizenship in all parts of the Union."[59] His optimism was in keeping with his earlier views as an active reformer, when he had so confidently looked toward emancipation. In the earlier period, however, he had labored as an abolitionist for a cherished goal; now he looked nostalgically back in a vain effort to retain the commitment of a period which had already faded.

In 1879, as Republicans celebrated the twenty-fifth anniversary of their formation, Whittier recalled the steps he had followed in seeking the end of slavery. Having failed to move Democrats and Whigs, he and others "broke away from them and voted an independent ticket. . . . From the outset I looked to the ballot-box as, under God, the chief instrumentality for averting the progress of slavery, differing in this respect from some of my esteemed associates in the anti-slavery cause." Despite slavery's strength, he concluded that political abolitionists had brought "the mightier ballot box of a kingless people to bear upon it."[60] After breaking with Garrison, he had joined with Radicals like Alvan Stewart as a founder of the Liberty party. He had then opted for a more moderate course than Stewart, joining the Free Soil and Republican movements. As a pacifist, he had modified his staunch abolitionism to fit the broader appeal of those seeking slavery's containment, and had reluctantly supported a war which he knew would end what he con-

59. Woodwell, *Whittier*, 435; Whittier to Apphia Horner, November 28, 1868, Whittier to Julia Ward Howe, August 12, 1869, Whittier to Gail Hamilton, May 22, 1878, Whittier to Robert H. Terrell and George Washington Williams, January 9, 1888, in Pickard, ed., *Letters*, 3:183–4, 196, 393, 548.

60. Whittier to Unidentified Correspondents, September 13, 1879, in Pickard, ed., *Letters*, 3:411.

sidered the most serious blight on American democracy. As the bard of freedom, the gentle Quaker humanitarian had eloquently voiced the goals and aspirations of an ever-increasing number of his countrymen. His commitment to emancipation and equality was as firm as any American's during the tumultuous decades leading to the Civil War, and he rarely wavered, from the day he helped found the Liberty party until the war ended slavery.

FOUR

BLACK MEN HAVE NO RIGHTS WHICH WHITE MEN ARE BOUND TO RESPECT

Charles Langston and the Drive for Equality

WE KNOW LITTLE of the childhood of Charles Henry Langston except that it was far from typical for an African American born in 1817 in Louisa County, Virginia. His mother, Lucy Langston, who was part black and part Native American, had been a slave but was freed by her white plantation owner, Ralph Quarles, before Charles's birth. Quarles and Lucy Langston lived together openly, but Virginia law forbade their marriage. Nor did they register their four children, because the state required the banishment of free blacks. Thus their children, although not slaves, lived in Quarles's slave community with twenty others who were his slaves. In this unusual setting Quarles raised his children as part of his family, providing well for them financially and educating them with the help of tutors. Charles's older sister Maria and brother Gideon were young adults when both parents died of natural causes in 1834, while the aggressive yet well-disciplined Charles was a boy of sixteen. A younger brother, John Mercer, had been born in 1829 and was thus too young to have lasting memories of his parents or his life in Virginia. Having raised his own children free, Quarles believed slavery should end by the voluntary action of individual owners. In his will he freed his slaves and divided his 2,030 acres equally among his three sons, thus providing some financial security even though Virginia law would now require they leave the state. Within months of their parents' deaths, Charles and his two brothers moved to the free state of Ohio.[1]

Charles Langston's background is unique among those in this study, for as a black man his concerns and perspective caused him to place as high a priority on the status of free blacks as he did that of slaves. Light-skinned and legally free from birth, he could relate to the plight of fugitives in Oberlin, Ohio, without directly experiencing the constant fear that he might be forced back into slavery. Able to overcome the educational disadvantage of most northern blacks, he used his Oberlin education as a springboard to a lifetime working to reverse the denial of basic civil rights that whites took for granted. Too young and somewhat isolated in Ohio from the protests which led to the formation of the Liberty party in the East, by the early 1840s he took up the issue of suffrage that might eventually allow blacks an equal place among those seeking change in the North. He supported each of the antislavery parties: Liberty, Free Soil, and Republican, and worked in Ohio to bring political and social equality even as he joined in the larger movement to weaken and end slavery. Langston's most prominent role came in the Oberlin-Wellington rescue of fugitive John Price in 1858 and in Charles's subsequent trial for violation of the Fugitive Slave Act. During the war he campaigned for a black soldier role and afterward continued his effort for black suffrage in Kansas. Unique among those in this study, he stands near the radical end of the spectrum occupied by Alvan Stewart and John Greenleaf Whittier, although his race precluded a role in Liberty party formation.

Before his death, Ralph Quarles had arranged for his friend William Gooch to be guardian of his children, knowing that he would move them to a free state. True to his word, Gooch and his wife moved with the Langstons to Chillicothe in late 1834, a town with a significant black population. The next year, Charles and older brother Gideon became the first African Amer-

---

1. There is no biography of Charles Langston, but much can be learned from William and Aimee Lee Cheek, *John Mercer Langston and the Fight for Black Freedom, 1829–1865* (Urbana: Univ. of Illinois Press, 1989), and from John Mercer Langston, *From the Virginia Plantation to the National Capitol* (Hartford: American Publishing Co., 1894; reprint, Johnson Reprint Corp., 1968). See also William Cheek, "John Mercer Langston, Black Protest Leader and Abolitionist," *Civil War History* 16 (June 1970): 101–20, and the brief entry by Thaddeus Russell in *American National Biography*, 13: 163–4.

icans to enroll in the preparatory department of the recently established Oberlin Collegiate Institute, west of Cleveland. Both were baptized and admitted as members in the mostly white First Congregational Church of Oberlin. When the Gooches moved to Missouri, the Langstons remained in Ohio; John was cared for by New England abolitionist Richard Long in Cincinnati, while the older siblings struck out on their own. Through the late 1830s and early 1840s, Charles taught at black schools in Chillicothe and Columbus and was instrumental in the enrollment of several of his students at Oberlin. In 1841, he reenrolled at Oberlin, where he remained for the next two years. He continued to earn a meager living as a teacher and emerged as a leader of Ohio's small black community. In the next years he championed the abolition press of Ohio, serving for a time on the editorial board of the short-lived black paper *Palladium of Liberty,* in Columbus. In 1843, he attended the first of many black conventions and was chosen secretary of the meeting which endorsed the Liberty party. The delegates also recommended the Cincinnati abolition paper *The Philanthropist,* whose editor, Gamaliel Bailey, was a strong supporter of the third party.[2] At the 1844 convention Langston gained prominence by proposing resolutions which characterized his emerging role as an abolitionist. One sought the repeal of Ohio's highly discriminatory black laws, which not only denied to African Americans the right to vote, to testify in court against whites, and to be educated in integrated public schools, but also required them to post a $500 bond when migrating into the state. The latter was rarely enforced but symbolized the racial views of the dominant white residents. Langston's second resolution sought equal education for African Americans in Ohio public schools, and a third expressed another concern of his by endorsing statewide prohibition.[3]

By the late 1840s Langston had become increasingly impatient for a change in the racial atmosphere, perhaps in part the result of being attacked by a white Ohio mob in 1848. In May, he had joined the lecture tour of Martin Delany in northern Ohio promoting black rights and temperance and seeking subscriptions to Frederick Douglass's newspaper, the *North Star.* After a meeting in Columbus the pair reached the small village of Mar-

---

2. Russell, "Charles Henry Langston," 13:163–4. See also Cheek and Cheek, *John Mercer Langston,* 19–43. For the proceedings of "The Colored Convention of August 4, 1843 in Columbus," see *The Philanthropist* (Cincinnati), October 4, 1843.

3. Steven Middleton, *The Black Laws in the Old Northwest: A Documentary History* (Westport, Conn.: Greenwood Press, 1993), includes all of the Ohio black laws (see pages 9–141). Russell, "Charles Henry Langston," 164.

seilles to the northwest. There, thugs broke up their rally in the schoolhouse and later threatened to drag them out of their hotel. Reduced to sneaking out of the hotel and out of town in the middle of the night, Langston thus endured the same kind of mob violence that white abolitionists such as Alvan Stewart and John Greenleaf Whittier had faced a decade earlier.[4] The experience made him wonder whether reform ever could be achieved and the attitudes of antiabolitionists as well as slaveholders changed. Yet he was still ready to give the political antislavery movement his support even though he and fellow blacks could not directly participate in it.

As an Ohioan, Langston was not a part of the larger Negro Convention Movement of the 1840s, which was centered in New York and Massachusetts. There, the split between those aligned with the Garrisonians, led initially by Frederick Douglass, and those endorsing the Liberty party, led by Henry Highland Garnet, continued through 1847. The latter group was aided by New York philanthropist and Liberty leader Gerrit Smith, who had donated 120,000 acres to three thousand African Americans, thus making many of them eligible voters in New York, where blacks needed to own property worth $250 in order to qualify to vote. Numerous blacks responded in support of the third party, and by 1848 Douglass was moving in the direction of the Free Soil party even as he broke with Garrison and initiated the *North Star,* in Rochester.[5] And when these conventions climaxed at a Cleveland rally in September 1848, Langston was present. The convention, chaired by Douglass and attended mostly by Liberty supporters, found the Free Soil platform of containment of slavery unsatisfactory. Equally disappointing, the new party was silent on the question of equality for blacks in the free states. Thus the Cleveland delegates stopped short of endorsing Free Soil candidates, but concluded that the party was the best that they could hope for; they recommended it to black voters even though they were "determined to maintain the higher standard and more liberal views which have heretofore characterized us as abolitionists."[6] Delegates chose Langston to be the Ohio representative to the group's national committee to carry

4. *North Star* (Rochester, N.Y.), July 14, 28, 1848; Cheek and Cheek, *John Mercer Langston,* 111–2.

5. For an account of these early meetings, see Howard H. Bell, "National Negro Conventions of the Middle 1840's: Moral Suasion vs. Political Action," *Journal of Negro History* 42 (1957): 247–60; see also John Stauffer, *The Black Hearts of Men: Radical Abolitionists and the Transformation of Race* (Cambridge, Mass.: Harvard Univ. Press, 2001), 135, 139.

6. *Report of the Proceedings of the Colored National Convention . . . Cleveland, Sept. 1848* (Rochester, 1848); *North Star* (Rochester, N.Y.), September 29, 1848.

on the work of the convention. In October, he was among "the few Free Soil men" of Chillicothe who greeted and listened to Free Soiler Joshua Giddings, a member of the House of Representatives from Jefferson, when he reported on third-party activities and attacked the "proslavery character" of Whig candidate Zachary Taylor.[7] Through support of the convention resolutions on the Free Soil party, Langston reflected the dilemma felt by all the delegates and the realization that the Free Soil party was all they could hope for at that time.

With the presidential election over, Langston and other Ohio African Americans turned to their own condition and the continuing impact of the state's discriminatory laws. Black leaders met for four days in Columbus in January 1849 at Bethel Church and hotly debated what actions they should take in the face of southern slavery and northern discrimination. The delegates chose the thirty-one-year-old Langston as the meeting's president. The young leader immediately faced a more divisive issue than Ohio's black laws: whether the delegates should encourage black migration from a nation so unmoving on race relations or, instead, resolve to stay and fight for their rights. It was Charles's younger brother, John Mercer, who, at nineteen, shocked the delegates by exclaiming: "I for one, sir, am willing, clearly as I love my native land, (a land which will not protect me however,) to leave it and go where I can be free." He and another delegate described their willingness to leave the country and "form a separate and independent one, enacting our own laws and regulations, trusting for success only in the God of Liberty and the Controller of human destiny." The younger Langston did not name a specific place for such an effort, but he was voicing the opinion of a small but growing group of more militant blacks led by Martin Delany of Pittsburgh that hope for meaningful change in the United States was futile. But few Ohio blacks were ready to consider such a drastic alternative and, instead of approving his proposal, the overwhelming majority resolved: "Our minds are made up to remain in the United States, and contend for our rights at all hazards." As the presiding officer, Charles Langston did not enter the debate, but at this time he stood with the majority and against his brother. At the same time, the Langston brothers fully agreed on the evil of slavery and northern discrimination and the need to continue the fight against both.[8]

7. *North Star* (Rochester, N.Y.), November 3, 1848.
8. "Minutes and Address of the State Convention of the Colored Citizens of Ohio convened at Columbus, Jan. 10th, 11th, 12th, and 13th, 1849," in Philip S. Foner and George E. Walker,

Langston and his colleagues chose each January as the time to meet and Columbus as the most frequent location in order to focus on the annual legislative session in the state capital. It was a process they would repeat each winter until the late 1850s. The convention also sought to establish a permanent organization to function between meetings, but it would not be until 1853 that Langston was chosen executive secretary and business agent for their new civil rights organization, the Ohio State Anti-Slavery Society, with offices in Cleveland.[9] Throughout these years Langston and fellow blacks focused on the discriminatory laws of Ohio, but while making modest gains, they failed to achieve what they wanted most, the right to vote. Their efforts did, however, coincide with a partial repeal of the black laws in 1849.

At their January 1849 convention the delegates, led by Langston, had agreed to petition the legislature "to repeal all laws making distinction on account of color," and resolved "now and forever," their refusal "to vote for or support, any man for office who will not go for us."[10] Thus they urged the Free Soil party and its Ohio leader, Salmon P. Chase, to hear their cries for help. Yet when the legislature repealed the $500 bond law and that barring the testimony of black witnesses in court, it was due more to a political bargain between Democrats and Free Soilers in the state legislature than it was to black pressure. The arrangement also included the beginnings of public education for black children, albeit on a segregated basis. The bargain, achieved by Free Soilers, resulted from neither Democrats nor Whigs being able to organize the legislature because a small number of Free Soil representatives held the balance of power. In a coalition arranged by Chase, Free Soilers threw their support to the Democrats, giving the latter the legislative control they sought. In return, the Democrats supported the partial repeal of the black laws and the election of Chase to be U.S. senator.[11] It is unlikely that many of the legislators who concluded their bargain in February 1849 were even aware of, much less persuaded by, the arguments of Langston and his colleagues in their petitions and address. That Chase and a few Free Soil-

---

eds., *Proceedings of the Black State Conventions, 1840–1865* (Philadelphia: Temple Univ. Press, 1979), 1:223, 225 (hereafter cited as *Proceedings*).

9. "State Convention . . . 1849," "State Convention . . . 1850," *Proceedings*, 1:229, 256 n.; Cheek and Cheek, *John Mercer Langston*, 249, 327.

10. "State Convention . . . 1849," *Proceedings*, 1:228–9.

11. Frederick J. Blue, *Salmon P. Chase: A Life in Politics* (Kent, Ohio: Kent State Univ. Press, 1987), 68–72; Robert McCormick and Frederick J. Blue, "Norton S. Townshend, A Reformer for All Seasons," in *The Pursuit of Public Power: Political Culture in Ohio, 1787–1861*, Jeffrey Brown and Andrew Cayton, eds. (Kent, Ohio: Kent State Univ. Press, 1994), 147–8.

ers, such as Norton Townshend of Lorain County, were committed to racial equality is clear. It is equally true that for Chase, personal advancement was at least as important as racial equality. *North Star* editor Frederick Douglass gave credit to "our colored brethren in Ohio" for forcing "the dominant class in their own state to notice and respect their efforts," but he and Ohio leaders such as Langston knew that their voices would not truly be heard in the white community until they organized more effectively. As Langston and six others explained in their address: "We ask that the word 'white' in the State Constitution be stricken out at once and forever."[12] Langston thus knew he had potential friends in Chase, Townshend, and other Free Soilers, but that political reality demanded that blacks continue to act together if further progress were to be made.

As the deepening sectional crisis intensified the differences between North and South, Charles Langston stepped up his role in Ohio's black conventions and helped make the group more visible. The Slave Power victory in the Fugitive Slave Act of 1850, continued discrimination in Ohio as delegates at a state constitutional convention in 1851 overwhelmingly rejected black suffrage, and third-party apathy in the presidential election of 1852 were the special targets of Langston and his fellow reformers. Attendance declined at their annual conventions of 1850, 1851, and 1852, but the delegates pled with both the black and white communities to hear their message. After Congress enacted the Compromise measures of 1850, Democrats and Whigs labored to convince voters in both North and South that the most important sectional issues had been resolved and that there was no further need for agitation. But to many in the North, the Compromise contained serious flaws, the most obvious being the Fugitive Slave Act, which denied the accused a trial by jury and required northern law officials as well as citizens to assist southerners in the capture and return of alleged fugitives. With the law barely four months old, black delegates at their January 1851 convention in Columbus approved Langston's resolution to draft a petition to Congress asking for the "unconditional repeal" of the law. The resulting petition called the Act "a hideous deformity in the garb of law—unconstitutional" and "an outrage upon humanity."[13]

12. *North Star* (Rochester, N.Y.), June 29, 1849; "Address of the State Convention . . . 1849," *Proceedings,* 1:233.

13. For a full discussion of the Compromise debates and enactment, see Holman Hamilton, *Prologue to Conflict: The Crisis and Compromise of 1850* (Lexington: Univ. of Kentucky Press, 1964). Black convention debates and resolutions are found in "Colored Convention . . . January, 1851," *Proceedings,* 1:260, 267.

When the state legislature in 1850 called a constitutional convention to write a new document to replace the original, but dated, constitution of 1802, Langston and his fellow delegates were both alarmed and hopeful. Knowing that several states had attacked minority rights and added new racial restrictions at such conventions, they feared that the gains of 1849 could be jeopardized. But they also knew that suffrage would be a major issue, giving them a golden opportunity to plead their case. At their January 1850 meeting they had sought the right "to address the Constitutional Convention" and resolved that the right to vote was "of the highest importance to our happiness and future prosperity and our lawful birthright under the established principles of freedom."[14] As the constitutional gathering approached, but in the shadow of Congress's enactment of the Fugitive Slave Act, Charles and his brother John wrote to Senator Salmon P. Chase asking whether "the public sentiment of the country [was] such as to preclude the successful attainment of our Political rights and equality in this State at present." Having just fought futilely against Congress's capitulation to the Slave Power, the first-term senator responded gloomily that "the people of color of Ohio" should not "expect equality of rights with the whites" in the near future.[15]

The results of the constitutional convention were, from the perspective of Ohio blacks, dubious at best. In a battle of petitions, Free Soilers and their allies exceeded the numbers and signatures of their antiblack antagonists. But on racial matters the delegates approved nothing of a positive nature, and the efforts to exclude blacks from the state, to reinstate the requirement that blacks post a bond upon entering the state, and to provide state aid for the American Colonization Society revealed that Langston and his colleagues had been accurate in fearing a retreat from the rights won in 1849. Black leaders could rejoice that such discriminatory proposals did not pass, although 41 percent supported the proposal to ban blacks from Ohio. And the delegates also rejected proposals expanding black rights. The efforts of Norton Townshend to include blacks in the state militia and to desegregate the public schools were rejected, and, most pointedly, the proposal for black suffrage lost overwhelmingly, 66–12. The Langston brothers had had an interview with Democratic governor Reuben Wood asking for his written endorsement of black suffrage, but despite the governor's dependence on Free

14. "Colored Convention, . . . Jan., 1850," *Proceedings,* 1:251–2.

15. Charles and John Langston to Chase, September 12, 1850, Chase to Charles and John Langston, November 11, 1850, Chase Papers, Library of Congress.

Soil support in his recent election, he refused their request. Chase had been all too accurate in his forecast, for suffrage in Ohio would be delayed until long after slavery was abolished. Not until after the ratification of the Fifteenth Amendment in 1870 would Ohio black men vote for the first time.[16]

Nevertheless, the black conventions continued to resist these disturbing trends in the years before civil war. Although arguing for positive change, the Langston-led meetings also seriously debated the concept of blacks either migrating to Canada or seeking a homeland in newly acquired western territories or outside of North America. At the same time the delegates were unanimous in their rejection of the scheme of some Ohio whites to help fund the American Colonization Society's efforts in Liberia, arguing that that society was a proslavery, southern-dominated organization. Of more immediate concern was the need to help fugitives escape to Canada and the real danger of free blacks being kidnapped from Ohio and other free states into slavery under the shield of the Fugitive Slave Act. At a Columbus gathering in late 1850, Charles Langston and others urged fugitives to escape across Lake Erie and for the state's twenty-five thousand blacks to protect themselves against illegal seizures.[17] The Langstons also asked Chase his opinion on whether territories recently seized from Mexico might be made available for black migration; should they "quit the land of our birth and seek an asylum in a foreign clime" or remain "until success shall crown our efforts." Chase saw no hope for Congress making western territories available, but suggested they consider "Jamaica, Haiti, Liberia, and other countries where the population is prepared" to welcome them.[18] However unrealistic such options might have appeared, the Langstons could not dismiss the concept entirely with things so unpromising in their own country.

Charles Langston was frequently in contact with fugitive slave Henry Bibb, who had organized a Canadian black settlement and who urged others to join the migration north. At their January 1852 convention in Cincin-

16. See Charles Thomas Hickok, *The Negro in Ohio, 1802–1870* (1896; reprint, New York: AMS Press, 1975), 53–4; Frank U. Quillin, *The Color Line in Ohio* (Ann Arbor: G. Wahr, 1913), 61–3; David A. Gerber, *Black Ohio and the Color Line, 1860–1915* (Urbana: Univ. of Illinois Press, 1976), 3–24. See also *Anti-Slavery Bugle* (Salem, Ohio), August 17, 24, 1850, February 22, 1851. For the debates of the constitutional convention, see J. V. Smith, ed., *Report of the Debates and Proceedings of the Convention for the Revision of the Constitution of the State of Ohio*, 2 vols. (Columbus: S. Medary, 1851).

17. *Cleveland True Democrat*, September 30, 1850; *Ohio State Journal* (Columbus), October 16, 1850; Cheek and Cheek, *John Mercer Langston*, 171.

18. John and Charles Langston to Chase, September 12, 1850, Chase to John and Charles Langston, November 11, 1850, Chase Papers, Library of Congress.

nati, Langston headed the committee on emigration, which reported its resolve "that in the voluntary emigration of the colored people of the United
States we see the only relief from the oppressions of the American people."
Reversing his earlier opposition to leaving the country, Langston suggested
that such a move might hasten the end of slavery. He and his committee did
not confine their proposal to Canada; they also suggested Central or South
America. The delegates rejected the concept, however, and instead approved
a motion that "It is not expedient for the free people of color of the United
States to emigrate to any place out of these States while one slave is in
chains." Bibb regretted that the delegates had "concluded to stay in the
States to be spit upon, as well as disfranched and oppressed."[19] The Langstons themselves would vacillate on the emigration issue until the mid-
1850s, but both ultimately determined to continue the struggle against slavery and discrimination from their Ohio base.

Charles and John Langston continued to wage the battle for suffrage and,
although still denied the vote, played an active role in antislavery politics in
the election of 1852. Free Soilers (now renamed Free Democrats) continued
to advocate support of containing but not abolishing slavery, just as they had
in their 1848 campaign under Martin Van Buren. They were now substantially weakened by the return of the Van Burenites of New York and other
antislavery Democrats to their original party throughout the North. But if
reduced to the more idealistic reformer-politician, the third party was no
more willing than it had been in 1848 to endorse suffrage and other forms
of racial equality in the North. The Free Democratic convention, meeting
in Pittsburgh, nominated John P. Hale of New Hampshire and George W.
Julian of Indiana after rejecting both the candidacy of former Liberty party
leader Gerrit Smith of New York and his equal rights plank. A mass meeting
of blacks in Cleveland followed in early September 1852 and was attended
by both Langstons; as in 1848, the delegates endorsed the third party but reminded it of the need to work for equal rights. Equally discouraging, Ohio
Free Democrats failed to endorse this goal. Nationally, the third-party showing in 1852 was only half that of 1848 even with such a moderate platform,
for Democrats and Whigs convinced most voters that the Compromise of
1850 had eliminated the need for an antislavery third party.[20] Although the

19. "Colored Convention . . . ," January 1852, *Proceedings,* 1:279; Bibb is quoted in *Voice
of the Fugitive,* February 12, 1852, in Cheek and Cheek, *John Mercer Langston,* 197.

20. Blue, *The Free Soilers,* 246–7, 261–2; Johnson and Porter, eds., *National Party Platforms,* 18–20; *Cleveland Plain Dealer,* September 9, 1852; *Anti-Slavery Bugle* (Salem, Ohio),
September 18, 1852.

Ohio Free Democrats finally agreed to support black suffrage in early 1853, the state's African Americans saw no hope for improved racial conditions in Ohio in the immediate future.[21]

To better articulate their needs and demands, the Langstons lent strong support to the ongoing efforts of the Ohio Colored Citizens conventions to establish a newspaper. Committees had been appointed by earlier conventions to use the joint-stock principle to raise the necessary capital, but until 1853, potential investors had failed to respond. Following that year's meeting, William Howard Day, an Oberlin graduate from Lorain, became editor, with Samuel Ringgold Ward of the Canadian settlement and J. W. C. Pennington of New York named corresponding editors. As close colleagues of Day and believers in the need for such a press, both Charles and John Langston invested significantly. The paper, *The Aliened American,* began publication in April 1853 in Cleveland to speak for "Colored Americans of the Free States," for "this class of native-born citizens . . . treated worse than foreigners—have had no mouthpiece to speak for them." Now, "the voice of twenty-five thousand oppressed" Ohioans "has called us forth." During the next year, before Day's health forced the paper's suspension, *The Aliened American* provided the important mouthpiece for black causes, political and otherwise, which had previously been lacking.[22]

Even as they despaired over conditions in their own country, the Langston brothers moved away from their earlier interest in migration to an area outside of the United States or even immigration to a western part of their own country. The first indication of their change of position came at the annual black convention in Columbus in January 1853. Encouraged by the Ohio Free Democratic endorsement of black suffrage a week earlier, the delegates made little mention of migration and devoted their resolutions to their pursuit of equal rights. The members created a statewide black political and civil rights organization, the Ohio State Anti-Slavery Society, with the elder Langston submitting a draft of its constitution and bylaws.[23] The Langston brothers further confirmed their commitment to improving conditions at home and showed that they had rejected immigration by their attendance at a Douglass-led national black convention in Rochester in July

21. *National Era,* January 20, 27, 1853; Blue, *The Free Soilers,* 271.

22. Martin E. Dann, ed., *The Black Press, 1827–1890: The Quest for National Identity* (New York: Capricorn, 1971), 24; *The Aliened American,* April 9, 1853, in Dann, ed., *The Black Press,* 50–2.

23. *Official Proceedings of the Ohio State Convention of Colored Freemen . . . Columbus . . . , 1853* (Cleveland, 1853); Cheek and Cheek, *John Mercer Langston,* 214–5.

1853 that advocated only domestic reform. The following year the Langstons worked successfully to undermine Ohio support for Martin Delany's black nationalist convention in Cleveland. At the same time, both Langstons continued their professional careers. In September 1854, after long and arduous study, John passed the Ohio bar exam, having read law under attorney Philemon Bliss, a prominent Republican judge. Neither Bliss nor Langston told the three-member panel which examined the light-skinned Langston that he was African American, for he had to "be construed into a 'white man'" to be admitted to the bar. Nonetheless, however he achieved it, he became the state's first black attorney. It was an achievement also indicative of his commitment to domestic issues as well as his emergence as the state's most prominent black reformer.[24]

Temporarily eclipsed by his younger brother's growing prominence, Charles Langston would remain in the background for the next four years. John, now an Oberlin attorney, played a significant role in the formation of the state's Republican party in 1854 and 1855, campaigning strenuously for the election to Congress of his mentor, Philemon Bliss, and traveling throughout northern Ohio in support of Republican candidates and issues. We know less of Charles's activities during the mid-1850s, except that he worked during these years as an agent for the Ohio State Anti-Slavery Society, living in Columbus, and earning a meager living as a teacher at a black elementary school. In 1856 he became principal of the Columbus Colored Schools. Three years earlier, he and two others had proposed a vocational school for blacks, which led to the founding of Wilberforce University in Wilberforce, Ohio.[25]

The election of the first Republican governor of Ohio, Salmon P. Chase, in 1855 along with a Republican-controlled legislature gave Ohio blacks new hope in their battle for the vote. At the annual black state convention in January 1856, Charles Langston helped write a petition to the state legislature again appealing for suffrage and other rights. Comparing the plight of African Americans to the American colonists on the eve of the Revolution, he argued that both groups suffered taxation without representation. The petition reminded Ohioans: "We are not Africans, but Americans, as much so as any part of your population." The state "does us a great injustice . . .

---

24. *Proceedings of the Colored National Convention, Held in Rochester, July 6th, 7th, and 8th, 1853* (Rochester, N.Y., 1853); Langston, *From the Virginia Plantation*, 125; Cheek and Cheek, *John Mercer Langston*, 218–21, 233–4.

25. Russell, "Charles Henry Langston," 13:164.

by refusing to acknowledge our right to the appellation of Americans which is the only title we desire." Dispelling any hint of a desire to leave, the petition concluded: "We are a part of the American People, and we and our posterity will forever be a constituent part of your population." Langston and his fellow delegates renewed their condemnation of the Fugitive Slave Act and, with the presidential election of 1856 approaching, also applauded the Republican party, even though, like its Free Soil predecessor, "it does not take so high antislavery ground as we could wish." They obviously preferred "immediate and unconditional abolition" to the Republican containment platform, but noted that the new party would still do "great service in the cause of Freedom."[26]

Yet even when the legislature failed to act in behalf of equal rights during its 1856 session, Charles Langston and his colleagues did not despair, hoping that the presidential election that fall would energize their cause. The Republican party nominated western hero John C. Frémont, but, not surprisingly, omitted an equal rights plank. Still, Charles occasionally joined his brother in trying to radicalize the Ohio electorate in behalf of "Frémont and Freedom," and to urge supporters to move beyond containment to abolition and suffrage.[27] Frémont carried Ohio and his party retained its control over the legislature. But despite renewed appeals from the annual black convention in January 1857, Governor Chase, with an eye on a presidential nomination in 1860, failed to urge equal suffrage. Enough Republicans in the legislature joined the Democratic minority again to block a suffrage bill. Party members did condemn the Supreme Court's Dred Scott decision of March 1857 denying citizenship to blacks and the right of Congress or a territory to ban slavery.

Frustrated by these latest setbacks, Charles Langston joined with other Columbus blacks in inviting Governor Chase to a public meeting of African Americans to speak on the decision and express opposition to "the great wrong . . . against all of the colored people of this country." The decision had "swept away the last vestige of colored men's rights and reduced them to the pitiable condition of mere articles of merchandise." Ohio blacks had looked to the Court for "a rebuke and restraint of the Slave Power" and now looked to the governor for leadership in bringing a reversal of the decision.[28]

26. "Proceedings of the Colored Convention . . . 1856," *Proceedings,* 1:310–2, 308.

27. *Anti-Slavery Bugle* (Salem, Ohio), August 2, 9, 16, 1856.

28. Charles Langston et al. to Chase, April 13, 1857, Chase Papers, Library of Congress. The Chase Papers do not indicate whether he responded to their invitation, nor is there any indication that he addressed the rally.

The legislature did respond with a law protecting the legal rights of Ohio blacks against the danger of kidnapping by slaveholders and their sympathizers. With Langston as executive secretary of the Ohio State Anti-Slavery Society, Ohio blacks hoped to provide an ongoing quick response to any black person so threatened. In 1857, Chase won reelection as governor, but Democrats regained control of the legislature, ending any immediate prospect of suffrage legislation. Even worse, lawmakers repealed the protection extended to blacks the previous year.[29] In the meantime, Langston, having recently moved to Cleveland, continued to toil for his cherished goals until a series of dramatic events relating to the fugitive issue catapulted him from an obscure black reformer into the spotlight.

Although he was an integral part of the network of defense established by the Ohio State Anti-Slavery Society to aid blacks threatened with capture under the Fugitive Slave Act, Langston was not expecting the excitement of late 1858 and early 1859. Not surprisingly, the scene for a fugitive rescue was Oberlin and surrounding areas, for the college town was the most committed in the state to the Republican party, equal rights, and resistance to the hated 1850 law. In the election of 1856 in the township which included Oberlin, John C. Frémont received 444 votes to 77 for Democrat James Buchanan. The town was known to be a haven for fugitive slaves, and in the 1850s more than twenty-five lived and worked there, many of them openly and in defiance of the federal law and the Buchanan administration's determination to enforce it.[30] Oberlin was also the home of attorney John Mercer Langston, who had been elected clerk by the township in 1855, the first black elected to public office in the nation. The town itself had more than four hundred African Americans out of a population of more than twenty-one hundred. It thus had the largest percentage of blacks of any town in Ohio.[31] Republican officials in Oberlin even permitted light-skinned blacks such as John Mercer Langston to vote, in defiance of the state prohibition. In 1856, he had proudly cast his vote for Frémont. Not surprisingly, local Democrats urged the federal government to make an example of this bastion of Republican and abolitionist strength, and Buchanan appeared ready to do so.

29. *Proceedings of the State Convention . . . Columbus, Jan., 1857* (Columbus, 1857); Cheek and Cheek, *John Mercer Langston,* 323–4; Blue, *Chase,* 117–8; Middleton, *Black Laws,* 130. The Ohio constitution denied the governor any veto power.

30. *Anti-Slavery Bugle* (Salem, Ohio), December 13, 1856; Nat Brandt, *The Town That Started the Civil War* (Syracuse, N.Y.: Syracuse Univ. Press, 1990), 45.

31. In 1860, the 36,673 blacks living in Ohio constituted 1.6 percent of the state's population. See Census of 1860, Lorain County Ohio, Russia Township, National Archives.

The opportunity arose in September 1858 when Kentucky slave catcher Anderson P. Jennings conspired with a Kentucky associate along with a deputy marshal and a deputy sheriff from Columbus in an Oberlin tavern run by prominent Democrat Chauncey Wack. Their plan was to seize a fugitive named John Price who had lived and worked at odd jobs in Oberlin for at least six months. They would use a thirteen-year-old boy, Shakespeare Boynton, son of a wealthy farmer, to lure Price to his father's property for work. Intercepting the two en route, they forced the fugitive into their carriage and then hurried nine miles south to Wellington to await the late afternoon train to Columbus. There, Price would be arraigned as a fugitive and returned to his Kentucky owner. Word of Price's abduction quickly spread in Oberlin, and black and white townspeople, students, and professors alike rode en masse to Wellington, determined to force the release of the kidnapped fugitive. Attorney Langston was away from home that day on business, and thus missed the excitement, but his brother Charles, visiting from Cleveland, heard the commotion, strapped a revolver on his hip, and rode south with the others.[32]

The crowd outside the Wadsworth House in Wellington where Price was held had quickly swelled to five hundred, including between thirty and forty Oberlin blacks, among them, John Copeland who would die the next year at Harpers Ferry. Seeking safety, the Kentucky slave catcher, Jennings, hastily retreated to the attic of the hotel and held Price in a small loft. Langston immediately emerged as the spokesman for the crowd and tried first to persuade law officials to arrest Price's captors for kidnapping, for as he told the assembled mass: "it was best to take legal measure if any and not to do anything by force." Refusing to consider a kidnapping charge, Deputy Marshal Jacob Lowe, knowing Langston to be "a reasonable man," had him come to an attic room, where he pleaded with him to urge the crowd to disperse. Langston's response was that the crowd was "bent upon a rescue at all hazards," and that he would be wise "to give the boy up." When Lowe refused,

---

32. There are numerous accounts of the kidnapping and rescue of Price as well as the trials that followed. The most important primary source is that of Jacob R. Shipherd, *History of the Oberlin-Wellington Rescue* (Boston, 1859; reprint, New York: Da Capo Press, 1972). See also John Mercer Langston, "The Oberlin-Wellington Rescue," *The Anglo-African Magazine* 1 (July 1859): 209–16. The most complete secondary accounts are those of Cheek and Cheek, *John Mercer Langston*, 316–42; and Brandt, *The Town That Started the Civil War*. See also Steven Lubet, "Slavery on Trial: The Case of the Oberlin Rescue," *Alabama Law Review* 54 (spring 2003): 785–829; and Roland M. Baumann, "The 1858 Oberlin-Wellington Rescue: A Reappraisal" (Oberlin, Ohio: Oberlin College, 2003).

Langston got up and, as he left, according to Lowe's later testimony, said: "We will have him any how." By then the 5:13 train for Columbus had already left Wellington. Immediately the crowd moved in, rushed the guards, and, following a struggle, seized Price, placed him in a buggy driven by Simeon Bushnell, and raced to Oberlin. The rescuers hid Price first in the home of Oberlin bookseller James M. Fitch, and then in the attic of Oberlin professor and future president James H. Fairchild. Several days later, unnamed rescuers escorted Price to Canada, where he would reside safely beyond the reach of law officials. In the meantime John Langston, on returning home and hearing the news, rushed toward Wellington only to meet the jubilant rescuers on their way back. That evening he joined in the celebrations and speech-making as the throng denounced the Fugitive Slave Act, the Slave Power, and the Buchanan administration, little suspecting that Charles Langston would soon be the focus of a trial with repercussions far beyond Ohio.

Federal officials, with an assist from local Democrats, wasted little time in gathering evidence and moving against what they perceived as flagrant and defiant violations of the Fugitive Slave Act, which prohibited resistance to the return of an alleged fugitive. In nearby Cleveland in November 1858, U.S. District Judge Hiram V. Willson impaneled a grand jury of twelve Democrats in the overwhelmingly Republican district. Among them was Lewis Boynton, the father of Shakespeare Boynton! On December 6, after several weeks of testimony conducted by Judge Willson before a grand jury openly prejudiced against Oberlin and Republicans in general and blacks in particular, thirty-seven men were indicted, twenty-five of them from Oberlin or, like Charles Langston, with close Oberlin ties. As the *Cleveland Morning Leader* put it, those indicted ranged "from snowy white to sooty." The most prominent Oberlinites were Professor Henry Peck, attorney Ralph Plumb, and bookstore owner James M. Fitch, none of whom had actually gone to Wellington, but who the Buchanan administration wanted to make examples of for aiding and abetting those who were part of the actual rescue. Four of those indicted were Oberlin students. Of the twelve blacks, Charles Langston was the most prominent; they included three fugitive slaves, six former slaves, and three men who had been born free. A local paper later described Langston not only as an abolitionist, but a temperance advocate and western agent for the Sons of Temperance: "Hair full and somewhat curly. Wears full beard . . . known to be a firebrand and orator . . . not large nor apparently firm of body, but well endowed intellectually . . . impetuous and aggressive; under discipline and opposition, he was always restive . . . his knowledge and power in an emergency never failed him."[33] During the proceedings the anti-Oberlin sentiment revealed itself further when none of the twelve indicted from Wellington was held longer than a few days but most of those from Oberlin were jailed for the duration of the trials. None indicted was a Democrat, although at least one member of that party had publicly boasted of having been part of the rescue. The jailings and trials that followed would become one of the most prominent fugitive slave cases of the 1850s.

Most of the accused surrendered quickly and appeared in the Cleveland court with their team of four prominent area Republican attorneys. All pled innocent and were released until their trials. Langston appeared on Christmas Eve, although he had reportedly warned court officials beforehand "to make their peace with God before they lay hands on him." Those who failed to appear included, not surprisingly, the three who were fugitive slaves and free black John Copeland who, according to rumor, had escorted Price to Canada.[34] Defense preparations included a meeting on January 11, 1859, in an Oberlin hotel, a gathering soon dubbed the "Felon's Feast," which quickly turned into a celebration of the accused. Charles Langston did not attend, but his brother spoke of their determination to defy enforcement of the law, "to go to prison, or if necessary, go out on the battlefield to meet the Slave Oligarchy." Throughout late 1858 and early 1859, area newspapers reported events according to their political leanings, with the Republican *Cleveland Morning Leader* applauding the rescuers and the Democratic *Plain Dealer* urging strict enforcement of the law and conviction of those who dared violate it. The latter made no effort to disguise its antiblack feelings.[35]

The trials began on April 5, 1859, with the prosecution headed by U.S. Attorney George Belden. The jury of twelve was chosen from the remaining pool of sixteen Democrats left from the grand jury proceedings. The prosecution chose Simeon Bushnell to be tried first, believing him to be the easiest to convict since he had driven the buggy carrying John Price from

33. *Cleveland Morning Leader,* December 12, 1858; *Portage County (Ohio) Democrat,* May 11, 1859; Langston, *From the Virginia Plantation,* 21–2; Brant, *The Town That Started the Civil War,* 112–20.

34. *Cleveland Plain Dealer,* December 16, 18, 1858; Cheek and Cheek, *John Mercer Langston,* 330; Brant, *The Town That Started the Civil War,* 129.

35. *Cleveland Morning Leader,* December 14, 1858, January 13, 17, 1859; *Cleveland Plain Dealer,* December 7, 1858.

Wellington to Oberlin and because he had been among the most outspoken against the federal law and in urging the crowd to gather at the Wellington hotel. Bushnell's ten-day trial included elaborate defense efforts to ridicule the legality of the Fugitive Slave Act and the case against their client. But the prosecution had only to show that he had helped a known fugitive escape to convince the Democratic jury to find him guilty once Judge Willson had dismissed all defense motions as frivolous and irrelevant. The judge then stunned the defense by announcing that the same jury would then hear the case of Charles Langston. In the meantime, in an effort to draw further public attention to their cause, most of the remaining rescuers refused to post bail and were thus held in the Cleveland jail pending their trials.[36]

The trial of Charles Langston opened on April 18 amidst complex legal maneuvering initiated when attorneys for the twenty jailed rescuers appealed to the Ohio Supreme Court for their release. Judge Willson did give in to defense pressure and dismiss the original jury, but the new one was little different, containing nine Democrats and three others "who had no objections to the Fugitive Slave Law." Many of the same witnesses against Bushnell repeated their charges against Langston. Much of the evidence centered around what he had said when he left the attic room in the Wadsworth House where Marshall Jacob Lowe was holding Price. Several repeated the charge that, as he refused Lowe's request to pacify the crowd, he had made the incriminating statement that it was no use, for the crowd would have him anyway. After days of testimony and several recesses, one when the state supreme court ruled against the release of those awaiting trial, the case finally went to the jury on May 10. Judge Willson's charge to the jury made clear again his determination for a guilty verdict, and the jury obliged within thirty minutes.[37]

The next day Willson sentenced Bushnell to sixty days in prison and a fine of $600 plus court costs. Before proceeding with the next case, prosecutor Belden announced that what he had feared would happen had indeed come to pass: Republican officials in Lorain County, which included Oberlin and Wellington, had arrested the four who had arranged for Price's abduction, charging them with kidnapping. Willson then announced that the remaining trials would be postponed until the next court term in two months. Still refusing to post bail, the rescuers remained in the Cleveland federal jail. Before

36. The most complete accounts of the trials are in Shipherd, *Oberlin-Wellington Rescue*; Brant, *The Town That Started the Civil War*, 143–65; and Lubet, "Slavery on Trial," 795–829.
37. Shipherd, *Oberlin-Wellington Rescue*, 94–107, 114–69.

sentencing Langston the next morning, Willson indicated his willingness to let the convicted man address the court. Langston had long prepared for this moment, and the words he spoke had been carefully rehearsed in his mind for days. On that day he became, in the words of his brother, the "representative of the Negro Race" whose entire life had been "a free offering to the Anti-Slavery Cause."[38]

Langston delivered his message with force and total conviction, and his words represent perhaps the most effective and dramatic antebellum challenge to the lack of justice permitted northern blacks.[39] He began by noting that, as a black man, he had not received a fair trial, for "judging from the past history of the country," he could not expect "any mercy from the laws, from the constitution, or from the courts of the country." He had been taught to believe that men were innocent until proven guilty, but he had come to know that that guarantee did not apply to those of his race. John Price was assumed guilty even though his kidnappers were not required to show him to be a fugitive; he was, said Langston, "*a man, a brother,* who had a right to his liberty under the laws of God, under the laws of Nature, and under the Declaration of American Independence." Langston thus "supposed it to be my duty as a citizen of Ohio—excuse me for saying that, sir—an *outlaw of the United States,* to do what I could to secure at least this form of Justice to my brother whose liberty was in peril." Denying having ever uttered the incriminating "we will have him any how" statement, he attacked the law under which he had just been convicted as "an unjust one, one made to crush the colored man and one that outrages every feeling of humanity as well as every rule of right."

In a sweeping defense of black rights and an attack on the jury system, he took note of the Constitution's guarantee of "a trial before *an impartial jury,*" but concluded, "I have had no such trial." Whites shared "deeply fixed *prejudices.*" Since his peers had been excluded, he had been "tried by a jury who were prejudiced" and by a system of justice equally prejudiced. Thus he should not be subjected to such a system, for "I have *not* been tried, either by a jury of peers, or by a jury that were impartial." Most tellingly, he concluded that under the Fugitive Slave Act "BLACK MEN HAVE NO RIGHTS WHICH WHITE MEN ARE BOUND TO RESPECT." Langston then reminded Judge Willson that under the terms of the Fugitive Slave Act a conviction

38. Langston, "The Oberlin-Wellington Rescue," 211.

39. The entire speech is found ibid., 211–5; and in Shipherd, *Oberlin-Wellington Rescue,* 175–8.

provided for a jail term of six months and a fine of a thousand dollars; yet if called on to defend another like Price he would do all he could "for any man thus seized and held." For Langston, the way to remedy inequality before the law was through legislative and political action; increasing Republican party strength could most effectively challenge the discrimination he and his race had endured so long. As he sat down to "great and prolonged applause," the judge, clearly moved by his eloquence and the force of his argument, sentenced him to only twenty days and a $100 fine plus costs.

The drama of the situation had not ended. Bushnell and Langston began serving their sentences while the others remained in jail pending trial. On May 24, 1859, a throng estimated at between thirty-five hundred and ten thousand supporters of the rescuers from counties throughout the state gathered for a rally on Cleveland's Public Square. Following fiery speeches, the demonstrators marched en masse to the nearby county jail. There the sheriff permitted the prisoners to speak from the prison courtyard, with Langston urging the crowd with impassioned words: "We are taught that this is the land of the free; yet we are imprisoned for breaking the bonds of the oppressor, giving liberty to the captive and letting the downtrodden and the oppressed go free." He followed with the rhetorical questions: "Shall we submit to this outrage on our rights?," "Are you here to-day to obey the Fugitive Slave Law?," and "Are you here to sustain the dicta of the Dred Scott decision?" Each time they thundered an emphatic "No!"[40] Other speakers quieted the crowd by urging caution, and remarkably those assembled did remain calm; finally the demonstrators returned to Public Square to hear the words of Ohio Republican leaders, including Congressmen Joshua R. Giddings and Edward Wade and Governor Chase, with the latter urging caution while waiting for the state supreme court to rule on the Langston-Bushnell appeals for a habeas corpus ruling. The court finally ruled on May 30, and by a 3–2 vote rejected the rescuers' appeal and refused to intervene. Langston was released on June 1, having served his time, while the others remained, still refusing to post bail. Finally, in early July the two sides agreed to suspend further proceedings, with Lorain County officials dropping the charges against the kidnappers and the federal government those against the remaining rescuers.[41] The events of 1858–1859 in north-

40. *Anti-Slavery Bugle* (Salem, Ohio), June 4, 1859.

41. Shipherd, *Oberlin-Wellington Rescue*, 247–57; Brant, *The Town That Started the Civil War*, 203–37; Cheek and Cheek, *John Mercer Langston*, 334–6; Lubet, "Slavery on Trial," 825–7.

ern Ohio had further polarized North and South as the country moved toward ultimate separation and war. In the process, Charles Langston, in defending the rights of his race against the Fugitive Slave Act and in demanding political action to overturn it, had proudly played a central role.

Judge Willson had ruled with leniency in sentencing Langston, but federal officials in Cleveland, led by prosecutor George Belden, demanded he pay the $100 fine plus $872 in court costs immediately. Of that total, $659 was to cover the expenses of government witnesses brought to Cleveland ironically to testify against him. Belden also began charging interest on these charges from the day that Willson had sentenced Langston. Officials then moved to attach his Columbus property to cover the costs, which quickly exceeded $1,000. Belden then ordered the sale of Langston's property, valued at $1,200, but when no bidders appeared the federal government was unable to collect.[42] This relentless pursuit by the Buchanan administration was further thwarted by the Democratic party's defeat in the presidential election of 1860 and the coming to office of Republican Abraham Lincoln. At the same time, Langston kept up his attacks on slavery and the Buchanan efforts to enforce the Fugitive Slave Act. Nor did he relent in his demands for black political rights. As the executive secretary of the Ohio State Anti-Slavery Society, he used his Cleveland office to publicize the ongoing kidnapping attempts against Ohio blacks by circulating petitions demanding enactment of a new Ohio personal liberty law along with black suffrage. These petitions called on the Ohio legislature to abolish "kidnaping and man stealing on the Soil of the State of Ohio," and to remove all "distinctions between the citizens of the State on account of color."[43]

While Langston had awaited his trial, in March 1859 John Brown visited Oberlin, met with both Langstons, and, in a public meeting, had called on his listeners to help liberate slaves with force if necessary. Later in the year, several of Brown's lieutenants, including John Brown Jr., came to Oberlin in an effort to recruit supporters for the coming raid at Harpers Ferry. Neither John nor Charles Langston was willing to enlist, but they did suggest names of those who might participate.[44] They also helped to recruit Lewis Sheridan

42. "Court Charges," May, 1859, in Carter and Ripley, eds., *Black Abolitionist Papers*; *U.S. v. Charles Langston*, National Archives, RG 21; Brant, *The Town That Started the Civil War*, 221, 250.

43. *Anti-Slavery Bugle* (Salem, Ohio), October 29, 1859; Cheek and Cheek, *John Mercer Langston*, 366.

44. Langston, *From the Virginia Plantation*, 192; Shipherd, *Oberlin-Wellington Rescue*, viii; Cheek and Cheek, *John Mercer Langston*, 352–4.

Leary and his nephew, John A. Copeland, both young Oberlin blacks, the latter, one of the Price rescuers. Although the elder Langston later became discouraged about Brown's plans, believing that there were too few involved for it to be successful, he nonetheless gave his full support to Brown and may have contributed financially. After the raid, as Brown awaited execution in Virginia, Langston praised his actions as "the result of his faithfulness to the plain teaching of the word of God." Angry with his fellow Republicans, who had timidly renounced Brown and his actions, he noted bitterly that Giddings, Hale, Gerrit Smith, and others "have denied any knowledge" of the scheme; he wondered if they were more concerned with the thought of "bloody gallows" or of "a political grave yawning to receive them." As for himself, he had "no political prospects, and therefore no political fears; for my black face and curly hair doom me in this land of equality to political damnation." On December 2, the day of Brown's execution, Langston addressed two thousand mourners in Cleveland, saying bitterly that Brown had been "murdered by the American people, murdered in consequence" of the "union with slavery."[45] A year later, and just four months before the outbreak of war, he was no less bitter or determined to use force to end slavery: "Let Republicans by their *votes* stop the extension of slavery. Let Radical Abolitionists make the Constitution of the United States purely Anti-Slavery. . . . Let colored men by their words and actions demonstrate the equality of the races. But above all let the friends of physical revolution continue to plot insurrection."[46]

As events in 1860 and 1861 moved inexorably toward the election of Abraham Lincoln, secession, and war, Langston renewed his efforts to secure the right to vote and then for blacks to enlist in Union armies. In neither case was he immediately successful, but his determination remained strong. His major efforts were through his Ohio State Anti-Slavery Society. By 1860, this group had finally become a viable organization, albeit one with limited resources which could pay him only a small salary while it maintained a permanent Cleveland office from which he worked as executive secretary. His demands for suffrage met with the usual frustration, with Democrats and conservative Republicans in the legislature again blocking any change in voting requirements. Nonetheless, he and his brother cam-

45. *Cleveland Plain Dealer,* November 18, December 3, 1859; *The Anglo-African Magazine,* December 3, 1859, in Carter and Ripley, eds., *Black Abolitionist Papers.*

46. Langston letter to Boston commemoration of John Brown, November 28, 1860, *The Anglo-African Magazine,* April 6, 1861, in Carter and Ripley, eds., *Black Abolitionist Papers.*

paigned hard for the Republican party. Charles had favored William H. Seward of New York for the 1860 presidential nomination, while John preferred Governor Chase, but after the party convention they united enthusiastically behind Lincoln.[47] When war began in April 1861, Langston, along with countless other Ohio blacks, attempted to enlist. Within two weeks of the president's call for troops, he wrote to state officials in behalf of himself and other "colored citizens of Cleveland, desiring to prove our loyalty to the Government," and offering themselves "to defend the Government of which we claim protection." Ohio adjutant general Henry B. Carrington rejected the offer by tersely noting that "the Constitution will not permit me to issue the order."[48] In the first fifteen months of the fighting, Langston and other African Americans, along with the more radical Republicans, viewed the war as a struggle to end slavery and secure racial equality, while the Lincoln administration held to its more limited goal of preserving the Union.

As the president moved gradually toward an emancipation policy in 1862, Langston's career shifted to meet the changing situation. For much of the next three years he lived in Leavenworth, Kansas, having learned of the Kansas situation after brief contacts with John Brown in the late 1850s. The ongoing struggle of Kansas blacks for a measure of equality may have been the factor which motivated his move. In Leavenworth, he taught recently liberated slaves who had migrated there, many of them from nearby Missouri; he also continued his enfranchisement efforts. At a black convention in Leavenworth on January 1, 1863, Langston urged state approval of black suffrage, but to no avail.[49] After Lincoln issued the Emancipation Proclamation, Langston, knowing now that the end of slavery was close at hand, returned to Ohio for a time in 1863 and worked with his brother in the recruitment of Cleveland-area African Americans for service in the all-black Massachusetts 54th Regiment. They then expanded their recruiting efforts into southern Ohio as well as Illinois, Indiana, and Kansas. Later in 1863, they began recruitment for an Ohio black regiment when state officials, led

---

47. See Langston to Editor, *The Anglo-African Magazine,* June 20, 1860, in Carter and Ripley, eds., *Black Abolitionist Papers;* Cheek and Cheek, *John Mercer Langston,* 366–73.

48. C. L. Langston et al. to Carrington, April 1861, Carrington to Langston, April 21, 1861, *Liberator,* May 10, 1861, in Carter and Ripley, eds., *Black Abolitionist Papers.*

49. Eugene H. Berwanger, "Hardin and Langston: Western Black Spokesmen of the Reconstruction Era," *Journal of Negro History* 64 (1979): 105; Richard B. Sheridan, "Charles Henry Langston and the African American Struggle in Kansas," *Kansas History* 22 (winter 1999–2000): 273.

by Governor David Tod, finally relented in their opposition and requested African American assistance.[50]

At the war's end Langston settled permanently in Kansas, serving as general superintendent of refugees and freedmen for the Freedmen's Bureau there. By 1865 they numbered more than twelve thousand. His work included the encouragement of education and industry among the thousands of new black residents of the state. He continued to labor for black suffrage by urging the state Republican party to include it in its platform, only to see Kansas voters follow the Ohio example and reject it by an almost two-to-one margin in 1867. He also sought state approval for blacks to serve on juries. Here he employed the same argument he had used in his 1859 Cleveland trial, the right he had been denied then, of a trial by a jury of his peers. In 1869, at age fifty-one, he married for the first time; his wife was Mary Patterson Leary, the widow of the martyred Harpers Ferry recruit, Oberlin's Lewis Sheridan Leary.[51] The ratification of the Fifteenth Amendment in 1870 finally brought Langston the right to vote which he had sought for a lifetime and which he now eagerly exercised even as he remained active in the local Republican party; Kansas granted jury rights to blacks in 1874. Long before that Langston had settled into his life as a Kansas grocer and farmer in Lawrence, but he remained active in behalf of newly arrived African Americans, working to aid the exodusters of 1879–1880. Frustrated by continued procrastination on black rights and further examples of party discrimination against himself and fellow African Americans, Langston left the Republicans in the mid-1880s and joined the Prohibition party, receiving that party's nomination for auditor in 1886. His grandson, Langston Hughes, recalled later that, with his continuing political involvement, his farm and grocery were often neglected.[52] He was seventy-five when he died in 1892, having long been eclipsed by his brother John Mercer, whose many accomplishments included being minister to Haiti and brief service in Congress as a representative from Virginia. In his quiet and nonconfrontational way, Charles Langston had, nonetheless, played a significant role in the political

50. Cheek and Cheek, *John Mercer Langston,* 391–7.

51. Berwanger, "Hardin and Langston," 105–7, 109. For an account of Langston's role in Kansas, see Sheridan, "Langston," 22:268–83. Langston and his wife had four children, including son Nathaniel Turner and daughter Caroline Mercer, who would later become the mother of noted poet and playwright Langston Hughes.

52. Berwanger, "Harden and Langston," 107; Sheridan, "Langston," 282; Langston Hughes, *The Big Sea* (New York: Hill and Wang, 1940), 12–3.

process before, during, and after the Civil War. Seeking to go far beyond the limited goals of the Free Soil and Republican parties, he stands at the radical end of the antislavery political spectrum. He achieved his greatest prominence in defiance of the Fugitive Slave Act. At the same time, his perseverance had kept him in steady pursuit of emancipation and equal rights.

FIVE

THE BARBARISM OF SLAVERY

Owen Lovejoy and the Congressional Assault on Slavery

THE EARLY NINETEENTH-CENTURY Maine frontier was the scene of Owen Lovejoy's childhood, a setting which fostered both a stern Puritan morality and a devout evangelical piety.
His grandfather, Francis Lovejoy, who had
served in patriot armies during the War for
Independence, had moved from New Hampshire to Albion, Maine, in 1790. There Owen's
father, Daniel, had grown up, become a Congregational minister, and with his wife, Elizabeth, raised a large family that included older
brothers Elijah and Joseph, born in 1802 and 1805.
Owen was born in early 1811 on the eve of the second
war with Great Britain and experienced a childhood of few luxuries, as his
father struggled without appreciable success as both minister and farmer. In-
stability characterized the Lovejoy household, although Biblical lessons
taught by his mother at their farmhouse hearth and tutoring in the classics
by Elijah prepared the young boy for the religious education that would follow. Despite the poverty of the Lovejoy household, each of the boys managed
some college education, while those remaining at home helped their parents
keep the family farm solvent. Owen's turn came in 1830 when he left to attend Bowdoin College in Brunswick, Maine, only to have to return home in
1833 when his father died.[1]

1. The only modern biography of Lovejoy is Edward Magdol, *Owen Lovejoy: Abolitionist
in Congress* (New Brunswick: Rutgers Univ. Press, 1967). Other brief accounts of his early life

Owen Lovejoy's journey to the political antislavery movement can be traced directly to the violent death of his brother Elijah at the hands of an antiabolition mob in Alton, Illinois, in 1837. Settling in Princeton, Illinois, as a Congregational minister in the early 1840s, Owen used his pulpit to urge his congregation to aid fugitives and support political abolitionism. Soon a Liberty party activist, he used his ministry and the lecture circuit to win converts to antislavery. Political success came in 1856 with election as a Republican to Congress, where he addressed his concerns to both constituents and southerners in the House. Pressuring more moderate Republicans, such as Abraham Lincoln, he antagonized defenders of slavery to the point of near violence in Congress on the eve of the Civil War. As a member of the Radical wing of his party, he sought the most vigorous prosecution of the war as the best means to destroy slavery and punish the Slave Power. More tolerant of Lincoln's hesitancy to accept Radical abolitionism, as the president's friend he used his influence to urge him to change even as the war left him no alternative. Death in 1864 precluded a central Reconstruction role but left an almost unmatched antislavery heritage.

Owen's guidance and direction had come more from his mother and from Elijah than from his father; in 1827 his brother had established a classical academy in St. Louis, where he combined education with political journalism and support of Henry Clay. In 1832, Elijah had returned to the East to prepare for the ministry at Princeton Theological Seminary. His total immersion in Presbyterian theology was revealed in his letter to Owen at the time of their father's death. Despite the younger Lovejoy's own emerging Christian faith, Elijah had admonished him that "though our dead father's life failed to convert you," Owen should let "his death accomplish it." He urged him to "make haste and be at peace with God through faith and repentance and a belief in the Lord Jesus Christ."[2] Not offended by his brother's self-righteousness, Owen resolved to commit his life to his faith and soon enrolled in the Bangor (Maine) Theological Seminary while teaching school to support his own training. Before completing the curriculum, in 1836 he joined his brother in Alton, Illinois, with the intention of finishing his theological studies there under his brother's tutelage. During the early

---

are found in Merton Dillon, *Elijah P. Lovejoy: Abolitionist Editor* (Urbana: Univ. of Illinois Press, 1961); and Lovejoy and Lovejoy, *Memoir of the Rev. Elijah P. Lovejoy.* See also the entry on Lovejoy by Frederick J. Blue in *American National Biography*, 14:6–7.

2. Elizabeth Lovejoy to Owen Lovejoy, 1834, Lovejoy Papers, William Clements Library, University of Michigan; Elijah Lovejoy to Owen Lovejoy, August 26, 1833, in Lovejoy and Lovejoy, *Memoir of the Rev. Elijah P. Lovejoy*, 64–6.

1830s, the two, along with their brother Joseph, had been won over to abolitionism, Owen an apparent convert of Theodore Weld, Joseph as a follower of William Lloyd Garrison, and Elijah more of a gradualist.[3] Despite different routes to deep antislavery commitment, the three agreed on slavery's immorality and the need for its immediate eradication. It would be in Alton that Elijah would pursue his beliefs until being murdered by antiabolitionists and Owen would vow to dedicate his life to avenging his martyred brother with the abolition of the hated institution of slavery.

By the time Owen joined his brother in Alton the crisis there had already reached an explosive stage. Elijah, by now a Presbyterian minister, had begun publishing his newspaper, the *Observer,* first in St. Louis, where he emphasized his growing hatred of Roman Catholicism, and what he called papal tyranny, beliefs typical of the era's militant Protestantism. In a city with a large Catholic minority which soon demanded he cease publication, Lovejoy further incensed the pro-southern populace by attacking slavery. At first he had taken a gradualist stance, even endorsing the colonization of blacks in Africa as a possible solution, a position rejected out of hand by the Garrisonians. But when mobs attacked eastern abolitionists like Alvan Stewart and his colleagues in 1835 in Utica and even in Boston, where antiabolitionists dragged Garrison through the streets, Lovejoy became more militant. The violence soon spread to St. Louis, where a mob lynched a free black in May 1836, and Lovejoy used his newspaper to condemn the act. The crowd then turned its aggression against the *Observer,* smashing the press and forcing Lovejoy to relocate across the Mississippi in Alton. Here in a free state with far fewer Catholics, he assumed he could pursue his journalistic attacks on slavery and Catholicism without fear of physical abuse. By the time Owen arrived in late 1836, Elijah had rejected colonization, and with Owen's help he prepared to form an abolition society.[4]

Alton proved as unreceptive to Lovejoy's antislavery rhetoric as St. Louis had been to his anti-Catholicism. With strong trade ties with the nearby slave states of Missouri and Kentucky, many of the people of Alton were not prepared to stand aside and watch Lovejoy's abolitionist organizing meeting in October proceed without opposition. The Lovejoy brothers and Presbyterian minister Edward Beecher, president of nearby Illinois College, planned

3. Dillon, *Elijah Lovejoy,* 15–31; Magdol, *Owen Lovejoy,* 27.
4. Lovejoy and Lovejoy, *Memoir of the Rev. Elijah P. Lovejoy,* 111; Dillon, *Elijah Lovejoy,* 80–8; Magdol, *Owen Lovejoy,* 3–15.

to organize the Illinois State Anti-Slavery Society, but obstructionist tactics temporarily blocked the creation of the new organization, and tensions escalated. Mobs had already stopped publication of Lovejoy's *Observer;* yet when Elijah had considered giving up his efforts, Owen had urged him to seek the support of his subscribers and continue.[5] The younger brother had gone to Cincinnati to order a new press to replace the one the mob had destroyed, when prominent city leaders demanded that Elijah take his agitation elsewhere. When the new press arrived on November 6, the Lovejoys had to form their own guard after city officials refused protection. The drunken and enraged mob attacked the next night. With one of their own already dead in the exchange of gunfire, they shot and killed Elijah in retaliation. The country had its first abolition martyr, irreversibly changing the course of the antislavery movement and giving its supporters a new rallying cry. Two days later, after his brother's funeral, Owen promised: "I shall never forsake the cause that has been sprinkled with my brother's blood." He was convinced that with his dramatic death Elijah had accomplished more than "living and unopposed he could have done in a century."[6] Owen now determined to devote himself to abolition.

Lovejoy took the first step in this direction the next year when he and his brother Joseph coauthored a biography and tribute to Elijah, *Memoir of the Rev. Elijah P. Lovejoy; who was murdered in defense of the Liberty of the Press at Alton, Illinois, Nov. 7, 1837.* The volume included an introduction and tribute by Congressman John Quincy Adams, who was then leading the House fight against the Gag Rule. The brothers provided an account of the childhood of the Lovejoy siblings and included Elijah's letters to family members. It concluded with his efforts in St. Louis and Alton, climaxing in his murder. Numerous Lovejoy editorials from the *Observer* were followed by tributes and eulogies by abolitionists. The *Memoir,* advertised in many antislavery newspapers, sold well and enhanced Elijah's status as a martyr; the Lovejoy brothers had helped to mobilize northern public opinion not only against their brother's murderers, but more importantly against slavery itself. Among the tributes was one by New York abolitionist Alvan Stewart, who urged his audience not to "forget that the life of the slave is

5. Lovejoy and Lovejoy, *Memoir of the Rev. Elijah P. Lovejoy,* 261; Dillon, *Elijah Lovejoy,* 120.

6. *Chicago Tribune,* June 12, 1874; Lovejoy and Lovejoy, *Memoir of the Rev. Elijah P. Lovejoy,* 261–93; Dillon's *Elijah Lovejoy* provides a full account of the final confrontation that led to his murder (see pages 159–79).

one continued scene of martyrdom, equal in anguish and horrour to that of Lovejoy."[7]

After overseeing the publication of the *Memoir* in New York, Lovejoy determined "to set my face West with all possible speed."[8] Joshua Leavitt had urged him to become the Illinois agent of the American Anti-Slavery Society, a position which would have required constant travel. Lovejoy instead preferred the more settled life that a pastorate would provide while still allowing him to speak out against slavery. He completed his studies for ordination in the Episcopal Church of Illinois and prepared to accept a call in Alton. But when the bishop demanded he sign a pledge not to discuss slavery, Owen refused and instead accepted a pastorate at the Hampshire Colony Congregational Church in the small town of Princeton two hundred miles northeast. The church was the first of that denomination established in Illinois. Arriving in Princeton with all of his possessions in his saddlebags, he insisted that there be no restrictions on what he preached. Returning to the denomination of his father and following his brother's violent death, the freedom to oppose slavery openly was far more significant than the differences in theology between the Anglican and Congregational churches. Yet even in northern Illinois, far removed from slave territory and only a hundred miles from Chicago, not all of the twenty-seven-year-old minister's new congregation were prepared to accept his sermons on the immorality of slavery. On one occasion when several parishioners rose in protest to leave in the middle of his message, he rejoined: "I intend to preach this until you like it and then because you like it."[9] Apparently he succeeded, because he would retain the Princeton position for seventeen years even as he led the area in support of fugitive slaves. He would lead the area's Liberty and Free Soil parties until finally being elected to Congress on a Republican antislavery platform in 1856.

In the late 1830s, Lovejoy quickly established himself in Princeton not only as a Congregational minister, but most controversially as a conductor on the Underground Railroad, for he soon made the small town a haven for escaping slaves. Initially he boarded with Butler and Eunice Denham and their two young daughters. Butler Denham died during the summer of 1841,

---

7. Stewart, remarks at Rochester, January 10, 1838, in Lovejoy and Lovejoy, *Memoir of the Rev. Elijah P. Lovejoy*, 363.

8. Lovejoy to Elizabeth Lovejoy, March 22, 1838, Chicago Historical Society.

9. Magdol, *Lovejoy*, 32–6; Ruth Haberkorn, "Owen Lovejoy in Princeton, Illinois," *Journal of the Illinois State Historical Society* 36 (1943): 285.

and seventeen months later Owen and Eunice were married. Together they raised her daughters and a large family of their own. The thirty-three-year-old mother needed little encouragement to support Owen's determination to keep his brother's legacy alive. In early 1842, he urged his parishioners to join the antislavery crusade with him: "Come life or death I will devote the residue of my life to the anti-slavery cause. The slaveholders and their sympathizers have murdered my brother, and if another victim is needed, I am ready."[10]

Lovejoy's leadership soon established Princeton as a regular stop for fugitives from Missouri or Kentucky as they followed the route to the hoped-for Canadian sanctuary. On several occasions he took escapees hidden under the hay of his wagon toward Chicago, where fellow abolitionist Zebina Eastman received them and guided them further north to eventual safety in Canada. Lovejoy made no effort to hide his role, openly and defiantly advertising in the Chicago journal *Western Citizen* to "inform the ladies and gentlemen of color of the South who wish to travel North for the benefit of their condition" that transportation to freedom was available and that "passengers will be carried all the way through for Nothing." His advertisement concluded: "Extras fitted out at any hour of the day or night, and articles of clothing furnished gratuitously to those who have fallen among Southern banditti and been stripped." When New York abolitionist leader Gerrit Smith published his "Address to the Slaves," urging them to flee their southern shackles and seek freedom in the North, some in the Old Northwest felt Smith had gone too far. But not Owen Lovejoy. Endorsing Smith's appeal, he responded that since slaveholders had stolen their freedom, fugitives were only reclaiming that freedom when they escaped to the North. Moreover, in securing their escape, they would be justified in stealing their master's horse.[11]

On occasion his efforts in behalf of fugitive slaves were interrupted by state officials and Lovejoy found himself in court defending his actions. In 1843, he was indicted under Illinois law for aiding two slave women, Agnes and Nancy, whom he had hidden in his home before guiding them to safety. Alvan Stewart had hoped to come to Princeton to defend him, but when he

---

10. Quoted in H. C. Bradsby, ed., *History of Bureau County, Illinois* (Chicago: World Publishing Co., 1885), 335.

11. *Western Citizen* (Chicago), June 1, 1843; Vernon Volpe, *Forlorn Hope of Freedom: The Liberty Party in the Old Northwest, 1838–1848* (Kent, Ohio: Kent State Univ. Press, 1990), 115–6.

was unable to leave Utica, Lovejoy was represented by a Chicago abolitionist attorney, James Collins. In October Lovejoy was tried in the Bureau County court but convinced the jury that the slaves' owner had voluntarily brought them to Illinois. Lovejoy thus won his acquittal; Agnes and Nancy were judged not to be fugitives since slavery could not exist in a free state and the two women had become free when their owner brought them there.[12] In 1849, a fugitive slave named John Buckner was captured in Princeton, but with Lovejoy's aid he escaped and found safety in the abolitionist's home. As a hostile crowd gathered, Lovejoy disguised the slave in women's clothes and successfully arranged his escape.[13] Such incidents continued sporadically into the 1850s even as Lovejoy devoted increasing effort to the political antislavery movement.

As a young man Owen Lovejoy had been somewhat of a free spirit, and he had shown no particular interest in politics while he lived in New England and even after moving to Illinois. Caught up in the drama which led to his brother's death in 1837, he was apparently unmoved by the issues dividing Jacksonian Democrats and the Whigs of Henry Clay and Daniel Webster. There is some evidence that, at least as a young man, he shared his brother Elijah's antipathy for papal power, although he was never openly anti-Catholic. Like many abolitionists he accepted the policy of questioning the candidates and supporting those least objectionable to the antislavery cause. But because such a policy rarely produced satisfactory results, he was among the earliest advocates of a third party dedicated to the destruction of slavery. In Illinois, a state with strong southern ties and in which Garrisonians were not as numerous or influential as in New England and New York, the more important obstacle to the third-party approach was voter apathy or outright opposition. Lovejoy may also have been motivated by the refusal of several of the leading Protestant denominations to denounce slavery, complaining on one occasion of "the criminal apathy of the American church on the subject." His brother Elijah's Presbyterian Church had become deeply divided over the issue of slavery's morality as well as a myriad of doctrinal differences. In 1837, it had come under the control of the Old School faction, which rejected any role for the church in abolitionism. In contrast, Owen's Congregational Church permitted local congregational autonomy instead of denominational control, and as a result, many Illinois congregations had strong antislavery foundations. Some, including Lovejoy's Hamp-

12. "People v Lovejoy," 1843, in Haberkorn, "Lovejoy," 295–6; Magdol, *Lovejoy*, 40–4.
13. Haberkorn, "Lovejoy," 292–8; Magdol, *Lovejoy*, 47–50.

shire Colony Congregational Church, insisted on an uncompromising stand against slavery, denying fellowship with anyone guilty of what the members considered proslavery sins. The Rock River Congregational Association, which included the Princeton congregation, urged its members to "break away from the proslavery parties" and to "go to the polls in the fear of God." Lovejoy added his own sense of urgency in noting that "religion and politics have been separated long enough." As Illinois abolitionists moved to form the state Liberty party, it would be strongest in towns with a Congregational church, including Princeton.[14]

Lovejoy's Illinois State Anti-Slavery Society included both those opposed to political action and those fully supportive of the Liberty party, which abolitionists had first established in Albany, New York, in April 1840. Lovejoy helped organize the party's first statewide gathering, which met in Princeton that summer. There he joined with Edward Beecher of the dissenting New School Presbyterian faction, giving the party a distinctly evangelical tone. Some of the delegates resisted the third-party approach and prevented an endorsement. A separate meeting finally nominated a Liberty ticket in support of James G. Birney's candidacy, and those present agreed to vote only for abolitionists. Still, the Illinois Liberty party did little campaigning in 1840 and its vote was minuscule in the excitement of the Harrison–Van Buren contest. It would not be until 1842 that party leaders could organize on a permanent basis.[15] At that time at a meeting in Chicago in May, Liberty leaders welcomed journalist Zebina Eastman, whose weekly *Western Citizen* would become the organ of the third party, thus providing an all-important element to a permanent third-party effort.

On Sunday, July 21, 1842, Lovejoy delivered an impassioned sermon to his Congregational flock in Princeton outlining why the Garrison resistance to abolitionists' voting and political antislavery activism was self-defeating and why Christians needed to reject the proslavery two-party system and play an active third-party role: "The notion is losing ground that religion must be confined to the sanctuary and the sabbath." Furthermore, he argued, "there is no reason why Christianity should not exert its influence in political affairs . . . no reason why Christians should not act as Christians at the polls as well as elsewhere." Frustrated by a federal government headed

14. Lovejoy et al., *Genius of Liberty* (Lowell, Ill.), July 10, 1841; *Western Citizen* (Chicago), January 20, 1843; Volpe, *Forlorn Hope of Freedom*, 24, 67–8.

15. Theodore C. Smith, *The Liberty and Free Soil Parties in the Northwest* (Cambridge, Mass.: Harvard Univ. Press, 1897), 42, 47; Volpe, *The Forlorn Hope of Freedom*, 48, 53.

by Virginia slaveholder John Tyler, Lovejoy urged his congregation "to carry our religion to the polls." Honest men must not "endorse and give currency to crime." Indeed, "the present Chief Magistrate is a slaveholder and consequently a robber and oppressor of the poor," and yet Christian voters have placed him in office: "John Tyler might have profaned the name of God on his plantation, and the influence of his profanity been limited and done comparatively little injury; but when Christians take him from the obscurity of his farm and place him at the head of the nation then . . . his influence is vastly extended and mightily enhanced." Clearly Christian voters must no longer "vote for slaveholders and profaners," for their actions "demoralize and corrupt with awful poison." Voters must withhold their support from men "who will not use their utmost exertion" to combat slavery. "I do not decide what you shall do, nor for whom you shall vote," he continued, but it was clear that they should withhold their votes from slaveholders and their allies among Democrats and Whigs. No one could miss his point that they must also reject the Garrisonian stance of staying out of politics entirely. Only by supporting the Liberty party could voters use their "political influence in the fear of God and in accordance with the principles of justice."[16]

In August 1843, Lovejoy traveled to Buffalo to attend the Liberty convention which made plans for the coming presidential campaign. There, party leaders chose him as one of the convention's secretaries and he worked actively in formulating party strategy. In addition to party leaders, including Gerrit Smith, James Birney, and Alvan Stewart, he met black delegates Henry Highland Garnet, Charles Ray, and Samuel Ringgold Ward and came away with a new appreciation of the plight of free blacks in both North and South. He returned from the meeting, which had renominated Birney for president, proclaiming it had been "a great, grand most glorious convention. . . . The resolution was undoubtedly correct which declared we are not the *third* but the *first* party." That fall, Lovejoy actively campaigned for the Liberty congressional candidate, John H. Henderson, who ran surprisingly well in an election won by Democratic leader "Long John" Wentworth.[17]

Liberty strength in the Old Northwest grew gradually during the mid-1840s as Lovejoy intensified his own efforts for political abolitionism even while he continued to minister to his Princeton congregation. In the presi-

16. *Western Citizen,* January 20, 1843.

17. Ibid., October 5, August 31, 1843; Charles H. Wesley, "The Participation of Negroes in Anti-Slavery Political Parties," *Journal of Negro History* 29 (1944): 32–72; Magdol, *Lovejoy,* 63–4.

dential campaign of 1844, third-party candidate James G. Birney increased his vote by nine-fold from 1840, and in Illinois, with Lovejoy chosen a Birney elector, the third-party total multiplied from fewer than 200 in 1840 to 3,469 in 1844. This was hardly enough to make an impact on the Polk-Clay contest, but sufficient to offer encouragement for the future. The following year, Lovejoy traveled to Cincinnati for the Southern and Western Liberty convention. The conclave, designed by Ohio Liberty leader Salmon P. Chase to advance his goal of a Liberty coalition with antislavery Democrats and Whigs, instead turned out to be a gathering of two thousand Liberty delegates. Lovejoy enthusiastically agreed with Birney and others at Cincinnati who sought to maintain the purity of Liberty-abolitionist principles in the face of Chase's efforts to move to the more moderate stance of containing slavery. At this point, the Illinoisan was among those who agreed with Alvan Stewart that the Constitution should be interpreted as an antislavery document.[18]

In 1846, with the nation deeply involved in war against Mexico, a war which Liberty leaders viewed as designed to expand slavery into the Southwest, Lovejoy accepted the Liberty nomination for Congress in his northeastern Illinois district. Although Democrats and Whigs could safely ignore the Liberty challenge in most northern districts, the Fourth Illinois District, which included both Princeton and Chicago, presented a significant third-party challenge. Although Democratic incumbent "Long John" Wentworth won a clear majority, Lovejoy's 4,247 votes was not far behind that of the Whig candidate. He had campaigned strenuously against the war, and in a district caught up in the enthusiasm of the spirit of Manifest Destiny and expansion, Lovejoy was frequently harassed and even made the target of egg-throwing mobs. Yet his vote equaled the total given all other third-party candidates in Illinois.[19] Among the successful Whig candidates for Congress in 1846 was Springfield attorney Abraham Lincoln, who Lovejoy had not yet met, but who had also campaigned against what both believed was the Democrats' war to expand slavery. After his own defeat in early October, Lovejoy rushed to Massachusetts to assist the campaigns of Liberty candidates there.

The war against Mexico brought a steady stream of American victories in 1847, and with it the inevitability of the addition of vast new territories.

18. Smith, *Liberty and Free Soil Parties*, 88; Volpe, *Forlorn Hope of Freedom*, 128, 114–5; Blue, *Chase*, 50–3.

19. *Western Citizen*, June 23, October 13, November 14, 1846; Magdol, *Lovejoy*, 73–8.

Congressional antislavery Whigs, such as Lincoln of Illinois and Joshua Giddings of Ohio, and Democrats, such as David Wilmot of Pennsylvania, thus stepped up their support of the Wilmot Proviso, which would prohibit the expansion of slavery into these regions. Liberty leaders now faced the dilemma of whether to join in a growing political antislavery coalition movement based on preventing the spread of slavery or, instead, maintain the integrity of their party's abolitionist stance. Chase again led those who sought broad antislavery union, but they faced opposition from eastern Liberty leaders joined by a significant number from the Old Northwest. Lovejoy was among the latter, who feared the compromise of their abolitionist principles. Party leaders had planned an October 1847 convention in Buffalo to choose their candidates for 1848, a move Chase had tried unsuccessfully to delay in hopes of pursuing a broader third-party movement which might include dissident northern Democrats and Whigs. Lovejoy led the Illinois delegation in Buffalo and successfully urged maintaining the Liberty position without compromise. The delegates chose John P. Hale as their presidential candidate; Hale had been elected to the Senate with a Liberty-Democratic coalition in the New Hampshire legislature. The choice for vice president was between Lovejoy and an Ohioan, Leicester King. Although the Illinoisan had a slight lead on the first ballot, he withdrew in King's favor in order to preserve party harmony.[20] He thus entered the crucial presidential election year of 1848 as an established third-party leader and one pledged to maintaining Liberty abolitionism. He explained confidently that the Liberty goal must not be just to force modest "anti-slavery action from the other parties, but to obtain control of the government in order thereby to abolish slavery."[21]

Even as Lovejoy spoke of the need to defend the Liberty stance on slavery, changes in the political situation were evolving that would lead him to adopt the more moderate containment stance and to approve the expansion of the platform to include related issues. Antislavery factions within both the Democratic and the Whig parties appeared ready to bolt should, as expected, their national organizations reject the Wilmot Proviso and nominate candidates for the 1848 presidential race not pledged to the containment of slavery. Democratic and Whig conventions that spring confirmed these expectations, leading antislavery men to begin the search for a new political home. Such a coalition effort would clearly welcome Liberty members in a

20. *National Era*, November 11, 1847; *Western Citizen*, December 14, 1847; Smith, *Liberty and Free Soil Parties*, 120.

21. *American Freeman* (Milwaukee), November 3, 1847.

major third-party effort assuming they would abandon their insistence on an abolition platform. In early August, Lovejoy again ran for Congress on the Liberty ticket, and when his vote fell from his 1846 showing, he, like so many other third-party leaders, became even more convinced that a more moderate antislavery party with a broader appeal was the practical way to accomplish the eventual end of slavery. By this time he also recognized that resistance to broadening a third-party appeal by taking positions on other issues, such as tariffs, land policy, and internal improvements, would only hamper a coalition effort.[22]

The Buffalo convention of the new Free Soil party in August 1848 confirmed Lovejoy's decision to abandon the more idealistic Liberty platform. As an Illinois Liberty delegate, he enthusiastically supported Hale's nomination for president but reluctantly joined with other Liberty leaders to endorse the convention's choice of former president Martin Van Buren. Only the small New York Liberty faction headed by Gerrit Smith and William Goodell resisted the trend and persisted in a pure abolitionist party, which they called the Liberty League. In contrast, Lovejoy defended his abandonment of immediate abolition in favor of free soil, explaining that "the principles of Liberty are in this movement, undergird it and surround it—the immediate object aimed at is one which we cordially approve and the ultimate object is identical—the extinction of slavery." He campaigned strenuously that fall for the Free Soil ticket of Van Buren and Charles Francis Adams and the party's containment platform. He said little about the Free Soil omission of a plank endorsing equal rights, including suffrage, for African Americans.[23] Although the party fell far short of the support that enthusiastic backers had predicted, Van Buren won close to three hundred thousand votes, or about 10 percent of the national vote. In Illinois, Lovejoy could take heart that the Free Soil vote had climbed to more than 12 percent of the total, up from the 3 percent showing of James G. Birney as the Liberty candidate in 1844.[24]

In the months ahead, Lovejoy gladly accepted the challenge to labor on for his antislavery goals as a Free Soiler. Yet the party faced significant defections in its brief six-year history as those less dedicated to antislavery suc-

22. *Western Citizen*, June 27, 1848.

23. Ibid., August 22, 1848; Sewell, *Ballots for Freedom*, 163–4; Blue, *The Free Soilers*, 81–103.

24. Svend Petersen, *A Statistical History of the American Presidential Elections* (New York: Frederick Ungar, 1963), 27–30.

cumbed to the compromise spirit and the lure of political influence that could be found only within the two-party system. In 1849, numerous anti-slavery Democrats returned to the fold while antislavery Whigs and former Liberty members struggled to maintain the third-party's vitality. Lovejoy helped convince most Illinois Free Soilers against rejoining the Democrats. The Compromise of 1850, with its hated Fugitive Slave Act, gave him further cause to resist the national trend toward the abandonment of antislavery principles, but most voters appeared unmoved by his appeal. Even as Congress moved toward the sectional truce, Lovejoy sought to arouse his congregation's commitment to "human equality" with a June sermon, "The Morning Cometh."[25]

In 1852, Lovejoy led the Illinois delegation to the third-party nominating convention in Pittsburgh. There he voted with the overwhelming majority in rejecting Gerrit Smith's efforts to include abolition and racial equality in the platform, knowing that such positions could only further erode the party's already dangerously low voting base. More and more the practical politician, Lovejoy may still have believed privately in equal rights, but, because of the racial climate in the North in general and in Illinois in particular, he understood that Smith's idealistic stance could only cost votes. During the 1850s he would say little about political rights for those he hoped to see free, although during the Civil War he did advocate civil rights for African Americans and even proposed legislation designed to guarantee it. He enthusiastically endorsed the convention's choice of John P. Hale and George W. Julian of Indiana for its ticket. Although the Free Democrats, as they now called themselves, had rejected the more radical demands of the Smith faction, the party was a more dedicated group of reformers than it had been in 1848.[26] Lovejoy proudly campaigned for the Hale-Julian ticket that fall even as he kept up his persistent demands for the repeal of the fugitive slave law. Although Hale's vote was only half of what Van Buren had received in 1848 and the Illinois third-party total fell proportionately, Lovejoy and others could point to the future of antislavery politics with hope and enthusiasm. In 1853, Lovejoy worked without success to modify the Illinois black code.[27]

---

25. The sermon is in the Lovejoy Papers; see also Haberkorn, "Owen Lovejoy in Princeton, Illinois," 300.

26. *Western Citizen,* August 17, 1852. For the third-party campaign in 1852, see Blue, *The Free Soilers,* 232–68; for Lovejoy's Civil War legislation, see Michael Vorenberg, *Final Freedom: The Civil War, the Abolition of Slavery and the Thirteenth Amendment* (Cambridge, UK: Cambridge Univ. Press, 2001), 51.

27. Petersen, *A Statistical History,* 31–2; Magdol, *Lovejoy,* 99.

But later that year, when Illinois senator Stephen A. Douglas introduced his bill to repeal the ban on slavery north of 36°30′ in the Louisiana Territory, northerners appeared finally ready to embrace a stronger antislavery stance and a more viable party as its advocate. Lovejoy would be among the leading Illinois supporters of the new Republican party.

After months of congressional debate on Douglas's Kansas-Nebraska proposal, President Franklin Pierce signed the senator's bill into law in May 1854, ending all semblance of the sectional truce which moderates had fought to keep alive since the passage of the 1850 Compromise measures. Angry northern antislavery leaders and voters of all parties now joined in the anti-Nebraska movement. They pointed toward creating a new northern antislavery party to replace the Whig organization they believed had been so ineffective in blocking this latest triumph of the Slave Power. Calls from antislavery members of Congress for a new party led to struggles throughout the North. Many Whigs, fearful of deserting a position in an established party within the two-party system, resisted change, while Lovejoy and his third-party colleagues led the Illinois drive for a new party dedicated to repealing the Kansas-Nebraska Act and preventing the spread of slavery. In October 1854, Illinois advocates, following the lead of such Old Northwest states as Ohio, Wisconsin, and Michigan, met in Springfield to discuss the new party concept. Lovejoy led these efforts but was rebuffed by the moderate Whigs, such as Lincoln, and the delegates could not agree on a firm commitment to form what in other states was called the People's or Republican party.[28] Still, the anti-Nebraska forces succeeded in many Illinois legislative contests; among those elected to the lower house was Owen Lovejoy, who won his first elective office.

The Princeton Republican played a key role in the 1855 legislative session in Springfield. With Lincoln among the candidates for the federal Senate seat, Lovejoy vacillated among several aspirants during the early balloting; finally he supported the eventual winner, Judge Lyman Trumbull, a former Democrat who was vehement in his opposition to Douglas's bill and at this point more committed to the new antislavery party than Lincoln. In February 1855, Lovejoy introduced a series of antislavery resolutions to instruct Illinois members of Congress to vote to prohibit territorial slavery, to oppose the admission of new slave states, and to seek repeal of the Fugitive Slave Act. Although only the first of these passed the legislature, the support for all three was substantial, giving their backers new hope and a dynamic

28. Smith, *Liberty and Free Soil Parties*, 295.

leader. Lovejoy's February 6 speech electrified the Illinois House and those in the crowded galleries who had flocked to hear the fiery orator arraign Douglas and his Kansas-Nebraska Act, calling the senator an "instrument that the slave power has used in the fraud."

Responding to a question from the gallery as to whether he was an abolitionist, Lovejoy replied dramatically, "I am an abolitionist, I glory in the name."[29] He recognized that a call to end slavery was premature and would serve only to antagonize voters, but he believed that his resolutions were the best way to begin an all-out political attack on slavery. To those who questioned "why don't you abolish slavery in all the states," he answered: "I do not go for it simply because I have not the power. . . . But we have the power to prohibit slavery in the Territories, as they are under the jurisdiction of us, the people of the United States." Reflecting the racial views of his era, Lovejoy believed that oppression had humbled the enslaved: "He is degraded, I know. He is often vicious, I grant it—He is often ignorant, repulsive, I do not deny it, but he is still a man." Wisdom suggested to him that only by halting the spread of the evil which had caused this degradation could the process be reversed.[30]

In 1856, party leaders officially formed the Republican party with two conventions, the first a mass meeting in Pittsburgh in February to activate their supporters, and the other in Philadelphia in June to nominate candidates and adopt a platform for the presidential campaign. Lovejoy would be central in both meetings even as he laid plans for another race for a seat in the U.S. House of Representatives. At the Pittsburgh gathering his invocation attacked Franklin Pierce for signing and implementing Douglas's bill. He asked God "to enlighten the mind of the President of the United States and turn him from his evil ways, and if this was not possible, to take him away so that an honest man might take his place." In a later address, referring to the violence in Kansas between pro- and antislavery forces, he asked, "Who would not lose his life in such a cause. In defense of Kansas . . . I will shoulder a gun and go as a private. If I use my Sharp's rifle I will shoot in God's name. I am for war to the knife and the knife to the hilt if it must be so." In late May, Lincoln and other moderates now joined with Lovejoy and other former Radicals in officially organizing the Illinois Republican party at a convention in Bloomington. At the Philadelphia convention the next month

29. *Free West* (Chicago), February 15, March 15, April 5, 1855; Magdol, *Lovejoy,* 118–26.

30. *Free West* (Chicago), April 5, 1855.

Lovejoy led an Illinois delegation of both radicals and moderates. He was satisfied with the containment platform introduced by David Wilmot even though he would have preferred a stronger attack on slavery. He opposed a motion to invite the anti-Catholic Know-Nothing faction into the new party coalition, more to protect the Catholic German vote in Illinois for the Republicans than as an expression of anti-Catholicism. In discussing the encroachments of the Slave Power on the rights of northerners, he compared southern attacks on free speech to those of the "spiritual supremacy of Papal hierarchy" in Europe in the seventeenth century. He was thus unable to overcome entirely the anti-Catholic heritage of the age and of his brother. At the same time he was enthusiastic over the party's nominee, the dashing military leader and explorer John C. Frémont.[31]

Back in Illinois, Lovejoy prepared an active campaign in Frémont's and his party's behalf while concentrating on his own nomination and election to the U.S. Congress. Although some in the new party considered him too radical an abolitionist, one who would divide Republicans, delegates chose him as their candidate at a meeting in Ottawa in July. As antislavery sentiment spread through the state in the wake of the Frémont nomination and the earlier caning of Republican senator Charles Sumner on the Senate floor by a South Carolina congressman, Lovejoy appeared assured of an easy victory over his Democratic opponent. His chances improved even further when the conservative candidate of the fast-dying Whig remnants withdrew from the race in September. After campaigning throughout the state with other Republicans, such as Lincoln, for the Frémont ticket, Lovejoy easily defeated his opponent, a Douglas Democrat, by more than six thousand votes.[32] While Democrats retained the presidency with James Buchanan's surprisingly narrow victory over Frémont, Lovejoy would be a part of a Congress in which Republicans would quickly make clear their determination to block the further demands of the Slave Power.

Lovejoy quickly mastered the many roadblocks that the Democrat-controlled House put in the path of a freshman representative, especially an abolitionist well-known to be determined on challenging slavery at every opportunity. Having secured a loan from Gerrit Smith to cover living expenses, he boarded with fellow Republicans in the capital city. Ignoring the unwrit-

31. George W. Julian, "The First Republican National Convention," *American Historical Review* 4 (January 1899): 314–6; *New York Times*, February 22, 23, 1856; *Chicago Tribune*, October 18, 1856; Magdol, *Lovejoy*, 152; Sewell, *Ballots for Freedom*, 277 n. 50.

32. Magdol, *Lovejoy*, 166.

ten rule that first-term congressmen should remain in the background, Lovejoy wasted no time in establishing his antislavery credentials. His early speeches lambasted the Buchanan administration's efforts to secure the admission of Kansas as a slave state and to enforce rigidly the Fugitive Slave Act and the Supreme Court's recent Dred Scott decision guaranteeing slavery in the territories. In a speech entitled "Human Beings, Not Property," he argued that: "The demon of Slavery has come forth from the tombs. . . . It claims the right to pollute the Territories with its slimy footsteps and then makes its way to the very home of Freedom in the free states." This it did by attempting "to hamper a free press, to defile the pulpit, to corrupt religion, and to stifle free thought and free speech!" Yet the most immediate threat to freedom was in the Kansas Territory: "Yes sir, while the border ruffians are striving by alternate violence and fraud, to force slavery into Kansas, the President and Chief Justice, by new, unheard of, and most unwarrantable interpretations of the Constitution are endeavoring to enthrone and nationalize slavery, and make it the dominant power in the land." The will of Kansans to prohibit slavery must be honored: "What now is the country's duty, destiny and true glory? . . . to extend the area of slavery; to hunt down fugitive slaves and take them back manacled to bondage; to break down the dykes of freedom?" Rather, the United States must "exemplify before the Nations of the earth the principles of civil and religious freedom and equality."[33] Lovejoy's Illinois constituents reacted enthusiastically to his words, and he was encouraged that his efforts and those of fellow Republicans had blocked the admission of Kansas as a slave state and any further victories of the Slave Power in Congress.

Lovejoy had little time to rest after the end of the first session of the Thirty-fifth Congress. On his return to Illinois he had first to secure his renomination and then became deeply involved in the most famous American political debate of the nineteenth century, the Lincoln-Douglas struggle for an Illinois Senate seat. Conservative Republicans led by Judge David Davis sought to replace the Princeton Republican with a more pliable moderate but were thwarted at the district nominating convention in Joliet in late June 1858. In his acceptance speech Lovejoy again made clear his desire to see slavery "exterminated" someday. But for the time being, he was "content to fight slavery in modes pointed out in the Constitution, and in those modes only." He thus disarmed his antiabolitionist critics by confirming he would not "seek extermination in unjustifiable modes." In the same address, he re-

---

33. *Congressional Globe,* 35th Cong., 1st sess., 752–4.

moved any doubt over his preference for Lincoln as the Republican most qualified to challenge the famous Douglas. By the summer of 1858, Lovejoy and Lincoln had made their political peace and sought to bury any memories of past differences over third-parties, which the latter consistently resisted joining. Said the congressman: "I am for him because he is a true hearted man" who would "remain true to the great principles upon which the Republican party is organized."[34] Although the two men remained far apart on how best to attack slavery, each knew he needed the other to forward individual and party goals.

The seven open-air debates between Lincoln and Douglas, which not only guaranteed Illinois voter attention but that of all Americans, included the opening encounter at Ottawa in Lovejoy's Third District.[35] Senator Douglas assumed that by linking his opponent with the views of the Princeton congressman in the time-honored tactic of guilt by association, he would succeed in painting Lincoln as a dangerous abolitionist. Reminding the audience of Lovejoy's radical views on slavery, Douglas hoped to drive a wedge between Republican factions and secure the support of the more moderate for himself. At the second debate at Freeport, with the congressman again on the platform with Lincoln, Douglas attempted to link his opponent with extremism. But in the northern Illinois towns of Ottawa and Freeport, Lovejoy's more advanced views, which he had voiced in both the state legislature and in Congress, were popular. The Douglas strategy backfired. Lovejoy thus assured Lincoln that legislative districts in his area would return Lincoln-Republicans to Springfield.[36] In the November results Lovejoy won a decisive victory, increasing his margin of 1856 and securing close to 60 percent of the popular vote over his Douglas-backed opponent.[37] His district returned a Republican delegation to the legislature, but it was not sufficient to prevent the Democrat-controlled body from reelecting Douglas to the Senate. Although the lawmakers had denied Lincoln the chance to join Lovejoy in Congress, a close friendship and alliance had evolved between the two that would be critical in the explosive days ahead.

In and out of Congress Lovejoy continued his attacks on slavery and the Slave Power. In February 1859, he again arraigned the Buchanan adminis-

34. *Bureau County Republican* (Princeton, Ill.), July 8, 1858.

35. For a detailed account of Lovejoy's role in the Lincoln-Douglas debates, see Magdol, *Lovejoy,* 209–19.

36. Lovejoy to Lincoln, August 4, 1858, Lincoln Papers, Library of Congress.

37. Edward Magdol, "Owen Lovejoy's Role in the Campaign of 1858," *Journal of the Illinois State Historical Society* 51 (1958): 416.

tration for its proslavery stance in Kansas and its efforts to acquire Cuba as a potential slave territory and future state or states, "for the benefit of slave breeders and human-flesh mongers."[38] In a speech he labeled "The Fanaticism of the Democratic Party," he not only condemned the party of slaveholders but defended his personal defiance of the Fugitive Slave Act and the assistance he had given to an aging runaway in 1854. He exclaimed that he would aid "every fugitive that comes to his door and asks it. Proclaim it then upon the housetops." All slave catchers should be aware: "Thou invisible demon of slavery, dost thou think to cross my humble threshold and forbid me to give bread to the hungry and shelter to the houseless! *I bid you defiance in the name of my God!*"[39]

In the new Congress which convened in December 1859, Republicans succeeded in organizing the House after a drawn-out struggle, a victory which gave Lovejoy the chair of the Committee on Public Lands. He would use that post to promote a homestead bill, a measure dear to his own constituents but strenuously resisted by southerners as detrimental to Slave Power interests because it would promote the interests of small, mostly northern farmers. A compromise land measure finally emerged from a Senate-House conference only to be vetoed by James Buchanan in June 1860, a victim of North-South antagonism. Before the president's action, Lovejoy had devoted his greatest effort to a speech he delivered in April 1860 attacking slavery and its defenders.

Lovejoy's speech of April 5, 1860—with House members in full attendance and the galleries crowded—was his most dramatic and controversial in a lifetime devoted to the destruction of slavery. At forty-nine, he was at the peak of his oratorical brilliance and able to bring the most enthusiastic applause and admiration from antislavery leaders while creating the most hostile reaction from the defenders of slavery. His address in the fateful year of 1860 would produce a response as explosive as Charles Sumner's "Crime Against Kansas" oration of May 1856, although it stopped just short of the violence that the Massachusetts senator's provoked. Twenty years of experience on the stump, in the pulpit, and now in Congress had given Lovejoy a reputation which by 1860 exceeded that of his martyred brother. Representing a solidly Republican district, he had little concern that he might antagonize his constituents enough to lose his seat in the fall election. He could thus speak his mind and conscience with little fear of the political conse-

---

38. *Congressional Globe*, 35th Cong., 2nd sess., 1127–32.
39. Ibid., Appendix, 199–203; Haberkorn, "Owen Lovejoy in Princeton, Illinois," 301.

quences. His oration, which he labeled "The Barbarism of Slavery," would be punctuated by shouts and threats from southern Democrats. This in turn occasioned a near riot as members prepared to use pistols or knives to defend their honor, their section, and their beliefs on slavery.[40]

In his address, Lovejoy went well beyond the platform of his Republican party. Taking issue with the party's containment stance, he implied that abolition everywhere should be the goal, for "if slavery is right in Virginia it is right in Kansas. If it is wrong in Kansas, it is wrong everywhere." More importantly, he challenged the morality of slavery in a manner rarely heard on the floor of Congress, where members, whatever their belief, usually avoided a direct and frontal attack on slaveholders and their peculiar institution. He began by taking the offensive in the most dramatic terms: "Slaveholding has been justly designated as the sum of all villainy. Put every crime perpetuated among men into a moral crucible and the resulting amalgam is slaveholding." It "has the violence of robbery, the blood and cruelty of piracy. It has the offensive and brutal lusts of polygamy, all combined and all concentrated in itself, with aggravations that neither one of these crimes ever knew or dreamed of." Like Sumner four years earlier he thus raised the image of sexual assault. It was perhaps the inference of rape and the debilitating effect on slave mothers and families that most outraged southern Democrats, for as Lovejoy spoke he moved closer to the Democratic side of the aisle, provoking southern demands that he come no closer and cease his attacks. William Barksdale of Mississippi shouted to the chair: "Order that black-hearted scoundrel and nigger-stealing thief to take his seat and this side of the House will do it." Republicans led by John F. Potter of Wisconsin rushed to Lovejoy's defense, with Potter adding, "this side *shall* be heard let the consequences be what they may." When the chair finally regained order and the members resumed their seats, albeit with their hands still on pistols and knives, Lovejoy continued his arraignment of slavery and its defenders.

The scuffle had emboldened Lovejoy rather than cause him to back away from confrontation. He condemned southerners for suppressing freedom of speech, saying, "I cannot go into a slave state and open my lips in regard to the question of slavery." "No," came a southerner's retort: "We would hang

---

40. Lovejoy's speech is in *Congressional Globe*, 36th Cong., 1st sess., Appendix, 202–7. For discussions of the implications of the speech, see George Bohman, "Owen Lovejoy on 'The Barbarism of Slavery,' April 4, 1860," *Anti-Slavery and Disunion, 1858–1861: Studies in the Rhetoric of Compromise and Conflict* (New York: Harper and Row, 1963), 114–32; Michael D. Pierson, *Free Hearts and Free Homes: Gender and American Antislavery Politics* (Chapel Hill and London: Univ. of North Carolina Press, 2003), 173–7; Magdol, *Lovejoy*, 233–43.

you higher than Haman!" Responding to southern efforts to force him to renounce John Brown, he responded, "I disapprove of his acts, that is true; but
I believe that his purpose was a good one." Most significantly, he charged
that "the practice of slaveholding has a tendency to drag communities back
to barbarism." To stop this process and the debilitating impact it had on
the slave community, the South must legalize the slave family. Lovejoy demanded to "know by what right you can say my child will be your slave?"
Rather, "I say in God's name, my child is mine." The impact of sins of "brutal lust," of separated parents torn from their children by forced sales, was
the worst of the crimes of slavery. While southerners led by Roger A. Pryor
of Virginia continued to demand Lovejoy be silenced, the Illinoisan concluded to the cheers and congratulations of his supporters and the groans of
his detractors.

The Democratic party was about to convene in Charleston to nominate
a presidential candidate as Lovejoy spoke, and his words had done little to
calm the already heated passions in both parties. He appeared not to care,
writing to his wife of his speech: "I poured on a rainstorm of fire and brim-
stone as hot as I could . . . I believe that I never said anything more Savage
in the pulpit or on the stump."[41] Press reaction was predictable. Southern
journals unanimously condemned the speech, and even the *Boston Courier,*
claiming to speak for northern Democrats, suggested that "there is in the
whole speech no sign of the statesman, no recognition of the essential differences on the question." It was instead an example of "bad manners, bad
taste, and bad temper." Horace Greeley's *New York Tribune* attacked the
southern fire-eaters who had provoked him and congratulated Lovejoy for
defying them. In Princeton, Lovejoy was acclaimed for his courage and honesty.[42] As the country pointed to the presidential election, Lovejoy's speech
had helped set the tone for the dramatic campaign ahead.

The remaining four years of Lovejoy's life were in some ways anticlimactic and highly predictable after the stirring speech of April 5, 1860. At the
same time, those years represented the culmination of all he stood for as he
continued his agitation for emancipation and a measure of equality and witnessed the implementation of the former and the partial achievement of the
latter. A close friend of Lincoln by 1860, Lovejoy vigorously supported his
election and then, as congressman and friend, continued to pressure the

41. Lovejoy to Eunice Lovejoy, April 6, 1860, quoted in Magdol, *Lovejoy,* 241.
42. *Boston Courier,* April 27, 1860; *New York Tribune,* April 6–8, 1860; *Bureau County
Republican* (Princeton, Ill.), April 19, 1860.

president to move more quickly in the direction of his long-sought goals. His speech in the spring of 1860 added to his popularity among his own constituents, and he needed little campaigning to retain his seat that fall, winning by a margin of eleven thousand. Lovejoy had spent much of the summer and fall stumping throughout Illinois for candidate Lincoln and the Republican platform, which labeled owning people as property immoral and attacked the abuses of the Slave Power.[43] This, after remaining in Washington until late June helping to shepherd a homestead bill through the House, over determined southern opposition. As he celebrated his own and Lincoln's victory at a rally in Princeton in November, he recognized that no matter how far apart he and the president-elect had been on slavery and how many differences still existed between his own abolitionism and his party's and its leaders' anti-extentionist position, the achievement of his cherished goals had now become a realistic possibility.

In the four-month interregnum before Lincoln took office in March 1861, Lovejoy was among the most outspoken opponents of the right of southern states to secede and of the need for any form of compromise to keep them loyal. As South Carolina withdrew in December, claiming possession of Federal property within its borders, the congressman resisted any plan of the outgoing Buchanan administration to comply. His House resolution called such state action unconstitutional and concluded: "It is the duty of the President to protect and defend the property of the United States." Southern members refused to vote on his resolution, which passed the House with no opposing votes.[44] Furthermore, he promised to resist any effort to appease the South with proposals to enforce the Fugitive Slave Act or guarantee slavery where it already existed. For too long, whenever southerners threatened secession there was "a Judas to betray, a Peter to deny, and a hired soldier to drive the nails" which sacrificed freedom, "bleeding and quivering to the accursed wood of Compromise." When Republicans such as Thomas Corwin of Ohio and Secretary of State-designate William H. Seward proposed significant retreats from the party's platform, Lovejoy made it clear that he would not be part of such a sellout: "In this new arrangement all the radicals like myself are to be left out! I wish you a very merry time of it my

43. *Bureau County Republican* (Princeton, Ill.), November 8, 15, 1860.
44. *Congressional Globe*, 36th Cong., 2nd sess., 109. For a discussion of the various plans of compromise in and out of Congress and their ultimate failure, see Kenneth M. Stampp, *And the War Came: The North and the Secession Crisis, 1860–61* (Baton Rouge: Louisiana State Univ. Press, 1950), especially pages 122–58.

masters. A very interesting play, *Hamlet* with Hamlet left out of it." To suggestions that Lincoln was prepared to compromise, Lovejoy responded that his friend would never "betray the principles of the Republican party which were made distinctly and squarely in the last campaign of inflexible, unalterable opposition to the extension of slavery." But even should "the President-elect and his future cabinet advise compromise I will not follow their lead one step."[45] As winter turned to spring, Lovejoy would be satisfied as compromise efforts floundered and Lincoln delivered his inaugural address promising to resist secession and maintain control of Federal properties in the seceded states.

Lovejoy would quickly develop a supportive but, at times, critical view of Lincoln's prosecution of the war, even as he urged Congress and the president to move toward emancipation. Before the inauguration he, like so many Republicans, had offered advice on the new cabinet's makeup. While some Radicals, such as Senator Benjamin Wade, were openly critical of some of Lincoln's choices, Lovejoy remained silent on those he disapproved of while openly urging him to include those of his own philosophy, such as Salmon P. Chase. He suggested that the inclusion of the Ohioan would please the "overwhelming majority of the Republican party."[46] When the fighting began in the spring and summer of 1861, Lovejoy proposed repealing the fugitive slave law and treating captured slaves as contraband as the first steps toward emancipation. Although the House rejected these initiatives and Lincoln promised not to interfere with slavery, Lovejoy and his allies in and out of Congress had taken the initial steps, which they hoped would lead to a general emancipation process. Not surprisingly, he wanted no part of a resolution proposed by Kentuckian John J. Crittenden that suggested that the war was being waged to maintain the Union and not to challenge slavery.[47] Rather, Lovejoy fully endorsed fellow abolitionist Gerrit Smith's philosophy of the war's purpose: "The liberation of slaves has obviously become one of the necessities and therefore one of the rights of the country. Let the President . . . proclaim such liberation and the war would end in thirty days."[48]

There would be no quick end to the fighting, however, anymore than there would be a quick end to slavery. Having helped raise an Illinois regiment of infantry, Lovejoy determined to aid directly in the war effort himself

---

45. *Congressional Globe,* 36th Cong., 2nd sess., Appendix, 84–7.
46. Lovejoy et al. to Lincoln, January 18, 1861, Lincoln Papers.
47. *Congressional Globe,* 37th Cong., 2nd sess., 333, 5.
48. Smith to Lovejoy, *New York Tribune,* July 28, 1861.

once Congress had adjourned in August. He thus eagerly accepted his commission as a colonel and was even more pleased to learn of his assignment as an aide to General John C. Frémont in Missouri for a ninety-day tour of duty. During his brief enlistment, he consulted closely with Frémont on slave-related issues, served on the general's claims commission, and, while he supported the return of physical property of disloyal Missourians, made sure that any slaves coming into Frémont's camp became free.[49] Even before Lovejoy left Illinois, Frémont had issued his controversial order of August 30, 1861, freeing the slaves of rebels within his Missouri command. Frémont's policy jeopardized the president's need to keep border slave states such as Missouri loyal to the Union, and Lincoln thus revoked the general's order in September and removed him from his command in early November. Lovejoy did not record his reaction to the president's conservative approach to emancipation at the time, and even after his return to Illinois in the late fall he was careful to note that the Republicans must support the president's war policies even though he believed that the general had been right in his action.[50] Until emancipation finally became a goal of the war a year later, Lovejoy would resist in Congress any effort to force generals to return fugitives to their rebel owners.

His service complete, Lovejoy returned to Washington in December for the second session of the Thirty-seventh Congress. There, he, along with like-minded Republicans, maintained a relentless pursuit of emancipation and the use of black troops in Union armies. It was clear to him that the Confederates could not be defeated "without liberating their slaves and putting muskets in the hands of all who will fight for us." Once they were free, Lovejoy would let them "work under the stimulus of cash instead of the stimulus of the lash." Hesitant to be openly critical of the administration, he nonetheless believed that the president was "advancing step by step" and would soon see the wisdom of the abolitionists' demands.[51] Most slaveholders in Congress had left when their states seceded, but a few from border states remained, and the fiery Lovejoy was quick to engage those, such as Charles Wickliffe of Kentucky, in verbal battle over emancipation issues. In such encounters, the Illinoisan more than held his own.[52] More significantly, Love-

49. Lovejoy to *Bureau County Republican* (Princeton, Ill.), October 31, 1861. For a full account of Lovejoy's brief tour of duty in Missouri, see Magdol, *Lovejoy,* 294–6.

50. *Bureau County Republican* (Princeton, Ill.), December 5, 1861.

51. Ibid.

52. See Magdol, *Lovejoy,* 309–17, and *Congressional Globe,* 37th Cong., 2nd sess., for a full account of these debates.

joy along with Thaddeus Stevens of Pennsylvania and other Radicals led the House efforts to abolish slavery in the District of Columbia and to free all slaves in the territories, measures which Lincoln signed in the spring of 1862. The congressman could also rejoice in the enactment of the Homestead Act, a concept he had long fought for and one which pleased his Illinois constituents.

Lovejoy could also celebrate the central role he played in congressional enactment of the confiscation laws, which helped push the president toward a more general emancipation policy. During the summer of 1862, as Congress debated expanding the confiscation concept, Lovejoy again came to Lincoln's defense against those demanding that he move faster. In an address at the Cooper Institute in New York in June, the congressman responded to the critics: "If he does not drive as fast as I would, he is on the right road, and it is only a question of time." Recognizing the pressures Lincoln faced, he argued, "The wonder is not that he should make mistakes but that he should make so few." Finally, he suggested that he had no doubt of Lincoln's "antislavery integrity, his ultimate antislavery action," and urged his listeners to give the president their "cordial, loyal and sympathizing support."[53] The passage of the Second Confiscation Act in July freed slaves entering Union lines and authorized the president to enlist blacks as well as seize the property of those supporting the Confederacy. As Lovejoy entered his strenuous fall campaign for reelection, he could take heart in Lincoln's Preliminary Proclamation of Emancipation, issued on September 22, knowing that his lifelong goal of emancipation was shortly to be achieved and that he had played a significant role in its enactment.

When the news of Lincoln's Preliminary Proclamation arrived, Lovejoy was busily campaigning. The Illinois legislature had reapportioned his district so that it now included more Democratic areas, including the city of Peoria. To compound the difficulty of his situation, Illinois voters, like those throughout the North, were weary of the war and in a mood to reject Republicans responsible for prosecuting it. Nonetheless, his strenuous campaigning paid off with a slender 641–vote margin over a former Republican, T. J. Henderson, and he could thus look forward to the Thirty-eighth Congress as a four-term member.[54] There, he hoped to play a significant role in the completion of the war effort and the final enactment of emancipation.

Lovejoy returned to Washington in December for the third session of the Thirty-seventh Congress determined to renew the battle against slavery and

53. *New York Tribune*, June 12, 1862.
54. *Bureau County Republican* (Princeton, Ill.), November 13, 1862.

its supporters when Wickliffe of Kentucky sought relief for southerners whose slaves had escaped. His bill would have required the army to return fugitives to their owners. Lovejoy renewed his efforts of the previous year in opposing enlisting the army into "the base business of chasing and capturing fugitive slaves," for in his eyes "every slave has a right to run away."[55] When Lincoln issued his final Emancipation Proclamation on January 1, 1863, Lovejoy paused only briefly to celebrate and then immediately accelerated his efforts to defend the evolving policy of raising black troops for Union armies. Again he clashed with Wickliffe and other border state Democrats and could rejoice when the bill authorizing such troops passed the House in early February 1863 by better than a three-to-two margin. But he could not go along with Radicals such as Thaddeus Stevens, who, looking ahead to the defeat of the Confederacy, sought to treat the rebel states as conquered provinces with which Congress could do as it pleased. Said the Illinoisan, individual rebels rather than southern states must be punished, for "we are not fighting a nation but a horde of traitors and rebels."[56] Here he appeared to be in closer accord with the president's more lenient approach to reconstruction than that of his Radical brethren. His hatred of slavery and hostility to its planters did not extend to a desire to punish the entire South.

Even as Lovejoy remained a center of focus in Congress, he was stricken with smallpox in late February, an illness which led to a rapid deterioration of his health. His condition meant that he was unable to return home immediately when Congress adjourned in March, although once he did it would be weeks before he could appear again in public and speak on his cherished wartime goals. By fall he was well enough to defend Lincoln against Radicals, who continued to press for a harsh reconstruction policy, and by December he was back in Congress. Before leaving Princeton he addressed his congregation in a "Thanksgiving Prayer," asking God to "grant that this unholy and causeless rebellion may be speedily and effectually put down and that our Government may be firmly established upon the basis of universal freedom." He thanked God "that thou hast given us a President . . . whose integrity and honesty are above the suspicion even of his enemies."[57]

In Congress, Lovejoy proposed a bill to require equal pay for all troops in an attempt to force an end to the pay discrimination suffered by black sol-

55. *Congressional Globe*, 37th Cong., 3rd sess., 23–4.

56. Ibid., 598, 689–90, 243.

57. Lovejoy, "Public Prayer," November 26, 1863, in *Bureau County Republican* (Princeton, Ill.), December 3, 1863.

diers. He persisted in his outspoken resistance to treating the Confederate states as conquered provinces. Believing that the Federal government possessed the authority to abolish slavery in the states without amending the Constitution, he proposed such a bill, which also included a guarantee of civil rights for blacks.[58] All the while, his health again deteriorated. Lincoln and several cabinet members visited Lovejoy in his boardinghouse, and as he lay near death he dictated his final letter. In it, he hoped that "when slavery has been swept away," there would be "a revival of religion . . . which shall go around like its divine author, healing the sick, cleansing lepers, giving eyes to the blind, ears to the deaf, and charity to *all.*"[59] When he died in late March of Bright's disease at fifty-three, he was mourned in his district, by his colleagues in the House and Senate, and in Republican journals throughout the country. There was even some grudging respect shown for him in the Democratic press. Reflecting on the ten years in which he and Lovejoy had been Republican colleagues, Lincoln called him "the best friend I had in Congress."[60]

Lovejoy had not lived long enough to see the war's end and the final destruction of slavery with the Thirteenth Amendment, but he had helped to hasten its demise. A dedicated abolitionist even before his brother's murder in 1837, he had rejected the Garrisonian approach and had quickly joined the Liberty party, placing himself at the radical end of the political spectrum. He had seen the need to modify his stance and had recognized the Free Soil and Republican containment policy as the necessary first step toward emancipation. In so doing, he prodded Lincoln to move toward a policy of freedom while reluctantly accepting the president's caution. Yet even as he supported the president he maintained his closeness with Radicals in his party. As such, he was remembered not only as a firm abolitionist, but as a supporter of equality for African Americans. Lincoln noted "that while he was personally ambitious, he bravely endured the obscurity which the unpopularity of his principles imposed and never accepted official honors, until those honors were ready to admit his principles to him."[61]

58. *Congressional Globe*, 38th Cong., 1st sess., 20; Vorenberg, *Final Freedom*, 5.

59. Lovejoy to John Andrew, February 22, 1864, in *Bureau County Republican* (Princeton, Ill.), May 5, 1864.

60. Francis B. Carpenter to Eunice Lovejoy, May 18, 1865, Lovejoy Papers, Bureau County Historical Society.

61. Lincoln to John H. Bryant, May 30, 1864, *The Collected Works of Abraham Lincoln*, ed. Roy P. Basler (New Brunswick: Rutgers Univ. Press, 1953), 7:366.

SIX

FREEMEN TO THE RESCUE
Sherman M. Booth and the Fugitive Slave Act

LIKE MANY EARLY Liberty party leaders, Sherman Booth had his roots in the burned-over district of New York, that area so affected by religious fervor and agitation for moral reform in the early nineteenth century. Unlike those who would remain in New York, Booth began his reform interests as a temperance crusader there and then lived for a decade in Connecticut as a Liberty party activist before gaining fame as a fiery Free Soil and Republican editor and politician in Wisconsin. He was born in the tiny crossroads of Davenport on September 25, 1812, the oldest of the three sons of Selah and Orra Booth. When his mother died in 1819 his father married her sister Sophie, and the young Sherman continued to make his home with them until he was twenty-one. We know little of Booth's religious upbringing or faith except that he received some of his early education from a local minister before he attended the district school and a local academy. Thus Booth had significant contact with evangelical Protestantism and was likely affected by its theology and practices even if religion did not become central to his life. He was a member of the Congregational Church of Davenport, and remained a Congregationalist throughout his life, although he later indicated his preference for "*the church*—of whatever name—which makes its members better neighbors and citizens, better men and women, better husbands and wives, better parents and children."[1] His father introduced him to Congregationalism's strong abolitionist leanings. On one occasion, on learning that his brother-in-law had purchased a slave, Selah Booth complained so loudly that when his wife told him to be silent, he replied: "Talk so loud? I wish I could talk loud enough so that they would hear me in South Carolina."[2]

Sherman Booth came to abolitionism from his northeastern roots in New York and Connecticut. As a Liberty party organizer and advocate while a student at Yale, he became an antislavery journalist, first in Connecticut and then in Wisconsin, where he moved in time for the Free Soil campaign of 1848. Best known as the founder of the Wisconsin Republican party, he falls on the more radical end of the political spectrum, joining the Liberty movement in the early 1840s at approximately the same time as Owen Lovejoy. Unlike Alvan Stewart, he found the Free Soil and Republican position of containment and the divorce of the federal government from slavery satisfactory even if not as advanced a stance as he might have preferred. Like Charles Langston, Booth was best known for his role in the rescue of a fugitive slave, Joshua Glover. The Glover case gave Booth the identity he sought and catapulted him into a leadership role among state Republicans and an eventual showdown with the Buchanan administration at the end of the decade. Personal scandal involving a morals charge laid him open to ridicule and accelerated his fall from political influence at the time of the Civil War. Having entered the antislavery movement via the Liberty party rather than a major party may also have worked to his disadvantage as Republicans seized control of government. His declining influence, however, did not come before he had played a central role in the growing antislavery movement in Wisconsin. Although he never held office, the controversial Sherman Booth represented the thinking of an increasing number of northerners in their willingness to use the political process to challenge Slave Power control over national affairs.

1. There is no biography of Booth. Brief accounts of his life can be found in Dwight Agnew et al., *Dictionary of Wisconsin Biography* (Madison: State Historical Society of Wisconsin, 1960), 42–3; Diane S. Butler, "The Public Life and Private Affairs of Sherman M. Booth," *Wisconsin Magazine of History* 82 (spring 1999): 166–97; Yale, Class of 1841, *Semi-Centennial of the Historical and Biographical Record of the Class of 1841 in Yale University* (New Haven, Conn.: Tuttle, Morehouse and Taylor, 1892), 46–53.

2. Milwaukee *Sentinel,* August 11, 1894.

As a young man, while alternating between farming and teaching at district schools and Jefferson Academy, Booth became involved in the fledgling temperance movement, first in the Davenport area and then as a lecturer throughout the Hudson River Valley. At twenty-five, he was an agent of the New York State Temperance Society, impressing crowds with his booming voice as he told of the evils of drink and appealed to their consciences for total abstinence. In 1838, he entered Yale, supporting his education by teaching in New Haven area schools. Before graduating he helped organize the city's Liberty party, having changed his focus from temperance to political antislavery, where it would remain for the next two decades. He called his oration at the Yale commencement ceremony in 1841 "Responsibilities of the Citizen at the Ballot Box" and stressed the importance of a political attack on slavery and the Slave Power. Upon graduation he moved to nearby Meridian, Connecticut, where he became the state agent for the Liberty party and worked closely with Ichabod Codding, the editor of the abolitionist *Christian Freeman,* published in Hartford. Together, Booth and Codding emphasized their disdain for the Garrisonian moral suasion approach to antislavery while defending what they believed was the immediate and more practical need for third-party antislavery agitation. Even before graduation, he attended an abolitionist convention called by Garrisonians, whose purpose was to attack the new Liberty party. The third party had received more votes in New England than expected in the recently concluded presidential election of 1840. Booth and his Liberty colleagues packed the meeting and, after three days of heated discussion, defeated all attempts to censure their political efforts. It was during these debates that Booth first revealed his feisty character and impressive ability as an abolitionist orator.[3]

While a student at Yale, Booth became involved in the *Amistad* case. Led by Joseph Cinque, fifty-three African slaves on board the Spanish slave ship *Amistad* had revolted in 1839 and taken control of the ship in the Caribbean before finally being seized by an American naval vessel off Long Island. An international controversy had ensued, with the Africans being jailed in Connecticut, the Spanish claiming interference with their rights, and the administration of President Martin Van Buren seeking to placate southerners and the Spanish by returning the slaves to their owners. Abolitionists, led by Lewis Tappan and Joshua Leavitt, sought to awaken Americans to the injustice of slavery by forcing a federal trial. The case eventually reached the

3. *Dictionary of Wisconsin Biography,* 42, 80–1. See also *Semi-Centennial,* 47–8.

Supreme Court before Cinque and his fellow slaves were freed and returned to their African homeland in 1841.[4] The case united opponents of slavery of all kinds, Liberty members and Garrisonians alike. Because the African mutineers were being held in a county jail near New Haven, wealthy New York merchant and philanthropist Tappan hired several Yale students, including Booth, to tutor the imprisoned Africans in English. Their lessons included the reading of New Testament scriptures and singing of Christian hymns, talents which the Africans later used to astonish several large audiences in an effort to raise funds for their return to Africa. During much of 1840 and 1841 Booth taught his students for three hours a day until the Africans sailed for home.[5] The experience was one further step in his growing commitment to antislavery activism.

It was as a Liberty party leader in Connecticut that Booth found his niche both in organizing the party and learning journalism. Codding taught him the latter, and Booth joined the staff of the *Christian Freeman,* a position he held for the next five years. During that time he traveled throughout the state, speaking in virtually every Connecticut town as the Liberty party's agent, using what little influence he had as a lobbyist to recover the right to vote for the state's small African American population. Suffrage had been taken away in Connecticut's 1818 constitution, a decision endorsed by voters by more than a three-to-one margin in an 1847 referendum. Like Charles Langston in Ohio, Booth met only frustration, for not only did he fail in the suffrage campaign but the state's Liberty party remained tiny and without significant influence. Thus when Codding decided to give up his Hartford newspaper and move west to Wisconsin, Booth eagerly agreed to join him in 1848. Codding and others had established the Liberty journal *American Freeman* in Prairieville (Waukesha), a paper which Booth purchased shortly after his arrival. In May 1848, the same month in which Wisconsin obtained statehood, Booth moved the paper to Milwaukee, the largest city, and there began a colorful career as a western abolitionist and journalist devoted to third-party politics.[6]

4. Howard Jones, *Mutiny on the* Amistad: *The Saga of a Slave Revolt and Its Impact on American Abolition Law and Diplomacy* (New York: Oxford Univ. Press, 1987).

5. *Semi-Centennial,* 48; David E. Swift, *Black Prophets of Justice: Activist Clergy Before the Civil War* (Baton Rouge: Louisiana State Univ. Press, 1989), 197; Jones, *Amistad,* 197, 253 n. 5; Butler, "Booth," 169–70.

6. *Semi-Centennial,* 48; Swift, *Black Prophets of Justice,* 197–200; *Dictionary of Wisconsin Biography,* 42, 80–1; Booth, "Reminiscences of Early Struggles in Wisconsin Politics and Press," *Wisconsin Press Association* 44 (1897): 106; Michael J. McManus, *Political Abolitionism in Wisconsin, 1840–1861* (Kent, Ohio: Kent State Univ. Press, 1998), 5–6, 39.

Almost immediately upon his arrival Booth stirred up controversy among Wisconsin Liberty men. Committed as he had been in Connecticut to immediate and total abolition, he quickly antagonized those seeking a coalition with the more moderate antislavery men who advocated the Wilmot Proviso's containment of slavery stance. At the time of Booth's move to Wisconsin, antislavery factions of both Democratic and Whig parties throughout the North were in negotiation with Liberty party leaders led by Salmon P. Chase of Ohio. The coalition they desired would be based on preventing the spread of slavery but not in challenging it where it already existed. Booth reacted strongly against this movement, which would climax in August 1848 with the formation of the Free Soil party. In the first issue of his *American Freeman* he suggested that the Constitution, if properly interpreted, "would abolish slavery, establish justice and secure the blessings of liberty for every human being within the limits of this Republic."[7] Although not concerned with the specifics of constitutional arguments against slavery as advocated by Alvan Stewart, he nonetheless rejected the Proviso because it would permit "slavery to live and run riot forever throughout the entire South." In contrast, the Liberty party platform existed "not simply to prevent the further growth of slavery, but to *put it out of existence*." To Booth, "A WILMOT PROVISO MAN IS NOT AN ABOLITIONIST," and any movement to Free Soil would "betray the interests and ruin the hopes of enslaved millions." As the Free Soil convention approached, Booth remained firmly committed to a presidential ticket headed by a Liberty candidate, either John P. Hale or Gerrit Smith, on an abolitionist platform. Such a platform must also seek rights for northern blacks "by protecting the equal rights of all."[8]

There were few signs before the convention opened that Booth accepted the view that Liberty members must back away from total abolition if the third-party movement were to have any hope of success. Chosen a delegate to the party's Buffalo convention, he believed strongly that if Martin Van Buren, the leading contender for the nomination, maintained his opposition to abolition of slavery in the District of Columbia, Liberty delegates "can't go for him." Furthermore, if "Hale and the Liberty party unite on such a nomination we are out of the Liberty Party in a twinkling." In such an instance he would support "*the man* of our choice—Gerrit Smith" and his abolitionist principles on an independent ticket. In the meantime he would work to help the various factions "struggle through the low grounds and

7. *American Freeman* (Milwaukee), May 31, 1848.
8. Ibid., June 7, 14, July 26, 1848; McManus, *Political Abolitionism in Wisconsin*, 40–1.

misty atmosphere of Expediency up to the high ground of Principle and the bright sunlight of Truth."[9]

Once in Buffalo, however, Booth got caught up in the spontaneous enthusiasm of the huge throngs of supporters of Free Soil. As a convention secretary and member of the platform committee, he accepted the containment concept and abandoned, albeit grudgingly, his prior insistence on immediate abolition wherever slavery existed. The platform, which was largely the work of Salmon P. Chase, called for "No more Slave Territory" and the abolition of slavery wherever the federal government "is responsible for its existence," an indirect demand for abolition in the District of Columbia. Although it avoided any mention of equal rights for free blacks, the platform at least placated Booth and most Liberty delegates. Although he voted for Gerrit Smith's nomination for president on the informal ballot, Booth later admitted that the convention "did wisely in nominating Martin Van Buren." While far from enthusiastic over the ticket of Van Buren and Charles Francis Adams, he believed that their victory "would be hailed as the triumph of Freedom, and the end of slavery encroachments and slavery extension throughout the Union."[10] Although the platform fell far short of Liberty principles and the candidates were not those Booth would have preferred, he professed to believe with Joshua Leavitt that "The Liberty party is not dead, but translated." Forty years later, he still argued that "the old Liberty party men had not abated one jot of tittle of their fealty to freedom," but privately he must have recognized that Liberty principles had been seriously compromised. Although a small faction called the Liberty League persisted in nominating Gerrit Smith on an abolition platform, Booth, along with the vast majority of Liberty members, opted for the less idealistic course, recognizing that only with a prominent candidate and a moderate stance on slavery could progress be made in the ongoing struggle against the Slave Power.[11]

Van Buren's showing of 26.6 percent of the popular vote in Wisconsin put the Free Soil party in a strong bargaining position. It won one of the three U.S. congressional seats and held the balance of power in the lower house of

9. *American Freeman* (Milwaukee), June 21, 1848.

10. Ibid., August 23, 1848; *Wisconsin Freeman* (Milwaukee), November 1, 1848. The platform of the Free Soil party is in Johnson and Porter, eds. *National Party Platforms*, 13–4.

11. Booth, "Reminiscences," 113; Volpe, *Forlorn Hope of Freedom*, 133–4. For Leavitt's role and the dilemma faced by all Liberty supporters, see Davis, *Leavitt*, 244–9. For an account of the Free Soil convention, see Blue, *The Free Soilers*, 70–80.

the state legislature. Booth now hoped to lead the party into an antislavery coalition with the state's Democratic party. He recognized that many in the Wisconsin third party had been Democrats until 1848, and thus he felt that the third party's future would be most secure if a coalition with Democrats could be arranged. Yet as a former Liberty leader, he was wary of being out-maneuvered by more experienced Democrats. As he told Chase: "I will urge the union on right principles."[12] But as the state election of 1849 ap-proached, his worst fears materialized, and the coalition fell apart. Many Free Democrats, as they now called themselves, returned to their old party without having won even modest antislavery concessions. Booth reacted in fury, lambasting those "short-sighted politicians" who "speak of the Free Democratic party as organized for a temporary purpose." Rhetori-cally, he asked: "Has the Ordinance of 1787 been established over our new territories—slavery and the slave trade in the District of Columbia been abolished—an effectual check been put to the admission of any more slave states . . . ?" He concluded bitterly that there was "just as much necessity for the existence and continued action of the National Free Democratic party to-day, as there was when it was first organized in Buffalo."[13]

The Free Democratic vote in Wisconsin fell in 1849 by more than 60 per-cent from its previous year's total, teaching Booth a hard lesson in political reality. Even worse, the proposal on the ballot to extend suffrage to the state's tiny black minority was defeated. It did get more positive than nega-tive votes, but state officials ruled it defeated because it did not get the re-quired majority of all votes cast. Booth charged that the ruling was a "back-handed blow," but it was clear that many voters had been too apathetic to vote on the proposal.[14] Garrison had long warned that involvement in the political process would bring a compromising of principles, a prediction which now appeared all too accurate. Gerrit Smith's Liberty League alone had been true to its abolitionist beliefs, yet it remained tiny and ineffectual. For the Wisconsin editor, the better course was now to persevere in the Free Democratic efforts against Democratic and Whig willingness to give in too easily to Slave Power demands.

Booth found the political events of 1850 to be even more disheartening than those of the previous year. As Congress debated Henry Clay's propos-

12. Booth to Chase, April 4, 1849, Chase Papers, Library of Congress.

13. *Wisconsin Free Democrat* (Milwaukee), November 21, 1849; McManus, *Political Abo-litionism in Wisconsin*, 60–5; Blue, *Free Soilers*, 173–6.

14. *Wisconsin Free Democrat*, November 21, 1849; Booth, "Reminiscences," 113.

als for a North-South compromise which would sacrifice both abolitionist and Free Democratic principles, Booth maintained his position that the central government "should prohibit slavery under its exclusive jurisdiction, vis the District of Columbia, and in the Territories and that the several State Governments should abolish Slavery within their respective jurisdictions."[15] The Compromise measures which became law later in the year abolished only the slave trade in Washington and rejected the Wilmot Proviso, instead endorsing popular sovereignty, meaning that it would leave the issue of slavery in the territories to the territorial legislatures. Most damaging to antislavery interests, Congress approved a new fugitive slave law which denied the alleged fugitive a trial by jury and required that both free-state law officials and private citizens assist in the return of the accused. A federal commissioner would hear each case, and his fee would be twice as much if the accused were found guilty rather than innocent. Said Booth in disbelief: "The commissioner has five dollars for each fugitive released and ten dollars for each one delivered up to the slave-catchers." He concluded that "if the people of this country submit tamely to such a law, they deserve to be enslaved themselves. . . . Let the rallying cry be *Repeal!* REPEAL! REPEAL!" When Milwaukee blacks resolved "to come forward at any alarm given and rescue our fugitive brethren even unto death," Booth gave his enthusiastic approval and predicted that "the first kidnapper who lays hands on one of them, we expect will be shot dead."[16]

For the next three years, Sherman Booth maintained a constant attack on the hated fugitive law and worked tirelessly to persuade first Democrats and then Whigs to join Free Democrats in presenting a united antislavery political front to Wisconsin voters. He was only partially successful, for members of both major parties faced constant pressure from national party leaders to adhere to the Compromise settlement. At first, Booth was uncertain himself over the viability of maintaining a separate third-party organization, asking Chase whether they should join with Democrats "to mold" their party into an antislavery machine, "or still maintain a separate organization." In effect, Wisconsin Democrats answered the question for him by treating the Free Democrats "as dogs and outcasts."[17] As a result, Free Democrats turned successfully to the Whigs for support in the reelection of third-party con-

15. *Wisconsin Free Democrat,* April 17, 1850.

16. Ibid., October 23, 1850, March 16, 1851, October 16, 1850.

17. Booth to Chase, February 2, 1850, Booth Papers, State Historical Society of Wisconsin; *Wisconsin Free Democrat,* August 7, 14, 21, 1850.

gressman and former Liberty member Charles Durkee of Kenosha, who defeated his Democratic opponent in a two-way race. Booth could take some solace, for at least in the southeastern part of the state, which included his own Milwaukee, voters were still willing to rally behind strong antislavery political leadership.[18]

Wisconsin Whigs were now Booth's main hope for an antislavery coalition, while the state's Democrats conformed to the national party's desire to appease southern Democrats. Thus in 1851, with Booth the key player behind the scenes, Whigs and Free Democrats united behind the Whig candidacy of antislavery and temperance activist Leonard Farwell for governor. Having cajoled the Free Democratic convention into accepting Farwell, Booth then used his newspaper and personal influence to persuade enough antislavery Democrats to support the candidate for him to squeeze through to a narrow victory over his Democratic opponent.[19] Booth had by now emerged as the key third-party strategist, with each success enhancing his reputation. Nationally, he kept in close touch with third-party leaders and represented Wisconsin Free Democrats at the planning convention in Cleveland in September 1851. That meeting sought to keep antislavery enthusiasm alive in an atmosphere of gloom, for during these months the Compromise spirit dominated both North and South.[20]

In 1852, Booth was again willing to cooperate with whichever party would adopt an antislavery stance: "Whenever the Democratic Party will dissolve its alliance with slavery . . . we shall act with it. Or should the Whig Party take the ground of Human Rights . . . we shall cooperate with it."[21] Not surprisingly, however, his efforts for a coalition collapsed in a presidential year. Not only did Whigs support their presidential candidate, Winfield Scott, but Booth was unable to retain their support of incumbent congressman Charles Durkee. Instead, Whigs nominated their own candidate, and Durkee finished second in a close three-way race. Both on the stump and with biting editorials, Booth campaigned hard for the national Free Demo-

18. *Dictionary of Wisconsin Biography*, 110–1; *Wisconsin Free Democrat*, October 30, 1850; Smith, *Liberty and Free Soil Parties*, 214–5.

19. *Wisconsin Free Democrat*, October 21, 29, 1851; Booth, "Reminiscences," 115–6; Smith, *Liberty and Free Soil Parties*, 234–5; McManus, *Political Abolitionism in Wisconsin*, 75–7.

20. *National Era*, October 2, 9, 1851; Blue, *Free Soilers*, 234.

21. *Wisconsin Free Democrat*, January 1, 1852; Richard N. Current, *The Civil War Era, 1848–1873*, vol. 2 of *The History of Wisconsin* (Madison: State Historical Society of Wisconsin, 1976), 210–2; McManus, *Political Abolitionism in Wisconsin*, 78.

cratic ticket of John P. Hale and George W. Julian, having first supported them as a delegate at the party's nominating convention in Pittsburgh. When the candidates visited Wisconsin in October, Booth was their key cheerleader at each of their rallies. Hale spoke in six cities and Julian in four.[22] Although the Hale-Julian ticket finished a distant third in the balloting with only 13.6 percent of the Wisconsin vote, Booth instinctively realized that the Whigs had been the real losers. He commented bluntly and only slightly prematurely that their party had been "blotted from the political map and henceforth ceases to be a political organization."[23] He was thus able to pressure Whigs into support of former Liberty leader Edward Holton of Milwaukee for governor in 1853. Democrats won the governorship, but as the Whig party declined even further, Booth appeared ready to lead Wisconsin antislavery forces in the formation of a more effective antislavery political coalition.[24]

The following year, 1854, was the most momentous in Booth's career as an antislavery advocate, for not only did he play a pivotal role in the formation of Wisconsin's Republican party, but he also became the central figure in the state's most significant fugitive slave rescue case. As Stephen A. Douglas's Kansas-Nebraska bill repealing the ban on slavery in those territories was debated in Congress early in the year, Booth flew into action. He accepted the challenge of the handful of antislavery members of Congress who, in their "Appeal of the Independent Democrats," not only protested the bill as a surrender to the Slave Power, but urged the creation of a more effective northern antislavery party to oppose it. Booth's initial call for a uniting of antislavery forces of all parties to protest the bill brought little response, but he persisted relentlessly until others finally replied.[25] Despite their opposition to the bill, many antislavery Whigs and Democrats were leery of joining forces with so radical an advocate as Sherman Booth. But they finally swallowed their reluctance and by summer, after the hated Nebraska bill had become law, joined forces with Booth and his Free Democrats in a new political organization.

The road to the creation of the Wisconsin Republican party was far from smooth and involved a stormy relationship between Booth and Rufus King,

22. *Wisconsin Free Democrat*, October 13, 20, 1852; Blue, *Free Soilers*, 257, 263.

23. *Wisconsin Free Democrat*, November 3, 1852.

24. *Dictionary of Wisconsin Biography*, 175–6; Smith, *Liberty and Free Soil Parties*, 279–83; McManus, *Political Abolitionism in Wisconsin*, 80–3.

25. *Milwaukee Free Democrat*, January 30, 1854.

Whig leader and editor of the *Milwaukee Sentinel*. In 1853, the two had formed a tenuous coalition which had swept Milwaukee city elections; they then cooperated in pushing through a statewide temperance referendum. But their cooperation ended abruptly with King labeling Booth a fanatic on the prohibition issue and refusing further coalition efforts. Nevertheless, the fusion movement accelerated with Booth organizing the state's first anti-Nebraska meeting in Milwaukee on February 13, 1854.[26] He urged that the state legislature condemn the pending Kansas-Nebraska bill, and in the final congressional vote of approval in May both Wisconsin senators and all three representatives voted against Douglas's bill. Booth was instrumental in calling a statewide meeting of protest, inviting "ALL MEN opposed to the Repeal of the Missouri Compromise, the extension of Slavery and the Rule of the Slave Power." The rally convened on July 13, 1854, in Madison with King and other leading Whigs endorsing his call. Booth chose the date as the anniversary of the passage of the Northwest Ordinance in 1787, which banned slavery in the Old Northwest, reminding his readers that "the time has come for the union of all free men for the sake of freedom."[27] One thousand angry Wisconsinites attended this gathering, which formally created the state's Republican party, with Booth among those who addressed the group. Booth thus was most responsible for the party's creation, having diligently worked to create the coalition which led to the party's formation. In the fall, the new party easily won control of the state legislature, which in turn elected former Liberty leader Charles Durkee to the U.S. Senate. Booth had sought the Republican nomination to Congress from the Milwaukee district but was denied by party leaders, who viewed him as too controversial a candidate.[28] By that time his central role in the rescue of fugitive slave Joshua Glover had guaranteed Booth a place even more contentious than that of Charles Langston in the Oberlin-Wellington rescue case in Ohio.

Federal authorities had seized Glover, then working in a sawmill, in Racine, Wisconsin, on March 10, 1854. A Missouri fugitive, he had escaped from his owner, Bennami Garland, two years earlier. Upon his arrest he was taken fifty miles north to be held in a Milwaukee jail, awaiting a hearing by a federal commissioner. From there, under the terms of the Fugitive Slave

26. Current, *The Civil War Era*, 216–7; *Dictionary of Wisconsin Biography*, 207, 44; *Milwaukee Free Democrat*, February 4, 6, 8, 9, 10, 11, 1854.

27. *Wisconsin Free Democrat*, June 9, 1854; Booth, "Reminiscences," 114.

28. McManus, *Political Abolitionism in Wisconsin*, 87–90, 229–30 n. 4; Current, *The Civil War Era*, 218–9.

Act, he would presumably be sent back to slavery. Protesters immediately held rallies in Racine and Milwaukee, with Booth riding through the streets of the latter, allegedly crying "Freemen to the Rescue. Slave catchers are in our midst." At the rally at the courthouse, which was attended by more than five thousand, Booth urged only "legal and peaceful methods" against the seizure rather than force, but the crowd responded to the more fiery demands of others and rushed the jail, securing Glover's removal and safe flight to Canada. Booth triumphantly told his readers that "in Wisconsin the Fugitive Slave Law is repealed! The first attempt to enforce the law in this state has signally, gloriously failed! . . . PERISH ALL ENACTMENTS ESTABLISHING SLAVERY ON FREE SOIL."[29] Four days later federal authorities arrested Booth. At his hearing, although he denied the "freemen to the rescue" statement attributed to him, he demanded that accused blacks be allowed a trial by jury. He further inflamed federal officials by suggesting that rather than seeing fugitives returned to the South, he would prefer to "see every Federal Officer in Wisconsin hanged."[30] As he and one other participant faced trial, the Kansas-Nebraska bill was signed into law by President Franklin Pierce on May 30. For Wisconsin opponents of slavery, the Slave Power had revealed its dangerous strength with these two almost simultaneous events.

As Booth awaited trial, he increased his fiery rhetoric, calling on "all the People of this State who are opposed to being made SLAVES or SLAVE CATCHERS and to having the free soil of Wisconsin made the hunting ground for *Human Kidnappers*" to "defend our State Sovereignty, our State Courts and National constitutions against flagrant usurpation of U. S. Judges, Commissioners and Marshalls and their attorneys."[31] For his trial in late May, Booth retained the young Republican attorney Byron Paine of Milwaukee to defend him before Wisconsin Supreme Court Justice Abram D. Smith. Paine claimed that the Fugitive Slave Act under which his client had been charged was unconstitutional because the Constitution did not give Congress the power to force the states to assist in the return of fugitives and because it

29. *Milwaukee Free Democrat*, March 13, 1854; Booth, "Reminiscences," 111.

30. The Glover rescue and subsequent Milwaukee rally is studied in detail in numerous sources. Among them are: Michael J. McManus, "Freedom and Liberty First and Union Afterwards: States Rights and the Wisconsin Republican Party, 1854–1861," in *Union and Emancipation: Essays on Politics and Race in the Civil War Era,* ed. David W. Blight and Brooks D. Simpson (Kent, Ohio: Kent State Univ. Press, 1997), 29–56; Current, *The Civil War Era,* 219–21; Alexander M. Thomson, *A Political History of Wisconsin* (Milwaukee: C. N. Casper Co., 1902), 96–108; Butler, "Booth," 175–8.

31. *Milwaukee Free Democrat*, April 1854; Current, *The Civil War Era,* 221.

denied the accused the right to a trial by jury.[32] Smith startled the state and pleased antislavery leaders beyond measure in accepting Paine's argument, granting Booth his freedom on a writ of habeas corpus, and declaring the Fugitive Slave Act unconstitutional as a violation of states' rights.[33] Six weeks later the entire state supreme court sustained Smith's decision, laying the foundation for a full-blown showdown with the federal government. Not to be outdone, federal officials immediately rearrested Sherman Booth, leaving the accused in the center of a major confrontation over fugitives and states' rights for the next several years.[34]

The federal trial opened in Madison in January 1855 with Paine again representing Booth, who was charged with violation of the Fugitive Slave Act. Judge Andrew G. Miller left the jury little choice when he advised that their feelings toward the act were irrelevant despite the action of the state supreme court, and that if Booth had violated it they must find him guilty. The jury concluded that Booth had aided in Glover's rescue and so convicted him, a decision at once overturned when the state court approved Booth's application for a writ of habeas corpus and confirmed its earlier ruling on the act's unconstitutionality.[35] In leaving Milwaukee for the trip to Madison for his appeal, Booth was cheered away by a crowd of two thousand supporters accompanied by bands and a cannon salute. Before departing he gave the gathering another rousing speech pledging continued defiance to the fugitive act. Later in 1855, the U.S. Supreme Court agreed to hear the case, but with the state court still defiant and refusing to transmit its decision to Washington, further judicial action was delayed indefinitely. In another closely related case, Glover's Missouri slaveowner, Bennami Garland, sought compensation from Booth for his lost slave, and the jury, following the terms of the Fugitive Slave Act, fined Booth $1,000 plus costs, which totaled another $246.[36]

As the litigation dragged on, Booth's Republican party stood by the editor. Not all Republicans were willing to defend the state court's defiance of

32. See Joseph A. Ranney, "'Suffering the Agonies of Their Righteousness': The Rise and Fall of the States' Rights Movement in Wisconsin, 1854–1861," *Wisconsin Magazine of History* 75 (winter 1991–1992): 89–91.

33. "In re Sherman Booth," 3 Wis. 13 (1854), *Wisconsin Reports*, 134–44.

34. McManus, "Liberty and Freedom," 37; Butler, "Booth," 182–3; Ranney, "States' Rights Movement in Wisconsin," 91–5.

35. See "In re Booth and Rycraft," 3 Wis. 144 (1855), *Wisconsin Reports*, 144–9; Ranney, "States' Rights Movement in Wisconsin," 95–6; McManus, "Liberty and Freedom," 37–8.

36. *Arnold v. Booth*, 14 Wis. 195 (1855), *Wisconsin Reports*; Butler, "Booth," 185.

the federal government, however, and state politics became entwined in electoral struggles over which justices would be elected to the state supreme court and who would serve the state in the U.S. Senate. Throughout it all Booth actively backed candidates pledged to maintaining the original ruling of the Fugitive Slave Act's unconstitutionality. Most dramatic was the legislature's election of antislavery Republican James R. Doolittle to the Senate in 1857.[37] That same year, in further defiance of the federal government's fugitive act, the legislature, at Booth's urging, enacted a personal liberty law which guaranteed habeas corpus and jury trial protection to alleged fugitive slaves.[38] Although Booth's own legal difficulties had yet to be resolved by the federal supreme court, his role in Republican politics remained as central as ever. His influence had been most evident as the party faced its first campaign for governor in 1855 and for president in 1856. He would not always get his way, but his strong presence continued to dominate party affairs on antislavery matters.

In the gubernatorial election of 1855 Booth sought his party's nomination in an effort to prevent the anti-Catholic nativists and their American or Know-Nothing party from gaining control of the Republican organization and diverting it from its antislavery focus. But the outspoken editor had antagonized too many fellow Republicans, and he finally agreed to abandon his candidacy to avoid creating additional dissension. He was eager for nativist support but only if antislavery was emphasized. Said Booth, the Republican party must be "free from the taint of Know Nothingism," and at the party convention the platform endorsed by Booth rejected "any sympathy . . . with the Know Nothing organization."[39] The Republican candidate for governor, Coles Bashford, won a disputed election which was eventually decided in the courts. Aiding Booth and fellow Republicans in their efforts to maximize antislavery concern in 1855 and 1856 was the escalating violence in Kansas. There, free state and proslave forces fought it out both at the ballot box and with firearms, allowing Booth to focus attention on the efforts of the Slave Power to block the will of the majority. At a Milwaukee meeting of the Kansas Emigrant Aid Society, Booth led the efforts to raise money for rifles to assist the free state settlers. In May 1856, the violence spread to the U.S. Senate, where a southern politician beat antislavery sena-

---

37. See *Wisconsin Free Democrat*, January 24, 26, 1857.

38. McManus, "Liberty and Freedom," 43–4; Ranney, "States' Rights Movement in Wisconsin," 101–2.

39. *Wisconsin Free Democrat*, September 6, 1855; McManus, *Political Abolitionism in Wisconsin*, 105–8.

tor Charles Sumner into bloody unconsciousness following the latter's emotional speech attacking proslavery efforts in Kansas and Congress. Booth exclaimed that "the outrage upon a Northern Senator" had "thoroughly aroused the people," who, said the editor, must "stand by Sumner and free speech."[40]

The Sumner beating set the tone for the presidential election that fall. Booth used all of his influence to convince Wisconsin voters to rally behind John C. Frémont, candidate of the new Republican party. To the fiery editor the party was carrying on the antislavery tradition inaugurated in 1840: "The principles of Freedom, which the Liberty party of 1840 and 1844 asserted as the basis of their organization, the Free Democratic party of 1848 and 1852 repeated and affirmed, and the Republican party of Wisconsin adopted and endorsed" must be maintained. The party would insist that no further territory "shall be cursed with Human Slavery; not another Slave State shall enter the American Union" and "the Fugitive Slave Act which converts one part of our citizens into Slave Catchers and the other into Slaves shall be repealed." Despite the slanderous attacks on their candidate by Democrats, "if the friends of Frémont will work . . . this State can be carried for freedom by a decisive majority."[41] Voters were clearly moved, and with 80 percent of those eligible casting votes, Frémont easily carried the state. Although Democrat James Buchanan won the presidency, northern voters had served notice that their willingness to tolerate Slave Power control of the federal government had limits. Again, Sherman Booth would take the lead in opposing the pro-southern Buchanan administration. In addition, the U.S. Supreme Court, in a controversial 1859 decision, brought the fiery editor's fugitive slave case to a close.

Before the Supreme Court ruled on Booth's case, it handed down its most significant decision relating to slavery, that involving another Missouri slave, Dred Scott. Scott had sued for his freedom based on his prior residency in a territory where slavery was illegal. In ruling against Scott in March 1857, the Court, headed by Maryland slaveholder Roger Taney, decreed that Congress could not prohibit slavery in the territories, thus undermining the containment stance of the Republican party. Booth was determined that antislavery moderates led by Timothy Howe would not gain control of the party in the wake of the Dred Scott decision. Thus, after denouncing the Taney ruling, he called a mass meeting in Madison in June to rally support for the state's

40. *Wisconsin Free Democrat*, June 4, 1856; McManus, *Political Abolitionism in Wisconsin,* 118–9.

41. *Wisconsin Free Democrat*, June 11, October 8, 1856.

recently passed personal liberty law and its continuing defiance of the Fugitive Slave Act. Among the outside speakers whose attendance Booth had arranged were abolitionists Gerrit Smith and John Brown. The resolutions approved included one stipulating that slave catchers apprehended in Wisconsin should be prosecuted as kidnappers.[42] While the Howe faction attempted to steer the party away from what it called a scheme to "abolitionize" the party, the platform approved in the fall reaffirmed the resolutions of the mass meeting. Booth's only serious setback in that election was voter rejection of a black suffrage referendum. He had campaigned hard for the proposal, but faced not only blatant Democratic appeals to racism but silence from many Republican leaders. Both of these factors added to the proposal's rejection by close to 60 percent of the voters.[43]

The stage was now set for a final ruling from the U.S. Supreme Court on Wisconsin's efforts to block enforcement of the Fugitive Slave Act and prevent the imprisonment of Sherman Booth. Early in 1859, the state Republican party had given the editor further encouragement with the nomination of his friend and former defense counsel Byron Paine for the state supreme court. Even Paine's subsequent victory, however, would be small consolation to the party in light of the long-expected ruling of Taney's court against Booth and the state of Wisconsin. Booth had refused to appear in Washington or be represented in court and instead had submitted a copy of the Paine argument and the state court's rulings. Not impressed, Chief Justice Taney, on March 7, 1859, in *Abelman v. Booth,* spoke for the Court in first denouncing Wisconsin's refusal to send the trial record of its 1855 ruling freeing Booth, then reversing the state court on all counts. In rejecting Booth's position, Taney based his argument on the supremacy clause of the U.S. Constitution, which gave the central government the authority to enforce decisions of federal courts. A state's assertion of supremacy, he insisted, would instead "subvert the very foundations of this Government." Not only did Taney deny the Wisconsin court the authority, but he concluded with a curt defense of the constitutionality of the Fugitive Slave Act.[44]

---

42. Ibid., March 23, June 18, 1857.

43. Current, *The Civil War Era,* 260–7; McManus, *Political Abolition in Wisconsin,* 146–7, 151–6; Michael J. McManus, "Wisconsin Republicans and Negro Suffrage: Attitudes and Behavior, 1857," *Civil War History* 25 (1979): 36–54.

44. *Ableman v. Booth,* 62 U.S. 514, 515 (1859); *U.S. v. Booth,* 2 Howard 506–26 (1859); Ranney, "States' Rights Movement in Wisconsin," 103–4; Current, *The Civil War Era,* 270–1; McManus, *Political Abolitionism in Wisconsin,* 173–4.

The decision, although predictable, nevertheless sent shock waves through the state. A federal district judge in Milwaukee ordered Booth's re-arrest, but he remained free for a time and his stature as a martyr to freedom was even enhanced. The Republican-controlled legislature, in a straight party line vote, added to the furor by passing a resolution condemning the Taney ruling "as nothing short of despotism." In labeling the Court's action as arbitrary and unconstitutional, it used the Virginia and Kentucky resolutions of 1798–1799 as precedent to defend its states' rights stance.[45] Milwaukee attorney and German-American Carl Schurz, a Booth ally and emerging Republican spokesman for the states' rights stance, even suggested that the state secede when he argued that the federal constitution "is not worth the paper it is printed on" if it were to be construed as denying a state's right to its own interpretation.[46] But Schurz spoke for only a limited number of Republicans in the state; many had been willing to question a court ruling, but few would push that challenge to an open confrontation with the federal government. As popular furor over Taney's decision cooled, party regulars denied Schurz their nomination for governor in 1859, and on March 1, 1860, Sherman Booth finally surrendered to federal authorities. Officials decided to hold him in the Milwaukee customs house, fearing that local jails might be vulnerable to pressure from the public.[47] Six years after his controversial role in Joshua Glover's rescue, Booth began serving his sentence for violation of the Fugitive Slave Act.

The Court's decision in 1859 was only one of several problems Booth faced that year, and although he remained a hero to his many supporters, his popularity was in decline. The issues confronting Booth included a running battle with Republican governor Alexander Randall and a morals charge and trial which subjected his private life to public scrutiny and substantially damaged both his reputation and political influence. Booth's personal problems began only a week before Roger Taney's ruling in *Abelman v. Booth.* The editor's family life had appeared to outsiders to be in keeping with traditional values. His first wife, Margaret Tufts, whom he had married in

45. *Wisconsin Free Democrat,* March 21, 1859; Ranney, "States' Rights Movement in Wisconsin," 104; Current, *The Civil War Era,* 270–1.

46. Hans L. Trefousse, *Carl Schurz: A Biography* (Knoxville: Univ. of Tennessee Press, 1982), 70; *Dictionary of Wisconsin Biography,* 320; Current, *The Civil War Era,* 271; Ranney, "States' Rights Movement in Wisconsin," 104.

47. *Wisconsin Free Democrat,* August 22, 1859; Butler, "Booth," 186; Ranney, "States' Rights Movement in Wisconsin," 110.

Connecticut in 1842, had died in 1849, and none of the couple's three children had survived childhood. Immediately after Margaret's death he had married Mary Corss, then visiting Milwaukee from Connecticut. The wedding had occurred within days of his first wife's death despite protests from Mary's mother and her efforts to force her daughter to return to New England. Booth appeared unconcerned with her protests and prevailing social custom and was determined to do as he pleased.[48] Nevertheless, the couple had lived in apparent marital harmony for the next decade and were raising three children born in the 1850s. On February 28, 1859, while Mary was out of town, Booth seduced a fourteen-year-old babysitter whom Mary had arranged to stay in their home to help care for the children during her absence. The girl, Caroline Cook, later charged that she had tried unsuccessfully to refuse his overtures. In early April, the state indicted Booth on a charge of seduction and having an "illicit connection" with her. At the sensationalized trial in July before a crowded courtroom, Booth's attorneys admitted that he had gotten in bed with Caroline but unconvincingly denied he had sexually abused her. The gender-biased laws of Wisconsin required the prosecution to prove seduction and that the girl be of previous "chaste character." Booth's attorneys thus attacked Caroline as "a lewd woman" and succeeded in convincing five of the all-male jury that Booth was indeed innocent. He thus won acquittal without having to take the stand in his own defense. Mary always assumed her husband guilty of adultery and soon left him. When Democrats arranged to have the 294-page court proceedings published, not only was any semblance of marital harmony destroyed, but his political career was exposed to ridicule.[49]

Booth's life appeared to be in a shambles as he awaited incarceration over his fugitive slave conviction. Democrats, having long-suffered under abusive and moralistic attacks against what Booth called their subservience to the Slave Power, now derided him as a "deceitful, bigoted hypocrite."[50] Even some Republicans, including both those moderate and more radical in their opposition to slavery, saw him now as a political liability and began to avoid identification with him. Carl Schurz, a formerly intimate antislavery ally of Booth's, was thoroughly disgusted with his behavior, and those Republicans who had long felt his abolitionism too extreme and domineering for their liking seized on the opportunity to disassociate themselves from him. Most

48. Butler, "Booth," 172–4.
49. Current, *Civil War Era*, 272–3; Butler, "Booth," 187–9.
50. McManus, *Political Abolitionism in Wisconsin*, 181.

Republicans remained loyal, however, and publicly defended his political role even as they remained silent on his private weaknesses. As criticism and legal expenses mounted, Booth sold his interest in the *Free Democrat* to antislavery allies, although he continued, even while in prison, as a corresponding editor.[51]

A further bizarre event occurred while Booth was imprisoned, as staunch supporters sought ways to force his release. In August 1860, they actually spirited him out of the customs house.[52] Booth remained at large for two months, sometimes even appearing in public at Republican rallies for Abraham Lincoln and for Republican candidates for state office. He finally surrendered in October to continue serving his sentence. Coincident with Booth's problems, the 1860 presidential contest led Wisconsin Republicans to shift their concern from states' rights defiance of the Buchanan administration over the fugitive issue, to support of their national platform and candidate, Abraham Lincoln. As a result, Sherman Booth's imprisonment for violation of the Fugitive Slave Act no longer appeared so urgent. With Booth's popularity already waning due to his personal problems, few paid much attention when, on March 2, 1861, two days before leaving office, James Buchanan agreed to remit Booth's remaining fines, thus allowing him to go free.[53] The president had apparently feared the potential political cost to the Democratic party had he remained incarcerated. The possibility of Booth's posing a threat to Democrats appeared remote, however, for only the public's distraction with the presidential campaign of 1860 and the secession crisis of the next winter saved the embattled Booth from further humiliation. Republicans had long since decided that he had become more of a political liability than an asset as they turned their attention to southern secession and the impending civil war.

Sherman Booth would never regain the prominence and respect he had once held in Republican circles, but the Civil War did allow him to recoup some of his lost prestige. At the start of hostilities, Republican governor Alexander Randall offered him a commission to lead Wisconsin troops against the Confederacy. Booth wisely rejected the offer, recognizing that he was totally lacking in military experience. He admitted: "I know nothing of

51. Trefousse, *Schurz*, 311 n. 48; *Wisconsin Free Democrat*, March 26, 1859; Current, *Civil War Era*, 273–5; Butler, "Booth," 189–90.

52. Thomson, *A Political History of Wisconsin*, 100.

53. Andrew Miller to James Buchanan, April 20, 1860, in Thomson, *A Political History of Wisconsin*, 102–3; Butler, "Booth," 192; Ranney, "States' Rights in Wisconsin," 112–3.

military tactics, but I know how to talk for my country."[54] He thus employed his booming oratory throughout the state during the war years urging support for, and enlistment in, Union armies. He claimed later that he had made "a thousand speeches for putting down the Rebellion and Slavery." Popular support of the war was far from unanimous in Wisconsin, as elsewhere in Union states, and on one occasion, after speaking at the Methodist church in a small southwestern Wisconsin town, Booth was attacked and pelted with eggs. Always willing to dramatize his role, he later noted that as "a free citizen," his "only offense was that he had asked loyal men to unite in defense of their country against traitors."[55] He also initiated a new antislavery paper, *Daily Life,* which he published in Milwaukee until April 1865, selling his interests at the time of the surrender of the Confederacy and the assassination of President Lincoln. The Civil War thus allowed Wisconsinites to forget some but not all of the controversies which had swirled around the fiery editor during the late 1850s.

As the war ended, Booth could claim one final victory in his relentless devotion to political antislavery. The issue of suffrage for black men had reemerged as a central and controversial issue in the months immediately following Appomattox. Not surprisingly, Wisconsin Republican leaders equivocated when the issue appeared on the ballot in 1865. The party retained the governorship that year, but black suffrage lost by more than eight thousand votes. Yet Booth and his longtime ally Byron Paine saw in the situation a new opening. On election day Booth had accompanied a black Milwaukean, Ezekiel Gillespie, to the polls, where predictably election officials rejected him because he was of "mixed African blood." Paine then brought suit on behalf of Gillespie, claiming that the voters had actually approved black suffrage in 1849 even though election officials then had ruled otherwise on the grounds that less than a majority of the voters had cast votes on the suffrage question. In March 1866, the state supreme court accepted Paine's argument and ruled in Gillespie's behalf.[56] Wisconsin thus joined a short list of northern states that granted suffrage to black men before the Fifteenth Amendment provided for it nationally. Booth could rightfully claim success on an issue of central importance which he had first pursued in Connecticut twenty-five years earlier.

54. *Semi-Centennial,* 51.
55. Booth, "Reminiscences," 116–7.
56. *Gillespie v. Palmer et al.,* (1866), Wisconsin Supreme Court, *Wisconsin Reports,* 20: 544–62; *Semi-Centennial,* 51; Current, *Civil War Era,* 569–72; Butler, "Booth," 194–5.

After the Civil War, Sherman Booth lived his remaining years in relative obscurity until, at age ninety-one, he died in 1904. Those years witnessed the death of his estranged wife, Mary, in 1865 and his marriage at fifty-five, two years later, to the twenty-five-year-old Augusta Ann Smith. The couple had five children and lived for a time in both Chicago and Philadelphia. During those years Booth worked for several newspapers, most notably the *Chicago Tribune*.[57] Late in the century he spoke from the steps of the courthouse in Milwaukee, the scene of the dramatic events surrounding the rescue of Joshua Glover in 1854, and urged his listeners to be patient with those southerners who still "mourn the defeat of 'the lost cause.'"[58] Yet during the exciting and crisis-filled years of 1840 to 1865 Booth had rarely been able to display such patience himself. His life revealed both personal weakness and overly harsh tactics in dealing with those not as committed as he was to antislavery. As a member of all three antislavery parties, Booth was a representative of the more radical political approach in challenging the federal government's submission to Slave Power control. His record was one of dedication to the tactics of political abolitionism and equal rights, and one which few could match in terms of commitment.

57. *Semi-Centennial,* 51–3.
58. *Milwaukee Sentinel,* May 31, 1897, in Butler, "Booth," 196.

SEVEN

FREE MEN, FREE SOIL, AND FREE HOMES
Jane Swisshelm's Search

ONE WOULD BE hard pressed to find a more flamboyant personality and action-filled life than that of Jane Grey Swisshelm. Her humble origins gave little hint of the colorful life she would lead, yet before she was twenty she had begun to defy the restrictions placed on American women in the early nineteenth century. Her challenge included denying her husband's control over her and her property, the questioning of women's subordination in society in general and of female slaves in particular. As one of the first female journalists, she questioned orthodox religion and capital punishment, and became an advocate of temperance, peace, and abolition. The strong-willed Swisshelm thus accepted direction from few and found herself attacked and defended with emotional excesses that at times exceeded her own devotion to whatever cause was at stake. Rarely did her spirits flag, nor did she compromise her principles. She was most certainly a dissenter who became most closely identified with the growing political attack on slavery.

Jane Swisshelm's role in the political antislavery movement was as controversial as everything else she did. It was conditioned by her gender. She was denied the traditional male role of voting and being a central part of the decision-making process within antislavery political organizations, yet in some ways her status freed her to take stands that most male party leaders dared not take on the Constitution and abolition. Being a woman, while restricting her role, also allowed her to be as radical as any in the antislavery parties she supported. Personal issues prevented her from an early advocacy of the Liberty party, but by 1844 she broke with her Whig journalistic mentor in Pittsburgh to endorse James G. Birney for president. By 1848, with her own newspaper she advocated the Free Soil cause, and six years later she was among the first to urge support of the Republican movement. Yet one wonders, had she been born a decade earlier and not encumbered by an oppressive marriage, would she have been in the forefront of early Liberty leaders as well? There too she would have found that her gender would have precluded a central and influential role even as it opened approaches to antislavery politics not obvious to men.

She was born Jane Grey Cannon in Wilkinsburg, Pennsylvania, near Pittsburgh, on December 6, 1815. Her parents, Thomas and Mary Scott, were Scotch-Irish and raised their daughter in a comfortable, yet austere, setting. Thomas owned significant real estate in Pittsburgh when he moved the family to nearby Wilkinsburg. There the family resided in a substantial home and he opened a store. Yet when he died in 1823, creditors closed in and seized most of his assets. When a degree of prosperity was restored, Jane could attend a nearby boarding school. The spread of tuberculosis, however, brought her home within a few weeks. At the same time, her older brother, William, one of the few males she later recalled with affection, died of yellow fever in New Orleans.[1]

Her childhood was filled with ghosts and spirits and graveyard walks with her grandmother, who "talked to me about God and heaven and the angels." As a very young child she was subjected to the preaching and theology of the Presbyterian minister John Black, who was of the Scottish Covenanter tradition. In this evangelistic atmosphere she claimed to have been "converted" during a religious revival at the age of three and had

1. There is no biography of Swisshelm, although she left a revealing and disjointed autobiography, *Half a Century* (1880; reprint, New York: Sourcebook Press, 1970). Pierson, *Free Hearts and Free Homes,* includes a revealing analysis of Swisshelm's attacks on slavery and her role in antislavery politics. Peter Walker, *Moral Choices: Memory, Desire and Imagination in Nineteenth-Century Abolition* (Baton Rouge: Louisiana State Univ. Press, 1978), 87–205, offers a more negative evaluation of her role as an abolitionist and her feelings toward women's rights. See also Harriet Sigerman's brief biographical sketch of Swisshelm in *American National Biography,* 21:217–8.

learned at that early age to read the New Testament![2] Although she became a member of the Covenanter Church by six, she could not attend regularly because of the great distance to church. At an early age she was impressed with the strict, almost repressive theology of Black. The Covenanters were a secessionist sect from Scots Presbyterianism and insisted on strict enforcement of Sabbath activities and the sinfulness of all mankind. They dressed in austere black and thrived on the tradition of early leaders having been imprisoned and then banished from Scotland. But perhaps more important to young Jane Cannon was Black's unequivocal stand against slavery, which included denying communion to slaveholders. Although abolitionists were rare in western Pennsylvania, Jane remembered Black fondly. It was he who helped inspire her as a young girl to collect signatures on a petition demanding abolition in the District of Columbia. Her interest in antislavery had long since supplanted any earlier fears regarding slaves resulting from a neighbor who supposedly owned several bondsmen. Among them was Adam, "the poor old ragged slave, with whom my nurse threatened me when I did not do as she wished."[3]

Despite limited formal schooling, Jane, at age fifteen, organized her own school in 1830, one most distinguished for its prohibition of corporal punishment, the first to do so in Allegheny County. At eighteen she followed Reverend Black into the New Light school of Presbyterianism, which, among other differences with the more conservative of the denomination, stressed abolitionism. In 1836, against her own better judgment, she married James Swisshelm, a Methodist farmer who had recently rescued her from drowning and who, she recalled later, "had elected me as his wife." And so began a stormy twenty-year union that found her frequently at odds with both her husband and his mother. It was her mother-in-law, Elizabeth, who urged her to put all else aside except making James happy and doing as he wished. Nor was Elizabeth happy with Jane's Presbyterianism, insisting that she abandon it and join her husband in the Methodist Church, despite his earlier promises not to interfere with her faith. Not surprisingly, James scoffed at his wife's artistic inclinations. At first she accepted her wifely duties meekly, despite her preference for portrait painting, noting bitterly in her memoirs that she reluctantly "put away my brushes" and spent "my best years and powers cooking cabbage." She admitted reluctantly that "a man

2. Swisshelm, *Half a Century*, 9, 15.
3. Ibid., 9, 10, 32–3.

does not marry an artist but a housekeeper."[4] It was James Swisshelm's move to Louisville to go into business with his brother in 1838 that brought to an early climax Jane's early rebellion against wifely submission and the subjugation of female slaves.

Her two years in Louisville opened her eyes first to the extreme abuse of female slaves, for on her arrival she found "a great army of woman whippers . . . whose business it was to insult every woman who ventured on the street without a male protector by a stare so lascivious as could not be imagined on American free soil." She learned that they all lived "by the sale of their own children and the labor of mothers extorted by the lash." They lived by violence and never used "other implements of toil than a pistol, bowie-knife or slave whip." They even beat "the old mammys from whose bosoms they had drawn life in infancy." On witnessing the plight of a slave mother and her mulatto children, she "promised the Lord then and there, that for life, it should be my work to bring 'deliverance to the captive and the opening of the prison to them that are bound.'" Viewing children eight and younger in chains, owned by "an Elder in the Second Presbyterian Church," further convinced her of her calling.[5]

Her first attempt to pursue her principles was to establish a school for African American children in her Louisville neighborhood. Despite a large enrollment, threats from the white community meant the quick abandonment of the effort. Seeking other work, she found that custom in Kentucky prevented white women from working, although she eventually found employment as a corset maker. With her husband's work failing, she learned of her mother's struggle against cancer and determined to return to Pennsylvania to minister to her in her dying days. In a chapter she named "Rebellion— Age 24," Swisshelm described her dilemma concerning her religious convictions when James denied permission for her to leave. In defying the New Testament injunction for wives to obey their husbands, she determined that the moral law took precedence and boarded a ship for Pittsburgh. Although James and his mother appealed to her to return to aid in his struggling Kentucky enterprise, she defied them and ministered to her mother until she died in January of 1840. In the days ahead James threatened to sue her mother's estate for wages due Jane for her nursing care "as the owner of my person and services." Jane appeared more bitter against the law permitting his suit

4. Ibid., 40–1, 49.
5. Ibid., 53, 57, 59.

"passed by Christian legislators" than against her husband, and her concern for women's rights was heightened. Finally James agreed to return to Pittsburgh and the two appeared briefly content.[6]

Now in her mid-twenties, Jane's interest in reform intensified. While teaching at a school in Butler, Pennsylvania, she wrote letters in support of petitions to abolish state capital punishment. These were her first public writings, but because she was a woman they had to be published anonymously. By 1842, she and James settled in his family home, called Swissvale, where she wrote stories under a pseudonym and then turned to writing articles on slavery and "on woman's right to life, liberty and the pursuit of happiness" for a Liberty party paper in Pittsburgh, *The Spirit of Liberty*. She was far from content, however, as marital problems intensified, and, despite her writings, "still there did not seem to be anything I could do for the slave." During James G. Birney's campaign for the presidency in 1844, she wrote in defense of the Liberty party, signing her letters with initials only, more in deference to her advocacy of women's rights than abolition. She knew that "abolitionists were men of sharp angles," divided over "the right of women to take any prominent part in public affairs." When *The Spirit of Liberty* failed, she began writing for a Whig journal, *The Pittsburgh Commercial Journal,* edited by Robert M. Riddle. Her letters on slavery were "direct and personal," for "the old Kentucky saint who bore the torture of lash . . . knew nothing of the abstraction of slavery or the fine spun theories of politeness which covered the most revolting crimes with petty words." To Swisshelm, the war against Mexico was to expand slavery and "the work of beating poor little Mexico—a giant whipping a cripple."[7] Throughout, Riddle stood behind her views as her notoriety spread.

Before the war began in 1846, Swisshelm, angered by the lack of women's property rights in Pennsylvania, had begun the study of law with Samuel Black as her mentor; he was the son of her old minister. But when Black accepted a military commission in the war, she refused to greet him by hand on the street, saying, "There is blood on it; the blood of women and children slain at their own altars, on their own hearthstones that you might spread the glorious American institution of woman-whipping and baby-stealing."[8] Black would later die in battle. For Jane Swisshelm, it was a logical next step to join in support of the Liberty and Free Soil parties even as she pursued

6. Ibid., 60–71, 72–3.
7. Ibid., 74–5, 89, 91, 93.
8. Ibid., 96.

women's property rights. By 1848, she was ready to do so with her own newspaper.

The catalyst which moved Swisshelm to inaugurate her own journal was the demise of Pittsburgh's Liberty organ, *The Albatross,* in the fall of 1847. At Riddle's insistence she had refrained from contributing her writings to *The Albatross,* arguing that his *Journal* had so many more readers, many of whom might be converted to the antislavery cause in contrast to the tiny number of already-committed Liberty readers of the third-party press. Riddle immediately supported her proposed newspaper, even allowing her to work from a desk in his offices and agreeing to print her journal. James Swisshelm gave his blessing, especially when he understood that she "would use my own estate and if I lost it, it was nobody's affair." While she did not own the paper, Riddle gave her full editorial control. The paper would be called the *Visiter,* with Samuel Johnson as her authority for the unique spelling. When Riddle later questioned her as to why she wore "those hideous caps," her response was that she sought not appeal to her readers "by any feminine attraction." Instead, "what I wanted of them was votes! Votes!! Votes for the women sold on the auction block, scourged for chastity, robbed of their children and that admiration was no part of my object." Thus with great fanfare and crowds waiting in the street for the first issue, she published the *Pittsburgh Saturday Visiter* on January 20, 1848.[9]

Jane Swisshelm thus joined the handful of female editors in the late 1840s and was unique in her combination of concern for the plight of the female slave and her children with that of women in general. The two issues were always closely connected in her mind, and in rejecting the continued dependence on the Garrisonian moral suasion approach, she was part of an emerging trend among women. Through the 1830s Garrison had joined his concern for women's rights with abolition and had thus won the support of most women reformers. But with the emergence of a political antislavery movement, Swisshelm joined a growing number of women in enthusiastic support.[10] While most of her gender could work only in more indirect ways, she could use the *Saturday Visiter* to express herself. Swisshelm had also rejected Garrison's attack on the Constitution as being proslavery, "for I had abandoned that in 1832, when our church split on it and I went with the New School, who held that it was then anti-slavery." Among her major concerns

9. Ibid., 105–7, 110–1.

10. For the changing role of women in the antislavery movement, see Jeffrey, *The Great Silent Army of Abolitionism,* especially pages 134–70.

were property rights and the right to vote; only rarely did she attack the vast array of other social and legal inequalities faced by those of her gender. Yet in endorsing the political antislavery movement and specifically the Liberty party, she accepted the reality that Liberty leaders "had given formal notice that no woman need apply for a place among them." True, the Gerrit Smith wing of the party urged the inclusion of women's rights in the party's platform, but she believed "there was division enough," and accepted the fact "that I belonged to no party." Still, that did not prevent her from supporting John P. Hale, the Liberty nominee for 1848, and then the new Free Soil party's nominee, Martin Van Buren, when Hale withdrew. For her, the only approach to abolition was "direct political action."[11]

The *Visiter* continued for the next five years and was consistent in its endorsement of the moderate Free Soil stance supporting the containment of slavery and the divorce of the federal government from it, rather than the abolitionism of Smith's tiny Liberty League faction, which struggled on in the face of the Van Buren candidacy. Taking the practical approach that containment was all the North would accept in 1848, she defended herself against Liberty attacks claiming she had abandoned abolitionism. She agreed that the Buffalo platform of the Free Soilers "is too low, but it is as high as the people are able to step at once from the bottomless gulf into which they had sunk." The Liberty attempt to force complete abolitionism "confines them to doing one thing—sitting like a city on a hill."[12] Swisshelm argued vehemently that rather than abandoning the abolition cause, her approach was designed to cause the demise of the Democratic party, "one of the great pro-slavery parties of the Nation," and by withholding votes from the Whigs, force them into an antislavery coalition with Free Soilers even though their platform did not go far enough on slave-related issues. Unconcerned over charges that Van Buren's motives might have more to do with revenge against proslavery Democrats than antislavery principle, she argued that in his "hostility to the spread of slavery," he was "a long step in advance of other parties." In her view, "checking the advance of an enemy was one step toward driving him off the field." Clearly, "this Free Soil party could do more to check its [slavery] advance than a hundred of the little Liberty Party with that pure patriot, Gerrit Smith, at its head." Only a moderate attack on

11. Michael D. Pierson, "Between Antislavery and Abolition: The Politics and Rhetoric of Jane Grey Swisshelm," *Pennsylvania History* 60 (July 1993): 305–21; *Pittsburgh Saturday Visiter,* January 20, 1848; Swisshelm, *Half a Century,* 112–3.

12. *Pittsburgh Saturday Visiter,* June 21, 1851; Walker, *Moral Choices,* 145.

slavery would win the support of large numbers of northerners who rejected immediate abolitionism out of hand. She concluded: "In doing right, take all the help you can get, even from Satan."[13]

If moderation was her approach in choosing an antislavery party, her views of slavery, the Constitution, and the Fugitive Slave Act were more radical. Part of her antislavery philosophy was a deep concern for female slaves and an abhorrence for male slaveowners and the politicians who facilitated their control over the slave community. Like Alvan Stewart and a handful of other Liberty men, she believed the Constitution to be an antislavery document. Far from being a political theorist, she never developed her constitutional philosophy, arguing simply that "the Constitution of these United states is anti-slavery." Instead of endorsing slavery, "the document was framed 'to secure liberty,' not recognize slavery." Furthermore, "if justly interpreted . . . it would emancipate every slave that breathes under the Stars and Stripes." This was because it "expressly forbids that any person shall be deprived of life or liberty without due process of law." Swisshelm concluded: "The Constitution cannot establish both liberty and slavery to the same people at the same time." Her position was in sharp contrast to that of the Free Soil party, which assumed slavery to be constitutional in the existing slave states. Third-party leaders argued that Congress could prevent its expansion but could not challenge it where it already existed. Said Swisshelm in response, "We do not believe the Constitution guarantees the selling of women and the stealing of babies." If it "did allow such invasions of the home [it] would not be worth straw enough to burn it." As debates on territorial slavery in Congress heated in 1849, she challenged the party she had backed during the previous election, suggesting that "the Free Soil Party occupies a ridiculous position, canting about the enormous wickedness of slavery in New Mexico and its *sacred* guarantees in South Carolina." Sparing no party from her verbal abuse, she asked "how *sacred* would the Ohio Whigs, Democrats and Free Soilers think it if it guaranteed someone's right to sell them, their wives and children?"[14]

Clearly, for Swisshelm, there was a higher law than the Constitution if politicians insisted on interpreting it as a proslavery document. She thus

13. Swisshelm, *Half a Century*, 122–3.

14. *Pittsburgh Saturday Visiter,* August 28, 1852, February 17, 1849; Michael D. Pierson, "Gender and Party Ideologies: The Constitutional Thought of Women and Men in American Anti-Slavery Politics," *Slavery and Abolition* 19 (December 1998): 57; Pierson, *Free Hearts and Free Homes,* 57–60.

agreed with New York Whig Senator William H. Seward, who invoked the higher law doctrine against the Fugitive Slave Act, a part of the congressional Compromise package of 1850. In pitting the Constitution against the Bible, she argued that "divine commands take precedent over a solemn act of Congress." She was especially angered by those northern congressmen who voted for the bill. They had become "miserable slaves . . . themselves" by agreeing "to destroy the Divine law."[15] Noting that several Pittsburgh papers had called for resistance to the law, she was shocked "to see our good friend [Robert] Riddle take the preposterous ground of submission and obedience." The act was "as much opposed to the Constitution as it is to the Moral Law, the source of all obligation." Because Riddle made no effort to force repeal "we consider him fully committed as a friend of the law." Attacking the male power structure of Pittsburgh, she described a scene of "this entire company of 'good citizens,' fat alderman, pompous lawyers, supple merchants, editors great and small" as they combined "to run down and capture some runaway nurse or laundress" as "our law-abiding clergy" offered up "public prayers for the success of the chase!"[16] While Free Soilers might take issue with her views on the Constitution and slavery, they joined hands with her in condemning the Fugitive Slave Act, which denied accused slaves a legal defense and required northern assistance in their return.

The fugitive issue was brought home to Pittsburgh shortly after the law's enactment, and it was Swisshelm who led the attack on its enforcement. The case centered around an alleged fugitive slave named Woodson. Claimed by a Kentuckian named Rhoda Byers as her property, Woodson resided with his family in Beaver, Pennsylvania, where he was a mechanic and preacher. With the aid of Pittsburgh officials he was returned to his Louisville owner in March 1851. As Swisshelm mounted her attack on what she considered an illegal seizure, she described the Woodson household, where children asked their mother for their father and blamed northern judges: "Do the people of Pittsburgh endorse the doctrine that a man shall not live with his own wife and support his children? Is the family relation no longer to be sacred in our midst? Can anyone be torn from his family on the oath of one man and consigned to helpless slavery and is there no redress?"[17] Largely through her efforts, enough money was raised in Beaver and Pittsburgh to purchase Woodson's freedom and secure his return to his family in Pennsylvania.

15. *Pittsburgh Saturday Visiter,* November 16, September 7, 1850.

16. Ibid., October 12, 1850, March 1, 1851.

17. *Pittsburgh Saturday Visiter,* March 22, 29, 1851; Pierson, "Between Antislavery and Abolition," 309–10.

The sanctity of the family was the focus of Swisshelm's attack on the Fugitive Slave Act and indeed of much of her opposition to slavery. When Woodson had been returned to Kentucky slavery, Pennsylvania "judges, priests and authorities" had each gone home, "there to take his baby upon his knee to look into the face of his wife and forge the family ties that their hands have broken." Family unity was more valuable than political union, and all who valued it should reject the arrival of the northern official who came to their door: "Every wife and mother who feels the value of a husband's love, should spurn him from her door and every child who loves its father should taunt and mock him when he shows his face." Again she railed at local officials for their compliance in the demands of southern slaveholders: "Did the people of Allegheny County build the Court House for a slave pen?" If in fact northerners were to be subservient to southern slaveholders, "What is a Union worth that is to be maintained at this price?"[18]

Much of Swisshelm's spreading reputation had to do with her attack on the Fugitive Slave Act, both while it was still a bill under debate in Congress and after it became law. As the Compromise debates evolved in early 1850 she determined to go to Washington to witness it firsthand. She wrote to Horace Greeley, urging him to publish her letters on the Washington scene in his *New York Tribune*. When he agreed to pay her five dollars for each letter, she learned that it was "the first time a woman had been engaged" in this way. On arriving in the capital, Swisshelm immediately made contact with Gamaliel Bailey, antislavery editor of the *National Era*, and with antislavery politicians, such as Joshua Giddings, who took her with him for an audience with President Zachary Taylor. Not surprisingly, she was horrified by the degree to which she found Washington to be a slave market destroying slave families. She was shocked to find that the members of Congress abused their positions: "Their language and gestures as they expectorated hither and thither were often as coarse as their positions, while they ranted about the 'laws and Constitution' and cracked their slave whips over the head of the doughfaces sent from the Northern States."[19] As they debated the fugitive slave bill, she found (just as she later would in Pittsburgh) that most disturbing was northern compliance, especially Greeley himself. She sarcastically noted that "You, with the rest, Mr. Greeley, indulge 'a *generous spirit of compromise*.' It is considered very praiseworthy to do so." Thus she attacked the editor directly for compromising with slavery while "it is the

18. *Pittsburgh Saturday Visiter,* March 22, 29, 1851.
19. Swisshelm, *Half a Century,* 128.

mother and her children who are called to fit the bill."[20] She became the first female reporter admitted to the congressional reporters gallery, having persuaded a reluctant Vice President Millard Fillmore to accept her credentials. There on her first appearance she witnessed Senator Henry Foote of Mississippi pull a pistol in retreating from the advancing Thomas Hart Benton of Missouri. Her disgusted reaction was that she had "never seen a well-whipped rooster run from his foe, without thinking of Foote's advance." She added that "if I stay here long, my bump of veneration will become so enlarged that I shall take to worshiping in the cabbage-patch, for want of anything more nearly resembling a Congress of very wise men."[21] The scene further confirmed her lowly opinion of Congress and its submission to the Slave Power.

In her disgust with members of Congress she reserved her special fury for Daniel Webster, Whig senator from Massachusetts. Like other abolitionists, she was especially angered by his famed Seventh of March speech calling on northerners to accept the Compromise in order to preserve the Union. In Swisshelm's words, he "had counseled the people of the North to conquer their prejudices against catching slaves, and by his vote would open every sanctuary to the bloodhound."[22] In hearing rumors of a personal scandal, she investigated Webster's private life "and soon discovered that his whole panoply of moral power was a shell—that his private life was full of rottenness." Gathering what sketchy evidence she could, she learned of a "family of eight mulattoes, bearing the image and superscription of the great New England statesman, who paid the rent and grocery bills of their mother as regularly as he did those of his wife." She later claimed that Giddings, Bailey, and George W. Julian, all Free Soilers, confirmed the story but advised against publication for fear of retribution. Julian warned her that "No good can come from its publication; it would ruin you, ruin your influence, ruin your work. You would lose your Tribune engagement by which you are now doing so much good." Convinced that the public must know, she concluded, "I will publish it, and let God take care of the consequences," a step she took in a public letter she had published in the *Visiter*.[23] Her letter was

---

20. *New York Tribune*, April 15, 1850; Pierson, "Gender and Party Ideologies," 56.

21. *New York Tribune*, April 19, 1850; Swisshelm, *Half a Century*, 130–1. For a modern account of the Foote-Benton altercation, see Hamilton, *Prologue to Conflict*, 92–4.

22. Swisshelm, *Half a Century*, 131.

23. Ibid., 132–5; *Pittsburgh Saturday Visiter*, May 25, 1850, July 5, 1851; Bertha-Monica Stearns, "Reform Periodicals and Female Reformers, 1830–1860," *American Historical Review* 37 (July 1932): 691–2; Lester Shippee, "Jane Grey Swisshelm, Agitator," *Mississippi Val-*

soon republished in other journals, leaving Greeley no choice but to fire her, for she had violated the unwritten rule prohibiting publication of rumors of the private indiscretions of Washington politicians. She had no regrets about the letter's publication, even suggesting that it was a factor in denying Webster the Whig presidential nomination in 1852. Although her scandal mongering had little to do with the nomination, the story fit into Swisshelm's more significant attack on northern politicians and more directly with her conviction that the real victim of the peculiar institution was the female slave.

Jane Swisshelm and other Free Soil female antislavery advocates were unique in their emphasis on the social and moral evils of slavery rather than the economic or political aspects stressed by their male counterparts. As a woman, denied a direct role in the political process, she could be less restrained in arguing the immorality of slavery and the need for northerners to push for its abolition through political action. Most prominent in their concern over the abuses women found in marriage and the sanctity of the family were Harriet Beecher Stowe, Clarina Nichols, and Swisshelm. The latter gave an enthusiastic reception to Stowe's *Uncle Tom's Cabin,* which began serial publication in Bailey's *National Era* in 1852. In its indictment of the brutal impact of servitude on the slave family and the infamous Fugitive Slave Act of 1850, Swisshelm noted that the wisdom of "Congressional legislation has been confounded by the *foolishness* of two month's of labor of a woman's pen." The novel "gives the promise of doing more against slavery than all the works of kindred character that have preceded it."[24] She was also supportive of Nichols, who published the *Wyndam County Democrat* in Brattleboro, Vermont, and who, like Swisshlem, used her own experiences as a basis for her advocacy of women's rights and antislavery politics.[25]

For Jane Swisshelm, her contact with slavery in Louisville and her stormy marriage to James Swisshelm were the bases of her reform efforts. In Kentucky, not only did slaveholders abuse and rape their female slaves, but they turned their marriages to white women into travesties. Swisshelm's landlady

ley Historical Review 7 (December 1920): 214–5; Donald A. Ritchie, *Press Gallery: Congress and the Washington Correspondents* (Cambridge, Mass.: Harvard Univ. Press, 1991), 44–6. Rumors persisted into the Civil War that an Atlanta slave, a mulatto barber named Robert Webster, was the Massachusetts senator's illegitimate son. See Thomas G. Dyer, *Secret Yankees: The Union Circle in Confederate Atlanta* (Baltimore: Johns Hopkins Univ. Press, 1999), 87–8.

24. *Pittsburgh Saturday Visiter,* May 1, June 26, 1852; for a discussion of the moral arguments against slavery in *Uncle Tom's Cabin,* see Pierson, *Free Hearts and Free Homes,* 61–5.

25. Pierson, *Free Hearts and Free Homes,* 57–8.

described how her own husband beat his female slave "until she had to comply." She concluded that Kentucky "women scarcely appeared to think of the moral turpitude of the husbands, fathers, and brothers in becoming the forcible violators of female chastity." The divided families, the raped women, the sold children, the spread of prostitution—subjects invariably ignored by male writers—were the product of an immoral system of bondage; yet southern white women had little concept that what they endured was "anything very uncommon or very heinous."[26]

If the women of the South were reduced so by slavery, those in Pennsylvania were little better off. And in describing their plight and the need for property and divorce rights, Swisshelm was in effect describing her own situation. In an editorial called "The Women of Pittsburgh," she claimed that "their minds are penned to the earth by incessant toil, corroding household cares and the bigotry of creeds." Although she rebelled against society's male dominance, "scarcely one in fifty believes in her equal rights to life, liberty and the pursuit of happiness." In fact, "they turn up their hands in pious horror at anyone who dares assert their claim to an equal humanity. . . . They are content to be slaves."[27] Between August and December 1849, she published her own novel, *The Locust's Song,* in the *Visiter,* a transparently autobiographical tale, in which the heroine, Susan Morrow, was locked in wedlock to the jealous, unloving Judge Horace Watson. Susan's position, so similar to her own relationship with the abusive James Swisshelm, said the narrator, was that of a slave both to Watson and his uncaring elder sister, Matilda, with the judge initiating legal proceedings to gain Susan's father's substantial estate. She lived "a life of servitude," and her husband wielded the authority of a slaveholder. When she got the courage to leave, he filed to confiscate her wages. But she thwarted him in divorce proceedings and gained her independence and financial control, finally opening her home to the poverty-stricken Matilda. Swisshelm thus used her column and her novel to seek the rights denied to women throughout the North. In challenging the patriarchal legal rights system, Susan won control of her own income and property and to an equal education—to liberation in general.[28] In her weekly series, "Letters to Country Girls," Swisshelm developed her protest

26. *Pittsburgh Saturday Visiter,* November 10, 1849.

27. Ibid., March 16, 1850.

28. Ibid., August 4, 1849–December 8, 1849; Pierson, *Free Hearts and Free Homes,* 81–90. See also Sylvia Hoffert, "Theoretical Issues: Jane Grey Swisshelm, Elizabeth Keckley, and the Significance of Race Consciousness in American Women's Lives," *Journal of Women's History* 13 (2001): 8–32.

philosophy more fully, both for the private and public life of her female readers. Bringing these letters together in a separate publication in 1853, she argued that equal education for boys and girls was key, for "if parents would give their daughters the same training they do their sons, they could not be converted into slaves so easily." In addition to education, she suggested that women must defend themselves with the vote.[29]

Swisshelm had begun arguing as early as 1849 that women must have the right to vote and "to sit in legislative halls, not merely as ornaments . . . but as lawmakers." During the presidential campaign of 1852 she renewed her call. Again it was primarily to save the "poor mother whose shrieks of agony as her nestlings are torn from her bosom and are repaid by the driver's lash," that women must vote. Only through political action could slavery "be met and destroyed. It must be voted into eternal condemnation at the ballot box and if we may not vote we must influence others to sign its death warrant." Much later, in her reminiscences published in 1880, she urged that women should "take one step at a time" and seek suffrage first in municipal elections and "say nothing about suffrage elsewhere until it proved successful here."[30] But with slavery very much alive in the 1850s, she believed women needed the right to vote for president.

At the same time she refused to identify with women's rights advocates. There were in her eyes gender differences based on physical disparity. Special conventions seeking women's rights usually accomplished little, for all of the "talk produces no action except reaction." Still she was willing to support "women's admission to the rights of citizenship" as long as it was addressed at a separate time. "One thing at a time! Always do one thing at a time and you will get along much faster than attempting to do a dozen." Instead, women and men should work together for such goals as temperance, peace, and, most important, abolition. She would thus disappoint women's rights advocates who sought to combine abolition and women's rights. For Jane Swisshelm, elevating the woman's role within the home took precedence over all else whether for female slaves or free women.[31] Female reformers, she believed, should focus on the single issue of slavery and espe-

29. *Pittsburgh Saturday Visiter,* August 10, 1850; Swisshelm, *Half a Century,* 139–50; Swisshelm, *Letters to Country Girls* (New York: J. C. Riker, 1853), 80.

30. *Pittsburgh Saturday Visiter,* December 15, 1849, August 21, 1852; Swisshelm, *Half a Century,* 146–7.

31. *Pittsburgh Saturday Visiter,* November 2, 1850, July 5, 1851, April 24, 1852, November 2, 23, 1850; Pierson, *Free Hearts and Free Homes,* 71–2, 90–1; Walker, *Moral Choices,* 160.

cially its impact on women. To do otherwise would weaken their effect, for by seeking to change their own status through special conventions they would only dilute their impact on the abolition cause.

Among those whom she met and was impressed with in Washington was antislavery congressman George W. Julian of Indiana, and when he received the Free Democratic nomination for vice president in 1852 she was extreme in her endorsement of the ticket headed by John P. Hale of New Hampshire. She found that the two offered a "promise of incorruptible fidelity to anti-slavery." Since the Free Democratic convention met in Pittsburgh, Swisshelm attended and could give a firsthand report. She shared the feeling that "the present movement would make a deeper impression than any previous efforts of the opponents of slavery," and described the religious spirit that pervaded the delegates. The Hale-Julian ticket appeared in the *Visiter*'s masthead, and the paper published the full proceedings. Even though the party's showing was only half of what the Free Soilers' had been in 1848, she noted a year later that "the Visiter is a Free Democratic paper to remain so until Hale is elected president." Women's status could best be achieved, she believed, "by laboring with the Free Democracy." The grievous wrongs against women, free and slave, could best be "destroyed by political action" in which women shared in the right to vote. Some of her male counterparts might have shared in her goal of women's suffrage, but few had the courage and conviction to state it so publicly and pointedly. She concluded that because "we have got to overthrow the Slave Power sometime, why not go to work and do it at once" with a vigorous Free Democratic campaign.[32]

Swisshelm's enthusiastic support for third-party politics continued through much of 1853, especially as the Whig party began to disintegrate and there appeared an increased opportunity for a purely antislavery party within the two-party system. Immediately after the election of Democrat Franklin Pierce she suggested that "the Free Democracy alone can meet and combat the Disunion Slavery–propagandism of the demented South." A week later she announced the death of the Whig party due to "a complication of diseases, the chief of which was the military fever." The Pierce government had determined that "the protection of the Slave Interest is to be the central idea of government." The political system was in disarray and antislavery forces must be ready to take advantage. With her focus on antislavery politics, she continued to plead the cause of the female slave, describing in September 1853 the successful rescue of a fugitive who "is now placed

32. *Pittsburgh Saturday Visiter*, September 11, August 14, 21, October 2, 1852.

where she can earn her livelihood."[33] But by the end of the year her close tie with the third party began to sour. She had been led to believe at the convention of August 1852 that the *Visiter* would be made an official journal of the state Free Democratic party, with financial backing from the party. When that failed to materialize and her financial woes increased, she was ready to make her paper independent and "suspend being a political organ." Early in 1854 she sold it to Riddle, who combined it with a journal of his own and called it the *Family Journal and Saturday Visiter*. Swisshelm continued as editor, attacking slavery and alcohol and defending women's rights but no longer using the paper as a political journal.[34]

At one point the *Visiter's* circulation had reached almost six thousand, but it had since declined, in part the result of Swisshelm's bitter attacks on the Roman Catholic Church of Pittsburgh, which she claimed was in league with southern slaveholders. She had been especially angered by Bishop Michael O'Connor's proposal that the parochial schools of Pittsburgh share public school money, her position winning her little support among workers. Through the 1856 presidential election she continued to support the new Republican party and its candidate, John C. Frémont, although she was resentful that the party in Pittsburgh seemed to scorn her, "fearing that it might injure rather than aid the party to have a woman take a prominent place in it." She visited Senator Charles Sumner during the summer of 1856 in the Allegheny Mountains to the east, where he was recuperating from the beating administered by Representative Preston Brooks of South Carolina on the floor of the Senate that May. There she empathized with Sumner on the ways in which his beating symbolized the brutality of slavery. He also urged her to continue her journalism: "The slave never had more need of it; never had more need of you."[35] By early the following year, however, she was ready to cut her ties with Pittsburgh, and with editor Riddle and husband James, and seek a fresh start in Minnesota.

Swisshelm's decision to resign from her newspaper position had been building for some time. In 1853, she had noted her desire to turn her paper over to "some well known Liberty man." Finally, as her dispute with the Catholic Church deepened, she resigned, "feeling that my public work was over." Moreover, her life with James Swisshelm had grown more intolerable: "I had lived over twenty-eight years without the legal right to be alone one

33. Ibid., November 6, 11, 1852, April 2, September 24, 1853.
34. Ibid., December 31, 1853, January 21, 1854.
35. Swisshelm, *Half a Century*, 150–5, 158–61; Walker, *Moral Choices*, 160.

hour—to have the exclusive use of one foot of space—to receive an unopened letter." Thus, she explained, she had burned her journal and private letters as well as those from "some of the most prominent men and women of the era." With her infant daughter, Zoe, she determined to desert him and "leave him free to make a new choice and I could more easily earn a living alone." She concluded bitterly: "Our marriage had been a mistake, productive of mutual injury; but for one it was not too late to repair the wrong." Several years after she had left, James secured a divorce on the grounds of her desertion, but only after a protracted legal suit over her personal property. Like her heroine, Susan Morrow in *The Locust's Song,* divorce finally freed her from her own form of slavery. Like Susan, she was "in a word *free,* emancipated, disenthralled, as the American slave when he touches British soil."[36] In the meantime, her sister's husband helped secure land for her to farm near St. Cloud, Minnesota, where the next and equally action-packed events in her life would begin to evolve in 1857.

Swisshelm's plans for an isolated farm life were destined to fail, for on arrival in St. Cloud her sister and her husband convinced her to live in town with them because of Indian dangers for a single woman and small child in a remote area. Equally disconcerting, she had "found the grasshoppers busily engaged in destroying the crops." In her new setting in St. Cloud, a bustling frontier town north of Minneapolis on the Mississippi River, it was only a matter of time before the lure of antislavery journalism would again attract her. With financial support from publisher George F. Brott, she produced the first issue of the *St. Cloud Visiter* on December 10, 1857. Pleading poverty, she suggested that produce would be acceptable in payment for subscriptions: "We want potatoes, corn, turnips, hay, beef, game, firewood, furs—anything to eat or wear or use about the house." More seriously, she declared that both "the Bible and the Constitution of the United States are antislavery." The town's Democratic press, controlled by Sylvanus B. Lowry, quickly took offense at her abolitionism as she attacked slavery and those who defended it in subsequent issues. Lowry had made it clear that St. Cloud was not big enough for two papers and that he would tolerate her journal only if it supported the Buchanan administration and its pro-southern policies. The boss of the Democratic party of Stearns County, the Tennessee-born Lowry was a strong supporter of slavery. Swisshelm, never one to back away from a fight, responded that the *Visiter* "will not be the organ of any

36. *Pittsburgh Saturday Visiter,* June 11, 1853, December 8, 1849; Swisshelm, *Half a Century,* 164–5; Hoffert, "Theoretical Issues," 18.

party or sect" and that the Declaration of Independence and Fifth Amendment protected the rights of all men. "Human chattledom is unconstitutional." Furthermore, under Buchanan the country would return "to the middle of the thirteenth century, when kingcraft and priestcraft shall be triumphant and the masses shall be provided with masters to exact their labor." The prime object of the administration, she suggested, was the perpetuation and spread of slavery.[37] Battle lines had been drawn, and after further furious exchanges, Lowry decided to use brute force, concluding that vigilante justice was the only option remaining if he wished to silence her.

On the evening of March 24, 1858, Lowry, attorney James Shepley, and Dr. Benjamin Palmer broke into the *Visiter* office and destroyed the press, throwing some of it into the Mississippi and scattering the rest on the streets of St. Cloud. Swisshelm had sarcastically labeled Lowry "a Southern gentleman" dedicated to training others "to habits of veneration and obedience." Lowry's note left at the remains of the *Visiter* office said that the paper was "fit only for inmates of Brothels, and you seem to have had some experience of the tastes of such persons." Earlier, Shepley had labeled advocates of women's rights like Swisshelm "utterly depraved," and she had responded with a thinly disguised attack on his wife. A week later, Shepley and Lowry accepted blame, accusing Swisshelm of "a most infamous attack" on the former's wife.[38] But if Lowry and his cohorts assumed that the citizens of St. Cloud could be so easily intimidated as those of border towns with large pro-southern elements like Alton, Illinois, or Cincinnati had been twenty years earlier, they were mistaken.

All that Lowry accomplished was the temporary suspension of the *Visiter,* because, with financial assistance from local citizens and Republicans throughout the state, the paper reappeared six weeks after its violent demise. A mass meeting on March 25 began the fund-raising process. Swisshelm's May 13, 1858, issue thanked the community for its support against "one of the most outrageous acts which ever disgraced" a town. When the three pursued Swisshelm with a libel suit, an agreement followed in which she agreed to remain silent on the controversy in the *Visiter.* Not to be outdone, she simply ceased publication and organized a new paper called the *St. Cloud*

37. *St. Cloud Visiter,* December 10, 24, 1857, February 25, 1858; Arthur J. Larsen, ed., *Crusader and Feminist: Letters of Jane Grey Swisshelm, 1858–1865* (St. Paul: Minnesota Historical Society, 1934), 11–3. See also Sylvia Hoffert, "Jane Grey Swisshelm and the Negotiation of Gender Roles on the Minnesota Frontier," *Frontiers* 18 (1997): 21–6.

38. Larsen, *Crusader and Feminist,* 16; William W. Folwell, *A History of Minnesota* (St. Paul: Minnesota Historical Society, 1924), 2:40.

Democrat, in which she resumed her attack on Lowry and slavery. On August 5, 1858, an obituary in the *Democrat* announced the death of the *Visiter* since it had been pledged to silence "on the subject of the destruction of our office." But the *Democrat* would discuss "any subject we have in mind." Henceforth, it would "proclaim the doctrines of the old Jefferson school," including "liberty throughout the land to all inhabitants thereof." As Swisshelm later gloated over her victory for freedom of the press: "No famous victory was ever before turned into a more total rout by a more simple ambush, and by it I won the clear field necessary to the continuance of my work."[39] Jane Swisshelm's attacks on slavery and her defense of women could resume with renewed vigor.

The course Swisshelm pursued in the next months was a highly predictable one, combining personal attacks with Republican politics and adding a speaking tour to her approach to antislavery. In the fall of 1858, she singled out a St. Cloud Presbyterian minister, Thomas Calhoun, telling him she "could not conscientiously unite in church fellowship with a voluntary slaveholder." Calhoun had allegedly brought his slaves, a mother and son, to Minnesota and then taken them back to Tennessee, rather than free them. Later that fall she began a series of lectures at antislavery meetings at the town of St. Anthony. She repeated her most popular topics, "Women and Politics" and "Slavery as I Have Seen it in a Slave State," throughout Minnesota. In the former she urged "upon women their duty toward those outraged children of a common God who are bought, sold, and bartered." She explained that in the future "we may use the voice of speech as well as the voice of pen in advocating the cause." As she campaigned for Republican candidates for state office, Democrats burned her in effigy, calling her the "Mother of the Republican Party."[40] Following Charles Langston's Cleveland trial in the spring of 1859 she reprinted his speech condemning the Fugitive Slave Act and his denial of rights as a black man, adding: "This speech will be read as a memento to American injustice." In an open letter to John Brown she praised his courage as he awaited execution, concluding: "Adieu until we meet in that land where there are no tyrants and no slaves."[41] Nor did she relent in her defense of women and her superior qual-

39. *St. Cloud Democrat,* August 5, 1858; Larsen, *Crusader and Feminist,* 19; Shippee, *Swisshelm,* 217–8; Swisshelm, *Half a Century,* 189–95.

40. *St. Cloud Democrat,* September 27, October 14, 21, November 25, 1858; Swisshelm, *Half a Century,* 201, 204.

41. *St. Cloud Democrat,* June 16, November 24, 1859.

ities, suggesting that Jesus Christ displayed womanly qualities: "He never led an army. . . . He never boasted of his right to swallow gin and his capacity for obtaining more bottles of wine than others . . . never knocked anyone down for insulting him." On the other hand, "He comforted the afflicted, wept with the distressed, fed the hungry. . . . He in short was more womanly than any woman has ever been." She concluded: "Man is the link between woman and the animal world."[42]

As the election of 1860 approached, Swisshelm spoke for the more radical and antislavery-oriented wing of the Republican party. The party, she said must favor "FREE MEN, FREE SOIL and FREE HOMES." She endorsed a ticket of William H. Seward and Cassius M. Clay of Kentucky, suggesting they were the best way to abolition. Yet disunion would be preferable to continued union with slaveholders. Regretting the defeat of Seward at the Republican convention, she conceded that Abraham Lincoln's nomination "is probably the best that could have been made under the circumstances." She continued: "Our practical creed in support of Lincoln is 'NO MORE WOMAN-WHIPPING, NO MORE BABY STEALING UNDER THE SHADOW OF THE STARS AND STRIPES.'" Later in the year, with Lincoln elected and South Carolina on the verge of secession, she could not "see why anyone should object to their going tomorrow," for "the North would no longer have to maintain armies to put down slave insurrections."[43] Nonetheless, she viewed the coming of war as an opportunity to destroy the evil which had kept millions in bondage.

As the Civil War developed, Swisshelm's position adjusted to meet the ever-changing situation. Before the fighting began she attacked Seward's plan to guarantee slavery in the slave states to thwart secession "as a formal surrender in *all* the States." Now with the war under way and Fort Sumter in Confederate hands, she was no longer willing to accept secession. She declared that "the monarchies of King Cotton will find that the American nation has no king." In June she urged the government to "abolish slavery at once while our armies are able. . . . There never can be a better time than now to deliver the country from this curse."[44] In August she lauded Union general Benjamin Butler for refusing to turn his army into one of "slave catching police" in a misguided effort pursued by other Union generals to enforce the Fugitive Slave Act. Not surprisingly, she attacked Lincoln for re-

42. Ibid., January 20, 1859.
43. Ibid., March 15, May 31, June 14, November 22, 1860.
44. Ibid., January 31, April 25, June 6, 1861.

voking General John C. Frémont's order freeing slaves in his Missouri command, saying, "we have a right to know whether we are to raise armies to preserve the Union or protect slavery." The president's policies were "more like the production of a provincial lawyer than the commander-in-chief of the armies of a great nation at war for existence." Yet when the administration moved against slavery with its approval of the bill abolishing it in the District of Columbia in April 1862, she rejoiced that "today not a chain is clanked in the shadow of our national capitol." Thankfully, "Our chosen President has a backbone and stands on his own feet." Agreeing with Radicals such as Charles Sumner and George W. Julian that Lincoln was moving too slowly, she nonetheless would be patient as his emancipation policy evolved. She eagerly reprinted Julian's speech given in the House in May calling for confiscation and liberation.[45]

When President Lincoln issued his Preliminary Proclamation of Emancipation in late September 1862, to take effect on January 1, 1863, she was both joyous and critical: "Thank God that the word of Freedom for the slave and salvation for the country has come at last. Why three and a half months should intervene before it becomes actually operative we do not see." Having lost faith in Lincoln, she concluded "it will require something more than talk to convince us that he is not a coward and completely under the domination of Kentucky politicians." With the Proclamation finally issued, she again joined Radicals in urging the arming of blacks to serve in Union armies. Having long been a supporter of equality for African Americans (in 1849 she had noted that "the color of the envelope has little to do with the quality of the goods"), she now suggested that if blacks were armed "the crushing of the rebellion would be a sure thing." But, she concluded, Lincoln "will not do it unless he is forced by an outside pressure from the North." She constantly urged the president to reinstate General Frémont, while arguing that "proslavery" conservatives, such as Seward and General Henry Halleck, should be forced out.[46] In all respects regarding slavery and equal rights as well as women's status, Jane Swisshelm remained committed to the policies she had advocated since the 1840s. At the same time her concern for minority rights showed some glaring inconsistencies.

In 1862, when a Lakota uprising in southern Minnesota in defense of lands guaranteed to them in an 1851 treaty had resulted in the death of nu-

45. Ibid., August 29, October 31, December 12, 1861, April 24, July 10, 1862.
46. Ibid., October 2, 1862; *Pittsburgh Saturday Visiter*, August 11, 1849; *St. Cloud Democrat*, February 26, April 9, May 7, 1863.

merous white settlers, she urged punitive steps by the federal government against the Native Americans. With little understanding of Lakota culture and traditions or their feelings toward the aggressiveness of frontier settlers, she identified closely with Minnesota pioneers seeking Lakota lands. Attacking those who would defend the Lakota, she responded that "the unimaginable tortures and indecencies inflicted on brave men and good women, are something which the Christian supporters and excusers of the Sioux must yet account at the bar . . . where the wail of tortured infants will not be hushed." Later in 1862, she even proposed a "bounty of $10 for every Sioux scalp," for "they should be got rid of in the cheapest and quickest manner." Early the next year she gave up her leadership of the *St. Cloud Democrat* and sold the paper to her trusted lieutenant, William B. Mitchell. She then began a lecture tour first in Minnesota and then in eastern cities demanding swift retribution against the Lakota by the Lincoln government as she sought "some security for women and children on the frontier." Her lifelong commitment to the concerns of the family now took precedence over the invasion of Minnesota Indian lands by whites seeking to establish farms. In Washington, she sought an audience with the president on the issue but was told by a cabinet official that "Mr. Lincoln will hang nobody."[47] Her unrestrained and bigoted attacks on the Lakota may have pleased her Minnesota readers, for she continued to supply Mitchell with letters from Washington, but there is little evidence to suggest that she convinced the president, who in late 1862 reduced the planned executions of tribal leaders from over three hundred to thirty-eight.

Even if she could not understand the plight of Native Americans, Swisshelm maintained her belief in emancipation and black rights. While in Washington she met with her old Pennsylvania friend Edwin M. Stanton, now secretary of war, who offered her a minor clerkship in the War Department. She also worked as a nurse, ministering to Union troops in nearby hospitals, and for a time continued to write letters to Mitchell's *Democrat* describing the appalling conditions endured by wounded troops. In a letter to Greeley's *Tribune* she described how "hospital gangrene has broken out in Washington" within those wards she visited. Her ministry and agitation for change continued through the end of the war. Late in the war a friendship evolved with

47. Swisshelm, *Half a Century*, 231–2, 234; *St. Cloud Democrat*, September 1, 1862, June 11, 1863; Sylvia Hoffert, "Gender and Vigilantism on the Minnesota Frontier: Jane Grey Swisshelm and the U.S.-Dakota Conflict of 1862," *Western Historical Quarterly* 29 (1998): 343–62.

the Lincolns, and she became especially close with Mary Todd Lincoln. When dismissed from her War Department position by President Andrew Johnson for her bitter criticism of his administration, she was assured by Stanton that her legal right to ten acres of the Swissvale estate near Pittsburgh was valid and that she should "go at once and attend to your interests."[48] Even as she left for Pittsburgh she continued her agitation for a harsh Reconstruction policy, in keeping with her deep and abiding hatred of those who had benefitted from slavery and the suppression of those of her gender. She remained semiactive in reform causes, but failing health prevented more than limited lecturing in behalf of women's suffrage in the 1870s. She wrote her autobiography, *Half a Century,* mostly from memory since she had earlier destroyed her letters and journals. It was published in 1880, a vivid account of her crusade against slavery (especially its impact on the slave family) and in behalf of the improved status of women.[49] Her death in 1884 at age sixty-eight brought to a close a life of antislavery political agitation by a spirited, dedicated woman who had fought for her causes with a resistance to compromise equaled by few reformers of her age. While supporting the Liberty party later than some, she easily matched the commitment of the most radical to the antislavery cause. Lacking the status enjoyed by men, she had displayed a tenacious devotion to the attack on slavery unique among abolition reformers.

48. Swisshelm, *Half a Century,* 252, 362–3.
49. Larsen, *Crusader and Feminist,* 26–7; Sigerman, "Jane Grey Swisshelm," 218; *New York Times,* July 23, 1884.

EIGHT

MY TRIUMPH HAD NO TAINT OF COMPROMISE

George Washington Julian, Free Soiler–Republican

THE QUAKER BELIEF in the immorality of slavery helped persuade George Washington Julian to join the antislavery movement. His parents, Isaac and Rebecca, had moved to east central Indiana from North Carolina early in the nineteenth century and had settled among those deeply committed to abolition. Isaac served in the War of 1812 and dabbled in local politics even as he farmed near Centerville but then died in 1823 when George was only six. Rebecca raised the young boy and his five siblings in this austere region of rural poverty, but in an atmosphere of devout faith and commitment to equality. By age eighteen he followed the pattern of so many future leaders, teaching school while he read law. At this point he appeared unaffected by the abolition movement and by the formation of the Indiana Anti-Slavery Society in 1836. His quest for religious understanding, however, had led him beyond Quaker writings to those of Unitarian William Ellery Channing, and even earlier an older brother had read to the family from William Lloyd Garrison's *Liberator*. Of greater impact in arousing his awareness were Channing's antislavery teachings.[1]

1. For Julian's boyhood years, see Julian, *Political Recollections*, 11–2; Grace Julian Clarke, *George W. Julian* (Indianapolis: Indiana Historical Commission, 1923), 27–45. The

Yet as Julian began his law practice in 1840, it was as a typical young Whig caught up in the excitement of the log cabin campaign. As he later explained: "I began my political life as a Whig, casting my first presidential ballot for General Harrison in 1840." He knew little of his party's platform "but in the matter of attending mass-meetings, singing Whig songs and drinking hard cider, I played a considerable part." In his eyes, Harrison's Democratic opponent, incumbent Martin Van Buren, was a "Northern man with Southern principles." In this heavily Whig region Julian may not have even been aware of the appeal of the Liberty party and its candidate, James G. Birney. With hindsight he explained that "it was the singular mistake of the non-voting Abolitionists at this time" to oppose "the formation of an anti-slavery political party."[2] But in 1840, Julian himself showed no interest in the idea either.

George Julian's entrance into antislavery politics came in the late 1840s and, like many in the North, from a solid Whig background. His political journey places him in the center of the antislavery political spectrum. The northern Whig party was the original home of far more future abolitionists than the Democratic organization. The party had stronger northern roots than the Democrats, who appeared more under Slave Power dominance. It was more middle- and upper-class based, with fewer workers, who often felt economically threatened by the prospect of emancipation. Like so many young Whig attorneys, Julian held out great hope for Henry Clay and his program of economic nationalism, and only after Clay's open break with antislavery forces in the 1840s was he willing to consider bolting the party. Julian was never a part of the tiny Liberty organization. But like colleagues in Ohio and Massachusetts he embraced the Free Soil movement in 1848 and was even willing to tolerate the candidacy of Martin Van Buren. Elected to the House of Representatives which considered Clay's Compromise proposals, he remained loyal even as former Democrats abandoned Free Soil in 1851. He was the third-party nominee for vice president in 1852 and led the new Indiana Republican movement two years later. A member of the House throughout the 1860s, Julian became a leading Radical who used his membership on the Committee on the Conduct of the War to advocate emancipation and a harsh policy of retribution against the Confederate states. Hav-

---

only scholarly biography is that of Patrick W. Riddleberger, *George Washington Julian, Radical Republican* (Indianapolis: Indiana Historical Bureau, 1966) (see especially pages 1–18). See also Frederick J. Blue, "George Washington Julian," in *American National Biography*, 10: 315–6.

2. Julian, *Political Recollections*, 24, 25.

ing joined antislavery politics from a position in the two-party system, Julian enjoyed considerable influence through the early years of Reconstruction. At no point did he desert the cause of the slave, the freed population, or of a political approach to antislavery.

During the early 1840s, Julian practiced law with his brother Jacob, yet from the start he was more interested in politics than in law. In 1845, he ran successfully as a Whig for the state legislature and revealed a concern for reform by assisting in the passage of a bill abolishing capital punishment. But it was the antislavery movement that attracted an increasing amount of his time and attention. Reading heavily in Channing's Unitarian theology, he was impressed with the New Englander's belief in the immorality of slavery and its challenge to civil liberties, especially free speech. Long before the presidential election of 1844, Julian had been won over by the appeals to conscience of antislavery Whig congressmen John Quincy Adams and Joshua Giddings in their struggle against the infamous House Gag Rule blocking free discussion of slavery and debate of antislavery petitions.[3] By then fully aware of Birney's Liberty party challenge, he nevertheless remained a loyal Whig devoted to Henry Clay's candidacy, in large part following the example of Adams and Giddings. He explained his growing opposition to slavery as the result of "my Quaker training, the speeches of Adams and Giddings, the anti-slavery newspapers, and the writings of Dr. Channing." Clay's opposition to Texas annexation in 1844 convinced him that he must resist the election of Democrat James K. Polk "with all of my might." Unlike fellow Whigs who blamed the Liberty vote for having denied Clay victory, Julian noted that the third-party vote "was made up of Democratic as well as Whig deserters," and that without it "the result of this election would have been the same." Moreover, the Liberty movement "was absolutely necessary." In his eyes "their sole offense was the espousal of the truth in advance of the multitude, which slowly and finally followed in their footsteps." Unsuccessful in winning the Whig nomination for the state senate in 1847, Julian and his antislavery views had by then become well-enough known to alarm conservatives in his party.[4] The next year would find him ready to join a broadened third-party movement headed by his old nemesis Martin Van Buren.

Democratic and Whig presidential nominations in the spring of 1848 finally forced Julian to bolt the two party-system. In his view, the Demo-

3. Riddleberger, *Julian*, 28; Julian, *Political Recollections*, 26, 27.
4. Julian, *Political Recollections*, 38, 42–3; Riddleberger, *Julian*, 33–4.

cratic candidate, Senator Lewis Cass of Michigan, "had shown the most obsequious and crouching servility to his southern overseers," while Whig candidate Zachary Taylor "had never identified himself in any way with the Whig party." Even worse, he "was a very large slave-owner."[5] Clearly, neither could be counted on to support the Wilmot Proviso introduced in the recent Congress to prohibit slavery in any territory acquired from Mexico. These nominations and the rejection of the Proviso had been the catalysts for the new Free Soil party, which combined dissident antislavery Democrats and Whigs with the Liberty party, the latter having already chosen Senator John P. Hale of New Hampshire as its candidate for 1848. The three groups came together at an emotional gathering in Buffalo in August to form the Free Soil party. New York's antislavery Democrats, known as the Barnburners, were the most numerous and influential and were insistent that their candidate, Martin Van Buren, lead the new party. Equally disconcerting to Liberty leaders and some antislavery Whigs was the Barnburner insistence that the platform should go no further than the Wilmot Proviso principle of containing slavery. While this was acceptable to Julian, Van Buren's candidacy was not, at least at first. Third-party leaders in Indiana had chosen Julian as a Free Soil delegate to Buffalo, and his decision to join the movement caused a rift in his family and a loss of significant legal business. Julian's brother Jacob, a stalwart Whig, dissolved their partnership in anger, taking many of their Whig clients with him. "I set out anew, with the loss of my standing in the great Whig party, the alienation of a large body of political and personal friends, including all who under other circumstances would have been my best clients." Yet at Buffalo, Julian had thrust himself into the dramatic political atmosphere and quickly fell in line behind the ticket of Van Buren and Charles Francis Adams, the son of former president John Quincy Adams: "I had all along felt that I could not support Mr. Van Buren under any circumstances, but the pervading tone of earnestness in the Convention and the growing spirit of political fraternity" had dissolved his doubt.[6]

Julian campaigned with vigor and enthusiasm that fall. Speaking widely throughout Indiana for the Van Buren–Adams ticket, he also wrote letters to the *National Era* (the Free Soil organ in Washington), which he signed "A Northern Whig," attacking his former colleagues for their support of

5. Julian, *Political Recollections*, 51, 53.
6. Ibid., 59; Julian, Journal, September 19, 1848, in Clarke, *Julian*, 80–1; Riddleberger, *Julian*, 39.

a southern slaveholder. Taylor, he said, was "a mere party chieftain" controlled by the South. Having no qualifications for president other than military prowess, "he stands before the country as the chief of our national cut-throats."[7] Free Soilers nominated Julian for Congress the following year, and he appeared to have a good chance of winning since the Democrats, with little hope, did not nominate a candidate. The Whig nominee, Samuel W. Parker, assumed his antislavery credentials would carry him to victory, but the Quaker population appeared disenchanted with his endorsement of recently elected Zachary Taylor. Seeing their control threatened, Indiana Whigs stepped up their abuse of the Free Soil candidate, and in Julian's words: "I was subjected to a torrent of billingsgate which rivaled the fish market. . . . I was branded as the 'apostle of disunion' and 'the orator of free dirt.' It was the standing charge of the Whigs that I carried in my pocket a lock of the hair of Frederick Douglass, to regale my senses with its aroma when I grew faint. They declared that my audiences consisted of eleven men, three boys and a Negro." Still, Julian prevailed by 154 votes out of more than 9,000 cast.[8] He thus prepared to join the handful of dedicated Free Soilers in Congress for the momentous debates of 1849 and 1850.

Because of illness Julian was late in getting to Washington for the December opening of the Thirtieth Congress. Adding to the delay, he and his wife, Ann, required nine days to travel from Indiana via coach and steamboat. There he joined in the deadlocked House debates over a new speaker. With Democrats and Whigs evenly divided, the little band of nine Free Soilers appeared to have a strong bargaining position even as they backed their own candidate, David Wilmot. Eventually the House agreed on a plurality rule after Julian and several others refused to back Indiana Democrat William J. Brown. Their negotiating strength thus evaporated and the House chose Democrat Howell Cobb of Georgia. Free Soilers were also criticized for refusing to support Whig Robert Winthrop, a Massachusetts moderate who, like Brown, clearly would have been preferable to Cobb. Yet loyalty to the Wilmot Proviso dictated that they support Wilmot instead.[9] During the debates Julian quickly became friends with Joshua Giddings, who pointed him to the "abolitionist" boardinghouse of Mrs. Spriggs north of the capi-

7. *National Era*, August 31, 1848.

8. Julian, *Political Recollections*, 65–6; Smith, *Liberty and Free Soil Parties*, 190–1, 234; Riddleberger, *Julian*, 47; Clarke, *Julian*, 86.

9. *Congressional Globe*, 31st Cong., 1st sess., 1–15; Julian, *Political Recollections*, 72; Blue, *The Free Soilers*, 191–5.

tol. There he was welcomed by his antislavery brethren, who also included Senators Hale and Salmon P. Chase. Socially, they gathered weekly at the home of Gamaliel Bailey, editor of the Free Soil journal *National Era,* and discussed strategy to push their antislavery agenda. In these deliberations, Julian emerged as among the most dedicated and outspoken in defense of their principles and resistant to the demands of the Slave Power.

The nine-month debate in Congress which culminated in the passage of the several parts of the Compromise of 1850 were disheartening indeed to the tiny Free Soil contingent. Julian was especially alarmed to see how "extreme men in both Houses led the way in violent and inflammatory speeches." Slaveholders threatened that unless they "were allowed to extend their system" over the territories, "they would block the wheels of Government and involve the nation in the horrors of civil war. . . . [Albert G.] Brown of Mississippi said he regarded slavery 'as a great moral, social and *religious* blessing—a blessing to the slave, and a blessing to the Master.'" Yet while Julian found President Zachary Taylor's conversation "awkward and amusing," he was pleased with the old soldier's willingness to stand up to slaveholders such as Brown and grieved that during the recent presidential campaign "I did him much, though unintended, injustice." He was naturally impressed with the charm and "gracious cordiality" of his former idol Henry Clay, even though he believed his proposals to be "radically wrong." He listened to Daniel Webster's Seventh of March speech, viewing it as "his final act of apostasy from his early New England faith." He was amused and yet horrified by the confrontation between Thomas Hart Benton and Henry S. Foote on April 17, especially by the Mississippi senator's retreat with pistol in hand, "claiming later that he had 'advanced backward.'"[10] But as sentiment swung toward compromise, Julian determined to defend free soil principles with his first speech before the House.

When he finally got the floor on May 14, Julian was still hopeful that Congress might yet block further surrender to southern demands. In his carefully prepared words he was vehement in his attack on his southern colleagues. Free Soilers had frequently pointed to Thomas Jefferson's advocacy of the ban on slavery in the Northwest Ordinance of 1787, and Julian stressed how "southern gentlemen appeal to our Revolutionary history . . . not for the establishment but the subversion of liberty . . . by the indefinite extension over free lands of that system of bondage which the very soul of

10. Julian, *Political Recollections,* 80, 82–3, 83–4, 86, 91.

Jefferson abhorred." He asked how keeping slavery out of previously free territories would be "aggression upon the guaranteed rights of the South. . . . Would not the rights of the Master, as sanctioned by local law remain unimpaired?" As slavery expanded, Julian blamed not only southern aggression but "Northern cowardice," noting that "slavery propagandists and doughfaces must answer for their own political sins." It was, he said, "a contest between liberty and despotism." Free Soilers, in defense of containment, had "sundered their party allegiance and for this they are branded as 'fanatics' and denounced as traitors." Free Soil men had the same rights "in this country and on this floor as slave soil men." What "was a virtue in our fathers in 1787" had become "a crime in their descendants."[11]

Julian could be rightfully proud of his maiden speech even though he recognized that he changed no minds. He said later, "I got through the work better than I anticipated, was handsomely listened to and went home in triumph." The Free Soil press, led by the *National Era,* was lavish in its praise, but with the sudden death of Zachary Taylor in early July, the chances of blocking compromise legislation faded. The president's death removed a major obstacle to passage, for as Julian told his wife after attending the funeral: "He did not hesitate to antagonize the South by his action on California."[12]

The various pieces of Clay's Compromise became law in August and September with the signature of Millard Fillmore of New York. Free Soilers had suffered a devastating defeat on two fronts with the rejection of the Wilmot Proviso and the enactment of the Fugitive Slave Act. Julian and his colleagues railed in frustration at these latest examples of Slave Power control, for as he explained: "The impression here seems to be that the Free Soilers and their principles are dead and buried and that no more 'agitation' will ever be heard of." In a bitter speech in late September he answered southern charges that the Wilmot Proviso had been "conceived in sin and brought forth in iniquity." Instead, it represented the right of the people "to the common blessing of freedom. In its application to our territories, the Wilmot

---

11. *Congressional Globe,* 31st Cong., 1st sess., Appendix, 573–9. The speech is also included in Julian, *Speeches on Political Questions* (1872; reprint, Westport, Conn.: Negro Univs. Press, 1970), 1–33. The term doughface originated in the early nineteenth century to refer to northern politicians who cooperated with the South. They were said to be northern men with southern principles.

12. Julian, *Political Recollections,* 88–9; *National Era,* May 23, 1850; Hamilton, *Prologue to Conflict,* 106–7; Julian to Anne Julian, July 13, 1850, in Grace Julian Clarke, ed., "Home Letters of George W. Julian, 1850–1851," *Indiana Magazine of History* 29 (1933): 140.

Proviso is the Declaration of Independence embodied in a fundamental law for their government."[13] Even worse was the law which required northern compliance in the return of alleged fugitives. Julian promised he would resist the execution of the law "if need be at the peril of my life." There was "no earthly power that can induce us thus to take sides with the oppressor." He warned that the measure would convert every northerner "into a constable and jail keeper for slaveholders." He promised that Free Soil agitation would cease only when "the Federal government shall be entirely withdrawn from the support of slavery." When Congress adjourned Julian traveled to Boston, where he found renewed strength to overcome his dejection over the Compromise through meetings with Free Soilers such as Charles Francis Adams and Charles Sumner and abolitionists including Wendell Phillips. In full support of Senator William Seward's higher law concept, he celebrated the determination of antislavery men to renewed resistance. He believed that "Agitation of the slavery question had not been suppressed," as "thousands of fugitive slaves had fled to Canada or to remote sections of the Northern States" in defiance of the new law.[14] The remaining year of his congressional term would see Julian addressing other interests and concerns of his constituents as congressional leaders blocked discussion of issues directly related to slavery. But like other Free Soilers, Julian's dedication to the cause could not be silenced. For him the moral imperative to resist slaveholding interests had become all-consuming.

Back in Washington in December 1850 for the second session of the Thirty-first Congress, Julian, like other antislavery advocates, had to find ways to keep the issues alive, for the Slave Power so controlled Congress "that Northern men are not permitted to breathe an honest whisper against it." When Julian presented a petition from Indiana Quakers calling for repeal of the Fugitive Slave Act, "there was a hubbub and I was denounced for stirring up 'agitation.'" Yet working with Andrew Johnson of Tennessee in support of homestead legislation, he successfully combined free soil principle with his desire to provide federal lands for his constituents. He found Johnson to be "a sincere friend" who befriended him despite "my decided anti-slavery opinions." Through Johnson's efforts, "I finally obtained the

13. *Congressional Globe,* September 25, 1850, 31st Cong. 1st sess., Appendix, 1300–1301; Julian to Anne Julian, September 9, 1850, in Clarke, ed., "Home Letters," 147; Julian, *Speeches,* 34–49.

14. Adams to Julian, September 14, 1850, Giddings-Julian Papers, Library of Congress; Julian, *Political Recollections,* 101. For his New England trip, see Riddleberger, *Julian,* 70–2.

floor in opposition to the earnest wish and determined purpose of Speaker Cobb." He began by comparing the impact of slave soil in Virginia with free soil north of the Ohio River. In the former, the slave's "wife and children may be torn from him at any moment, sold like cattle to the trader. . . . The motive from which he toils is the lash." Across the river "the whole land teems with abundance." Labor "is rendered honorable and independent." But even there, "the curse of land monopoly or *white* slavery" was gaining strength as wealthy speculators sought to extend their control over federal lands. Congress must move to protect "the public domain yet remaining un-sold," for the poor and downtrodden. Free land for small farmers would benefit the "poor white laborers" of both North and South "while shaking the South's peculiar institution to its foundations."[15] Southern congressmen naturally agreed with Julian and viewed homestead as a means of excluding slavery from the territories. Not surprisingly, small farmers would have to wait for homestead legislation, for southern congressmen found sufficient northern allies to block Johnson's bill. Thus Julian returned to Indiana with further proof of Slave Power control of the national government, yet more determined than ever to resist.

Julian's term in Congress had persuaded him that more forceful tactics would be needed. This would include seeking reelection to Congress in 1851 and his party's vigorous pursuit of the presidency in 1852. He had earlier shown little desire to stay in Congress, but he now understood that southern domination could only be challenged by direct confrontation. His role in the previous Congress had convinced both Indiana Whigs and Democrats that he was a dangerous abolitionist agitator who must be purged. Many Democrats now withheld their support of two years earlier, and, despite a vigorous campaign on his part, Julian finished a close second to Whig Samuel Parker. As presidential politics heated up, Julian vowed, "I shall never desert the cause I have espoused."[16] For him, preventing the spread of slavery had become as important as total abolition had been earlier to Liberty party advocates. By 1852 the thinking and strategy of the two groups had merged into a united struggle against the Slave Power.

15. Julian to Anne Julian, January 6, 1851, in Clarke, ed., "Home Letters," 154; *Congressional Globe,* May 14, 1850, 31st Cong., 1st sess., Appendix, 573–9; January 29, 1851, 31st Cong., 2nd sess., Appendix, 135–8; Julian, *Political Recollections,* 104; Julian, *Speeches,* 50–66.

16. Julian, *Political Recollections,* 17–8; Riddleberger, *Julian,* 81–2; Smith, *Liberty and Free Soil Parties,* 233–4; Julian, Journal, in Clarke, *Julian,* 122 n.

Once out of Congress, Julian accelerated his role in Free Soil politics, attending a mass meeting in Cleveland in September 1851, a conclave which set the stage for the 1852 election. Now called the Free Democrats, the third party assembled in Pittsburgh in August 1852 without most of its former Democratic supporters, who had meekly returned to their old party. Reduced in numbers, Free Democrats were even firmer in their resolve to overturn the Compromise and especially the hated Fugitive Slave Act. They rewarded John P. Hale for his willingness to step aside for Van Buren in 1848 and nominated him for president. Party members prepared to support a resident of the Old Northwest to balance the ticket, most likely Samuel Lewis of Ohio. Some viewed Lewis as too radical, however, and in a surprise move chose Julian on the second ballot. The nominee feared ill-feelings from Lewis, but was relieved by the Ohioan's assurances to the contrary.[17]

Julian belonged to that faction of the party which was concerned over the omission of an appeal for equal rights for the free black population. Even though it had strengthened its stance against slave expansion, the party rejected the appeal of a small group of Radicals led by Gerrit Smith to seek for equal political rights for all persons.[18] By 1852 Julian was beginning to alter his views, but he was still uneasy with the concept of racial equality. Having heard an address by Frederick Douglass in Cincinnati that spring, he felt "strengthened in my desire to overcome the ridiculous and wicked prejudice against color which even most anti-slavery men find it difficult to conquer." During the campaign, he spoke to a largely black audience in Detroit and was impressed with the impact of his message on the wrongs of slavery and how it was "appreciated as it could be by no white audience." He had become more at ease in the presence of blacks, although not yet fully accepting of their rights. On a later occasion he suggested that opponents of slavery did not hate slavery strongly enough even though "we hate the negro with a practical vengeance . . . a blighting, scathing, ever-present hatred under which the colored race withers and is consumed in our midst."[19] Few Free Democrats in 1852 had come as far as he had, yet it would not be until the Civil War that Julian could totally embrace the concepts of racial equality.

17. Julian, *Political Recollections,* 123–8; Blue, *The Free Soilers,* 242–3; Lewis to Julian, August 19, 1852, Giddings-Julian Papers.

18. Blue, *The Free Soilers,* 246–9.

19. Julian, Journal, May 5, October 12, 1852, in Clarke, *Julian,* 123, 134; Julian, "The Slavery Question in its Present Relations to American Politics," June 29, 1855, in Julian, *Speeches,* 102–25.

The vigorous thirty-five-year-old Julian did strengthen the ticket in 1852 more than Samuel Lewis would have as the party embarked on what would be a futile effort to convince northern voters to abandon the Compromise and reopen supposedly settled old sectional issues. He was in full accord with the platform's labeling of the fugitive measure as "repugnant to the Constitution, to the principles of the common law, to the spirit of Christianity and the sentiments of the civilized world."[20] The candidates campaigned widely and traveled together in Wisconsin, where they anticipated a large third-party vote. Julian courageously spoke to unfriendly crowds in Kentucky at the invitation of Cassius Clay. In Terre Haute, after the party's gubernatorial candidate had been mobbed, Julian spoke without incident. Most voters appeared willing to give the Compromise additional time to heal sectional wounds, and the third party, without sufficient funds, organization, or press support, was largely ignored. Its total of 156,000 votes was slightly more than half of the Van Buren showing in 1848. In Indiana it won less than 4 percent of the vote; nationally, Democrat Franklin Pierce swept to an easy victory.[21] Julian and his party appeared to face a bleak future, although the shattering defeat of the Whigs and their ineffectual presidential candidate Winfield Scott gave some cause for optimism among the most dedicated like Julian, who believed that antislavery sentiments were about to rise.

Whig fortunes dipped sharply in the months after Pierce's election, but it was not clear at first whether the party's decline and the emerging void in the two-party system would be filled by an organization devoted to antislavery or to anti-Catholicism. Irish immigration had increased dramatically, and the fears of Anglo-Saxon Protestants had risen accordingly. Nativism had its political embodiment in the American or Know-Nothing party, which emerged first in Massachusetts in 1854 and wherever else Catholics were concentrated. In some parts of the North the bigotry of such thinking had a stronger appeal than the threat of slavery and its expansion. In some cases, Free Democrats were themselves torn, with a few, such as Henry Wilson of Massachusetts, active in American party politics and others willing to unite with them in coalition to defeat Democrats in state and national elections. For Julian, however, any taint of such cooperation was to be avoided. Part of his rejection of Know-Nothingism was due to its secrecy: "It fought in the dark. It pretended to act openly and in friendly conference with its enemies"

20. Johnson and Porter, eds., *National Party Platforms*, 18–20.

21. Clarke, *Julian*, 133–6; Julian, *Political Recollections*, 126–32; Blue, *Free Soilers*, 251–2, 255.

as a guise to its bigotry. It violated the great Christian "doctrine of human brotherhood." Immigrant labor was the source of great strength: "Let them come. . . . To proscribe him on account of his birthplace is mean and cowardly as to proscribe him for his religious faith or the color of his skin. It is the rankest injustice, the most downright inhumanity." But for Julian, the greatest threat that the movement represented was that it "ignores the slavery issue." By failing to attack slavery, it "becomes the practical foe of the anti-slavery cause. Nothing could have been more wisely planned or more opportunely concocted by the slaveholders and their allies." Thus while numerous political leaders in Indiana and throughout the North cooperated with Know-Nothings, Julian steadfastly rejected their appeal and the value of coalition in order to keep the focus on antislavery. Only a party directed solely to that end could meet his priorities. Otherwise, "the antislavery cause would be prostituted and trampled underfoot."[22]

As Whig numbers declined and Free Democrats combined with those less dedicated to antislavery than they, there was a danger of sacrificing antislavery principle. In Indiana, as in several other states of the Old Northwest, the temporary transition to the new Republican party was called the People's party. Dominated by former Whigs, such as Oliver P. Morton, who opposed endorsing even a containment of slavery position, the new People's party did not at first welcome those like Julian who insisted that they stand up to the Slave Power. They rejected the Wilmot Proviso philosophy and opposed even a partial repeal of the state's highly discriminatory black laws. Even though the party won nine of Indiana's eleven House seats in 1854, Julian explained to Giddings that Know-Nothings in the coalition had blocked a firmer stand against slavery. Through the next year, antislavery advocates found themselves denied positions of influence in the People's party. Yet as the presidential election year of 1856 approached, Julian fought vehemently within party circles in both Indiana and in national meetings to purge the antislavery movement of nativism. By then the Republican party was replacing the People's party, with Julian insisting that it must "break away from the vampires that have been sucking their blood for months." He would "compel them to walk up to a clean Republican platform on the single issue of slavery" or else go their separate way.[23]

22. Julian, *Political Recollections,* 142; Julian, "The Slavery Question in its Present Relations to American Politics," June 29, 1855, in Julian, *Speeches,* 102–25; Julian, Journal, March 5, 1856, in Clarke, *Julian,* 171–2.

23. Julian to Giddings, January 12, 1855, Giddings-Julian Papers; Julian, Journal, March 5, 1856, in Clarke, *Julian,* 171–2; Riddleberger, *Julian,* 103–9.

Republicans held two national conventions in 1856, one a mass meeting in Pittsburgh in February, and the other a delegate convention in Philadelphia in June. In Pittsburgh, Julian met old Free Soil congressional colleagues David Wilmot and Giddings and rising leaders such as Owen Lovejoy. He was especially encouraged at the strong feelings against nativism and praised a German-American delegate from Cincinnati whose "arraignment of Know-Nothingism as a scheme of bigotry and intolerance" helped set the tone of the meeting. Julian was a member of the committee which arranged the Philadelphia convention.[24] There, too, the delegates rejected nativism and nominated John C. Frémont for president on an antislavery platform. As Julian explained later, the convention "affirmed unequivocally the right and duty of Congress to prohibit slavery in all the Territories" and called for the repeal of the Fugitive Slave Act. He campaigned with enthusiasm in Indiana and was "welcomed by the Republican masses everywhere" and at least accepted even by those who earlier had tried "to drive me out of the party." As nativism waned, Frémont made a strong showing against the Democratic victor, James Buchanan of Pennsylvania. Julian felt that the Republican party had made a good beginning and he "was not at all cast down" by Frémont's defeat: "He was known as an explorer, and not as a statesman." Instead, the Buchanan administration was "necessary to display the abomination of slavery" for all in the North to see, and the Republicans would then be better prepared in four years to offer firmer antislavery leadership.[25]

As the nation moved toward disunion, Julian maintained his efforts in both the courts and party circles to insure that Indiana would not give in to slave interests. In late 1857, he defended a slave named West who had been captured by a Kentuckian claiming to be his owner. At the Indianapolis trial, the federal commissioner ruled against West despite Julian's branding of the Fugitive Slave Act as designed to "drag God Almighty from his throne." Julian and others attempted to aid in his escape, but West was recaptured and returned to Kentucky "under the cover of an infamous law and by the help of truculent officials."[26] Politically, Julian fought conservative Republican and native elements to keep his party's focus on antislavery. In party meetings and public lectures he complained that "the sad truth is that Indiana is the most pro slavery of all our Northern States. . . . Our people hate the negro . . . and their antislavery . . . is a superficial and sickly sentiment

24. Julian, "The First Republican National Convention," 4:319.

25. Julian, "On Indiana Politics," July 4, 1857, *Speeches*, 145; Julian, *Political Recollections*, 154, 156.

26. Julian, *Political Recollections*, 163–4; Riddleberger, *Julian*, 118–20.

rather than a deep-rooted and robust conviction." Still battling Know-Nothing elements, he sought a party organized "on the basis of the Philadelphia platform . . . as an enunciation of essential anti-slavery truth." But conservative elements led by Morton continued to resist and succeeded in blocking his nomination for Congress in 1858. Still, he would not compromise his belief that the federal government must endure to end "the perpetual enslavement of four millions of people and their descendants."[27]

Julian continued to find hope in the national party, and as the presidential campaign of 1860 approached, he supported Governor Salmon P. Chase of Ohio for the nomination. Yet when delegates chose the more moderate Abraham Lincoln, he found hope in the party platform, which, like the Free Soilers in 1848, supported containment. Although conservative Indiana Republicans opposed him, Julian received the nomination for Congress in his strongly antislavery district and won easily in the fall election. Personal tragedy struck during the campaign, and on November 15 his thirty-four-year-old wife, Anne, succumbed to tuberculosis, leaving a void in his life and three young children to raise on his own. But his own election and that of Lincoln renewed his antislavery determination. Despite his earlier misgivings over the president-elect, he returned from a visit to Springfield in January 1861 "much pleased with our first Republican executive."[28] Once in Washington, Julian fell in with the Radical faction in Congress which included Senators Benjamin Wade of Ohio and Sumner of Massachusetts and Representatives Lovejoy of Illinois and Thaddeus Stevens of Pennsylvania. They soon joined in voicing their displeasure with the Lincoln administration's war strategies.

For Julian and others of his persuasion, early military reversals were compounded when, in September 1861, the president revoked General John C. Frémont's order freeing the slaves in his Missouri command. Julian believed that the people of the North had supported Frémont "with inexpressible gladness and thanksgiving," and in Indiana the general's name was received with "prolonged hurrahs." For at last "the policy of 'a war on peace principles was abandoned.'" Instead, "slavery, the real cause of the war, was no longer to be the chief obstacle to its prosecution." Lincoln's reaction was thus "a terrible disappointment to the Republican Masses."[29] The Indiana

27. Julian, "On Indiana Politics," July 4, 1857, *Speeches,* 127–8; Julian to T. W. Higginson, October 24, 1857, Giddings-Julian Papers.
28. Julian, *Political Recollections,* 181–3.
29. Ibid., 198–9.

congressman helped lead a rising chorus of criticism in Congress over military defeats and strategy which culminated in December 1861 when Radical Republican leaders forced the creation of the Committee on the Conduct of the War. Chaired by Wade, it would include Julian among its seven members, four of whom were Radicals. It had "its birth in the popular demand for a more vigorous prosecution of the war, and less tenderness toward slavery." Julian was gratified by his appointment "because it afforded a very desirable opportunity to learn something of the movement of our armies and the secrets of our policy." A modern student of the committee has described Julian as "perhaps the most radical of the Republicans" appointed.[30] In the months ahead, Julian was among the most vehement critics of the Lincoln war effort even as he came gradually to appreciate the difficulty of the president's task.

The focus of Julian's challenge to Lincoln was the president's refusal at first to convert a war to save the Union into one to end slavery. This he did through speeches on the floor of the House and through his position on the Committee on the Conduct of the War. In remarks on January 14, 1862, he outlined the steps earlier Congresses had taken to appease slaveholders during times of peace, from the annexation of Texas to the abandonment of the Wilmot Proviso and the repeal of the 36°30′ line, and climaxing in the passage of the Fugitive Slave Act. Now, with the war raging, the time to stop compromising had come: "The overthrow of slavery is necessary to weaken the enemy and disable him from resisting us and supporting injustice." Confiscation of slave property was indeed constitutional. Arguments to the contrary were the "sickly higgling of pro-slavery fanatics, or the poorly disguised rebel sympathy of sniveling hypocrites." No better time could be found than the present to use the war powers of the government: "Never perhaps in the history of any Nation has so grand an opportunity presented itself for serving the interests of humanity and freedom. . . . Our failure to give freedom to four million slaves would be a crime only to be measured by that of putting them in chains if they were free."[31] Opponents of emancipation were, in Julian's eyes, part of a proslavery plot. If he did not label the president himself a conspirator in such a plot, many of his generals in the field were.

30. Ibid., 201; Bruce Tap, *Over Lincoln's Shoulder: The Committee on the Conduct of the War* (Lawrence: Univ. Press of Kansas, 1998), 28.

31. Julian, "The Cause and Cure of Our National Troubles," January 14, 1862, *Speeches,* 154–80; *Congressional Globe,* 37th Cong., 2nd sess., 229ff; Tap, *Over Lincoln's Shoulder,* 118.

Julian, Wade, and other Radicals on the Committee on the Conduct of the War used the committee as a forum to attack Democratic generals and their belief in slavery and to defend Republicans such as Frémont who tried to make it a war against slavery. Proslavery generals were responsible for key Union defeats and the failure to engage the enemy. Julian reserved his heaviest attacks for General George B. McClellan. Even after Lincoln had removed him as commander of the Army of the Potomac there were many who demanded he be reinstated: "Every man who loves negro slavery better than he loves his county, and would sooner see the republic in ruins than slaves set free, is the zealous advocate and unflinching champion of General McClellan." The general and others of like thinking had forced Lincoln's removal of Frémont and now blocked his return to active command. Earlier in 1862, Jessie Benton Frémont had urged Julian to "refuse to assist" those who slandered her husband, for "it is not one man they are striking at but a representative of a clean policy against slavery."[32] Democrats, said Julian, had initiated secession and brought on the war in the first place and now blocked its successful prosecution. Even after Lincoln had issued his Emancipation Proclamation, Democrats continued to oppose freedom: "The government which at first sought to spare slavery, now seeks to destroy it. At last it has a policy; and I hold that no man is fit to lead our armies or to hold civil position who does not sustain that policy. Our only hope lies in a vigorous prosecution of the war and the overthrow of Democratic rule." This surely precluded any cooperation with War Democrats in a Union party effort so prevalent in many northern states such as neighboring Ohio, a position which almost cost Julian reelection in 1862. With Democrats winning seven of the eleven Indiana seats and conservative Republicans bent on bringing Julian down, he could boast proudly later that "My triumph had no taint of compromise in it and nothing saved me but perfect courage and absolute defiance of my foes."[33]

Having enthusiastically endorsed Lincoln's emancipation policy, Julian now urged the president to "arm the colored men of the free States as well as the slaves of the South, and thereby give effect to the proclamation of freedom."[34] Again he was pleased as the president gradually moved toward the

32. Julian, "The Rebellion—Mistakes of the Past—The Duty of the Present," February 18, 1863, *Speeches,* 192–211; *Congressional Globe,* 37th Cong., 3rd sess., 1064–69; Jessie Benton Frémont to Julian, May 1, 1862, Giddings-Julian Papers.

33. Jessie Benton Frémont to Julian, May 1, 1862, Giddings-Julian Papers; Julian, *Political Recollections,* 216.

34. Julian, "The Rebellion . . . ," February 18, 1863, *Speeches,* 211.

use of black troops in 1863, and Julian now expanded his efforts to force confiscation of the lands of slaveholders, to be distributed to the freed population. In earlier efforts to weaken slavery and prevent land monopoly, Julian had used his position as chair of the Committee on Public Lands to help secure passage of the Homestead Act of 1862. The law "was a long delayed but magnificent triumph of freedom and free labor over the Slave Power." In 1864, he urged that the Homestead provisions be extended to blacks who had served as soldiers or laborers: "Let the government, which has so long connived at his oppression, now make sure to him a free homestead on the land of his oppressor. Let us deal justly with the African and thereby lay claim to justice for ourselves."[35] Unable to secure congressional approval of a confiscation measure, Julian and others faced the dilemma of whether to support Lincoln's reelection in 1864 or to urge someone more in agreement with Radical policies. Already at odds with the president on reconstruction policies, Julian initially showed interest in a movement to draft Treasury Secretary Chase for the nomination: "I was a decided friend of Mr. Chase, and as decidedly displeased with the hesitating military policy of the Administration." But finding the Chase committee "inharmonious and composed, in part, of men utterly unfit and unworthy to lead such a movement," Julian, like most Radicals, withheld his support and continued his less than enthusiastic support of the president.[36]

Julian and his Radical colleagues continued to exploit their positions on the Committee to move the war and reconstruction policies toward their own partisan and egalitarian ends. While they understood little of military strategy and in some ways may have hampered the war effort with their amateurish interference, they did expose some abuses and helped focus attention on the abolition and equal rights goals and the need to punish rebel abuse of black soldiers. Especially did they push for revenge measures against Confederates such as General Nathan B. Forrest, whose forces had refused prisoner-of-war status to black troops captured at Fort Pillow in Tennessee in April 1864. Instead of being allowed to surrender, the troops had been subjected to numerous atrocities and many were slaughtered. Wade favored retaliation, a position tentatively endorsed by Julian, but with his cabinet divided, the president refused to respond in kind. Julian later examined black Union prisoners in Annapolis released from Richmond prisons and "never before had been so touched by any spectacle of human suffering.

35. Julian, "Homesteads for Soldiers on the Lands of Rebels," March 18, 1864, *Speeches*, 212–28.

36. Julian, *Political Recollections*, 237–8.

They were in the last stages of life, and could only answer our questions in a whisper."[37]

Julian's unhappiness with Lincoln was compounded by military reversals in Louisiana in 1864 and the president's efforts to bring the state back into the Union without sufficient safeguards for black rights and the installation of Radical leaders in civil positions there. Julian supported the Radicals' plan of stringent Reconstruction in the Wade Davis bill that same year. When the president allowed the measure to die through a pocket veto, Congress responded with the Wade-Davis Manifesto, charging executive usurpation of congressional prerogatives to establish the terms under which states could be reconstructed. For a short time "the feeling against Mr. Lincoln waxed stronger and stronger," and Julian and others considered supporting a Frémont drive for the presidency. The realization that it "threatened a serious division in the Republican ranks" and that it could make possible the victory of Democratic candidate George B. McClellan convinced him that there were worse things than Lincoln's reelection. Julian was an astute enough politician to recognize that his own reelection to the House required him to remain in the Lincoln camp. Having survived a bitter primary battle against General Sol Meredith, he still needed to avoid conservative Republican defections in the general election. With the tide of the war turning in favor of Union forces, he like Lincoln easily defeated his Democratic opponent in the fall.[38] Despite his unhappiness with the nomination of Andrew Johnson for vice president, "a decided hater of the negro and of everything savoring of abolitionism," Julian was content with Lincoln's easy victory and believed that the people "had voted for liberating and arming the slaves of the South to crush out a slaveholders' rebellion." Yet, he could remember no previous presidential election "in which the element of personal enthusiasm had a smaller share." More encouraging was the president's appointment, in December, of Salmon P. Chase to be chief justice of the Supreme Court, "as a healing measure."[39] As 1865 opened with the final defeat of the Confederacy in sight, Julian believed that his war goals were close to success.

Most encouraging was the House passage of the Thirteenth Amendment, which would abolish slavery everywhere. Julian described it in his journal as

37. Ibid., 238–9; Tap, *Over Lincoln's Shoulder*, 193–206.

38. Julian, *Political Recollections*, 247; Riddleberger, *Julian*, 195–201.

39. Julian, "Radicalism and Conservatism—The Truth of History Vindicated," February 7, 1865, *Speeches*, 237–8; *Congressional Globe*, 38th Cong., 2nd sess., 654; Julian, *Political Recollections*, 247, 243, 248.

"the greatest event of this century" and "thanked God for the blessed opportunity of recording my name where it will be honored as those of the signers of the Declaration of Independence." An additional indication of racial progress was the admission of John Rock, "colored lawyer and scholar, to practice in the Supreme Court." Julian noted with amazement that "no objection was made, even by the old Dred Scott judges. . . . The world *does* move."[40] Still there were problems, as when Lincoln pocket vetoed a bill regulating the cotton trade, preferring to grant permits to favored supporters "in violation of law." Julian agreed with Wade that "this administration is more corrupt than that of Buchanan." Yet, in early April on a visit to New York, he learned of the fall of Richmond and found the people "wild with joy." Less than a week later he visited Libby Prison in Richmond with other members of the Committee and saw the "loathsome dungeons below, where our poor boys suffered so much. . . . The filth, vermin and disease which one must encounter there" filled him with even greater hatred of Confederate leaders.[41] Congress must now provide for "the reconstruction of the rebel States by systematic legislation which shall guarantee . . . the complete enfranchisement of the negro" and block "any executive interference with the people's will as deliberately expressed by Congress." This would include "the parceling out the forfeited and confiscated lands of rebels in small homesteads" to poor whites and blacks of the South.[42] Not surprisingly, Julian responded to news of the president's assassination with mixed emotions.

Back in Washington on April 14, Julian was "aroused from a deep sleep" to be told that "Lincoln was murdered. . . . About 7:30 the church bells tolled the President's death. The weather was gloomy as the mood of the people." Initially he responded negatively, noting the people's "hostility towards Lincoln's policy of conciliation and contempt for his weakness . . . were undisguised; and the universal feeling among radical men here is that his death is a godsend. It really seems so." Yet on April 18 he attended the slain president's funeral: "The procession has no parallel," including the presence of freedmen. "The President's hold on them is wonderful and indeed on the whole country. . . . He was a plain man of the people, indeed *one*

40. Julian, Journal, February 1, 12, 1865, in Grace Julian Clarke, ed., "George W. Julian's Journal: The Assassination of Lincoln," *Indiana Quarterly Magazine of History* 11 (1915): 327–8.

41. Ibid. (March 31, April 7, 12, 1865), 329, 330, 332.

42. Julian, "Radicalism and Conservatism—The Truth of History Vindicated," February 7, 1865, *Speeches*, 229–44.

of them and hence their devotion to him."[43] Now, like so many Radicals, he hoped for full cooperation from the new president.

Initially there was cause for optimism, and a positive relationship with the new president appeared possible. As Julian later explained: "Mr. Lincoln's latest utterances had been far from assuring or satisfactory. The question of reconstruction had found no logical solution and all was confusion respecting it." The key issues of black suffrage, punishment of rebel leaders, and the status of the former Confederate states awaited resolution. Andrew Johnson appeared in agreement with Radical members of the Committee on the Conduct of the War when they met with him on April 16, especially when he stated that "treason must be made infamous and traitors must be impoverished." Yet, said the Indiana representative, Johnson's "demeanor, at first seemed modest and commendable, but his egotism soon began to assert itself."[44] In all of the key areas of policy the president and Radicals in Congress held opposing views that quickly hardened into irreconcilable differences.

On the issues of black suffrage and punishment of rebel leaders, the Radicals were not always in full agreement among themselves, and the more determined, such as Julian, were at odds with both conservative Republicans and most Democrats. Julian had changed his view on black suffrage over the last fifteen years. Initially indifferent, he now emerged as the most insistent of supporters. Gratitude for the role played by African American troops was one factor: "They fought side by side with our white soldiers, fighting so well that our generals praised them for their bravery and endurance."[45] Practically speaking, denying the vote while restoring it to former rebels "would be to turn them over to the unhindered tyranny and misrule of their enemies." Especially opposed to his view was the conservative Republican party of Indiana headed by Julian's longtime nemesis Oliver Morton. Governor Morton, who was prone to changing his views when political expediency dictated, argued that education and landowning experience should be prerequisites to political rights for blacks. So too, the rivals disagreed on punishing former rebels. Julian would move first against Jefferson Davis: "I

43. Julian, Journal, April 15, 18, 1865, in Clarke, ed., "George W. Julian's Journal: The Assassination of Lincoln," 334–6.

44. Julian, Journal, April 16, 1865, in Clarke, ed., "George W. Julian's Journal: The Assassination of Lincoln," 335; Julian, *Political Recollections,* 258–9.

45. Julian, "Dangers and Duties of the Hour—Reconstruction and Suffrage," *Speeches,* November 17, 1865, 262–90.

would convict him, and then build a gallows and hang him in the name of God. . . . I don't ask vengeance. Davis has committed treason, and the Constitution demands his punishment." He would include Robert E. Lee and "a score or two of the most conspicuous of the rebel leaders."[46] President Johnson's plan included no hint of such punishment, and Morton was in full agreement. The differences between president and Radicals intensified when they faced the issue of reconstructing the seceded states.

Julian's hopes for reconstructing the South included the seizure of Confederate lands, and their distribution to freedmen in order to bring racial justice and permit the remaking of the region into a land of small farms. In the process, the states which had seceded should be treated as conquered provinces with Congress determining when they met its terms and could thus be readmitted. Included in those congressional requirements would be the granting of basic rights to former slaves, especially the right to vote. By 1866, Republicans in Congress had overcome Johnson's ability to block their plans and had begun overriding his numerous vetoes. Perhaps due to his Quaker inclinations, Julian accepted with reluctance the Republican-sponsored military occupation of the South. Abdicating the responsibility to the army was "a confession of Congressional incompetence to deal with a problem which Congress alone had the right to solve." In contrast, he enthusiastically supported the Fourteenth Amendment guaranteeing basic citizenship rights to African Americans. So too did he lead the drive for passage of the Southern Homestead Act of 1866, making 46 million acres of federal land available to poor southerners, thus furthering his hopes for the region to become a land of small farmers. It was a part of his lifelong fight against land monopolists, such as railroads and speculators, which threatened to deprive small farmers of their just part of the national domain. Congress accepted Julian's amendment to exclude anyone who had "born arms against the United States." The act remained in effect until repealed in 1877, when North-South compromises ended most aspects of Reconstruction.[47]

In 1866, Julian easily withstood conservative opposition at home to win a fourth term in the House as part of widespread Radical victories over Democrats and the Johnson government. But he could not block Morton's election by the legislature to be senator. As impeachment proceedings

46. Julian, *Political Recollections*, 265; Riddleberger, *Julian*, 213–8; Julian, "Dangers and Duties," 267–8.

47. Julian, *Political Recollections*, 307; *Congressional Globe*, 39th Cong., 1st sess., 715–8, 2nd sess., 1660–61; Riddleberger, *Julian*, 242–3.

against Johnson began in late 1867, Julian helped draw up impeachment charges and urged their approval by the House. In his view, "Andrew Johnson was no longer merely a 'wrong-headed and obstinate man,' but a 'genius in depravity.'" He confidently expected that the Senate would agree and remove the president from office; he was thus shocked and disappointed when Johnson was acquitted. As the Senate vote neared, "an indescribable gloom now prevailed among the friends of impeachment," and "a long breathing of disappointment and despair followed." Again Julian won reelection in 1868, although by a smaller margin, and in his final term he urged Congress to complete the reconstruction process by guaranteeing the black vote. His only misgiving concerning the Fifteenth Amendment was that it did not include women. In fact, he had attempted to amend the proposal so that suffrage could not be denied on account of "race, color, or sex." On that issue he was clearly well in advance of his times. He explained later that, "for the sake of the negro I accepted Mr. Lincoln's philosophy of 'one war at a time,'" even as he prepared for later battles "in behalf of the sacredness and equality of human rights." When Julian was finally defeated in 1870, Reconstruction issues had begun to recede into the background. The ratification of the Fifteenth Amendment in March had "perfectly consummated the mission of the Republican party." In the Republican primary of 1870, the Morton machine succeeded at last in causing his defeat. Two years earlier Julian had predicted such an outcome when he noted: "I did not surrender because it was morally impossible, and therefore in self defense I had to return blow for blow. That was my sin. I would not yield."[48]

In 1872, Julian joined many other reform-minded Republicans unhappy with the presidency of Ulysses S. Grant in bolting the Republicans and supporting the Liberal Republican party. That decision forced him to decline a Republican nomination for an at-large seat in Congress. Because "I could not support him I could not honorably accept a position which would commit me to his favor." He led the Indiana delegation to the Liberal Republican's Cincinnati convention and fought for the nomination of his old Free Soil friend Charles Francis Adams. Julian reluctantly accepted Adams's defeat and campaigned for Horace Greeley despite believing that Adams could have been elected. "The work of reform would thus have been thoroughly inaugurated and the whole current of American politics radically

---

48. Julian, *Political Recollections*, 314, 316, 317, 324–5, 330; Julian, "Review of Congressional Politics," October 25, 1868, *Speeches,* 463–72.

changed."[49] Like other Liberal Republicans, he believed that the Grant-led Republicans had turned their backs on reform and the South, leaving blacks at the mercy of the resurgent planter class. In later years Julian joined the Democratic party in support of Samuel J. Tilden and then Grover Cleveland. In 1885, the latter appointed him to be surveyor general of New Mexico, a position which allowed him to pursue his interest in land reform. Although Julian no longer played an active role in the issues involving race relations, his commitment to black rights remained firm. His second wife, Laura Giddings, the daughter of Joshua Giddings whom he had married during the Civil War, had died in 1884. In retirement, in 1892, he published a biography of Giddings in which he lovingly traced the career of a fellow reformer, first as a Whig, then a Free Soiler, and finally as a Republican.[50] Death for George Julian came at his home in Irvington, Indiana, in 1899 at age eighty-two. Although he had been a member of numerous political parties, he fits into the center of the political spectrum. He began as a Whig and continued as a Free Soiler and Republican before ending as a Democrat; his commitment was more to principle than party—a principle that was dominated by reform through antislavery politics before and during the Civil War and by an equal dedication to equality after the war.[51]

49. Julian, *Political Recollections,* 335, 340.

50. Julian, *The Life of Joshua Giddings* (Chicago: A. C. McClurg, 1892).

51. Julian provided a summary of his own career in politics on October 25, 1868, "Review of Congressional Politics," *Speeches,* 463–72. For a detailed account of the last phase of Julian's life after he left Congress, see Riddleberger, *Julian,* 279–321.

NINE

NEITHER SLAVERY NOR INVOLUNTARY SERVITUDE
David Wilmot and the Containment of Slavery

DAVID WILMOT'S PLACE on the antislavery spectrum falls toward the conservative end. In 1846 he authored his famous Proviso, designed to prevent the spread of slavery to Mexican War territories, for reasons some historians have judged selfish and racist—to punish the Polk administration for denying his faction of the Democratic party significant patronage and to secure the territories for the exclusive use of his white constituents. He also believed that, with Polk's election, his party had fallen under the dominant control of a landed aristocracy dominated by slaveholders and their many allies, North and South, who were determined to see slavery expand at the expense of small farmers. Wilmot, like many others who came to support the containment of slavery, believed that if slavery did not expand it would eventually die. Thus a movement to halt its spread would benefit not only white farmers but hasten the process of eventual emancipation. For David Wilmot, the Free Soil movement and ultimately the Republican party could better serve his constituents and antislavery than could the Democrats. At the same time, insistence on containment might force Democrats to hear other voices than those of the Slave Power.

Wilmot entered the political antislavery movement in 1848 from an established place in the two-party system as a Democratic congressman having previously shown little concern over the slavery issue. As a Jacksonian Democrat, his concern was consistently in behalf of economic opportunities for his small farmer constituents. With the Democrats defeated, he returned to the party fold the next year, believing that a third party was not practical. He remained a Democrat, albeit uncomfortably so, and said little in regards to the Compromise of 1850 or in behalf of the party candidate for president, Franklin Pierce, in 1852. Finally, as the Kansas-Nebraska bill was debated two years later, he was ready to sever his ties and become a Republican. He thus permanently cast his lot with antislavery politics, but within the two-party system. His earlier indecision leaves him at the conservative end of the spectrum, ahead only of those who had opposed the Free Soil party. His role as the author of the Proviso, however, established his credentials as a leader of the antislavery movement, albeit for politically expedient reasons as well as a means to force an eventual end to slavery. As a representative of anti-slavery Democrats, his views are significant even though sometimes at odds with other political antislavery leaders.

Wilmot was born in Bethany, Pennsylvania, in 1814.[1] His father, Randall, a merchant, had lived in Connecticut before moving to the Catskill Mountains area of New York, where he met and married Mary Grant. The young couple soon moved to the frontier region of Wayne County, Pennsylvania, in search of land and greater opportunity. Following Mary's death in 1820, David's father remarried and raised the young boy in relative comfort. He attended school first in Bethany and then at the Cayuga Lake Academy in Aurora, New York. In 1832, he left school and began the study of law under the direction of George W. Woodward in Wilkes Barre. A contemporary suggested that Wilmot appeared unsuited for the law: "He seemed to read very little and was apparently listless. He dressed without taste and his appearance was very careless." Yet upon examination he easily secured admission to the bar in 1834.[2] As a young Jacksonian, he appeared as much concerned with local politics as with the law, choosing the small county seat of Towanda in the sparsely settled county of Bradford in northeastern Pennsylva-

1. The only full-length biography of Wilmot is Charles B. Going, *David Wilmot, Free-Soiler* (New York: D. Appleton and Co., 1924). Although thoroughly laudatory of Wilmot, Going includes a wealth of his letters and speeches, and most are not available elsewhere because few of his papers survived. As a result, the Wilmot correspondence cited here is found in Going's biography. See also Jonathan H. Earle, "The Undaunted Democracy: Jacksonian Antislavery and Free Soil, 1828–1848," Ph.D. diss., Princeton University, 1996, 323–69; Frederick J. Blue, "David Wilmot," in *American National Biography*, 23:553–4.

2. Going, *Wilmot*, 8–10.

nia to begin his career. Towanda was part of a solidly Democratic district and ideal for a politically ambitious young attorney.

Wilmot's role in Towanda during his first decade there was that of a typical young attorney establishing his roots in a new community. In 1836, he married Anne Morgan, with whom he would have three children. In 1840, he helped charter Christ Church, an Episcopalian congregation. It was a part of a mainstream Protestant sect that rejected the evangelical approach. Episcopalians also typically rejected the radical abolitionism sometimes endorsed by evangelical congregations. There is little indication that Wilmot's religious beliefs directly affected his attitude toward the morality of slavery; yet his membership in a church that held an anti-Evangelical world view helps explain his distrust of abolitionism and other moral reform issues. His early role in politics rather reflected an intense support of Jacksonian Democracy and especially Vice President Martin Van Buren of New York. He quickly joined the local Democratic party, and began writing antibank editorials in the *Towanda Banner and Democrat*. When Van Buren assumed the presidency in 1837, Wilmot's defense of hard money and attacks on the Whig party intensified. By the time Van Buren sought reelection in 1840 in the midst of depression conditions, Wilmot had assumed an active role in the Bradford County Democratic party. In an area where few blacks lived, although some fugitive slaves crossed on the Underground Railroad, there was little interest in the new Liberty party. The county vote for James G. Birney was minuscule in both 1840 and 1844, as the Democrats retained their firm grip on local offices and the area continued to send one of its partisans to Congress.[3]

For Wilmot in the early 1840s the only political issues of import were economic, especially the controversial problems of banking and tariffs. Although not raised on a farm, he identified with his rural neighbors and with the agrarian interests closely associated with the Jacksonian economic program. In defense of equal economic opportunity and common-man democracy, which the Jacksonians claimed to represent, he firmly opposed Henry Clay's American System, which was designed to aid business. Like most Jacksonian Democrats, he felt that abolitionist efforts to divert attention to slavery and away from the need to resist a national bank and high protective tariffs were misguided. Thus Wilmot was a firm antiabolitionist, and when an antislavery group planned a rally in the courthouse in Towanda in 1843,

3. See David Craft, *History of Bradford County, Pennsylvania* (Philadelphia: L. H. Everts, 1878); Earle, "Undaunted Democracy," 346–7.

he led the effort to prevent it from assembling. A later political associate recalled: "I never shall forget the eloquence of the man. I stood spellbound under his words, and I never shall forget his appeal to his democratic friends not to permit us to assemble in the courthouse."[4] As his law practice prospered his interest in politics intensified, and it was his perseverance and oratory that eventually won him a party nomination for Congress in 1844. A New York journal described him as "inclined to be corpulent, with a full red face. . . . His voice is rich, full, melodious. He is called the most eloquent man in Bradford County. . . . he is almost slovenly in his dress and not over pious in his language. He is ambitious—is evidently more ambitious to shine as a politician than as a jurist." He carried the district by close to three thousand votes, receiving seven hundred more votes than presidential candidate James K. Polk.[5]

As Wilmot took his position in the Twenty-ninth Congress, there were already clear signs of a rift among Pennsylvania Democrats, reflecting similar divisions in New York. There, Van Buren Democrats were angered when the president denied them key appointments despite their firm support of Polk's election. Wilmot was especially angered when Pennsylvanian James Buchanan, who he felt was beholden to southern interests, became secretary of state. Even more ominous in the young congressman's eyes was Buchanan's success in blocking both the election of his legal mentor, George Woodward, to the Senate by the legislature and then Woodward's confirmation as a justice on the federal Supreme Court.[6] The Wilmot-Buchanan feud would persist even as the latter assumed the presidency in 1857. In 1845 the issues were especially critical, as Congress tackled divisive economic questions, such as tariffs and internal improvements, and faced the explosive issues of territorial expansion.

Wilmot showed few signs of rebellion against the administration during his first months in Congress. He supported a tariff reduction championed by Polk that was unacceptable among Pennsylvania manufacturers but popular among the agriculture and timber interests in his district of northeastern Pennsylvania. He was the only Pennsylvania representative to vote for the Walker Tariff of 1846, which reduced rates, doing so in violation of specific

---

4. Going, *Wilmot*, 34.

5. *New York Globe*, 1843, in Going, *Wilmot*, 35–6, 41; *Bradford Reporter* (Towanda, Pa.), November 20, 27, 1847.

6. Milo M. Quaife, ed., *Diary of James K. Polk, 1845–1849*, 4 vols. (Chicago: A. C. McClurg, 1910), January 22, 24, 1846, 1:194–6; Going, *Wilmot*, 41–3.

instructions from the state legislature. In a state dominated by rising manu-
facturing interests, even Democrats often supported the Whig program of
high tariffs and aid for internal improvements. More surprising to some in
light of his soon-to-emerge antislavery concerns was his support of a Democratic effort to restore the Gag Rule blocking House discussion of abolitionist petitions.[7] His position, however, was totally consistent with the views of
his constituents and with his personal distrust of abolitionism. The previous
Congress had repealed the infamous denial of the right to petition through
the determined efforts of John Quincy Adams and Joshua Giddings. Wilmot
joined a large block of Democrats, the majority of whom were southerners,
in a futile effort to prevent antislavery debates on slavery. Many of the petitions dealt with the plight of fugitive slaves, a group for which he had little
concern. He thus consistently worked to keep the focus on economic issues
and avoid the potentially disruptive issues which might threaten party unity.
The need for low tariffs and preventing a federal government role in internal
improvements, both of which would aid business, meant that on economic
issues President Polk could not have found a more loyal Democrat than
David Wilmot.

In December 1845, Wilmot opposed a Whig amendment to the Texas
statehood bill which would have banned slavery there. The congressman apparently believed the institution to be acceptable there as it was already
entrenched and legalized in the former republic's constitution.[8] As a loyal
Democrat, he believed Whig efforts to block slavery expansion in such areas
could only divert attention from Polk's economic goals. Only when it came
to the boundary settlement with Great Britain over Oregon did Wilmot
show any uneasiness with the administration, and even here he remained
loyal. An expansionist, he insisted in his maiden House speech in February
1846 that American territory include the valuable Puget Sound harbors.[9] He
made clear his desire for the entire territory north to 54°40′. But he was
content with the forty-ninth parallel compromise because it included the
necessary ports. While other northern Democrats, especially those of the
Old Northwest, protested what they regarded as the sacrifice of northern interests, Wilmot was still supportive of the president. Democratic unity was
soon to be further tested, however, with David Wilmot leading the revolt.

7. Going, *Wilmot*, 86; *Congressional Globe*, 29th Cong., 1st sess., 1049–53, 4.
8. *Congressional Globe*, 29th Cong., 1st sess., 64; Going, *Wilmot*, 49–52.
9. *Congressional Globe*, 29th Cong., 1st sess., Appendix, 184ff.

The occasion of Wilmot's break with the president occurred when, on August 8, 1846, Polk sought congressional approval of a $2 million appropriation to be used in negotiations with Mexico for lands to be acquired in the Southwest. In his proposal, Polk made no mention of his additional goal of California lands.[10] In conversation with several northern Democratic colleagues during a dinner recess that evening, Wilmot initiated the idea of amending the bill so that slavery would be excluded from any territory which might be acquired from Mexico. So was born the Wilmot Proviso.

Despite the fear of one congressman that such an amendment, even if passed by the House, would kill the bill in the Senate, Wilmot responded that he would rather see it defeated "than to see it passed without the Proviso." After dinner, others encouraged him to proceed. They included Democrats Jacob Brinkerhoff of Ohio, Preston King, George Rathbun, and Martin Grover of New York, Hannibal Hamlin of Maine, and James Thompson of Pennsylvania.[11] The group then agreed that there would be sufficient support from Northern Whigs and Democrats to assure House approval. When debate on the bill proceeded later in the evening, Wilmot fatefully introduced the amendment that the group of northern Democrats had agreed on. In doing so, he assumed a new role, for the Proviso was a benchmark in his career. Always the faithful Democratic loyalist, never questioning party strategy as presented by the president, he now would take a risk and challenge the party leadership in behalf of what he believed to be the best interests of his constituents.

A year later, in late September 1847, Wilmot outlined the sequence of events in a speech to his constituents, repeating his explanation to a Herkimer, New York, meeting of dissident Democrats.[12] Although Wilmot and his defenders attributed firm opposition to the expansion of slavery as his sole motivating factor, it is clear that there were additional issues which led him to urge a proposal which he knew would alienate the president. Other events of 1845 and 1846 had led him to join the New York Van Buren dissidents furious with Polk for denying them key patronage positions. Wilmot, too, had seen patronage denied to his supporters in Pennsylvania, due, he be-

10. *Congressional Globe*, 29th Cong., 1st sess., 1211; Chaplain W. Morrison, *Democratic Politics and Sectionalism: The Wilmot Proviso Controversy* (Chapel Hill: Univ. of North Carolina Press, 1967), 15–6.

11. Morrison, *The Wilmot Proviso Controversy*, 19–20, 180 n. 63.

12. *National Era*, October 21, 1847; Gardiner, *The Great Issue*, 59; Going, *Wilmot*, 134–5.

lieved, to the influence of Polk's secretary of state, James Buchanan. Wilmot explained: "I am fully determined to give no rest to the President until he does in some proper manner recognize the strong claims of my district."[13] He was unhappy with Polk's willingness to compromise with Great Britain over Oregon while seeking vast territories from Mexico. In essence, he had concluded that the president's policies were too proslavery and prosouthern, most especially in terms of territorial expansion in the Southwest. It was not the purpose of the Proviso "to encroach upon the rights of the South. It does not propose to abolish Slavery either in states or territories, now or hereafter. Its sole object and end is to protect free soil from the unlawful and violent aggressions of slavery." Only by preventing the spread of slavery to Mexican War territories could these tendencies be reversed.[14]

The amendment that Wilmot proposed on the evening of August 8 read: "That as an express and fundamental condition of the acquisition of any territory from the Republic of Mexico by the United States by virtue of any treaty which may be negotiated between them and to the use by the Executive of the Moneys herein appropriated, neither slavery nor involuntary servitude shall ever exist in any part of said territory except for crime, whereof the party shall first be duly convicted."[15] Although Wilmot was most likely the originator of the Proviso strategy in 1846, he and his colleagues were quick to point out that Thomas Jefferson was the real author. Jacob Brinkerhoff suggested that it should be called the "Thomas Jefferson proviso."[16] Fearing that southerners would seize on it as an abolitionist concept and hoping it would bring additional support if attributable to a slave-

13. *National Era*, October 21, 1847; Wilmot to Victor Piolett, July 4, 1846, in Going, *Wilmot*, 145–6.

14. *National Era*, October 21, 1847; Morrison, *The Wilmot Proviso Controversy*, 180–1 n. 70; Going, *Wilmot*, 134–5.

15. *Congressional Globe*, 29th Cong., 1st sess., 1217.

16. Much discussion ensued later as to whose idea the Proviso originally was. Brinkerhoff later claimed to be the originator, and some have suggested that the group chose Wilmot because he was thought to be most friendly to the Polk administration and thus would not provoke suspicion. But despite the vast amount written then and since, the consensus of twentieth-century historians is that Wilmot originally conceived the plan and thus the Proviso was properly named. See Morrison, *The Wilmot Proviso Controversy*, 180–1 n. 70; Going, *Wilmot*, 134–5; Clark E. Persinger, " 'The Bargain of 1844' as the Origin of the Wilmot Proviso," in American Historical Association, *Annual Report of the American Historical Association, 1911* (1913), 187–95; Richard R. Stenberg, "The Motivation of the Wilmot Proviso," *Mississippi Valley Historical Review* 19 (March 1932): 535–41; Eric Foner, "The Wilmot Proviso Revisited," *Journal of American History* 56 (1969): 262–79.

holding Founding Father and author of the Declaration of Independence, he noted that Jefferson "had brought it forth with a view to incorporate it into American legislation" in 1784 and it had become part of the Northwest Ordinance of 1787, banning slavery in the Old Northwest. Surprisingly, despite the fears of Brinkerhoff and Wilmot, little debate followed, perhaps because opponents viewed it more as a political maneuver than a significant threat to their interests. The amendment then passed, as did the bill by sectional votes later that evening. With adjournment of Congress looming on August 10, the Senate failed to act, leaving the issue unresolved until Congress reconvened at the end of the year.[17]

When Wilmot returned home to campaign for reelection in the fall of 1846, he knew he was vulnerable, but more the result of his tariff vote than his Proviso. Pennsylvania appeared united behind protectionism, but the congressman hoped that his district was an exception since farmers, workers, and lumbering interests in the area would benefit little from high rates. Thus he could explain in the language of a Jacksonian that, by his vote for the Walker Tariff bill, "I stood by the rights and interests of the mass, against the claims of a privileged few, by the cause of labor against the sordid aims of capital." The voters of the Twelfth District agreed, but by the narrowest of margins. As Whigs swept the state as the champions of protectionism, Wilmot carried his county by four hundred votes and his district by eight hundred.[18] The press and political leaders had given little notice to the Proviso in the controversy and had instead concentrated on protection. But if Wilmot was viewed by some as the courageous opponent of business in behalf of the common man, he would soon be in the center of sectional issues involving the expansion of slavery.

When the Twenty-ninth Congress convened for its second session, in December 1846, it was not Wilmot who reintroduced the Proviso. Late in the month President Polk had convinced him of the disruptive nature of the Proviso, at least as an amendment to war appropriation bills. The president appealed to his loyalty to the party, and momentarily Wilmot surrendered to political expediency.[19] But if he hesitated briefly, his close ally Preston King

---

17. *Congressional Globe*, 29th Cong., 1st sess., 377; Morrison, *The Wilmot Proviso Controversy*, 19–20.

18. Wilmot to Chauncy Guthrie et al., September 18, 1846, in Going, *Wilmot*, 152, 154–5.

19. Wilmot's version of these events is recorded in a speech he delivered in Congress on February 17, 1849. See *Congressional Globe*, 30th Cong., 2nd sess., Appendix, 139. See Morrison, *The Wilmot Proviso Controversy*, 27.

of New York did not, and it was King who proposed it as an amendment on January 4. The antislavery journal *The National Era*, edited by Liberty party leader Gamaliel Bailey, immediately reacted in its initial issue and suggested that the Proviso as proposed by King "may be regarded as defining the position of the Northern and Western sections of the Democratic party." Polk, angered that the now $3 million appropriation bill still languished, fumed: "Whilst they neglect to do this, they are agitating the slavery question, which has nothing to do with the practical business before them." Moreover, the Proviso's "introduction in connection with the Mexican War is not only mischievous but wicked." It was "an abstract question. There is no probability that any territory will ever be acquired from Mexico in which slavery could ever exist."[20]

When the appropriation bill finally reached the House floor for debate in early February, Wilmot no longer hesitated; rather, he regained the risk-taking role he had assumed the previous session by delivering a forceful and articulate endorsement and defense of the Proviso. Again he insisted it was not an abolitionist measure: "I have stood up at home, and battled time and again against the Abolitionists of the North." Instead, "I ask not that slavery be abolished. I demand that the Government preserve the integrity of *free territory* against the aggressions of slavery—against its wrongful usurpations." To those like the president who believed the issue an abstraction because slavery could not work west of Texas, Wilmot responded that slaveholders were determined to take their slave property with them: "Slavery follows in the rear of our army," he said.[21]

Moreover, Wilmot revealed another central element of his beliefs on slavery when, in his February address and on later occasions, he argued that, "Slavery has within itself the seeds of its own dissolution. Keep it within given limits, let it remain where it now is, and in time it will wear itself out." Endorsing a widespread belief that slavery must expand or die, he argued that as slaveholders drove their slaves they wore out the land: "Slave labor exhausts and makes barren the fields it cultivates. Crop follows crop, until the fertility of the soil is exhausted" and "the old fields abandoned." Thus the planter must seek "new and virgin soil, or release his slaves." If the institution were contained within its present boundaries, these practices "will at no distant day put an end to slavery and its concomitant evils." Other-

20. Polk, January 4, 5, 1847, in Quaife, ed., *Diary of James K. Polk*, 2:306, 308; *National Era*, January 7, 1847.
21. *Congressional Globe*, 29th Cong., 2nd sess., Appendix, 352–5.

wise, "the slave becomes valueless and emancipation of necessity follows." Nowhere did he mention the moral issue of slavery; nowhere did he refer to slaves as human beings who shared the concerns of all humanity. Rather, he concluded: "The unlimited extension and eternal perpetuation of slavery has become the leading if not the '*one idea*' of the South." In order "to perpetuate slavery for all coming time, its limits must be extended as the slave population increases."[22] Taking Wilmot's reasoning to its logical conclusion, adoption of the Proviso principle and its application to all territories where slavery did not already exist would be the first step toward eventual abolition, a step clearly in the interests of his small farmer constituents.

In attempting to preserve territories free of slavery, Wilmot emphasized that he argued in behalf of his own constituents and all free farmers and workers throughout the North, rather than the cause of the slave. Suggesting he had no "morbid sympathy for the slave," instead he pled "the cause of the rights of white freemen. I would preserve for free white labor a fair country, a rich inheritance where the sons of toil of my own race and own color, can live without the disgrace which association with negro slavery brings upon free labor." He concluded that "where the negro slave labors, the free white man cannot labor by his side without sharing his degradation and disgrace." Nor could Pennsylvania farmers compete with the slaveowners themselves in such territories. In a harsh comment attributed to him years later, he noted: "men born and nursed of white women are not going to be ruled by men who were nursed on the milk of some damn negro wench!"[23] Such views were clearly at odds with those of most abolitionists, those in this study and in the larger antislavery community. His approach showed a belief in racial superiority common in the nineteenth century, an attitude bereft of a moral sense or at least one of empathy to the plight of African Americans. Wilmot himself viewed containment as a significant step toward eventual abolition, but for reasons shared only by his faction of antislavery advocates. Having once fought against the monied Whig banking aristocracy as a Jacksonian Democrat, he now fought against the Slave Power—a landed aristocracy based on slave labor. Should he and his northern allies succeed in halting its spread, slavery would die and the opportunities for free labor expand. In this sense, he was still the Jacksonian populist representing small farmer interests against those of large farmers, especially slaveholders.

22. Ibid.; *National Era*, October 21, 1847. See also Earle, "Undaunted Democracy," 367–8.

23. *Congressional Globe*, 29th Cong., 2nd sess., Appendix, 314, 352–5; Going, *Wilmot*, 166–7, 175 n.

Wilmot was not in agreement with the growing Northern Whig contingent in the House who argued that going to war with Mexico had been a mistake. Rather, he believed the war to be "just and necessary," and had consistently voted for Polk's requests for the supplies and men to wage it. As a Democrat, he shared the expansionist vision which many Whigs rejected. But his support of the Proviso with allies like King made him, in the eyes of the president and party leaders, "an idle schemer" and "a disrupter of the party." Again, the northern-dominated House agreed with him, and in mid-February passed the bill with the Proviso included by a vote of 115 to 106.[24]

By now southerners of both parties were fully alarmed, and four days later John C. Calhoun offered resolutions in the Senate defining his section's position. Congress, he argued, "has no right to make any law" by which any state "shall be deprived of its full and equal right in any territory of the United States, acquired or to be acquired." Moreover, any such law which might "deprive the citizens of any of the States of this Union from emigrating with their property into any of the territories of the United States . . . would be a violation of the constitution and the rights of the States from which such citizens emigrated."[25] Although the Senate took no action on Calhoun's resolutions, southerners had in effect declared that the territories were jointly owned by the states, and slaveholders had the right to bring their slave property to any such region. The issue as presented by both Calhoun and Wilmot had more to do with property rights than human rights.

The Senate then approved the $3 million bill without the slave restriction. As the two bodies wrestled to resolve their differences, Wilmot again tried to amend the Senate proposal by adding his Proviso, to be applied now to *all* new territories, not just those to be acquired from Mexico. This time, however, he failed to win approval, and the House accepted the Senate version. The narrow margin in support of restriction had disappeared, with seven northern Democrats now opposed and six others not voting. Polk got his appropriation, perhaps as one critic suggested, because the administration had been "strong enough with its persuasions of its patronage" to convince wavering Democrats.[26] The president apparently had the needed votes without the antislavery faction, which he omitted from patronage considerations.

24. Going, *Wilmot*, 158; *Congressional Globe*, 29th Cong., 2nd sess., 303, 352.

25. *Congressional Globe*, 29th Cong., 2nd sess., 455; Morrison, *The Wilmot Proviso Controversy*, 34–5.

26. *Congressional Globe*, 29th Cong., 2nd sess., 367, 573; Going, *Wilmot*, 227; Morrison, *The Wilmot Proviso Controversy*, 37.

But if Congress had rejected the Proviso, Wilmot and his colleagues had succeeded in thrusting it into the center of a major national debate, where it would remain for the next three years.

Following the adjournment of Congress, maneuvering for the next presidential election began in earnest. Due to his sudden prominence, Wilmot would be central in the actions of northern antislavery Democrats. He had moved beyond his earlier role as an expedient, loyal politician to that of a risk-taking leader acting on a bigger stage than his Pennsylvania district. The Van Buren Democrats of New York, now calling themselves Barnburners, set the tone in the fall of 1847 as they struggled to win control of the state party organization and block their bitter rivals, the proslavery faction known as the Hunkers, led by Polk's secretary of war, William Marcy.[27] Unable to win control in a September party meeting, the Barnburners met separately in Herkimer, New York, in late October to rally support. Appropriately, David Wilmot addressed the body, forcefully outlining his role in the Proviso agitation and urging on the delegates in their efforts to seek party rejection of Hunker proslavery principles.[28]

By late 1847 those Hunker concepts were embodied in the proposal of Senator Lewis Cass of Michigan, who urged a doctrine known as popular sovereignty. As it related to territorial slavery, it would place the issue of slavery in the hands of the residents of each territory acting through their territorial legislatures. In effect, it would block the congressional ban on territorial slavery through the Wilmot Proviso as well as the constitutional protection for slavery as advocated by Calhoun and other southerners. As positions in North and South hardened, Wilmot and his Barnburner colleagues sought to convince elder statesman Martin Van Buren to be their presidential candidate on a Wilmot Proviso platform.[29] Should they be unable to persuade the Democratic party convention to approve their platform and candidate, bolting the Democrats to form a separate antislavery party might be the only way to maintain their principles.

27. The New York Democratic factions had received their nicknames as their feud had developed. Critics called the Van Burenites Barnburners after the Dutch farmer who supposedly burned down his barn to rid it of rats. In a similar manner, they claimed they were willing to destroy the party to achieve their antislavery principles. In contrast, the Hunkers were said to be those who "hunkered" after Polk's patronage. See Blue, *The Free Soilers,* 28, 31.

28. For Wilmot's speech, see Gardiner, *The Great Issue,* 59.

29. Wilmot to King, September 25, 1847, Wilmot to Martin Van Buren, October 6, 1847, in Going, *Wilmot,* 318–20. See Morrison, *The Wilmot Proviso Controversy,* 75–92, for a fuller account of these events.

Following the Herkimer meeting in October 1847, congressional responsibilities forced Wilmot to remain inactive in political gatherings and strategy sessions. Congress convened in December 1847, and remained in session until late the next summer. For the most part, Wilmot stayed in Washington, conscientious and dedicated to his duties and to the needs of his constituents. In March 1848 he went to Harrisburg to the state party convention, where the Buchanan-dominated meeting rejected endorsement of the Proviso. In May, he attended the Democratic national convention in Baltimore as a spectator and watched in dismay as the delegates rejected the claims of the Barnburners to be the sole representatives of New York Democrats. Equally disheartening was the party's refusal to endorse the Proviso and its nomination of popular sovereignty candidate Lewis Cass. He applauded as the Barnburners walked out and organized a meeting in late June in Utica— the first step in the formation of the Free Soil party. Earlier, he had returned home briefly at the time of the tragic death of his twelve-year-old son, Clarence, due to food poisoning. House duties kept him in Washington as Free Soil delegates gathered in Buffalo on August 9. There, antislavery Whigs (led by the Massachusetts faction known as Conscience Whigs), Barnburners, and Liberty men joined to endorse his Proviso and nominate the Free Soil ticket of Martin Van Buren and Charles Francis Adams.[30] If he could not be present, he stood ready to campaign for the ticket when Congress adjourned in August.

In Congress, Wilmot continued his attacks on slaveholders and their aristocratic institution. Early in the session he proposed a direct tax on property to help finance the war. It was a pure Jacksonian measure directed against all forms of capital property, that of both wealthy northern and southern property owners. But the tax angered southerners most, and they reacted in fury against what they perceived as a scheme that would tax planters most heavily for their slave property. Neither side reflected any awareness that human beings were involved as well as property interests. Administration officials saw it as an "idle scheme," and southerners in Congress described it as a "second Proviso," and as "*another* firebrand." Wilmot responded that he did not know "why a few thousand capitalists of the South who hold a certain species of property, should be exempt from taxation." Rather, he intended only "to exempt the humble laborer of the country from any portion of this tax." Wilmot's populist language might have appealed to struggling farmers and workers in his district, but it offered little to African Americans,

30. See Blue, *The Free Soilers*, 44–80; Going, *Wilmot*, 316–7.

few of whom lived in northeastern Pennsylvania. He attributed the abuse on him for his proposal as coming not just from southerners, but from a "scheming, ambitious candidate" for the presidency, Secretary of State James Buchanan.[31] While Wilmot's tax proposal found few supporters in the House, he did help to unmask further Buchanan's thinly disguised quest for a presidential nomination later in the year. Several weeks later, Democrats chose someone equally opposed to the Proviso in Lewis Cass.

With his party's rejection of the Proviso in mind and on the eve of the Free Soil gathering in Buffalo, on August 3, Wilmot delivered a blistering attack on the Democratic party and in defense of his principles. The contest between Cass and Buchanan centered around which candidate could be more subservient to the Slave Power: "The Presidency, in fact, was held up to the highest northern bidder, and the humiliating spectacle presented to the world of an ignominious rivalship between the leading men of the North in a race of subserviency to southern demands." Attacking Cass's popular sovereignty concept, he noted that territories possessed no "inherent political sovereignty" allowing them to decide on slavery. Rather, with the precedent of the Northwest Ordinance of 1787 and Missouri Compromise of 1820, the federal government had "exercised full and exclusive sovereignty over its territories." While the Cass doctrine had a populist aspect in it, small farmers, said Wilmot, needed federal government protection which the Proviso offered and popular sovereignty circumvented. Again, he reminded his colleagues of his belief that slavery in the states was "sacred from Federal interference; but the soil of freedom must not be invaded . . . by the direct action of this Government, nor by its utterance and silent acquiescence. Slavery has its abiding place, and freedom its home. Let the limits of each be sacredly observed. Here is the true compromise."[32] Antislavery Whigs and Democrats followed Wilmot's lead in support of the Proviso throughout the session, but to no avail, for southerners were fully prepared and had lined up sufficient northern Democratic allies to block it. As a young Whig representative from Illinois, Abraham Lincoln, later noted: "The Wilmot Proviso, or the principle of it, was constantly coming up in some shape or other. I think . . . I voted for it at least forty times during the short time I was there."[33]

---

31. *Congressional Globe*, 30th Cong., 1st sess., 304ff.

32. *Congressional Globe*, 30th Cong., 1st sess., Appendix, 1076ff.

33. Lincoln, Speech at Peoria, October 16, 1854, in Basler, ed., *The Collected Works of Abraham Lincoln*, 2:252.

Long before Congress adjourned in mid-August of 1848, all three party nominations were in place, and Wilmot rushed home, first to campaign for his own reelection and then to add his voice in Van Buren's behalf. Unlike his 1846 campaign, when the Proviso was rarely mentioned in the furor over his tariff vote, it was now the central issue. Wilmot had become a significant political leader. Buchanan forces were powerless to block his renomination by antislavery advocates in his northern Pennsylvania district, but dissident Democrats did choose their own candidate. Yet Wilmot campaigned as a Proviso Democrat rather than as a Free Soiler. Party labels were too strong for him to seek election as a Free Soiler, as at least twenty candidates did in districts throughout other parts of the North. More than half of them succeeded, but he feared that he might lose the votes of some of his constituents who might misinterpret his party-jumping. His concern was both as a practical politician seeking the best way to protect his political base and as an antislavery advocate angered by his party's proslavery stance.

As a Democrat, Wilmot easily won reelection in October, gaining 60 percent of the popular vote over Whig and Buchanan candidates. That accomplished, he did not hesitate to campaign vigorously for Free Soiler Martin Van Buren for the presidency. He spoke more than twenty-five times, both in his own district and throughout New York. Van Buren and the Proviso were synonymous in his eyes. He noted in late October: "I stand now where I have stood from the day I heard of the nomination of Mr. Van Buren at Utica—his firm and uncompromising supporter."[34] Liberty and Conscience Whig factions might regret the former president's nomination, but antislavery Democrats were pleased. Van Buren won only 10 percent of the national vote in 1848, as the country was not yet ready for a third-party appeal to the Wilmot Proviso. In New York, Free Soilers won 26 percent of the vote and helped Whig candidate Zachary Taylor to victory by denying Cass the support of many Democrats. But the Buchanan-Cass influence was much firmer among Democrats in Pennsylvania, and Free Soilers had little impact. There they won only 3 percent of the statewide presidential vote, proving the practicality of Wilmot's decision to seek reelection as a Democrat. Of Van Buren's meager eleven thousand Pennsylvania votes, more than three thousand came from Wilmot's district, a total which was only one-third of what Wilmot received in his October election. His appeal to his district's voters, combining the Proviso with the economic interests of small farmers and workers, was a strong one, but one which did not extend to significant num-

34. Wilmot to E. O. Goodrich, October 30, 1848, in Going, *Wilmot*, 266–7, 327.

bers in the state as a whole. Van Buren's vote in Wilmot's district was more than 26 percent of the state Free Soil total and far in excess of any other part of the state. Even in Jane Swisshelm's Allegheny County, Van Buren received less than 5 percent.[35] Wilmot's outspoken defense of the Proviso had persuaded his constituents to retain him in Congress, but most preferred to remain within the two-party system.

During the second session of the Thirtieth Congress, which convened in December 1848, Wilmot revealed again his devotion to containment but hesitated to embrace a frontal assault on slavery in the District of Columbia. The Free Soil party had been firm in its belief that Congress should abolish slavery in Washington, where it clearly had jurisdiction, even though the congressmen of the surrounding slave states of Virginia and Maryland feared it could become a haven for fugitives and, along with other southerners in Congress, were united in opposition. Even Free Soil candidate Martin Van Buren had hedged when asked his views on his party's platform. Some Free Soilers like Wilmot preferred merely to prohibit the slave trade there while leaving slavery intact.[36] Early in the session, Joshua Giddings, Free Soiler from Ohio, introduced a bill to hold a referendum on slavery among District residents. Because Giddings's bill would have allowed African Americans there to vote on the issue, Wilmot offered it "my strong repugnance," preferring only the "legal and qualified voters" to participate, a populist stance which reflected his resistance to extending rights to African Americans. Yet when southerners attempted to table and thus kill the bill, Wilmot voted in the 105–79 minority. His position was complex but consistent. He clearly opposed the slave trade in the District, arguing that it should be "prohibited at once—cut up root and branch," because "slave pens are erected within sight of the Capitol and all the disgusting details of the business exposed to view before the Nation and the world." To him, the inhumanity of slavery was less important than what others would think. But he would not support slavery's abolition there, arguing instead for "gradual emancipation, so founded as that no injustice should be done individual and private interests."[37] Wilmot bitterly opposed the slave trader and his traffic, but could understand the plight of the slaveholder. The plight of slaves and free blacks

35. For an analysis of the Free Soil vote, see Blue, *The Free Soilers,* 140–5; Going, *Wilmot,* 277; Earle, "Undaunted Democracy," 389.

36. For the Van Buren and Free Soil party position on slavery in the District of Columbia, see Blue, *The Free Soilers,* 74–5, 105–6.

37. *Congressional Globe,* 30th Cong., 2nd sess., 56, 84, 107, 416; Wilmot to *Bradford Reporter* (Towanda, Pa.), January 24, 1849.

living in the District was of less concern to him and to his constituents. Not surprisingly, the House failed to resolve the issue.

When Congress began consideration of the more pressing issue of territorial organization for California and the rest of the area recently acquired from Mexico, Wilmot showed his usual determination to see the territories organized with slavery prohibited. Ohio Free Soiler Joseph Root introduced the Proviso for the California and New Mexico territorial bills. Some, like the president, feared that if Congress remained deadlocked, those areas, possibly even including Oregon, might attempt to form a new Pacific nation.[38] Northerners of all three parties in Congress called his bluff and approved the Proviso by a solid majority in December. In February, with the matter still pending, Wilmot and the president bitterly attacked each other over Proviso strategy. Wilmot argued that Polk, in 1846, had been prepared to accept the Proviso, while the chief executive assailed the Pennsylvanian in his diary: "The baseness of Wilmot in this matter cannot be adequately described." In this charged atmosphere, Polk waited as his term expired in early March 1849, prepared to veto any bill with the Proviso included: "I took with me also to the Capitol a veto message of the Wilmot Proviso should any bill containing it be presented to me."[39] But the Senate refused to accept the House bill, and Congress adjourned, still deadlocked. The matter was thus left to the new president and a new Congress which would not convene until December.

The Thirtieth Congress had adjourned amidst signs of increased North-South tensions, and before its successor could convene, events in the West had made a settlement of the dispute all the more urgent. The discovery of gold in California had brought eighty thousand people to the region by the end of 1849, and Congress could no longer postpone territorial organization there. Agitation on slavery and the slave trade in the District of Columbia had intensified as well. Yet the new House of Representatives faced a crisis partly of Free Soil's making, leaving it temporarily unable to organize and · elect a speaker. Wilmot stood in the center of this latest controversy. With 12 Free Soil members along with 111 Democrats and 107 Whigs, neither of the major parties could get the required absolute majority to choose a speaker without Free Soil support. Democrats supported Howell Cobb of Georgia, Whigs, Robert Winthrop of Massachusetts, and Free Soilers, their most prominent spokesman, David Wilmot. In the initial balloting, party

38. Quaife, ed., *Diary of James K. Polk,* December 12, 13, 1848, 4:231, 233.
39. Ibid., 4:341, 364; *Congressional Globe,* 30th Cong., 2nd sess., 139.

lines held firmly, and the third party prevented a decision. The House could transact no business, the Senate marked time, and President Taylor held back his annual message.[40] Throughout the protracted balloting, Wilmot, the expedient politician who had never officially left the Democratic party, acted in every way as a Free Soiler. He told friends that if Democrats proscribed him "for my opinions, I will proscribe him [Cobb] for his opinions on the subject of slavery." Any northern Democrat who gave in and supported Cobb would succumb to "the tyranny of the South."[41] Third-party members appeared determined to maintain unity to prevent the choice of slaveholder Cobb or a Northern Whig like Winthrop who had consistently fought antislavery goals.

As balloting continued, Cobb's support among Democrats began to fall dramatically, and in his place William J. Brown of Indiana gained strength. On the fortieth ballot, Brown's 112 votes were only two short of the required majority. Among his supporters were Wilmot and five other Free Soilers, including former Whig Joshua Giddings. Immediately, southerners became suspicious and forced Brown to read aloud his pledge to Wilmot to include Free Soilers on key House committees. Brown quickly withdrew from the contest, and Free Soilers found themselves under attack from all sides.[42] Equally distressing, several Free Soilers of Whig background, led by George Washington Julian of Indiana, withheld their support of Brown. They thus prevented his election, and charged that the Indiana Democrat had consistently opposed the Proviso and other Free Soil priorities. Wilmot defended the arrangement, saying that "the particular men who should be placed on these committees" had not been stipulated; instead Free Soilers sought only those "who would not stifle the expression of the sentiments of the people of the North." He added that southerners in the past had sought and received similar guarantees from northern candidates concerning slavery.[43] But no amount of explaining could free Wilmot and his Free Soil colleagues of charges of political bargaining even though they had merely followed the examples of their critics.

---

40. *National Era*, December 6, 13, 1849; *Congressional Globe*, 31st Cong., 1st sess., 1–15; Blue, *Free Soilers*, 191–2.

41. Wilmot to Ulysses Mercur, December 3, 10, 1849, in Going, *Wilmot*, 355.

42. *Congressional Globe*, 31st Cong., 1st sess., 16–22; *National Era*, December 20, 1849; Brown to Wilmot, December 10, 1849, Wilmot to Brown, December 19, 1849, in Going, *Wilmot*, 361–2.

43. *Congressional Globe*, 31st Cong., 1st sess., 20–2; Going, *Wilmot*, 360–4.

Unable to sustain unity among themselves, the Free Soilers suffered further as the House finally elected its speaker. After twenty more ballots, Democrats pushed through a plurality rule over Whig opposition, and on the sixty-third ballot Cobb defeated Winthrop, 102–99, with Free Soilers still loyal to Wilmot.[44] Third-party members, in refusing to support Winthrop, thus allowed slaveholder Cobb to be chosen, subjecting themselves to charges of permitting the worse of two evils. Yet Winthrop, who had consistently opposed the Proviso, left them little choice. Despite the abuse Whigs subjected them to, Free Soilers were not totally without influence in the new committee structure which Cobb established. Giddings would serve on the Committee on Territories and Charles Allen of Massachusetts on the District of Columbia committee. Not surprisingly, Wilmot received a less significant post, that of the Committee on Claims.[45] Still, overall, the party fared better than it might have from Winthrop. In the efforts to find a compromise between North and South, Democrats and Whigs viewed Free Soilers with suspicion and disdain. Ostracized socially and denied any voice in the distribution of patronage, Free Soilers, including Wilmot, gathered weekly in the friendly atmosphere of the home of *National Era* editor Gamaliel Bailey. There they planned their strategy to fight for their Proviso and District of Columbia positions, knowing that it would be an uphill struggle.[46] In everything but party name, Wilmot had emerged as a Free Soil leader.

Congress began in earnest to deal with the crisis in January when Henry Clay presented his five-part Omnibus proposal in the Senate. It included the admission of California as a free state, thus skipping the territorial stage; territorial organization for New Mexico and Utah on a popular sovereignty basis; adjustment of the New Mexico–Texas boundary and assumption of the Texas debt by the federal government; abolition of the slave trade but not slavery in the District of Columbia; and a more stringent fugitive slave law. In the ensuing debates, the Senate would maintain the initiative with orators such as John C. Calhoun, Daniel Webster, Stephen A. Douglas, and William H. Seward dominating. In the House, Free Soilers pursued their antislavery principles with determination, but little impact. Wilmot presented close to fifty petitions, most of which were designed to contain slavery. He joined with Preston King in attempting to get the California bill with its antislavery constitution out of committee.[47] Occasionally, Free Soilers

44. *Congressional Globe,* 31st Cong., 1st sess., 63–6; *National Era,* December 20, 1849.
45. *Congressional Globe,* 31st Cong., 1st sess., 88–9.
46. Blue, *Free Soilers,* 196–7.
47. *Congressional Globe,* 31st Cong., 1st sess., Appendix, 511, 573–9.

were attacked by their proslavery critics. In defending himself and his district against the verbal abuse of a southern member, Wilmot accepted the term abolitionist for himself, but only "if it described those opposed to the extension of slavery." Repeating arguments he had urged ever since 1846, he called the extension of slavery "a political evil of the first magnitude." Slavery, he said was "aristocratic in all its tendencies and results— it is subversive to those great principles" which were "the foundation of all free Governments."[48] No longer a provincial Jacksonian Democrat, Wilmot had become a prominent Free Soil leader, although still loyal to the Jacksonian populist principle of equality of opportunity, so important to his constituents.

Wilmot offered little new to the nine-month debate, and in the end succeeded only in helping to delay passage of the separate parts of the Compromise of 1850. He was content when Congress finally admitted California "without condition," but disheartened with the victory of popular sovereignty over the Proviso in the Southwest. He found the District of Columbia settlement satisfactory, although many of his Free Soil colleagues had wished it to include complete abolition. And like many in the North, he found the Fugitive Slave Act a dangerous victory for the Slave Power, although he said little of its effect on the slaves themselves. He and his fellow Free Soilers had been unable to stop the trend toward compromise and could only regret the rejection of the Proviso. Wilmot, in fact, seeing that further resistance was futile, had rushed home to Pennsylvania in late August before the final votes occurred.[49] There he was engaged in the battle of his political life, for Buchanan Democrats were feverishly working to deny him renomination.

Wilmot knew early in 1850 that conservative Democrats were determined to bring him down. The *National Era* noted in February that Buchanan "and his creatures" viewed him as an obstacle to their man's presidential nomination. Arguing against substituting another Democrat, Wilmot contended that the Proviso principles "would be best promoted by my own reelection." Such an outcome, he said sincerely, "would carry with it an importance, far beyond any consideration due to my poor merits or talents as a man."[50] Yet it became clear that he could not survive the attacks of the Buchanan forces and their allies in his district. On the grounds that the nomination should go

48. Ibid., 31st Cong., 1st sess., Appendix, 511ff, 940ff.

49. Wilmot to F. D. Campbell, July 3, 1850, in Going, *Wilmot*, 420–1; see Blue, *Free Soilers*, 303, for the vote of other Free Soilers on each of the parts of the Compromise.

50. *National Era*, February 21, 1850; Wilmot to Horace Willey, August 15, 1850, in Going, *Wilmot*, 423–5.

to a Democrat from one of the counties in the district other than Wilmot's Bradford, he consoled himself by playing a key role in the choice of Galusha A. Grow of Susquehanna County, a former law partner who shared many of his principles. Grow was "a friend of the Proviso and of Freedom in the great struggle with the Slave Power." He was also a strong proponent of the homestead principle—the granting of federal land to small farmers—a concept that Wilmot had urged in Congress both because it would benefit his constituents and because it would help to keep slavery out of the territories. Grow won a narrow victory in the October election. Wilmot then completed his third and final term in the House in the uneventful second session of the Thirty-first Congress during the winter of 1850–1851. The Compromise spirit embraced moderates in both North and South, for the country as well as Pennsylvania Democrats had rejected Wilmot's policies and beliefs.[51]

Neither Wilmot nor his many supporters or detractors would have predicted that when he left Congress in March 1851 at age thirty-seven, after six years in Washington, his most significant years were behind him. He would serve as a Pennsylvania justice for the next decade and become active in Republican politics. In 1857 he ran unsuccessfully for governor, and he would be chosen for a two-year term in the U.S. Senate during the Civil War. But at no time did he regain the prominence he had enjoyed as the key advocate of the Wilmot Proviso in the 1840s. On leaving Congress and returning to private practice, he sought and received the Democratic party's nomination to be president judge of the Thirteenth District, comprised of Bradford and two other counties. When Whigs failed to nominate, he easily won election over an independent candidate and began a ten-year term at the end of 1851. Most of his Barnburner–Free Soil colleagues had long since returned to the Democratic fold as the Compromise spirit spread and their lack of influence in the two-party structure became obvious in early as 1849 and during the 1850 debates. Ever the practical politician, Wilmot had ceased attending Free Soil strategy sessions in Washington in 1850, so intent was he in regaining recognition from other congressmen as a Democrat. Political expediency had won out temporarily over antislavery principle. In 1852, the third party was reduced to its Conscience Whig and Liberty elements, many of whom Wilmot still distrusted due to their evangelical abolitionism. As a judge, Wilmot played little role in the presidential campaign

51. Wilmot to Constituents, September 27, 1850, in Going, *Wilmot*, 431–2, 423–36; Robert D. Ilesevich, *Galusha A. Grow, The People's Candidate* (Pittsburgh: Univ. of Pittsburgh Press, 1988), 34–5.

but did reject the Free Democratic ticket of John P. Hale and George W. Julian in favor of the Democratic pro-Compromise candidate, Franklin Pierce. He rationalized his support of Pierce, "not because we believe in him but because in our judgment it is the wisest course to prepare for the conflict which must come upon the extension of slavery in this country."[52] Free Soilers throughout the North could not help but feel that an important leader had defected from the antislavery cause. Wilmot believed otherwise, however, and, like other antislavery Democrats who had done the same, he could not long remain content in his old party.

When, in early 1854, Franklin Pierce fell in line behind Stephen A. Douglas's Kansas-Nebraska bill repealing the Missouri Compromise ban on slavery north of 36°30′ in favor of popular sovereignty, Wilmot was quick to denounce the president and the Douglas-wing of the party as "the mere tool and puppet of the Slave power." Admitting the error of his support of Pierce in 1852, he charged that "Freedom has been betrayed." Still, he said: "I am a democrat—deeply imbued with the doctrines of that political school," of Jacksonian democracy and its commitment to the goals of small farmers and workers. The party's past remained intact even though "this administration abused its name and principles" with this attempt "to prostitute the name and principles of democracy in its assaults upon the Constitution and liberties of the country." Because "Slavery demands entire submission to its policy as a condition of its support," it was time for antislavery Democrats to think of a more permanent break with the party than that of 1848.[53] This latest surrender of northern Democrats to the interests of the South was so dangerous as to cause Wilmot to question his lifetime commitment to the party of Andrew Jackson. Slave Power domination meant that he must find a new political home.

When the Kansas-Nebraska bill became law in May 1854, there followed two years of political turmoil that would result in the slow, agonizing death of the Whig party, while in the North two new parties, the Republican and the American, struggled to replace it. Having made his decision to bolt the Democrats, Wilmot played an active role in Republican formation, only partially restrained by his judicial position. Buchanan Democrats, furious with his role, sought unsuccessfully to limit his influence and even force his removal as judge. As the state legislature deadlocked over the choice of a senator in 1855, Wilmot received insufficient support, and while he professed

---

52. *National Era*, April 4, 1850; Going, *Wilmot*, 443.
53. Wilmot to *Bradford Reporter*, June 29, 1854.

not to be "eager for senatorial honors," it was clear he would have gladly accepted had it been offered. During the summer of 1855, he spoke frequently at political gatherings denouncing the aggressions of slavery as perpetrated by the Democrats and helped organize the state Republican party. Delegates chose him to chair the party at the state convention in Pittsburgh in September.[54]

In 1856, Wilmot redoubled his efforts as the new party organized for its first campaign for the presidency. In February, delegates from all of the free states met in Pittsburgh to plan for a nominating convention in Philadelphia in June. Party leaders chose Wilmot as the Pennsylvania representative on the party's executive committee. Before that meeting, he urged Pennsylvanians to unite to rescue the government "from the domination of an aristocracy founded upon property in slaves" which "threatens a war of extermination against the peaceful settlers of Kansas." Again his concern was the wealthy slaveholder interests which blocked the legitimate interests of small farmers. In Philadelphia, Wilmot chaired the platform committee and authored the plank which denied "the authority of Congress, of a Territorial legislature . . . to give legal existence to Slavery in any Territory."[55] He joined in enthusiastic support of party nominee John C. Frémont and urged the delegates to make his nomination unanimous. Wilmont himself was among several whom delegates considered for vice president, a group which also included Lincoln and Charles Sumner. They eventually chose William L. Dayton of New Jersey. In the summer and fall, Wilmot pushed judicial duties aside as he campaigned for Frémont throughout the state. James Buchanan, however, was too strong a candidate in his native state, given his powerful machine there, and while Frémont won a large majority in Wilmot's district, Democrats gave their man the state's electoral vote.[56] Still, the Republicans had made a strong showing in their first national race, and Buchanan would face their determined opposition in Congress. For his part, David Wilmot would continue to urge the Republican antislavery agenda in 1857 by seeking the governorship.

Running for governor in a Democratic-controlled state, the home of President Buchanan, was a thankless task. Yet despite misgivings, Wilmot accepted the nomination, determined to make the president's proslave Kansas

---

54. Wilmot to B. Laporte, January 22, 1855, in Going, *Wilmot*, 466, 469–77.

55. Wilmot to Friends of Freedom in Pennsylvania, March 15, 1856, in Going, *Wilmot*, 480–2; Johnson and Porter, eds., *National Party Platforms*, 27.

56. For Wilmot's role in the 1856 campaign, see Going, *Wilmot*, 478–94.

policy the key issue, rather than state matters. In his acceptance he noted: "The repeal of the Missouri restriction and the attempt to force Slavery upon Kansas by fraud and violence" involved "a conflict between the antagonistic systems of free and servile labor." It centered on "the independence, dignity and rights of the free white laboring man and his posterity. Slavery is the deadly enemy of free labor." Clearly, such a populist appeal was of greater significance to Pennsylvania farmers and workers than any issue of merely state relevance which Democrats might choose to raise. Not surprisingly, Democratic candidate William F. Packer declined Wilmot's offer that "we canvass so much of the State as is practicable, in company, addressing alternately the same meetings."[57] Wilmot did temporarily resign his judicial post to campaign, with the understanding that he would regain his seat should he lose. He spoke in more than forty locations between late August and the October election, but had little chance, as the well-oiled Buchanan machine sold its candidate to the voters by, among other things, reminding them of Wilmot's opposition to protective tariffs. Although he won his own district by thirty-five hundred votes, he lost the state by forty-two thousand; a third-party, American or Know-Nothing candidate cut further into Wilmot's total. Especially telling was his failure in Philadelphia, where he received less than 25 percent of the vote.[58]

While Buchanan forces celebrated Wilmot's defeat, they would not be fully satisfied until he was permanently removed from the bench as well. Thus in early 1858 they began impeachment proceedings, charging him with partisanship and favoritism. The Democratic-controlled legislative committee charged that he "frequently makes political speeches during Court week, that he is unfair to his political opponents in his political intercourse and partial to his friends." Even worse, "the due administration of justice is interfered with by the President Judge's partisan proclivities." Little hard evidence could be found to back such charges, and following Wilmot's able and forceful defense before a joint judiciary committee in late March the matter died. But not before Democrats tried one more tactic, also unsuccessfully, to abolish Wilmot's judicial district and combine it with those nearby. However unpopular he might have been with Buchanan Democrats, he retained the support of his constituents, who chose him again for the judicial seat in the

---

57. Wilmot to J. S. Bowen et al., April 22, 1857, Wilmot to Packer, July 14, 1857, Packer to Wilmot, July 27, 1857, in Going, *Wilmot*, 497–503, 505–6.

58. Ibid., 508, 513.

general election that fall.[59] Wilmot did keep his political leanings separate from his judicial role, even though he worked strenuously for Republican causes when not in court. Clearly, however, his heart was in antislavery politics, and as the momentous presidential election of 1860 approached, it was only a matter of time before he would leave the bench and return full-time to elective politics.

The first step in that direction came in February 1860, when the state Republican party convention chose Wilmot as an at-large delegate to the Chicago nominating convention. In Chicago, he became temporary president and thus delivered the keynote address. The speech was an emotional attack on the Slave Power: "Whose rights are safe where slavery has the power to trample them under foot?" There was more freedom in the empire of Russia or the "despotism of Austria," said Wilmot, than "within the limits of the slave States of this Republic." Having helped arouse the delegates with his passionate oratory, Wilmot watched as the principles of the Proviso became part of the platform. He was also instrumental in the decision of the Pennsylvania delegation to switch to Lincoln on the critical third ballot. The delegates were pledged to Simon Cameron and John McLean on the first two ballots, but Wilmot convinced many to turn to Lincoln on the deciding vote. On his return home, he campaigned strenuously for the Republican ticket of Lincoln for president and Andrew Curtin for governor. The latter's margin of victory was thirty-two thousand, while Lincoln carried the state by sixty thousand; each received large majorities in Wilmot's district.[60] The former Buchanan stronghold had turned Republican, and Wilmot was in position to play a key role in the new Lincoln administration.

Following the November 1860 election, weeks of deliberation and intrigue ensued as to the makeup of the Lincoln cabinet. There was little doubt that Wilmot was high on the president-elect's list, and many assumed that he would be the Pennsylvania representative among Lincoln's advisors in thanks for his loyal support and for having helped deliver the state's electoral votes to the Republican column. Thus, Wilmot joined the pilgrimage of countless prominent party leaders to Springfield for the obligatory interview with the president-elect. After consultations lasting more than five hours, he returned to Towanda with an apparent promise of a cabinet position in hand. The situation became more complex, however, when Simon Cameron

59. Ibid., 518, 523–6.
60. Ibid., 529–31, 540–1. For the Republican platform of 1860, see Johnson and Porter, eds., *National Party Platforms*, 31–3.

arrived to press his claims and convinced Lincoln that he rather than Wilmot should represent the state. Although Lincoln delayed the announcement of the more conservative Cameron to head the War Department until early March, it was clear much earlier that Wilmot had been displaced by his bitter rival. This despite a vigorous effort by Governor Curtin, Thaddeus Stevens, and Wilmot himself to press his claims over Cameron. The outcome was strongly rumored when the Republican-controlled state legislature met in January to choose a senator for a full six-year term. Cameron again flexed his political muscles and helped to secure the choice of his close supporter Edgar Cowan over Wilmot, who again learned the price of having made many enemies even among fellow Republicans. In part, conservatives and moderates in the party found his containment policy too aggressive an attack on slavery to suit them; in part it was pure political infighting between rival Republican factions. Thus it was somewhat ironic when in March 1861, upon Cameron's resignation of his Senate seat to join the Lincoln cabinet, the legislature chose Wilmot to fill the remaining two years of his term.[61] Whether or not his election was a consolation prize, he would be in Congress to vote into law the Proviso he had first advocated fifteen years earlier.

In the interregnum, while the cabinet and Senate choices were pending, Wilmot agreed to be a part of the Pennsylvania delegation to the Washington Peace Conference, which convened in early February. Chaired by former president John Tyler of Virginia, the conference had little chance of success. Seven southern states sent no delegates; having already decided to secede, their delegates instead attended the convention in Montgomery, Alabama, where the Confederacy was born. Many Republicans were skeptical, and only twelve states sent delegates to the peace conference. There were some prominent Republicans present, however, including Salmon P. Chase of Ohio, who Lincoln was about to appoint treasury secretary. The meeting was dominated by southern unionists and their moderate northern allies. They were influenced most by the plan of Senator John Crittenden, Democrat of Kentucky, whose compromise proposals included a constitutional amendment guaranteeing slavery in the existing slave states and extending the old Missouri Compromise 36°30′ line west to the Pacific, guaranteeing slavery south of the line and prohibiting it north. The Crittenden plan had already been killed in the Senate in mid-January, indicating that no compromise had much chance of success.

61. For the struggle to fill Lincoln's cabinet, see David Potter, *Lincoln and His Party in the Secession Crisis* (New Haven, Conn.: Yale Univ. Press, 1942), 146–55; for Wilmot's role, see Going, *Wilmot*, 543–54.

While the majority of the Pennsylvania delegation accepted the plan, Wilmot among key Republicans vehemently rejected it. As he told the delegates: "The issue was formed—Slavery or Freedom," during the recent election, and Lincoln's victory had settled it: "Any substantial change in the fundamental principles of government [such as legalizing slavery] is revolutionary. Yours may be a peaceable one, but it is still a revolution. The seceded States are in armed revolution. You are in direct alliance with them." Despite their efforts to "entrench slavery behind the Constitution," men of principle must give an emphatic no: "The Government has long been administered in the interest of slavery. The fixed determination of the North is, that this shall be no longer." The proposed Crittenden Compromise also called for ending congressional authority over the District of Columbia by making emancipation there dependent on Virginia's and Maryland's approval. Again, Wilmot was emphatic in his opposition, adding: "I hope to see slavery abolished in the District." Having opposed abolition in the District a decade earlier, Wilmot now reversed himself in light of southern secession and the likelihood of war, more than out of direct concern for slaves living there. Both the Crittenden and the peace conference proposals were rejected again in the dying days of the Thirty-sixth Congress. And when Lincoln and the new Congress rejected the proposals, the Senate by a 28–7 margin, Wilmot could look ahead to a different tone when the new administration assumed office in early March.[62] In the Senate Wilmot would find his views more in tune with the majority than he had at the peace conference.

As a member of Congress, Wilmot's undistinguished role was characterized by firm support of Lincoln's war policies. Rejecting the hardline stand of Radicals such as Benjamin Wade, George Julian, and Owen Lovejoy, Wilmot endorsed those measures which gradually weakened slavery rather than those which would have moved against it more aggressively. He arrived in March for the final ten days of the Thirty-sixth Congress and returned on July 4 for the new Congress convened by the president to face the secession and war crises. There Wilmot found old friends from the Proviso days, including Senators Preston King of New York and John P. Hale of New Hampshire, and Vice President Hannibal Hamlin of Maine. Newer colleagues, elected since he had left office, included Radicals such as Wade of Ohio and Charles Sumner of Massachusetts. Wilmot was appointed to the Foreign Relations committee chaired by Sumner. Illness kept him absent during much

62. Potter, *Lincoln and His Party*, 107–10, 171, 302; *Congressional Globe*, 36th Cong., 2nd sess., 112–4, 409, 1261, 1405.

of the session, but he returned in apparent renewed health in January 1862 and voted with Republicans in expelling several of their Senate colleagues for pro-Confederate sympathies, men he identified with the elitist, aristocratic slave system. They included John Breckenridge of Kentucky and Jesse Bright of Indiana.[63] Of more lasting significance were congressional decisions weakening slavery.

Throughout the first eight and a half months of 1862, Congress and the president jockeyed for position on the slavery issue. Before Lincoln issued his Preliminary Proclamation of Emancipation on September 22 which would free slaves behind Confederate lines as of January 1, 1863, the Republican-controlled Congress had enacted several measures weakening slavery and in some ways going further than the president. In each instance, Wilmot played an enthusiastic, if secondary, role. Ever the populist, he argued in committee that slaveholders, by their rebellion, had forfeited all claims to their slave property. Defending the confiscation concept, he maintained that those who opposed it "offer a premium to disloyalty and treason." Continuing to reflect the concerns of small farmers and workers rather than the slaves themselves, he continued, "We can never crush this rebellion except by laying our hands on the property of these slaveholders." In April, Congress approved a compensated emancipation plan for the District of Columbia. Even more significant to Wilmot, moreover, was the approval of his Proviso. Introduced in the House by Owen Lovejoy in May 1862, it passed the Senate on June 9, 28–10, and became law with the president's signature shortly after that.[64] Although no longer as critical an issue during a war dealing with slavery in the states, Wilmot could glory nonetheless in its passage, knowing that his 1846 proposal that "neither slavery nor involuntary servitude shall ever exist" in any territory of the United States had finally become law. In all of these issues he played a minor role, deferring instead to Senate Radicals like Sumner and Wade for leadership.

Much of the rest of Wilmot's life was anticlimactic. As his Senate term ended in early 1863, Pennsylvania Democrats, now in control of the legislature, denied him reelection. As a reward for his faithful Republican service, President Lincoln, in March 1863, immediately named him a judge on the newly created Court of Claims. He served with this court in Washington until his death at fifty-four in 1868. An effective and forceful orator, he preferred a relaxed and disorganized lifestyle and was a man of little personal discipline. Overweight because of his excessive appetite for food and alcohol, he cared little about his personal appearance and health, a factor which hastened his death. He was most significant in prewar years as a leading advocate of containing slavery, a principle he helped formulate with his Proviso and one which became the backbone of the Free Soil and Republican parties.

David Wilmot falls within the conservative end of the political, antislavery spectrum. His concern had always been for the free labor platform of Jacksonian Democracy—the interests of the small farmers and workers in his Pennsylvania district of farms and small towns. His brand of populism was a bridge between the original Jacksonian appeal and that of the 1890s. Equal opportunity for the common man meant economic individualism and a government that would protect such interests. Not strongly motivated by religious beliefs, he shared little of the moral concern over slavery and the rights of African Americans of most abolitionists, and in fact consistently opposed evangelical abolitionism. The issues which concerned and motivated Wilmot varied significantly from those of most others in the antislavery movement. Never an abolitionist before the war, his containment philosophy gave Republicans their key platform plank until he and the majority of the party moved with the president to abolition during the course of the bloodshed. Political antislavery for David Wilmot meant a course of moderation in behalf of small farmers and workers, yet one which helped point finally to slavery's destruction.

TEN

THE PLIGHT OF SLAVERY WILL COVER THE LAND

Benjamin and Edward Wade, Brothers in Antislavery Politics

RARELY IN AMERICAN history is it possible to find brothers so dedicated to the same cause as Benjamin and Edward Wade were in their opposition to slavery. Their personalities were sharply different and they suffered through periods of estrangement, in large part the result of differences on antislavery tactics. Yet they had much in common beyond their background and upbringing. Their early efforts as attorneys in northeast Ohio, their reconciliation in the mid-1850s, and their companion roles in the Republican party as it moved toward abolition during the Civil War suggests that a dual and comparative look at their careers is appropriate. Even though one went on to fame in the Senate during the war and Reconstruction and the other dropped out of Congress in 1861 and fell into relative obscurity, they were equally dedicated to the antislavery cause.

Such were the parallel lives of Benjamin and Edward Wade. They were born two years apart, Benjamin in October 1800 and Edward in November 1802, in western Massachusetts. When the Wade family relocated in Andover in Ohio's Western Reserve in 1821, the young brothers accompanied the family. Despite limited formal schooling, each studied law under the same nationally known attorney before admission to the bar and practice in Jefferson, Ohio. From there in the early 1830s, their careers diverged, with

Benjamin elected briefly to the Ohio legislature as an antislavery Whig while Edward quickly joined the abolitionist Liberty party. Benjamin would remain a Whig until the Republican party formed in 1854, while Edward pursued Liberty and Free Soil politics before becoming a Republican. Benjamin won election to the Senate as a Whig in 1851 and remained there as a Republican until denied reelection in 1868. During those years, he became a leading Radical, critical of both Presidents Abraham Lincoln and Andrew Johnson for what he believed was excessive leniency toward slavery and slaveholders. Edward was elected to the House in 1853 as a Free Democrat and served as a Republican until 1861, retiring due to poor health to return to his law practice. Their differences were intense and many during the years of estrangement, but with the help of colleague and friend Joshua Giddings, they reconciled and resumed their political ties, dedicated to the overthrow of slavery.[1] Theirs was truly a unique relationship and one that placed them in different yet similar places on the spectrum of political antislavery.

The Wade brothers joined antislavery parties more than a decade apart, yet had much in common in their ideologies. Both began their careers as Whigs, but Edward was the first to bolt, joining the Liberty party in 1842 and campaigning for James G. Birney for president in 1844. Benjamin, with an established position in the Whig party, stayed with that organization until it declined and disappeared in the mid-1850s. Edward signed the call for a new antislavery party in 1854, while Benjamin declined to add his name. Thus the latter's first role in an antislavery party was delayed until the Republicans became a part of the two-party system. He sought to protect his position as a senator first secured as a Whig in 1851, arguing that third-party membership would deny the movement a strong voice in Congress. Edward Wade fits in early in the leadership spectrum among those who were part of the Liberty party, while Benjamin was among the last to join an antislavery party. Yet, in his later years, he was among the most radical in pursuing abolition and racial equality during and after the war. The brothers shared a common hatred of slavery, and neither wavered in his intensity or desire to

1. For Benjamin Wade, see Hans L. Trefousse, *Benjamin Franklin Wade: Radical Republican from Ohio* (New York: Twayne, 1963); a laudatory biography was written by a friend, Albert G. Riddle, *The Life of Benjamin F. Wade* (Cleveland: William W. Williams, 1886); see also Trefousse, "Benjamin Franklin Wade," in *American National Biography*, 22:431–2. The more obscure Edward Wade is considered in brief entries in *Biographical Directory of the American Congress, 1774–1996*, comp. James L. Harrison (Alexandria, Va.: C. Q. Staff Directories, 1997), 1996, and William W. Williams, *History of Ashtabula County, Ohio* (Philadelphia: Williams Bros., 1878), 84–7.

thwart the Slave Power. Despite their personal and political differences, together they represent a total dedication to the destruction of slavery through the political process.

Benjamin and Edward were the youngest siblings in a struggling farm family of seven boys and four girls raised at Feeding Hills, near Springfield, Massachusetts. Their father, James, was a Revolutionary War veteran who, like his wife, Mary Upham, had Puritan ancestors. Benjamin and Edward, nicknamed Frank and Ned, received little formal education due to the family's poverty. They attended village schools during winter and worked at farm chores during the warmer months. Their mother provided them extensive instruction, but was often unable to impress her deeply held religious views on the rebellious boys; both remained outside of any organized religious sect for their entire lives. At least Benjamin held deist beliefs and refused to take the nonalcohol pledge expected in the family's Protestant congregation. As the older of the two boys, he was the natural leader and mentor for Edward. In 1820, four older siblings, Theodore, Charles, Samuel, and Nancy, broke with their Massachusetts heritage and followed many other New Englanders to the Western Reserve of Ohio. There they began farming on the 320-acre Wade homestead near Andover and teaching school in the winter. The following year, their parents and younger siblings joined them in an area of Ohio steeped in New England tradition. None ever returned to their birthplaces, although they remained dedicated to their Puritan and antislavery backgrounds.[2]

The two brothers followed similar paths during the 1820s, both farming while pursuing personal goals. Benjamin took a job as a cattle drover, taking a herd to Philadelphia in 1823, and received a wage of twelve dollars plus expenses for his efforts. Later he joined an Erie Canal work gang as a common laborer and then worked with an older brother, James, who was a doctor in Albany. He hoped for a law career, and due to his halting, stammering speech, received tutoring from Edward to help overcome his handicap. The younger brother, who had already written an arithmetic textbook, also planned to pursue law.[3] Together they clerked in the law offices of Whittlesey and Newton in Canfield in 1826. Elisha Whittlesey, the prominent National Republican congressman, had a reputation as the leading attorney and as the head of "the great private law school of Northern Ohio." Joshua Giddings had also studied under Whittlesey earlier and was soon to be Ben-

2. Trefousse, *Benjamin Wade*, 11–21; Riddle, *Benjamin Wade*, 39.
3. "Edward Wade," in Williams, *Ashtabula County*, 85.

jamin's law partner. Both Wades were quickly admitted to the Ohio bar and began practice in Jefferson, near the family home in Andover in the Lake Erie county of Ashtabula. Edward was elected a justice of the peace in 1831, married Louise Atkins in 1832, and became a prosecuting attorney the following year, living in various northern Ohio locations before settling in Cleveland in the late 1830s. Almost two decades after the death of his first wife, he married Mary B. Hall in 1852. Benjamin Wade remained in Jefferson and, because of his continued speech problems, mostly stayed in the office while Giddings did the court work. His first experience in court proved disastrous, becoming so red-faced and tongue-tied that he forgot what he wanted to say. Gradually overcoming his handicap, and with "a deep, raucous voice, his defiant laugh, and natural pugnaciousness," in time Wade became an effective attorney despite his often rude and unpolished manners.[4] The firm of Giddings and Wade quickly gained a reputation for effectiveness throughout the Reserve. By the mid-1830s, the Wade brothers appeared destined for bright futures in law, but they were also showing political interests.

Benjamin was the first to enter politics, and in running successfully for the state senate in 1837 he began a long career as a member of the Whig party, which dominated politics on the Reserve. By then his partnership with Giddings had ended and the two had become estranged and rivals in the courtroom. A bitter trial exchange in which Benjamin humiliated his former partner dissolved whatever friendship had remained. After Giddings won election to Congress as a Whig in 1837, Wade twice tried unsuccessfully to unseat him.[5] In the legislature Benjamin quickly revealed his pugnacious side and could not always remain loyal to his party's position even while faithful to its organization. It was the antislavery issue that exposed Wade's rebelliousness. On his arrival in Columbus, he immediately sought repeal of Ohio's discriminatory black laws, including the restriction against African Americans' presenting petitions to the legislature. As a member of an Ohio Senate committee looking into the annexation of Texas, he opposed adding more slave territory and recommended that the legislature pass strong anti-annexation resolutions based on the principles of the Declaration of Independence. Any hope of approval of his proposals ended in late 1838 when Ohio Democrats regained control of the legislature.[6] Nonetheless, in early

4. "Elisha Whittlesey," *Biographical Directory*, 2051; Trefousse, *Benjamin Wade*, 24; Riddle, *Benjamin Wade*, 81.

5. James B. Stewart, *Joshua R. Giddings and the Tactics of Radical Politics* (Cleveland: Case Western Reserve Univ. Press, 1970), 10, 16–7, 55, 95; Riddle, *Benjamin Wade*, 127–8.

6. *Ashtabula (Ohio) Sentinel*, January 27, 1838; Trefousse, *Benjamin Wade*, 30–3.

1839, black residents persuaded him to introduce their petition for a charter for their own school, a proposal which outraged legislators quickly shouted down and buried. He was also outspoken but unsuccessful in blocking legislative approval of a stringent state fugitive slave law designed to appease Kentucky slaveholders in the wake of an increasing tide of escapees crossing the Ohio River in search of freedom. In an impassioned speech, he noted: "Until the laws of nature and of nature's God are changed, I will never recognize the right of one man to hold his fellow man a slave. I loathe and abhor the cursed system; . . . this system of slavery is the foulest blot on our national escutcheon. . . . it is because I love and venerate my country, that I wish to wipe away this, her deepest and foulest stain."[7] It was a position that few of his antislavery constituents would find objectionable.

In seeking reelection to the state senate in 1839, Wade faced a coalition of Democrats and conservative Whigs and lost by close to 150 votes, a factor which helped convince him to avoid too close a tie with the abolition movement in the future.[8] Thus when the Liberty party formed in 1840, Wade wanted no part of a third-party organization, a position he would hold to throughout the next fifteen years. In the exciting presidential election of 1840, he campaigned for William Henry Harrison and the following year won election to his old senate seat by more than a thousand votes. In Columbus, he continued to speak for antislavery causes—but in more moderate tones—and easily retained his seat in the next election as well. In 1841, Benjamin married Caroline Rosecrans, and in 1843 the couple had the first of two sons. Despite his commitment to Whig causes in the mid-1840s, he briefly retired from politics to be with his family more and to concentrate on his law practice. Nonetheless, his interest in politics remained high and he campaigned strenuously for presidential hopeful Henry Clay in 1844.[9] Like many Northern Whigs, he believed that Clay's refusal to support the annexation of Texas was more important than his role as a Kentucky slaveholder. In rejecting the appeal of the Liberty party and its candidate, James G. Birney, Benjamin Wade broke with the course of brother Edward.

By the late 1830s, Edward Wade had settled forty miles west in Cleveland, where he developed a lucrative law practice. In 1837 he became president of the county antislavery society, and in the years ahead defended several fugitive slaves in court. In 1840, he had agreed with his brother in

---

7. Williams, *Ashtabula County*, 67–8; *Ashtabula Sentinel*, June 15, 1839.

8. Vernon Volpe, "Benjamin Wade's Strange Defeat," *Ohio History* 97 (1988): 129–30; *Ashtabula Sentinel*, November 23, 30, 1839.

9. Trefousse, *Benjamin Wade*, 41–55.

campaigning for Harrison over the nascent Liberty party under Birney. Equally strong in his antislavery beliefs, he nevertheless wrote a letter advising political abolitionists to support Harrison. Yet by 1842 he could no longer be a part of a party headed by slaveholder Henry Clay, and so he worked with others of like mind to organize the Liberty party in the Western Reserve. Thus at a Liberty party convention in Akron in 1844, delegates approved his resolution that "no law-abiding citizen can support Mr. Clay for President."[10] A year earlier, with Joshua Giddings under attack by both Democrats and moderate Whigs in his race for reelection to Congress, Edward had accepted the Liberty nomination to oppose him as well. The third-party press noted that "no Liberty man" could support Giddings "without voting with and for the Whig party." Instead, they must "come out and vote for Edward Wade." The congressman fought back with the traditional argument against all third parties, that the Liberty party was simply diverting Whig votes and aiding proslavery Democrats in the process. Giddings, by then a well-entrenched antislavery Whig who had been a central figure in the House repeal of the Gag Rule, easily defeated Wade and a Democratic opponent.[11] Still, Edward Wade, now opposed politically by both brother Benjamin and Giddings, resolved that the third-party was the only effective way to fight slavery.

As the Free Soil movement emerged in 1848, the political paths of the Wade brothers continued to diverge. On the constitutional issues surrounding slavery neither of the brothers showed any significant interest although both were attorneys. Equally committed to antislavery goals, they rarely agreed on political tactics, however. The previous year Benjamin had further strengthened his ties to Ohio Whigs when they rewarded him for past services by electing him judge in the third Ohio judicial circuit. It was a position he would hold with distinction for the next four years.[12] Edward found the absorption of the Liberty party by the new Free Soil organization much to his liking, and appeared unconcerned as Liberty abolitionism was replaced by Free Soil containment. In contrast, Benjamin maintained his resistance to third-party politics. Although unhappy when the Whigs chose Louisiana slaveholder Zachary Taylor as their nominee and ignored the Wilmot

---

10. Riddle, *Ashtabula County*, 84; Smith, *Liberty and Free Soil Parties*, 61, 72; David Van Tassel and John Grabowski, eds., *The Encyclopedia of Cleveland History* (Bloomington: Indiana Univ. Press, 1987), 1020–21.

11. Stewart, *Giddings*, 95–7; Smith, *Liberty and Free Soil Parties*, 59, 112.

12. Riddle, *Benjamin Wade*, 109–14.

Proviso in their platform, Benjamin claimed to find the earlier proslavery stance of Free Soil candidate Martin Van Buren even more objectionable. Few Western Reserve Free Soilers could understand Wade's temporizing, especially after Joshua Giddings bolted the Whigs and accepted the third party's nomination for reelection to Congress. Belief in Taylor's record as a soldier and his strong unionism, along with Wade's old Whig ties and belief in the two-party system meant to him that antislavery could still best be served from his base within his old party. Unstated was his realization that his judicial position depended on his remaining a Whig. Even as Van Buren and the Free Soilers won a plurality in most Western Reserve counties and Giddings swept to a reelection victory, Wade explained to his old mentor, Elisha Whittlesey, that the choice for him was between Taylor and Michigan senator Lewis Cass, a Democrat eager to please the South: "I assume it as a fixed principle that either Cass or Taylor must be the next president and between the two it seems strange that a Whig should hesitate. . . . I believe the free States safer with honest old Zach and a free territory Congress than with a miserable doughface with a Congress of like mind at his hands."[13] Political realities for him meant that slavery could be effectively challenged only from within the two-party structure.

Neither Wade held a political office as Congress debated and eventually passed Henry Clay's proposals in 1850. But both were vehement in their denunciation of the most controversial part of his Compromise provisions, the Fugitive Slave Act. At a Whig rally in Ravenna in late 1850, the older Wade announced his willingness to work with men of any party against "the most infamous enactment known to the statute books of this country." As a judge, he could not advise open resistance to a law, but in the next breath he recalled the Revolutionary War tradition of resistance to British tyranny, thus implying that northerners might consider mob violence in aiding escaping fugitives. A Union which had been "converted into a giant slave catcher" might not be worth saving. Said Wade: "The sooner we're rid of it the better."[14] As shocking as such an invective might be to some, antislavery Whig and Free Soil leaders saw great political potential in Wade. Thus when the Ohio legislature prepared to elect a senator in early 1851, Benjamin Wade instantly became a leading contender. Since 1848, the small Free Democratic (formerly Free Soil) contingent had held the balance of power in Columbus

13. Wade to Whittlesey, July 3, 1848, Whittlesey Papers, Western Reserve Historical Society.

14. *Ashtabula Sentinel,* November 30, 1850.

and was thus in a position to drive a hard bargain when senators and state officers were chosen. In 1849, they had combined with Democrats to elect one of their own, Salmon P. Chase, as senator. Now in 1851, although they lacked the power to force another third-party leader's election, they could insist on a Whig with the right antislavery credentials. Wade was clearly their man, and after a protracted legislative battle the Whig–Free Democratic coalition chose him in March. Giddings feared that Wade would be more true to his Whig party than to antislavery principle, but promised, "we shall all do what we can to encourage him to maintain his integrity." His fears appeared justified when Wade announced, "I do not intend to be an agitator in the Senate," and that he would always remain a Whig "because I believe that the best interests of the country are connected with the success of that party." During the 1852 presidential campaign, while Edward campaigned enthusiastically for Free Democratic candidate John P. Hale, Benjamin traveled throughout Ohio in behalf of Whig nominee Winfield Scott; yet he had helped to convince Whig delegates to their nominating convention to omit any platform endorsement of the Compromise measures, especially the infamous Fugitive Slave Act.[15]

To complete the Wade brothers' resurgence, Edward ran for Congress in 1852 as a Free Democrat in a newly created Cleveland district. The Democratic party strategy in the redistricting of congressional districts had been to try to eliminate Giddings from Congress by taking away several Free Democratic counties and adding Democratic ones to his district. But the gerrymander had backfired, and both Giddings and Wade triumphed. The latter won a close, three-way victory over Democratic and Whig candidates. Ironically, Benjamin Wade, as a partisan Whig, actually campaigned against both Free Democrats, his brother Edward and Giddings.[16] As the Thirty-third Congress convened in late 1853, Free Democratic representative Edward Wade now joined Whig senator Benjamin Wade in what would become a momentous session. Although of different parties and, at the time, bitter rivals both politically and personally, they could nevertheless agree on the need to stand firm against southern demands.

It was the introduction in the Senate in January 1854 of the Kansas-Nebraska bill, authored by Illinois Democrat Stephan A. Douglas, that set in motion a political process which sent the national Whig party to a slow

15. Trefousse, *Benjamin Wade*, 67, 81–2; Giddings to Chase, April 3, 1851, Chase Papers, Historical Society of Pennsylvania; *National Era*, May 1, 1851.

16. Smith, *Liberty and Free Soil Parties*, 258–9; Stewart, *Giddings*, 216.

and agonizing death and brought into existence the purely sectional Republican party. The latter would eventually win a place in the two-party system with its central platform plank, the containment of slavery, the position advocated by the third-party Free Soilers during the previous six years. Both Edward and Benjamin Wade played central roles in the dramatic turn of events, with Edward easily making the transition from Free Democrat to Republican, while Benjamin finally concluded that the Whig party could not survive and joined his brother in the new organization. What made the Kansas-Nebraska proposal so controversial was its repeal of the congressional ban on slavery north of the 36°30′ parallel originally established by the Missouri Compromise of 1820. For advocates of antislavery throughout the North, its passage would represent a rejection of the containment principle, which was part of the Wilmot Proviso, and the right of the federal government to keep slavery out of the territories. The Wade brothers agreed it would represent a major victory for the Slave Power.

In the eyes of many northern members of Congress of all three parties, the time to stand up for containment had at last arrived. But to a small group of those most determined to resist the expansion of slavery, the time was ripe for a statement of protest which might also serve as a rallying cry for a new and more effective party to unite northern voters behind the principle of containment. Accordingly, Senators Salmon P. Chase and Charles Sumner joined with Joshua Giddings to write what they called the "Appeal of the Independent Democrats in Congress to the People of the United States." Their protest was also signed by Gerrit Smith of New York, Alexander De Witt of Massachusetts, and Edward Wade. Although not among those who signed, Benjamin Wade was in full accord with the Appeal's sentiment.[17] Douglas's proposal to repeal the ban on slavery, said their statement, could only be viewed "as a gross violation of a sacred pledge; as a criminal betrayal of precious rights; as part and parcel of an atrocious plot to exclude from a vast unoccupied region, emigrants from the Old World and free laborers from

---

17. The reasons for Benjamin Wade's name not being on the final draft of the Appeal have never been clear. Nineteenth-century biographer Albert G. Riddle suggests that Wade signed the first draft, called "To the People of Ohio," but when it was revised and the name Independent Democrats was attached to it, the authors "omitted Mr. Wade's name" (Riddle, *Benjamin Wade*, 194). Modern biographer Hans Trefousse suggests that because Wade "had no use for Democrats, independent or otherwise," he declined to sign (Trefousse, *Benjamin Wade*, 85). Given Wade's distaste for third parties, it is also possible that his reluctance to sign had more to do with a refusal to be associated with a document that might imply support for a new third party while the Whigs still survived as part of the two-party system.

our own States, and convert it into a dreary region of despotism inhabited by masters and slaves." The bill would not have legalized slavery in the region to be organized, but would rather have left it to the territorial legislatures to decide under the principle of popular sovereignty. The Appeal, however, stressed instead that the bill violated "the original *settled policy* of the United States, clearly indicated by the Jefferson Proviso of 1784 and by the Ordinance of 1787," the "NON EXTENSION OF SLAVERY." Should the bill pass, "The plight of slavery will cover the land" and free labor "must necessarily be degraded."[18] A highly effective engine of sectional propaganda, the Appeal accelerated the transformation of the two-party system. Douglas reacted in fury at what he regarded as a total distortion of his bill and its goals, but the authors could not have more effectively tapped growing northern resentment against the South and its expanding slavery.

Although Benjamin Wade had not signed the Appeal, he was quick to join those who had as, together, they arraigned the bill, its author, Douglas, and its southern supporters. In his attacks, he was as firm and compelling as any of those who had signed, including brother Edward. On February 6, Benjamin attacked the bill in the Senate. Using the Declaration of Independence to defend the rights of slaves, he concluded: "You may call me an Abolitionist if you will, I care little for that, for if an undying hatred for slavery and oppression constitutes an Abolitionist, I am that Abolitionist." As the bill moved slowly toward passage, he traded jibes with slave state senators who were defending their way of life. When Senator George E. Badger of North Carolina attacked northerners for trying to prevent him from taking his "dear old black mammy to Kansas," Wade exploded: "We are willing you should take the old lady there—*we are afraid you'll sell her when you get her there.*"[19] Yet no amount of sarcastic humor could prevent the passage of the bill, which came by a large margin in the Senate in March and a narrow majority in the House in late May. Even before President Pierce signed the Kansas-Nebraska bill into law, the first steps had already occurred that would bring political turmoil.

While the House debated the Kansas-Nebraska bill in early May, both Benjamin and Edward Wade joined in a spontaneous meeting of approximately thirty members of Congress to consider the best course of action

18. *Congressional Globe*, 33rd Cong., 1st sess., 280; *National Era*, January 24, February 2, 1854.

19. *Congressional Globe*, 33rd Cong., 1st sess., 337–40; Riddle, *Benjamin Wade*, 199–200.

should it become law. All agreed that the existing party structure could no longer meet the emergency and stop the spread of slavery. *National Era* editor Gamaliel Bailey urged that old party organizations and labels be forgotten and a new party formed "in unselfish devotion to the cause of human rights." Massachusetts congressman Henry Wilson recalled later that those present were convinced that only a new party could resist "the continued aggressions of the arrogant and triumphant Slave Power."[20] Predictably, Edward Wade and his Free Democratic colleagues, who had been urging such an approach for months, were quick to indicate a willingness to drop their third-party organization and join a larger movement.

More surprisingly, Benjamin Wade soon announced that, in his eyes, the Whig party was dead. Earlier in the year he had indicated that southern Whig support of Douglas's bill had been the last straw and had destroyed his willingness to remain in the party which he had been a part of all of his adult life. His decision to abandon the struggling Whigs came almost two years before Abraham Lincoln and William H. Seward reached similar decisions in Illinois and New York. Ohio Whigs were in more immediate jeopardy, and Wade believed his political future more secure if he became an early member of the Republican party. Benjamin's official announcement came in a May 25 speech in the Senate when he proclaimed that "pride and self respect compel a man either to be a doughface, flunky, or an abolitionist and I choose the latter. I glory in the name." In June, both Wades joined Chase and others Ohioans in a call for a summer fusionist meeting in Columbus to choose candidates for statewide elections that fall.[21] Later that summer Benjamin exhorted a fusion meeting of antislavery Whigs, Democrats, and Free Democrats in Ravenna, Ohio, to "throw all party predilections to the winds and rally one great party of all the liberty loving men of Ohio from all parties. . . . Please tell all good Whigs for me, that I for one, counsel the whole party to forget a name, and join heartily in this great movement of the People." They must not look back "until the vile traitors have been punished and our country redeemed from the grasp of the meanest aristocracy that ever cursed a nation."[22] A new party was forming in reaction to the Kansas-Nebraska law, and both Wades were enthusiastic charter members in the ongoing political movement to stop the spread of slavery.

20. *National Era*, June 22, 1854; Henry Wilson, *History of the Rise and Fall of the Slave Power* (Boston: J. R. Osgood, 1877), 2:410–1.

21. *Congressional Globe*, 33rd Cong., 1st sess., Appendix, 763–5; *National Era*, June 22, July 27, 1854.

22. *Ashtabula Sentinel*, August 10, 1854.

That fall Edward Wade and Giddings were reelected to Congress, but on a Republican ticket. The fall campaign under the new party label even brought reconciliation between Benjamin Wade and both his brother Edward and Giddings, as the senator warmly endorsed the two men whom he had so roundly condemned two years earlier when they had run as Free Democrats. Personal differences now appeared all but forgotten. These had included Benjamin's intense dislike of Edward's second wife, Mary, whom he had married in 1852. Political unity among all antislavery forces was clearly necessary. Such a need was powerful enough to force even family feuds into the background.[23]

The two were also in complete accord in resisting the nativist challenge to their party. The Know-Nothing movement and its political arm, the American party, stressed ethno-cultural issues and gained strength wherever Roman Catholic, and especially Irish, immigrants concentrated. Their presence had created fear among Protestant majorities which supported temperance reform, typically resisted by European immigrants. The movement found supporters throughout the North and in limited parts of the South. In Ohio, its appeal was confined to Cincinnati and, to a lesser extent, Cleveland, but its political potential was significant. To the Wades, however, it was a dangerous concept and one to be scorned because of its bigotry and because it might deflect potential support from the antislavery movement. For Benjamin, it might also gain votes that might have gone to Republican candidates for the Ohio legislature and thus jeopardize his reelection to the U.S. Senate by that body. He was thus outspoken in his rejection of their anti-immigrant stance. When Congress considered a homestead bill in 1854 and a pending amendment would have denied government land to recent immigrants, Wade came to their defense by declaring that "these poor men do not deserve the harsh epithets which have been indiscriminately applied to foreigners." Admitting that a tiny minority might merit proscription, he objected "to the great mass of our worthy immigrants being compelled to suffer the sins of a vicious few."[24] Later attacked by a nativistic senator, the fiery Wade responded with a challenge to duel his antagonist. Cooler heads prevailed, but his outspoken opposition to the Know-Nothings for a time jeopardized his reelection hopes in the Ohio legislature in early 1856. In the end, Wade's courageous attacks on nativist bigotry may have actually strengthened his position, and he was easily reelected. In the same manner,

23. Benjamin Wade to Edward Wade, Nov. 13, 1854, in Trefousse, *Benjamin Wade*, 92–93.
24. *Congressional Globe*, 33rd Cong., 1st sess., 944, 1661, 1717.

Edward Wade had campaigned for Salmon P. Chase, the Republican candidate for governor, in the fall of 1855 and during the campaign attacked the Know-Nothing movement.[25] For both, the only issue of concern was containing slavery and the only party worthy of their support was the Republican.

Despite the strength of the Know-Nothing movement, sectional issues always took precedence over ethno-cultural ones in the 1850s. By 1856, the Republican party had secured its place in the two-party system and political nativism had begun to decline. In the presidential election of that year both Wades campaigned strenuously and enthusiastically for John C. Frémont and helped swell the Pathfinder's Ohio majority. Like other Republicans, they urged the repeal of the Fugitive Slave Act and were outraged by the Supreme Court's Dred Scott decision in 1857 challenging the very basis of their party's platform, the right of Congress to prevent the expansion of slavery into federal territories. A year earlier, Benjamin had been among the most vociferous in condemning South Carolinian Preston Brooks for his assault on Charles Sumner on the floor of the Senate. When southerners argued that the beating was not the business of the Senate, he reacted in fury: "I will vindicate the right and liberty of debate and freedom of discussion upon this floor." If denied, "let us come armed for the combat. . . . I am here to meet you." Again a duel, this time with Senator Robert Toombs of Georgia, appeared imminent, only to be averted. For several days, Wade, Henry Wilson, and other militant Republicans came to the Capitol with handguns hidden, yet conspicuous under their coats.[26]

As a member of the Committee on Territories, Wade was brutal in his attack on Stephen A. Douglas and his cherished principle of popular sovereignty. The Ohioan consistently condemned moderate Republicans who briefly considered political cooperation with Douglas after the Illinois Democrat broke with James Buchanan. The president's surrender to southern demands by rejecting popular sovereignty as a means of dealing with the ongoing Kansas crisis had caused Douglas to look for allies outside of the Democratic party, but Wade would have no part of a man he considered little better than a lackey of the South. As much as southerners and some in the North might consider Wade an uncouth and fanatical Republican agitator, it was clear that his compassion for the cause of antislavery was honest and heartfelt. In his eyes there could be no compromise with the demands of the Slave Power.

25. Trefousse, *Benjamin Wade*, 97–9; Stewart, *Giddings*, 231.
26. *Congressional Globe*, 34th Cong., 1st sess., 1304–1306; Stewart, *Giddings*, 238.

As the events of the late 1850s moved the nation closer to the brink of a sectional showdown, of the two Wade brothers, Benjamin generated the most attention. Yet Edward was not far behind, as his role in the Oberlin-Wellington fugitive rescue case revealed. Thirty-three Ohioans faced trial in 1859 in federal court in Cleveland, accused of violating the Fugitive Slave Act in assisting fugitive John Price's escape, and Edward helped organize the huge demonstration protesting their prosecution. He, along with Governor Chase and other Ohio Republican leaders, addressed the rally in Cleveland's Public Square demanding the release of Charles Langston and the others being held.[27] Yet as the momentous presidential election of 1860 approached, declining health forced Edward to announce his retirement from politics rather than seeking a fifth term in the House. Thus as Republicans appeared on the verge of winning control of both the presidency and Congress, Benjamin Wade would stand alone in carrying the family name in the ongoing struggle against slave expansion. He would prove more than equal to the task.

As the most important presidential election of the nineteenth century approached, Wade played an important role in setting the tone as well as determining whom the Republican candidate would be. In Senate debates before the election he attacked southerners threatening secession if the Republican nominee became president and argued that leaving the Union was illegal: "There is no way by which either one section or the other can get out of the Union." He pointed out that neither he nor his party had anything "to say of slavery in the states. . . . Within your own boundaries, conduct it your own way. . . . I shall do nothing to overturn it." But in the territories, "I will allow no such curse to have a foothold." Following the election he repeated his promise: "There is no Republican . . . who ever pretends that they have any right in your states to interfere with your peculiar institution"; but neither would any member of his party allow it to expand.[28]

Several Republicans had sought their party's nomination, with William H. Seward and Salmon P. Chase the leading contenders. Of the two, Wade strongly preferred Seward, believing Chase's background of favoring antislavery union with Democrats and his willingness to sacrifice principle for personal advantage made him undesirable. This feeling was intensified by his

27. *Anti-Slavery Bugle* (Salem, Ohio), June 4, 1859; Brant, *The Town That Started the Civil War,* 203–37; Stewart, *Giddings,* 269.

28. Riddle, *Benjamin Wade,* 227–8, 229–32; *Congressional Globe,* 36th Cong., 2nd sess., 99–107.

personal distrust and dislike of the Ohio governor. He had even allowed his own name to be advanced by several members of the Ohio delegation to the Chicago nominating convention, gravely weakening Chase's chances in the process. Although Seward lost out as well, Wade was most relieved to see Chase eliminated and content when the delegates chose Lincoln. He campaigned actively for the nominee and his party's containment platform and then prepared for the ongoing congressional struggle which he knew would surely follow, one in which he would play a central role.[29] Republicans had finally won the presidency, and he believed that there could now be no further extension of slavery.

During the months between Lincoln's election in November and inauguration in March, Wade was among those most resistant to compromise as a means of preventing secession. Nor did he tolerate those Republicans who appeared willing to bargain away parts of his party's platform to appease the slave states. In a mid-December Senate speech, with South Carolina on the brink of becoming the first state to secede, he responded: "I would not entertain a proposition for any compromise for in my judgment, this long, chronic controversy which has existed between us must be met upon the principles of the Constitution and laws, and met now." When Congress considered the Crittenden Compromise in January 1861 and then looked at similar suggestions emanating from the Washington Peace Conference in February, he vehemently resisted their proposals. On the last day of the Thirty-sixth Congress and just hours before Lincoln's inauguration, as Congress debated and eventually approved a constitutional amendment guaranteeing slavery where it already existed, Wade spoke in opposition and summed up why such a proposal must be rejected: "I understand the reason that impels you to leave us. . . . We of the free States love liberty too much, love justice too well, prize the great principles of free Government too highly, to have a despotism flourish even in our vicinity."[30] The onset of war averted ratification of the proposed amendment and, at least on the principles of standing firm against the Confederacy and preventing further slave expansion, Wade could look forward to a strong ally in the new president. On the issues of how to wage the war and deal with emancipation, however, agreement between the two would be more elusive.

For the first three months of the war the president was in total control of military strategy, in large part because Congress was not in session. But

---

29. Blue, *Chase*, 123–6; Trefousse, *Benjamin Wade*, 121–9.
30. *Congressional Globe*, 36th Cong., 2nd sess., 99–107, 1363–64, 1393–1401.

when the Thirty-seventh Congress convened on July 4, members like Wade came expecting a short war and a quick destruction of Confederate armies, and were ready to demand accountability if that did not occur. The Ohio senator had quickly enlisted in the army at his home in Jefferson, although, much to his disappointment, the state did not call his unit. Impatient for action, he returned to Washington in May, two months before Congress convened, and in mid-July went armed to the first battle at nearby Bull Run (Manassas), Virginia. Disgusted with the defeat of Union troops led by Irwin McDowell, he had even tried to block their retreat by threatening to shoot fleeing soldiers.[31] Events later in the summer further angered Wade and other Radical Republicans. Especially discouraging was the Union defeat at Wilson's Creek in southern Missouri and the death there of Union general Nathaniel Lyon. But even more disheartening was the president's order in September rescinding General John C. Frémont's effort to free the slaves within his Missouri command. Wade reacted in fury, writing to fellow Radical and Michigan senator Zachariah Chandler: "I have no doubt that by it, he has done more injury to the cause of the Union by receding from the ground taken by Frémont than McDowell did by retreating from Bull Run."[32] Further defeats on the battlefield that fall left Wade in total despair, with most of his frustration directed against the president.

When Congress convened again in December, Chandler and others quickly proposed creation of a joint congressional committee to oversee the direction of the war. It would be called the Committee on the Conduct of the War. Vice President Hannibal Hamlin chose its Senate members, who included Wade, Chandler, and Andrew Johnson of Tennessee. Prominent Radical George W. Julian of Indiana was named among four House members. Hamlin, at Chandler's urging, then appointed Wade to chair the committee, thus helping to assure that Radicals would control and direct its course.[33] For the remaining three and a half years of bloody combat, Wade would use the committee as his vehicle to force Lincoln into a more vigorous prosecution of the war. This he hoped to achieve by insisting on the appointment of generals opposed to slavery and the removal of those who appeared unwilling to engage Confederate forces and use their armies to assist in the demise of slavery.

31. Albert G. Riddle, *Recollections of War Times: Reminiscences of Men and Events in Washington, 1860–1865* (New York: G. P. Putnam's Sons, 1895), 45, 52.

32. Wade to Chandler, September 23, 1861, Chandler Papers, Library of Congress.

33. *Congressional Globe,* 37th Cong., 2nd sess., 22, 40, 110, 153; Tap, *Over Lincoln's Shoulder,* 22–4, 33–4; Riddle, *Recollections of War Times,* 177–8.

Much of Wade's criticism of military strategy (as well as that of other Radicals) was, in the words of a modern student of the committee, based on "simplistic, amateurish and unrealistic views of warfare" in the belief "that the South could be defeated in a single battle."[34] For Wade, it was largely a matter of West Point–trained generals, especially Ohioan George B. McClellan, who were responsible for the lack of forceful action against the Confederacy and for the "proslavery" approach employed. In the senator's view, the military academy had educated not only most Confederate generals, but, even worse, proslavery Union leaders. West Point, said Wade, "was the hot-bed from which rebellion was hatched. . . . from thence emanated your principal traitors and conspirators." There, a young man was taught "to despise his own democratic section of the country" and "to admire above all things, that two-penny, miserable slave aristocracy of the South." Wade even urged that the academy be abolished. Far more preferable to lead Union armies than a "traitor" like McClellan were those with abolitionist leanings and with military training acquired in the field, rather than at West Point. John C. Frémont was the perfect example. When Lincoln had forced the general's removal from his command after his efforts to free Missouri slaves, in Wade's view, he had been "sacrificed by a weak and wicked administration, to appease the wrath of an indignant" proslavery group of northerners. Wade rejoiced when, in 1862, pressure from the Committee on the Conduct of the War and others finally forced Lincoln to remove McClellan as well, but his unhappiness over the president's policies on slavery continued.[35]

Wade had always been among those Republicans who saw their party as the vehicle to bring about eventual emancipation. Before 1861, he had strongly endorsed containment as the role of the federal government, but, like other Radicals, he believed that secession and war meant that Congress and the Lincoln administration must now pursue total abolition. Along with Chase in the cabinet, Julian, Owen Lovejoy, and Thaddeus Stevens in the House, Sumner and Chandler in the Senate, as well as a growing minority in and out of government, he believed that Congress and the president could and must move in concert to destroy slavery wherever it existed. Like most Radicals, he rarely appreciated the delicate position of the chief executive; Lincoln could not move decisively without jeopardizing Union slave state

34. Tap, *Over Lincoln's Shoulder,* 45.

35. *Congressional Globe,* 37th Cong., 3rd sess., 324–34; 38th Cong., 1st sess., 3196–97; Wade to Charles Dana, February 3, 1862, in Tap, *Over Lincoln's Shoulder,* 92; Tap, *Over Lincoln's Shoulder,* 47.

loyalty and antagonizing moderate and conservative supporters throughout the North. Thus Wade and his colleagues became relentless in their pressure and, at every good opportunity, pushed legislation designed to undermine the institution that the Confederacy so depended on. After Lincoln's election, but before secession, Wade had urged emancipation on southerners in Congress, reminding them that "the first blast of civil war is the death warrant of your institution."[36] Now, with the war raging, he joined in support of bills to weaken slavery on the periphery of the Confederacy. In April 1862, Congress abolished slavery in the District of Columbia, thus completing a longstanding goal of antislavery advocates dating back to the 1830s. As chairman of the Senate committee on territories, Wade swelled with pride when his committee reported a bill ending slavery in all federal territories, one which the Senate passed in June and Lincoln quickly signed into law. It had taken a bloody war to bring it about, but the major goal of containment was at last achieved. Wade and his Radical colleagues would now accelerate their pressure to force Lincoln's hand on total emancipation.

Wade was a leading advocate of confiscating the slave property of those in rebellion, and in May he delivered an impassioned Senate speech in support.[37] The confiscation bill passed by the Senate in late June did not go as far as he wished it to, but he gladly voted for it as a necessary first step, knowing it would add further pressure on Lincoln. When the president signed the confiscation measures in July, the battle to end slavery was far from over, but its outcome now appeared inevitable. The process leading to a presidential policy of emancipation, too complex to describe here in detail, reached its next milestone in September 1862 with Lincoln's Preliminary Proclamation freeing slaves behind Confederate lines as of January 1, 1863. As much as Wade might have disparaged Lincoln for what he saw as the president's timid steps, and as much as he might have challenged him on congressional authority over that of the executive branch, the Ohio senator was ecstatic. To Julian, he rejoiced: "Hurrah for Old Abe and the proclamation."[38]

Shortly after Lincoln's emancipation policy went into effect, the Ohio legislature overwhelmingly reelected Wade to his third term in the Senate. In Congress, the senator maintained his relentless efforts to force greater compliance by Union military leaders in completing the emancipation process and accelerating the defeat of rebel armies. His chief vehicle in this effort

36. *Congressional Globe*, 37th Cong., 2nd sess., 1919.
37. Ibid., 37th Cong., 2nd sess., 1916–19; Trefousse, *Benjamin Wade*, 181–4.
38. Wade to Julian, September 29, 1862, Giddings-Julian Papers.

continued to be the Committee on the Conduct of the War. Although the Senate remained firmly Republican, Democrats had gained twenty-five seats in the House in the 1862 elections, and Wade blamed his party's loss on the timid and inconsistent policies of the Lincoln government. He and other Radicals were especially critical of Secretary of State Seward, believing him to be most responsible for the administration's vacillating policies. Wade had been a part of the group which had met with Lincoln in late December in an effort to force Seward's removal, only to be outmaneuvered by the president. In early 1863, Wade's temper again erupted over the president's dependence on West Point generals, and it was at this time that the Senate rejected his bill to abolish the academy by a lopsided 29–10 margin.[39] Such defeats did not deter the senator from his ongoing crusade, which also included the elevation of African Americans.

Emancipation, in Wade's eyes, was only the first step in achieving the equality of all black Americans, free or slave. The enlistment of black troops in Union armies was the next; it began slowly in 1862 and then accelerated, with Wade among the most vociferous in seeking to expand their numbers and achieving for them equal pay with white troops. Yet in seeking equality, Wade reflected many of the biases against blacks so characteristic of nineteenth-century America. In late 1860, he stated his beliefs in reaction to those who claimed "that the African is an inferior race." If that were true, he argued, "so far from giving me a right to enslave him," it required "that I shall be more scrupulous of his rights; but I know that, whether he be equal to me or not, he is still a human being; negroes are still men."[40] Earlier the same year he had endorsed colonization for free blacks, "a race of men who are poor, weak, uninfluential, incapable of taking care of themselves. . . . It is perfectly impossible that these two races can inhabit the same place and be prosperous and happy." Thus he felt it the government's responsibility to provide a place "whereby this class of unfortunate men may emigrate to some congenial clime." But African Americans should not be forced to migrate: "We will not drive them out, but we will use every inducement to persuade these unfortunate men to find a home there, so as to separate the races."[41]

However much Wade might have sought equal rights and treatment for both slave and free black populations in his public appeals, his references

39. *Congressional Globe,* 37th Cong., 3rd sess., 324–34; Tap, *Over Lincoln's Shoulder,* 144–54.

40. *Congressional Globe,* 36th Cong., 1st sess., Appendix, 150–5.

41. January 12, 1860, in Riddle, *Benjamin Wade,* 229–32.

to African Americans in private correspondence, especially to his wife, Caroline, revealed the vulgar side of his thinking. When he first arrived in Washington as a senator in 1851, he called the city "a mean God forsaken Nigger-ridden place." Nor did his views change after three terms in the Senate. Retired and back in Jefferson, in 1873, he bemoaned the problem of finding servants other than African Americans: "I wish that we could get a white woman of the English or Northern European breed. I am sick and tired of Niggers." In the same letter to Caroline, he called a black attorney he had been dealing with "a d–d Nigger lawyer."[42] Like so many reformers of the Old Northwest who hated slavery and the Slave Power, Wade wanted social justice for blacks but retained a personal aversion to contact with African Americans.

If his private remarks reflected white America's racist thinking, his public actions differed markedly from the views and actions of most. In sharp contrast, the public Benjamin Wade maintained a constant vigil to prevent discrimination against free blacks and the end of slavery for those still in bondage. For example, his reaction to the slaughter of black troops by Confederates under General Nathan Bedford Forrest at Fort Pillow, Tennessee, in April 1864 was one of total disbelief. His committee authorized him and Daniel Gooch of Massachusetts to travel to the scene and take testimony on what had happened. They interviewed more than seventy witnesses, finding evidence of the deliberate butchering of blacks by rebel troops. While their official report calling for Union retaliation exaggerated Confederate atrocities in order to rally northerners, it nonetheless revealed Wade's compassionate side through his defense of mistreated African Americans.[43] As Congress and the president continued to grapple with the best way to defeat the Confederacy and complete the process of emancipation, Wade remained the most vocal critic of anyone who he believed retarded the movement toward equality among the races.

By 1864, northern leaders could begin to look ahead to the end of the war and the process by which rebel states would reenter the Union. Again, Radicals found themselves in seemingly irreconcilable conflict with Lincoln, this time over the terms of Reconstruction. Not surprisingly, Wade was in

---

42. Wade to Caroline Wade, December 29, 1851, March 9, 1873, Wade Papers, Library of Congress; Trefousse, *Benjamin Wade,* 311–3. See also Trefousse, "Ben Wade and the Negro," *Ohio Historical Quarterly* 68 (1959): 161–76.

43. "Fort Pillow Massacre," Senate Report 63, *Congressional Globe,* 38th Cong., 1st sess., scattered pages; Tap, *Over Lincoln's Shoulder,* 194–200.

the center of the struggle between Congress and the president. The president's plan revolved around a quick and relatively painless process to begin when as few as 10 percent of the eligible voters in a seceded state took an oath of loyalty to the Union. Radicals such as Wade proposed instead a slower, harsher process, requiring a majority of southerners to declare their loyalty, and one in which Congress, rather than the president, would set the terms. To Wade, the idea that "only one tenth of the people" was needed for reentry was a principle "anomalous and entirely subversive of the great principles" of democracy. "Majorities must rule and until majorities can be found loyal and trustworthy for State Government, they must be governed by a stronger hand."[44]

The congressional plan was embodied in a proposal Wade coauthored with House leader Henry Winter Davis of Maryland, the Wade-Davis bill, which Congress approved in July 1864. When the president rejected the measure through a pocket veto and told southern states they could choose either his plan or that of Congress, Wade and his Radical allies reacted in fury. Their response was a bitter diatribe, the Wade-Davis Manifesto, indicting the president for what they regarded as political heresy. Lincoln, "by preventing this bill from becoming a law holds the electoral votes of the rebel States at the dictation of his personal ambition. . . . But he must understand that our support is of a cause and not of a man; that the authority of Congress is paramount and must be respected." Lincoln, said the Manifesto, "must confine himself to his executive duties—to obey and execute, not make the laws—to suppress by arms armed rebellion and leave political organization to Congress."[45] In light of later events vindicating Lincoln and many of his policies, Wade and his colleagues had overreached themselves in their challenge. But they had also expressed their deep frustrations over what they regarded as excessive executive leniency to the South and rebel leaders.

Republicans were most critical of the Manifesto because it came in the midst of Lincoln's uphill reelection battle in the late summer. Wade had considered supporting the third-party candidacy of deposed general John C. Frémont, but reluctantly fell into line behind Lincoln when Frémont withdrew and the Democratic challenge under former general George C. McClellan appeared to threaten everything that he stood for. He explained his thinking to Chandler in typical Wade rhetoric: "I never had doubt of our ability to elect him [Lincoln] by an overwhelming majority. I only wish we

44. *Congressional Globe*, 38th Cong., 1st sess., 3341–61.
45. *New York Tribune*, August 5, 1864.

could do as well for a better man. But to save the nation I am doing all for him. . . . were it not for the country there would be poetical justice in his being beaten by that stupid ass McClellan." The choice, said Wade, was either Lincoln "or Jeff Davis, for McClellan and all those who support him are meaner traitors than are to be found in the Confederacy."[46] As the war neared an end in early 1865, Wade continued his pressure on Lincoln, demanding harsh terms for the soon-to-be defeated Confederacy. He warned that there could be no peace without total abolition: "The radicals have their feet upon your necks, and they are determined that their feet shall rest on the neck of this monster until he breathes his last."[47] The president's backing of the proposed Thirteenth Amendment abolishing slavery everywhere eased Wade's mind only slightly, and he now increased his demands for black suffrage. Wade's efforts to goad the president into conformity with Radical demands did not end until Lincoln's assassination made Andrew Johnson president.

Heartened by the fall of Richmond in early April 1865, Wade had rejoiced with Robert E. Lee's surrender to Ulysses S. Grant at Appomattox on April 9, for the end of both the bloodshed and the slave system that had sustained the Confederacy were at hand. Yet he remained suspicious of what he believed was Lincoln's continued leniency toward the seceded states.[48] Having never understood or appreciated the difficulty and delicacy of Lincoln's task, Wade optimistically assumed that there would be a better relationship with the president's successor. On Easter Sunday, two days after Lincoln's murder, Wade and other members of the Committee on the Conduct of the War met with their old friend and colleague, President Andrew Johnson. Believing that the presidential policies of weakness and misguided conciliation were over, Wade proclaimed: "Johnson, we have faith in you. By the Gods there will be no trouble now in running the government." The president responded: "Treason is a crime and *crime* must be punished. . . . Treason must be made infamous and traitors must be impoverished."[49] The Radicals logically assumed that their ultimate goals, including full equality for the former slaves, were in sight.

What Wade sought was retribution against Confederate leaders who had put the nation through four years of bloodshed. He preferred that the fed-

---

46. Wade to Chandler, October 2, 1864, Chandler Papers.

47. *Congressional Globe*, 38th Cong., 2nd sess., 158–68.

48. Trefousse, *Benjamin Wade*, 245–6.

49. Julian, Journal, in Clarke, ed., "George W. Julian's Journal: The Assassination of Lincoln," 335.

eral government should "either force into exile or hang ten or twelve of the worst of those fellows. . . . We could all agree on Jeff Davis, Toombs, Benjamin Slidell, Mason, Howell Cobb. If we did no more than drive these half-dozen out of the country we should accomplish a great deal."[50] Yet even more important than Johnson's unwillingness to move against former Confederates with such harshness was his refusal to endorse political rights for African Americans.

The conflict between president and Congress became obvious when the Thirty-ninth Congress finally convened in December 1865. Wade still sought to work with the chief executive until well into 1866, when Johnson vetoed two key Radical measures, the Freedmen's Bureau bill and a civil rights proposal. Still, the senator would accept the readmission of former Confederate states if they would ratify the Fourteenth Amendment protecting basic civil rights. Only Tennessee complied, and when the president urged the others to refuse ratification, the break between senator and president was complete. In the fall congressional elections, Republicans increased their majorities to veto-proof levels. Even before the new Congress convened, the Thirty-ninth approved a measure dear to Wade's heart. He had earlier introduced a measure granting District of Columbia blacks the right to vote, and now he joined with Sumner in a renewed effort to secure its passage. In January 1867, Congress overrode a Johnson veto to make the bill law. Wade had been instrumental in securing a critical step in his drive for black suffrage throughout the nation, and one which he later referred to as among his most significant achievements.[51]

In order to assure its control over Reconstruction policy and prevent Johnson from seizing the initiative, Congress arranged for the new Fortieth Congress to convene immediately upon the adjournment of the Thirty-ninth in March 1867. As the old Congress completed its work, senators chose Wade to be president pro tem of the body, placing him next in line in presidential succession. The senator appeared at the peak of his power, and when the drive to impeach the president began later in the year, it seemed possible that Wade might actually become president.[52] Yet, with hindsight, it is clear that Wade had overreached himself, for in advocating black suffrage and, even more controversially, the right of women to vote, he had alienated large blocks of northern voters as well as some Republican Senate colleagues. During the political campaign of 1867 in Ohio, Republicans managed to re-

50. Riddle, *Benjamin Wade*, 268–9.
51. *Congressional Globe*, 39th Cong., 2nd sess., 109, 303, 313.
52. Trefousse, *Benjamin Wade*, 281–3.

tain the governor's office, but lost control of the legislature. During the campaign, Wade had urged voter approval of a black suffrage amendment to the state's constitution. Not only did the proposal fail, but Democratic control of the legislature guaranteed that, as his third term in the Senate ended, he would not be reelected. As Wade explained: "We went in on principle and got whipped."[53]

In many ways, the Senate impeachment trial of Andrew Johnson in the spring of 1868 marked the end of Benjamin Wade's political career. Despite rejection in Ohio, he would assume the presidency should Johnson be convicted. In the face of the senator's conflict of interest, many demanded he not vote on the impeachment charges, but he refused to abstain, claiming it was his duty to represent his constituents.[54] When the Senate failed to convict by one vote, some believed that the prospect of a Wade presidency helped persuade at least one moderate Republican to vote for Johnson's acquittal. The evidence is far from conclusive, but clearly Wade's self-serving action and extreme beliefs had been factors in the outcome. Wade would then return home to Jefferson to resume his private law practice for the first time in eighteen years. As the debates intensified over ratification of the Fifteenth Amendment granting suffrage to black males, he recognized that much work remained unfinished. Writing to African American leaders in 1869, he noted that much racial injustice remained "to be corrected." No longer a central figure, he urged that blacks "who have so lately been emancipated from the foulest oppression and injustice . . . take the lead in these great and necessary reforms."[55]

The Wade brothers of Ohio had worked tirelessly for racial justice through the political process. Edward, the more obscure of the two, was more advanced than his brother on the antislavery spectrum, and had moved through the Liberty and Free Soil parties before winning a seat in Congress in 1852. Serving for eight years, he had signed the call for a new antislavery party and had been part of the changes that brought Republicans to power and allowed them to abolish slavery at the war's end. Retiring in 1860, his health weakened until he died in Cleveland of an apparent stroke in the summer of 1866. His more famous and outspoken brother Benjamin had rejected third-party politics in part to protect his own status in the Whig party and in part because he believed that antislavery goals could be achieved only

53. *New York Times*, November 8, 1867.
54. Riddle, *Benjamin Wade*, 285.
55. *New York Times*, April 2, 1869.

through the two-party system. Yet he maintained with equal vehemence that slavery must be contained through the political process and the Slave Power brought down. Elected to the Senate as an antislavery Whig in 1851, he had become perhaps the most controversial of the Radicals, who through the years of Civil War and Reconstruction helped to force the end of slavery and the approval of political and civil rights for African Americans. Sparing no one in his verbal attacks, he reflected the limits that the times placed on racial justice. If he belongs on the conservative end of the antislavery political spectrum, he was far in advance of the general public and most politicians. He remained active in Republican circles until his death at seventy-seven in 1878 of typhoid.[56] Together, the Wade brothers had been an integral part of the political antislavery movement.

56. Williams, *History of Ashtabula County,* 85; Trefousse, *Benjamin Wade,* 320.

ELEVEN

QUITE A FEMALE POLITICIAN
Jessie Benton Frémont and the Antislavery Movement

JESSIE BENTON GREW up in a setting that prepared her almost to perfection for an activist
role in her fifty-year marriage to explorer,
politician, Civil War soldier, and business-
man John Charles Frémont. That setting also
provided the inspiration for her crusade in
antislavery politics, albeit one tightly circum-
scribed by the role and place of nineteenth-
century American women. In an era in which
women could neither vote nor hold office and
in which society assumed they would remain
silent and passive in the male world of politics,
Jessie came as close as any woman to breaking out
of the mold. Never directly rebuffed for her activist role
in behalf of her husband, she nonetheless angered politicians, including at
least two presidents, countless military men, and businessmen alike over her
aggressive "unfeminine" tactics. In the process she played a significant, albeit behind-the-scenes role in the political struggle against slavery and in behalf of African Americans. Never an abolitionist until the war years, she had
little awareness of the antislavery movement, either Garrisonian or political,
until her husband's run for the presidency as a Republican in 1856. Yet when
she did take up the cause from within the two-party structure, she did so
with a vigor that forced both major parties to take notice.

Before 1856, Jessie Benton Frémont's involvement in politics was as a

Democrat, for her father was a longtime member of Congress, first as a Jacksonian and then as a supporter of James K. Polk. She was thus the last to join an antislavery political party in the political spectrum of this study. Always the advocate of John C. Frémont, she supported his brief Senate career as he took his seat at the end of the Compromise debates in the fall of 1850. When his military heroics led to Republicans nominating him as their first presidential candidate, she joined the male world of politicians as Frémont's leading advocate and strategist, even helping to write a campaign biography. Despite remaining in the background, she endeared herself to supporters throughout the North in the "Frémont and Jessie" campaign. Denied the presidency in a close vote, the Frémonts returned to California until the Civil War brought them east again. When General Frémont attempted to free the slaves in his Missouri command, President Lincoln rebuffed his move and removed him from his position. Jessie rushed to Washington in his defense, again revealing her devotion to the dual cause of her husband and abolition. As his career declined, she returned to relative obscurity after the war, having played a meaningful role in the antislavery crusade as the most vocal woman in its behalf.[1]

Jessie Benton was born in 1824 at the Cherry Grove estate of her mother's family in western Virginia, one of three locations where she spent her childhood. Her mother, Elizabeth McDowell, had grown up in a slaveholder's family which possessed forty bondsmen; she inherited slaves when her father, James McDowell, died in 1835. The young Jessie spent many summers of her childhood in this setting, but much more of her early years were in Washington, where her father, Thomas Hart Benton, was an influential senator from Missouri and a supporter of Andrew Jackson. Second-born in a family of four daughters and two younger brothers, she quickly became her father's favorite. Never close to her mother because of Elizabeth's traditional domesticity, she endeared herself to the senator with her fiery, independent spirit. He thus attempted to raise her as the son he would have preferred. The young girl was soon accompanying him on his political rounds in Washing-

1. Pamela Herr's accounts of Jessie Benton Frémont provide the most insightful and historically sound studies of her colorful life. See Herr, *Jessie Benton Frémont: A Biography* (New York: F. Watts, 1987), and her brief account in *American National Biography,* 8:458–9. Herr and Mary Lee Spence have also edited a collection of her letters, *The Letters of Jessie Benton Frémont* (Urbana: Univ. of Illinois Press, 1993). See also Herr, "Permutations of a Marriage: John Charles and Jessie Benton Frémont's Civil War Alliance," in *The Intimate Strategies of the Civil War: Military Commanders and Their Wives,* ed. Carol K. Blaser and Lesley Gordon (New York: Oxford Univ. Press, 2001), 199–224.

ton and on occasion played and read in the Library of Congress while he worked. She thus learned of capital politics even as she became her father's confidante and personal secretary. Her third home was Benton's St. Louis political base, where she absorbed the spirit of the Missouri frontier and learned of the exciting American West, for which St. Louis was the jumping-off spot. Among her father's visitors whom she met was the aging William Clark, co-leader of the Lewis and Clark expedition of 1804–1806, now superintendent of Indian Affairs. Jessie was always more at ease in her father's Washington and St. Louis political world than that of her mother's family among Virginia slaveholders.

Not surprisingly, Jessie Benton chafed under the genteel and restrictive atmosphere at Miss English's Female Seminary in Georgetown where her parents enrolled her in 1838; the seminary was the favored girls' school among Washington politicos. Yet is was here at a school concert that the sixteen-year-old met a dashing young army surveyor, John Charles Frémont, already the favorite of her father because of the latter's interest in western exploration. Alarmed over the obvious romantic interest between the twenty-seven-year-old explorer and his teenage daughter, Benton apparently used his influence to have Frémont assigned to a surveying expedition in Iowa. The trip only delayed the romance, however, and on his return the two defied social convention and were secretly married in late 1841 when Jessie was seventeen. On learning of the union, the senator at first banished the young couple in anger, but soon reconciled and welcomed them into his household even as he used his political influence to champion the exploring desires of his son-in-law. He thus secured funding of a government expedition to the Rockies to explore the Oregon Trail through South Pass, with Frémont as its leader.

As the Frémonts planned for John's departure in May 1842, it was already clear to the couple that the pregnant young Jessie would assume a role in her husband's career going far beyond that of a typical nineteenth-century homemaker. Having already helped to write the report for the brief Iowa surveying expedition, she stood ready to do the same for subsequent government reports that would follow his expeditions. When the exploring party into the Rockies returned in success in late October, the impetuous young officer sought Jessie's assistance in effectively recounting the events and their significance. As Jessie put it years later in her memoirs: "The horse-back life, the sleep in the open air, had unfitted Mr. Frémont for the indoor work of writing—and second lieutenants cannot indulge in secretaries." After several false starts on the report brought him only frustration and illness, "I was let to try, and thus slid into my most happy life work." Jessie probably exaggerated her own role. Although not the report's author as she implied, she did edit and shape much of the original detailed draft which was in her husband's hand. She found it far from easy, but adjusting to the routine, she exclaimed: "Behold! Mr. Frémont's first book was finished."[2] With their home now in St. Louis, Jessie Frémont settled easily into an off-stage role as her husband's collaborator in a story of adventure which her writing skill brought to life and helped to make a success. So began a relationship that would take the couple deeply into the controversies of western exploration and war and then into antislavery politics.

Frémont's second expedition of 1843–1844 brought the young explorer even greater fame, again with the help of his wife. The goal was to explore the Oregon Country to the Pacific, but when petty jealousies led military leaders to seek to delay its departure, Jessie later claimed to have intervened to prevent delivery of a dispatch to John which might have held up or even halted the expedition. Frémont thus left on an ambitious 6,500–mile journey which included an unplanned return through Mexican California. Back in Washington, the two again collaborated over the winter months to produce an exciting account, "a superb blending of the technical and the intimate," which helped inspire thousands of Americans to head west and added to Frémont's growing fame as "the Pathfinder."[3] By the time his third expedition left for California in 1845, the nation was on the brink of war with Mexico over western lands. Expansionist Democrats under President James K. Polk were eager to add western and southwestern territories but faced Whig reluctance due to northern fears that it would become a war to add slave territory. Once on the Pacific, as war began between American and Mexican forces, Frémont's ambitions got the better of him as he sought glory and honor for both himself and his country. In Missouri, Jessie managed little enthusiasm for the war. Her opposition had little to do with slavery and

---

2. John C. Frémont, *Report of the Exploring Expedition to the Rocky Mountains in the Year 1842, and to Oregon and North California in the Years 1843–'44* (Washington, D.C.: Gales and Seaton, Printers, 1845); "Memoirs," 1901–1902, in Herr and Spence, eds., *Letters,* 12; Tom Chaffin, *Pathfinder: John Charles Frémont and the Course of American Empire* (New York: Hill and Wang, 2002), 143–4.

3. John C. Frémont, *Report;* Herr, *Frémont,* 110 (see also 88–91); Vernon Volpe, "The Origins of the Frémont Expeditions: John J. Abert and the Scientific Exploration of the Trans-Mississippi West," *The Historian* 62 (2000): 260–1; Chaffin, *Pathfinder,* 241–4.

future slave states, however, and much to do with the morality of aggressively seizing territory belonging to a weaker neighbor. A growing number of northerners of both parties had sought first to block the annexation of the slave republic of Texas and now feared a similar push into New Mexico. As she told a friend: "I have no sympathy for the war, nor has Mr. Frémont."[4] But in California as the war raged, her husband became embroiled in a personal struggle for command with his superior, General Stephen W. Kearny. The outcome left California in American hands and Frémont under arrest, to be marched east to face court-martial. Unable to stay out of the controversy, Jessie Frémont had hurried east to see President James K. Polk even before she knew of John's arrest.

Jessie's visit to Polk's office brought her little satisfaction. In June 1847, accompanied by Kit Carson, who had just returned from California with a letter from John outlining his predicament, she confronted the president. Her husband, she said, had been caught in the crossfire between General Kearny and Commodore Robert Stockton, who had appointed Frémont governor of California. Frémont had unwisely accepted the appointment, defying Kearny in the process. Anything but pleased with her visit, the president, who feared antagonizing his strong supporter Senator Benton, nonetheless refused to intervene, denying Jessie the "expression of approbation of her husband's conduct" that she sought. He believed that Frémont "was greatly in the wrong . . . in his controversy with Com. Stockton. It was unnecessary, however, that I should say so to Col. Frémont's wife." He clearly hoped that Frémont and Stockton would give in and that "it might not be necessary to institute any trial by a Court Martial." In August, Jessie finally met her husband in Kansas City, only to learn firsthand that the rumors of his arrest and pending court-martial were true. Meeting with Senator Benton en route to Washington, the three planned the defense that John would use in his trial. Jessie wrote again to the president pleading in her husband's behalf, but as the trial approached in November, Polk refused to stop the proceeding.[5] The president, a traditionalist and hardly one to give in to political pressure from a woman, was clearly perturbed by Jessie's aggressive intervention.

Jessie attended the daily sessions of her husband's three-month court-martial in Washington, which concluded with a guilty verdict and his dis-

---

4. Jessie Benton Frémont to John Torrey, March 21, 1847, in Herr, *Frémont,* 148.
5. Quaife, ed., *Diary of James K. Polk,* June 7, 14, August 17, 1847, 3:52–3, 61, 121.

missal from the army. After lengthy cabinet debates, Polk waived Frémont's dismissal and ordered him to return to duty. Rejecting Polk's offer as an admission of guilt, John resigned from the army in anger, a decision Jessie and her father fully endorsed.[6] The outcome, although leaving the Frémonts outraged, made John a persecuted hero in the eyes of much of the public. Together, he and Jessie could pursue both exploring and political goals with their reputations intact.

During the summer of 1848, Jessie's personal concerns overshadowed any interest she might have had in a presidential campaign dominated by proponents of the Wilmot Proviso seeking to block the expansion of slavery into territories recently seized from Mexico. Instead, the Frémonts faced a House refusal to fund a new western expedition, the birth of a dangerously ill baby boy, and plans for a privately funded expedition to seek an all-weather railroad route through the Rockies. When the baby, Benton Frémont, died in October, the grieving parents said their goodbyes to each other as John headed west and Jessie returned to Washington, promising to join him in California. Their reunion was delayed until June 1849, with Jessie enduring a two-month wait in Panama for a ship to San Francisco and John having suffered through a disastrous expedition and the loss of ten of his men in bitter winter snows in southern Colorado. But with gold fever raging in California and Frémont the owner of a huge tract of gold-bearing land, Las Mariposas near Yosemite Valley, the future again appeared bright for the Frémonts. California politics would finally introduce the couple to the issues of slavery and sectionalism.

As thousands rushed to California seeking gold, the new arrivals demanded statehood. But Congress failed to bring immediate satisfaction due to the North-South differences, of which California was only one point of contention. While Congress debated, Californians formed a provisional government, drafted a state constitution, and chose public officials to represent them. The constitutional convention which met in Monterrey in September 1849 drew up a document that made slavery illegal, an issue easily decided by miners who were less opposed to slavery on moral grounds than out of fear of competing with the chattel of slaveowners in the gold mines. Jessie remembered later that the issue was far more divisive than actually had been the case. As she hinted to the press first during the 1856 presidential cam-

6. Ibid., February 12–3, 16, 1848, 3:335–8, 340; see Herr, *Frémont*, 167–73, for an account of the trial and Jessie's role.

paign and then recalled in the 1890s, when asked in 1849 if she desired a slave as her servant, she had boldly informed the miners "that for no reason would I consent to own or use a slave." She even claimed that her home was "the headquarters of the antislavery party, and myself the example of happiness and hospitality without servants." In fact, she later recalled that during the delay in Panama, while she lay dangerously ill, she had had a vision in which her Aunt Edmonia appeared to her in a dream to tell her that she must "help to free the slaves" and work to prevent southern efforts to legalize slavery in California![7] Whether or not these recollections contained even a kernel of truth, or were more for propaganda effect, it is clear that Jessie's childhood experiences had turned her against slavery. Although she had little in common with her mother, Elizabeth, and her aristocratic Virginia background and had seen slavery on her grandfather's property, she closely identified with her mother's rejection of the peculiar institution. Freeing the slaves she inherited at the time of her father's death in 1835 "because of her conscientious feelings on the subject," according to Jessie's later account, Elizabeth had assisted the former slaves "and their children until they were self supporting."[8] Fully aware of the controversies over slavery that had raged in both Washington and Missouri, Jessie Frémont had, by the late 1840s, long since rejected any sympathy for southern slaveholders. The degree to which this attitude might later be translated into an active role in antislavery politics would soon be tested.

In December 1849, while Jessie and their seven-year-old daughter, Lilly, waited in San Francisco, John attended the sessions of the legislature in San Jose, where, due to his past prominence in national affairs and great wealth in California gold, he was elected one of the senators to represent the state as soon as Congress admitted it. She now eagerly anticipated her return to the East as the wife of a U.S. senator. It was a horrendous trip, first to Panama, where she was hospitalized with malaria for a month before resuming the Atlantic part of the voyage to New York. Once in Washington she recovered quickly in anticipation of the new life that awaited her. Party labels had meant little in California when John was elected, but most assumed that in Congress Frémont would identify with the moderate antislavery Demo-

7. Jessie Benton Frémont, "Great Events During the Life of Major General John C. Frémont, United States Army, and of Jessie Benton Frémont" (unpublished manuscript, 1891), 121–2, 126; Jessie Benton Frémont, *A Year of American Travel* (New York: Harper and Bros., 1878), 142–3, 147, 150–1.

8. Jessie Benton Frémont, *A Year of American Travel*, 141–2; Herr, *Frémont*, 16–8, 35.

crats of which his father-in-law was a leading member. He was, he said, a Democrat "by association, feeling, principle and education."[9] At this point there was little to indicate anything to the contrary, much less a leadership role in a yet-to-be established antislavery party.

As congressional debates on the Compromise proposals of Henry Clay dragged on through 1850, California statehood awaited the breaking of the North-South deadlock; the new senator could only bide his time. Finally, in late summer, the pieces of Clay's Compromise began to pass individually, with California statehood among the last enacted and Frémont and William Gwinn sworn in as its first senators. During the remaining two and a half weeks of the second session of the Thirty-first Congress, Frémont voted for the only Compromise bill still to be enacted, the ban on the slave trade in the District of Columbia, but against Whig senator William H. Seward's proposal to abolish slavery itself there.[10] He showed little interest in the antislavery demands of either Seward or the more radical Free Soilers led by Salmon P. Chase in the Senate and Joshua Giddings in the House. How his record might have evolved was a moot point because he had drawn the short-term Senate seat and had to return to California immediately to campaign for reelection to the next Congress. Reluctantly, Jessie set out with her husband on the difficult journey home and an uncertain future. Before leaving, neither Frémont expressed any concern about the disillusionment of Free Soilers over Congress's rejection of the Wilmot Proviso in relation to the Utah and New Mexico Territories or to the enactment of a new, proslavery fugitive slave law, all of which were parts of the Compromise package.[11]

Back in California, the Frémonts were caught in a political firestorm as the legislature deadlocked and appeared unable to choose a senator. Frémont's failure to win reelection and his decision to withdraw from the race after months of legislative debate were the result of his Democratic leanings, the opposition of a proslavery Democratic faction, and the growing resentment against wealthy land barons by landless miners and squatters. The evidence

9. Ruhl J. Bartlett, *John C. Frémont and the Republican Party* (1930; reprint, New York: Da Capo Press, 1970), 2.

10. Hamilton, *Prologue to Conflict,* 143 n. 13, 191 (appendix).

11. Most historians suggest that Frémont's record in the Senate established him as a significant antislavery advocate, but that can be claimed only if one interprets antislavery in its mildest forms. See Nevins, *Frémont,* 2:391; Andrew Rolle, *John Charles Frémont: Character as Destiny* (Norman: Univ. of Oklahoma Press, 1991), 138; and Herr, *Frémont,* 218, 220; Chaffin, *Pathfinder,* 417–8.

fails to show, however, that Frémont's containment of slavery position was a significant factor in his defeat, although the candidate himself believed that it had caused his defeat. As Jessie explained to her father's close friend Democratic editor Francis Preston Blair: "The state is decidedly Whig," and thus he must withdraw. In fact, California was closely divided politically and Frémont had failed to secure the support of all Democrats. But, she added, he would return "with renewed vigor by the next election."[12] Yet as she returned to domestic chores, which now included the raising of an infant son named after her husband, politics appeared no longer her priority. As she told her closest friend and confidante, Elizabeth "Liz" Blair Lee in November 1851: "The only politics we hear come from you and that is as much as we want." With California more and more her home of choice, the thought of a return to Washington politics repelled her. She concluded: "I should dissolve the Union sooner than let Mr. Frémont go away a year to Congress." Nor did John reveal any interest in national politics, as the excitement of California gold and the vast wealth they were accumulating took their full attention for the next four years.[13]

Much of their lives in the early 1850s involved the legal complications of the Las Mariposas grant, an area the size of the District of Columbia and rich in gold. In 1852 and 1853, they were in Europe trying to raise capital to develop the claim. In late 1853, John led his fifth and final expedition to search for and survey potential central Rockies railroad routes for the first transcontinental. It was again privately funded, with the Frémonts angry with the Franklin Pierce administration and its southern allies for its willingness to fund only a more southerly railroad route. Thus the president had rejected government support of the Frémont expedition. At this point, Frémont's anger with Pierce had everything to do with railroads and expeditions and little to do with the issues involving slavery, then so dominant in Congress. Not surprisingly, supporters found little interest in him among Democrats for that party's 1856 presidential nomination in a contest dominated by Senator Douglas and President Pierce. That his name was even mentioned was further indication of his moderate antislavery position and his stature as a military figure. The passage of the Kansas-Nebraska Act by Democratic majorities in May 1854, with its repeal of the ban on slavery

---

12. Nevins, *Frémont*, 2:396–7; Bartlett, *Frémont*, 6; Jessie Benton Frémont to Blair, August 14, 1851, in Herr and Spence, eds., *Letters*, 45–9.

13. Jessie Benton Frémont to Elizabeth Blair Lee, November 14, 1851, in Herr and Spence, eds., *Letters*, 50–2; Bartlett, *Frémont*, 6.

north of the Missouri Compromise line, meant that endorsement of the act would be a prerequisite for any serious contender for the party's nomination. Furthermore, leaders in a party controlled by southerners insisted on a candidate's endorsement of the Fugitive Slave Act of 1850. Jessie later recalled that one Democrat had noted: "the Democratic party was sure to win" and no wife of a candidate "could refuse the presidency." Yet the couple agreed that instead they would pursue a "mission of doing good. You cannot give in to the execution of all the laws," a reference to the Fugitive Slave and Kansas-Nebraska acts. Neither John nor Jessie could abide by either demand, and in 1855 they agreed to put their future with the fledgling Republican party, at the risk of alienating not only her southern relatives but also her father, who pledged himself to remain a Democrat. For Jessie, "there was only one decision possible."[14]

Jessie Frémont would play a critical, albeit behind-the-scenes role in John's drive for the Republican presidential nomination in 1856. Astute enough to understand the party's need for a moderate who was not overly partisan, she believed her husband to be the ideal candidate. Those dedicated to a truly firm opposition to slavery in all its forms had their favorites in Senator William H. Seward of New York and Governor Salmon P. Chase of Ohio. Although both Frémonts were coy about their aspirations, they and more moderate Republicans understood that the party's only chance was to avoid any suggestion of radicalism in either platform or candidate. Thus the two worked closely with like-minded party leaders, especially Francis Preston Blair. It was Jessie who assured her husband of Blair's willingness to provide "assistance" and then approached the aging editor, urging him to meet with John. Blair agreed and even drafted a letter in Frémont's name attacking Kansas-Nebraska's repeal of the ban on slavery north of 36°30′ as well as the actions of proslavery elements in the Kansas Territory.[15] She also curried the favor of Republican congressman Nathaniel Banks of Massachusetts, a friend of Blair and candidate to be Speaker of the House, a factor noted later during the campaign. Banks's election in early February 1856 provided a needed boost to the Frémont drive. The Frémonts had recently returned east from California for the campaign and had rented a house in New York City. By April, Jessie was enthusiastically playing the role of the

14. Jessie Benton Frémont, "Great Events During the Life of Major General John C. Frémont, United States Army, and of Jessie Benton Frémont," 204; Nevins, *Frémont*, 2:425.
15. Jessie Benton Frémont to Blair, August 27, 1855, in Herr and Spence, eds., *Letters*, 71.

wife of a man soon to become president. As she shared with Liz, "just now I am quite the fashion—5th Avenue asks itself, 'Have we a Presidentess among us—.' . . . So I go out nightly—sometimes to dinner and a party, both the same night and three times a week to the opera where I hold a levee in my box." She lamented that her social whirl would all end in May to prepare for the Republican convention the following month.[16] As the party's nominating convention approached, Jessie had helped to create a viable contender who moderate Republicans could rally around.

Frémont had also taken steps to identify with free soil elements in Kansas. He wrote a leader of the free-state party there, Charles Robinson, who had earlier been his supporter in California: "As you stood by me firmly and generously . . . in California, I have every disposition to stand by you in your battle with them (the pro slavery party) in Kansas." Frémont strategists got the letter printed widely in key journals, and with that any doubt over his antislavery credentials began to evaporate.[17] Thus with moderates in total control at the convention, the candidacies of Seward and Chase collapsed and Frémont delegates had only to beat back the challenge of the aging Supreme Court justice John McLean. John and Jessie had remained in New York during the convention, but when crowds gathered to celebrate the outcome, they not only cheered the candidate, but shouted: "Jessie! Jessie! Give us Jessie." When she finally appeared, as no other presidential candidate's wife had ever done before, the crowd was delirious with approval.[18] John's letter of acceptance published in early July said all of the appropriate things for a candidate of a party portraying itself as seeking the divorce of the federal government from slavery. Proslavery Democrats in the slave states and in Kansas, he claimed, had distorted the intentions of the Founding Fathers to keep slavery within its existing boundaries. The Free Soil faction responded with enthusiasm to his candidacy. Gamaliel Bailey gave a ringing endorsement in the *National Era,* and John Greenleaf Whittier added the voice of the poet in his praise of Frémont's antislavery convictions. In "The Pass of

16. Jessie Benton Frémont to Blair, November 3, October 21, 1855, Jessie Benton Frémont to Lee, November 27, 1855, April 17, 18, 1856, in Herr and Spence, eds., *Letters,* 73–4, 71, 78–9, 95–6, 97–9.

17. *New York Tribune,* April 10, 1856; Bartlett, *Frémont,* 17. For a full account of the political maneuvering of the various Republican factions and the Frémonts' role, see William E. Gienapp, *The Origins of the Republican Party, 1852–1856* (New York: Oxford Univ. Press, 1987), 307–30, and Chaffin, *Pathfinder,* 436–9.

18. *New York Tribune,* June 26, 1856.

the Sierra," Whittier used his western heroics as the background from which Frémont would lead the nation into the promised land of emancipation:

> Strong Leader of that mountain band
> Another task remains
> To break from Slavery's Desert land
> A Path to freedom's plains
>
> . . . .
>
> Rise up Frémont! And go before;
> The Hour must have its Man;
> Put on the hunting-shirt once more
> And lead in Freedom's Van![19]

Frémont's popular image among northern voters would hopefully do the rest, aided by the aggressive role of his wife.

Jessie's role in John's presidential campaign was largely unknown to the public but was of far greater significance than that of any other woman in nineteenth-century American politics. Publicly, John's July letter of acceptance was his first and last campaign statement. But as Republican campaign leaders devised a strategy to elect their candidate, the Frémonts worked feverishly, with Jessie taking the lead. Not only did the party, participating in its first national election, face all of the organizational difficulties of any new party, but it found itself in a three-way race. The southern-leaning Democrats, with their large block of northern voters content with appeasing the South to prevent further sectional unrest, nominated longtime party professional James Buchanan of Pennsylvania. He was joined by former president Millard Fillmore of the American or Know-Nothing party, a third party which threatened to cut into Republican strength with its nativist appeal. Jessie saw her most essential role as managing the candidate's correspondence, deciding which letters he should see and respond to and which she should keep to herself to shelter her sensitive husband from the mudslinging that was part of all campaigns. She worked with those writing campaign biographies of John, especially with John Bigelow, whose glowing portrait, *Memoir of the Life and Public Services of John Charles Frémont*, appeared in installments in his *New York Evening Post* and in book form during the

19. Ibid., July 9, 1856; Bartlett, *Frémont*, 20–1; *National Era*, October 2, 23, 1856; John Greenleaf Whittier, *Anti-Slavery Poems: Songs of Labor and Reform* (Boston: Houghton Mifflin, 1892), 187–9.

summer. Jessie wrote at least one of the chapters in Bigelow's biography herself, trying to counter the various scandalous rumors then in circulation about her husband. She worried about fine details, such as his portrait, which the publishers "have by their unjustifiable hurry ruined his mouth in the likeness of Mr. Frémont." Her concern, she said, was her wish that all should "share my admiration of Mr. Frémont's character as shewn in his face."[20]

Of greater import were Jessie's efforts to counter the smears directed against the candidate. Democrats raised questions about the couple's elopement in 1841 in defiance not only of her father, Senator Benton, but also of prevailing social convention. More significant, given the anti-Catholicism of the day and the bigotry of the Know-Nothing appeal, was the rumor that Frémont was a Catholic because his father had been French and because John, in his haste to marry Jessie in 1841, had engaged a Catholic priest to perform the ceremony. Although she believed the issue irrelevant, she hastened to point out to one inquirer that "Mr. Frémont was born and educated in the Protestant Episcopal Church" in Charleston and "that I am too an Episcopalian and our children were all baptized in that church." There was no effective response to Democratic reminders of his illegitimate birth, but she was quick to refute the rumor that he had once owned slaves. Said Jessie, "Neither has either of us owned any slaves, which is the other bugbear."[21] In correspondence with reformer Lydia Maria Child, a Garrisonian who by 1856 endorsed elective politics and became interested in Frémont's candidacy because of Jessie's prominence, she reviewed her past opposition to slavery. Noting her refusal to buy a slave while in California, she added: "I would as soon place my children in the midst of smallpox, as rear them under the influences of slavery." To Child she also recalled her Virginia mother's rejection of slavery: "She brought us up to think it good fortune to be free from owning slaves." She bemoaned to Liz the abuse that she and her husband were subjected to during the campaign, but most of all she helped plan the strategy that the party pursued, urging supporters, especially in Pennsylvania, to campaign for John and win the key home state of opponent

20. Margaret Clapp, *Forgotten First Citizen: John Bigelow* (1947; reprint, New York: Greenwood, 1968), 99–107; Jessie Benton Frémont to Charles Upham, June 25, 30, 1856, in Herr and Spence, eds., *Letters*, 108, 111. See John Bigelow, *Memoir of the Life and Public Services of John Charles Frémont* (New York: Derby and Jackson, 1856).

21. Jessie Benton Frémont to Dr. John Robertson, June 30, 1856, in Herr and Spence, eds., *Letters*, 110.

Buchanan: "Urge every available man to go to Pennsylvania and speak. The Democratic party will fill that state with documents of their own, but the human voice will exercise a magnetic power which will undo their work."[22] Throughout the summer months no one worked harder or as effectively for the Republican candidate than Jessie Benton Frémont.

In the process she helped forward both the Republican containment platform and the role women might play in politics. It was Jessie who caught the imagination not only of the voting male public, but of many women who took an active interest in politics for the first time. Said Lydia Maria Child: "What a shame women can't vote! We'd carry 'our Jessie' into the White House on our shoulders, wouldn't we." Child also wrote a novella, "The Kansas Emigrants," in support of the Republican candidate, and other women like her who had long shunned politics in their Garrisonian belief that it would compromise their antislavery principles now joined in urging Frémont's election. Although Child was the recipient of Democratic criticism for her role in politics, for the most part, talk of the "Frémont and Jessie" campaign overshadowed the attacks and left Republican vice presidential candidate William L. Dayton of New Jersey all but forgotten. And it left the Republican party within a thin margin of victory in its first presidential campaign.[23]

As the campaign ground on, Jessie found her delicate health in jeopardy, yet she refused to heed doctors' warnings to slow down. Deeply hurt by her father's refusal to communicate with her, she nonetheless plunged ahead in John's behalf. With the breech between father and daughter apparently complete, she urged Blair not to "let him say things personally injurious to Mr. Frémont."[24] Benton did make numerous campaign speeches for Buchanan, arguing that the election of a Republican would divide the Union and result in civil war. There was no effective way to counter such arguments, and Jessie was realistic enough to understand that when state elections in October in Pennsylvania and Indiana went against the Republicans,

22. Jessie Benton Frémont to Lydia Maria Child, late July/August 1856, Jessie Benton Frémont to Lee, August 12, 1856, in ibid., 121–3, 124–8.

23. See Nevins, *Frémont*, 2:443; Herr, *Jessie Benton Frémont*, 241. For a full discussion of Jessie's appeal to the electorate in 1856, both as a physically attractive woman and as a politically active antislavery woman, see Pierson, *Free Hearts and Free Homes*, 129–33. Pierson also analyzes Child's plot, 153–5, 158.

24. Jessie Benton Frémont to Lee, August 20, 1856, Jessie Benton Frémont to Blair, August 25, 1856, in Herr and Spence, eds., *Letters*, 130–2, 132–5.

Buchanan would prevail in November. Long before the votes were counted and the Pennsylvanian had defeated Frémont by an electoral count of 170 to 114 and a popular majority of 1.8 million to 1.34 million, she had reconciled herself to the outcome. She lamented her wish that Frémont "had been the one to administer the bitter dose of subjection to the South." Like a surgeon, he would "have cut off their right hand Kansas from the old unhealthy southern body." The presidency, she concluded, "would have called out great qualities in him."[25] Far from the abolitionists that Whittier would have preferred, Jessie and John nonetheless accurately represented Republican thinking in support of containment in 1856. To what degree they would move beyond such a stance and approach that of more Radical Republicans was a question for the future.

During the four years following Frémont's defeat, John and Jessie focused on his California claims and on personal problems and relationships and, for the most part, retreated from sectional and gender issues. As the nation drifted toward a showdown between North and South under the weak and vacillating direction of James Buchanan, who appeared eager to comply with virtually every southern demand, and as the Republican party in Congress and the states resisted his policies and pointed to the next presidential election, the Frémonts appeared little interested in the developing crisis. Based on their public actions and private correspondence, they appeared unconcerned over the increasing control over government by the Slave Power. They scarcely noted the Supreme Court's endorsement of the southern position on property rights in slaves and on territorial slavery in the Dred Scott decision of March 1857, so vilified by Republicans throughout the North. Although women had been inspired by Jessie's prominence during the 1856 campaign and had held Frémont rallies of their own, Jessie appeared unaware of the resolution of the National Woman's Rights Convention in New York presided over by Lucy Stone, and held shortly after the election. The members urged the Republican party "to do justice" to women because it had appealed "constantly, through its orators, to female sympathy" and used "for its most popular rallying cry a female name."[26]

Personal rather than political issues dominated Jessie's thinking and actions. Only thirty-two in early 1857, deeply discouraged by the election results, hurt by rumors of John's infidelity, and driven by her desire to reconcile with her father, she resolved to put her own life in order. With difficulty,

25. Jessie Benton Frémont to Lee, October 20, 1856, ibid., 139–40.
26. *New York Times*, November 26, 1856.

Benton and the Frémonts agreed to try and forget the political bitterness of the previous year. Jessie was both relieved and pleased that she could renew her ties with her aging father and that her husband held no grudge against him. In fact, John appeared at times more willing to accept what had happened than she was. To Liz she admitted that Benton's opposition had been "a sort of Brutus stab." Thankfully, "family harmony and peace for my father's old age has come out of defeat." As she explained to Blair, election defeat meant that "We're all dead men in the political world so we have all our talents free for private life." Yet if John appeared content, she concluded that her political interest had not been totally silenced. She resolved: "I want the party to prevail."[27]

John preferred now to return to California, but she had little interest in joining him.[28] Instead she took their three children to France for six months, only to find that, whatever their differences, she missed her husband and longed to be with him. On her return in March 1858, she visited her father again and, despite her realization that he was dying of cancer, reluctantly left for California with her husband. The next two years were, for the Frémonts, a time of trial and tribulation in the tiny mining town of Bear Valley, California. Horace Greeley arrived in the summer of 1859 and urged John to consider entering the 1860 presidential contest, but neither he nor Jessie were tempted. During her two and a half–year stay in California, she had befriended two young writers, a Unitarian minister, Thomas Starr King, and Bret Harte. Her support and encouragement of their writing and oratory was for her the best alternative to the role as a writer she would have preferred for herself, but which her gender denied her.[29] In June 1860, after Republicans in Chicago had chosen their candidates, she claimed total contentment with her California life and seemed glad that her husband appeared accepting of "home life." She rejoiced that they were now "a complete and compact family."[30] Yet she followed the campaign enthusiastically, and news of the election of Abraham Lincoln which arrived via pony express in November would quickly end whatever domestic tranquility the Frémonts had enjoyed and send them east into the maelstrom of sectional and political conflict.

27. Jessie Benton Frémont to Lee, March 1, 1857, Jessie Benton Frémont to Blair, January 31, August 30, 1857, in Herr and Spence, eds., *Letters*, 151–4, 148–50, 167–71.

28. Jessie Benton Frémont to Blair, January 31, 1857, in ibid., 148–50.

29. Herr, *Frémont*, 304, 312–4.

30. Jessie Benton Frémont to Lee, June 2, 1860, in Herr and Spence, eds., *Letters*, 227–9.

Before leaving for the East, Jessie personally involved herself in behalf of a black employee, Albert Lea, who faced hanging after conviction for the murder of his wife. The evidence appeared conclusive, and Jessie sought only to have the sentence commuted to life imprisonment. In a letter to the *Alta California,* she outlined Lea's "faithful services" to Frémont beginning with John's third expedition and continuing at Bear Valley until the murder. Her intervention in Lea's behalf perhaps underscored the Frémonts' deepening commitment to challenging the racial injustice of nineteenth-century America. Although Lea's trial and execution did not openly suggest racial bias by the jury or judge, Jessie believed that the governor had refused to commute his sentence because of his race.[31] Her eagerness to defend Lea, albeit unsuccessfully, showed a compassion rare among people of her standing and suggests that her lack of involvement in slave-related issues since the 1856 campaign had merely been a brief hiatus. Surely her every effort in the coming war years would reveal a commitment equal to that of any abolitionist. These actions also showed her continued willingness to go to any length in her husband's behalf. For Jessie the two goals were of equal importance and always emerged simultaneously. Ever since he had entered sectional politics in 1856 her concern over antislavery was a means to advance his political fortunes and vice versa. Late in joining the movement, her dual interests made her among the most vehement in attacking the Slave Power.

The fall of Fort Sumter in April 1861 accelerated Jessie's plans to join her husband in the East, where he eagerly awaited appointment to lead a Union army. In May he learned he would command the Department of the West, and Jessie and their children immediately left San Francisco for New York. Although friends suggested they stay in Washington during the fighting like other wives and family of military leaders, she would have none of it. His headquarters would be in St. Louis, "and I will be with him everywhere— I will."[32] Once there, they faced a crisis of major magnitude, for Missouri, a Union slave state, had large numbers of rebel sympathizers. The task of civil and military leaders was to keep the state secure for the Union. The president believed that meant not tampering with slavery, at least at first, in order to keep as many Missourians loyal as possible. To the Frémonts, on the other hand, the war had altered their earlier reluctance concerning

31. Jessie Benton Frémont to *Alta California,* February 26, 1861, ibid., 235–7; Herr, *Frémont,* 317–8.

32. Jessie Benton Frémont to John A. Anderson, June 11, 1861, in Herr and Spence, eds., *Letters,* 319.

forced emancipation. The Confederacy's decision to fight to defend slavery meant that rebels must be brought into line and perhaps have their chattel seized and freed.

Such a policy was not obvious at first in the military crisis faced by General Frémont. Union troops and supplies were insufficient in Missouri due to the government's decision to concentrate on Eastern battle theaters. Union general Nathaniel Lyon, badly outnumbered at Springfield, chose to stand and fight at Wilson's Creek in August, a decision which not only cost him his life, but the surrender of much of southern Missouri to rebel forces. As Frémont scurried to rally Union forces throughout the state, Jessie, in effect, coordinated activities at the St. Louis headquarters. Critics were quick to label her "General Jessie." It was Jessie who acted as liaison with the Western Sanitary Commission in organizing makeshift hospitals for the many wounded brought to St. Louis from the Wilson's Creek battlefield. It was she who wrote much of Frémont's confidential correspondence, advised him, and met important visitors in his stead. It was she who wrote to Lincoln of the pending disaster at Wilson's Creek, pleading for additional troops and supplies. It was, in her words, "one of the most pleasant memories of that the most wearing and most welcome work of my life."[33] But her determination and enthusiasm had accentuated other issues, which only deepened the crisis the Frémonts would soon face.

An integral aspect of their precarious situation was the deteriorating relations between the Frémonts and the Blairs in the late summer of 1861. Francis Preston Blair's sons, Montgomery and Frank, were Missouri politicians who had been key in keeping their state loyal; both were moderates who opposed expanding a war to save the Union into one to free the slaves, however. President Lincoln had appointed Montgomery Blair to be his postmaster general, and his brother, Frank, was a Republican congressman who returned to St. Louis in the summer of 1861 expecting to receive a high military appointment and lucrative war contracts for himself and his many Missouri friends. When Frémont helped deny these to him due in part to their differences over slavery, Frank wrote damning letters to the president questioning Frémont's military ability and implying the commander's negligence in Lyon's defeat at Wilson's Creek. Lincoln eventually sent Montgomery to investigate the situation, and within days the Frémonts and Blairs had turned against each other with a vengeance that quickly dissolved a friendship of

33. Jessie Benton Frémont to Lincoln, August 5, 1861, ibid., 262; Jessie Benton Frémont, *The Story of the Guard: A Chronicle of the War* (Boston: Ticknor and Fields, 1863), 43–4.

decades. Not only were Jessie and John at odds with the Blair brothers, but Jessie now faced the anger of their father, Francis, and their sister, Liz, the latter with whom she had corresponded so intimately for so many years.[34] The details of their many differences are not critical to a description of Jessie's antislavery politics, but they reflect her firm dedication to abolition goals. And while not the immediate cause of the feud, it was John and Jessie's handling of the slavery issue in Missouri which exacerbated the bitter feelings.

What followed on August 30 was the most momentous act of John's career and one which had the full support of Jessie and soon the entire antislavery community. Feeling that the administration had given him a free hand in his Western Department due to its preoccupation with the Eastern theater, General Frémont, facing a military crisis in light of the defeat at Wilson's Creek, declared martial law throughout the state. He decreed that rebels captured behind Union lines could be court-martialed and shot, their property seized, and their slaves immediately freed. It was by no means a step he took lightly or without having carefully thought it through. He had consulted closely with Illinois congressman and abolitionist Owen Lovejoy, then serving briefly as a colonel in an Illinois regiment in St. Louis and assigned to him as an aide. Before his announcement he had called in Jessie and Edward Davis, a Quaker abolitionist, to read to them what he had just drafted. Both heartily approved his action and fully understood what had created the need for such a drastic step. Missouri was not only threatened militarily, but rebel sympathizers jeopardized its civil functioning as well. Martial law would put Frémont in command rather than the provisional governor, the states' rights, proslavery-oriented Hamilton R. Gamble. Not surprisingly, Fremont distrusted Gamble and all those whom he believed to be aiding the enemy. Not only would military control strengthen his own hand in Missouri and thus facilitate forcing the state into conformity with the Union cause, but it would be the first step toward making the war into one to destroy slavery.[35] Although she claimed not to have known of his plan until he handed her the order he had written, it was clearly a decision that

---

34. Vernon Volpe, "The Frémonts and Emancipation in Missouri," *The Historian* 56 (1994): 348; Herr, *Frémont*, 331–2, 340–2; Herr, "Permutations of a Marriage," 207–9.

35. Frémont, "Proclamation," August 30, 1861, in *The War of the Rebellion: A Compilation of the Official Records of the Union and Confederate Armies* (Washington, D.C., 1880–1901), 1st series, 3:442; see Volpe, "The Frémonts and Emancipation in Missouri," 339–54; see also Nevins, *Frémont*, 2:499–500; Louis S. Gerteis, *Civil War St. Louis* (Lawrence: Univ. Press of Kansas, 2001), 147, 88–9, 142–3.

was as much Jessie's as it was his. And it would be she who took on the burden of defending his action before an angered president.

Lincoln's reaction to Frémont's order was swift and predictable. At this early stage of the war, the president feared that any direct move against slavery would antagonize the Union slave states, not only Missouri, but especially Kentucky and perhaps Maryland and lead them to join the Confederacy. Nor would it please northern moderates on whom he depended for support. Of equal importance in a policy matter as critical as emancipation, the decision rested solely with the chief executive and could not be entrusted to various field commanders acting unilaterally. Yet not wanting to undercut Frémont entirely, he hoped to settle the issue painlessly by urging the general to modify his martial law proclamation so as to remove the slave property provision and thus not antagonize "our Southern-Union friends."[36]

Together, the Frémonts determined to defy the president's request, for emancipation was, in their view, a military necessity justified by the need for "strong and vigorous measures." Moreover, as Jessie later viewed the order, it had "struck the first blow for freedom for the slave and declared war as well as on secession."[37] Whether or not they naively believed that the president would submit to their policy is not clear, but the sincerity of their convictions is apparent. Although critics viewed it as political expediency and designed to win favor with abolitionist elements of the Republican party, the war had served as a catalyst to move both Jessie and John from a moderate to a more radical antislavery stance. They were now abolitionists themselves. Unfortunately for them, Lincoln had received messages from both Frank and Montgomery Blair disparaging the general and all aspects of his Missouri command. Thus when John accepted Jessie's urging that he send her to Washington to plead their case before the president, Lincoln's predisposition to rescind the emancipation order had been reinforced dramatically.

Jessie Frémont's interview with Lincoln on September 10, 1861, was a meeting almost without precedent in the annals of the nineteenth-century presidency. The only previous confrontation initiated by a woman against a

36. Lincoln to John C. Frémont, September 2, 1861, in John G. Nicolay and John Hay, *Abraham Lincoln: A History* (New York: Century Co., 1890), 4:418; Bartlett, *Frémont,* 74.

37. Volpe, "The Frémonts and Emancipation in Missouri," 339. Jessie's account is found in "Great Events During the Life of Major General John C. Frémont, United States Army, and of Jessie Benton Frémont," 268. See also John C. Frémont to Lincoln, September 8, 1861, in Nicolay and Hay, *Lincoln,* 4:418–9; Herr, "Permutations of a Marriage," 209–11.

president was Jessie's meeting with James K. Polk in 1847 over John's pending court-martial. The difference was that this involved an issue of major national import, that of emancipation. Whether she realistically expected to change Lincoln's mind is not clear. What is clear is that her challenge, if anything, reinforced his decision to revoke the general's policy. As Jessie later recalled, the meeting was tense at first, and when she reminded Lincoln that emancipation might deter England and other European states from recognizing and even aiding the Confederacy, the president responded condescendingly: "You are quite a female politician." Refusing to give her a direct response, Lincoln then ignored two further written requests that he respond to her personally, and, instead, sent word directly to St. Louis ordering Frémont to rescind his order. The president believed he had valid reasons to delay emancipation and then to take the initiative himself. Believing that Frémont should have consulted Frank Blair before acting so precipitously on his own, Lincoln, according to Jessie, responded angrily to her plea, claiming that "it is a war for a great national object and the Negro has nothing to do with it."[38] However one interprets her recollection of the interview, the meeting served only to exacerbate their differences and accelerate Frémont's removal from command. The president had dismissed her in advance at least in part because she was a woman and because Frémont's policy did not suit his overall war strategy. She had unwisely challenged his authority because she unflinchingly supported her husband and because she believed his policy would effectively hasten emancipation. In the end it is also possible that Frémont's order, based on military necessity, and her intervention in its behalf may have moved Lincoln to an emancipation policy based on the same premise more quickly than otherwise might have been the case.

Lincoln delayed Frémont's removal until early November, but in the intervening weeks the controversy touched off a major debate that would last well into the following year. Abolitionists were virtually unanimous in their support of Frémont and in their condemnation of the president's handling of the issue. Horace Greeley endorsed Frémont's action and reported that as many as twenty-three slaves had been freed before Lincoln rescinded the order. Antislavery Republicans in Congress led by Benjamin Wade and including Charles Sumner, Owen Lovejoy, George W. Julian, and others ral-

---

38. Jessie Benton Frémont, "Great Events During the Life of Major General John C. Frémont, United States Army, and of Jessie Benton Frémont." It is also found in Herr and Spence, eds., *Letters*, 264–9. See also Lincoln to John C. Frémont, September 11, 1861, in Nicolay and Hay, *Lincoln*, 4:420; Nevins, *Frémont*, 2:517.

lied to Frémont's cause and were joined at least privately by Treasury Secretary Chase. Leading abolitionists, such as Wendell Phillips, William Lloyd Garrison, and other editors throughout the North, including Jane Swisshelm, rallied to the embattled general's cause. The Quaker poet John Greenleaf Whittier added his voice in "To John C. Frémont," which concluded:

> Thy error, Frémont simply was to act
> A brave man's part, without the statesman's tact,
> And, taking counsel but of common sense,
> To strike at cause as well as consequence
>
> . . . .
>
> Still take thou courage! God has spoken through thee,
> Irrevocable, the mighty words, Be free!
> . . . .[39]

Jessie read him the lines to bolster his sagging spirits as he prepared for one final Missouri battle in late September. She told Whittier later that "His face lit up with such a different kind of look from the angry, baffled resentful kind of face he had just had. His natural serenity came back and the whole tone of his mind was altered. Thanks to your true brave words." The Committee on the Conduct of the war heard Frémont's testimony in early 1862, and, led by Wade and Julian, endorsed his every move, including his emancipation order, suggesting that he had "rightly judged in regard to the most effective means of subduing this rebellion." For Jessie, the chance for him to appear before the committee was "the end of our silence and now will come justice and retribution."[40] Not wishing to make him more of a martyr to abolitionism than he already was, Lincoln, in March, named him to command Union forces in the Mountain Department of eastern Kentucky and Tennessee and western Virginia.

Throughout the crisis Jessie led the fight in her husband's behalf. Moderates had rushed to the president's defense even before he had revoked the emancipation order and removed its author. Led by the Blairs, they had put much of the blame on Jessie, suggesting personal ambition more than anti-

39. *New York Tribune*, September 15, 16, 17, 18, 1861; *Liberator* (Boston), September 20, 27, 1862; Blue, *Chase*, 181; Whittier, "To John C. Frémont," *Anti-Slavery Poems*, 222–3.

40. Tap, *Over Lincoln's Shoulder*, 81–100; "Report of the Joint Committee on the Conduct of the War," Part 3: "Department of the West," *Senate Executive Documents*, 37th Cong., 3rd sess., document 108, 6; Jessie Benton Frémont to Whittier, October 17, 1863, Jessie Benton Frémont to Thomas Starr King, December 29, 1861, in Herr and Spence, eds., *Letters*, 356–9, 305.

slavery conviction had motivated both Frémonts. As they left Missouri for New York, Jessie planned her next step in John's defense. While he awaited a new command and prepared to testify before the Committee on the Conduct of the War, she wrote a spirited account of the Missouri events in the form of a novel, *The Story of the Guard,* an heroic account of Frémont's military maneuvers in Missouri designed to answer the charges of corruption and incompetence in his leadership there. She wrote with understatement and subtlety, not wanting to be too blunt in her attack on the administration: "I would not let it have the look of sentimentalizing public opinion and it will follow public justice to the general."[41] Although it only indirectly addressed the slavery issue, the novel served as an effective defense of her embattled husband and a bold step for a woman to take even during a time of war.

As John prepared for his new command from his headquarters in Wheeling in western Virginia, Jessie helped organize and direct his office much as she had done in St. Louis the previous summer. The western counties of Virginia sought approval of their separation from Virginia and the Confederacy, and Jessie lent her efforts in behalf of the Unionist element there. Frémont's presence, she predicted in April, "will be to kill the *conditional* union sentiment and bring out the healthy feeling." A month later, she pled with her friend George W. Julian, Radical member of the Committee on the Conduct of the War, not to "*let troops be withdrawn from this Dept,*" again suggesting that the administration was sabotaging her husband's efforts. She added that "the working and middle class call for emancipation and we are doing a good political work here."[42] As John left for the field in mid-May, Jessie returned to New York to await the outcome. Things did not go well, however, and when Frémont's forces failed in their pursuit of Stonewall Jackson's army, Lincoln, in frustration, combined Frémont's army with two others under General John Pope, a longtime critic of Frémont and a man that John considered his inferior. Having been passed over by Lincoln for this critical command, Frémont resigned rather than be humiliated. Had he stayed, said Jessie later, "they would have prepared defeats and destroyed his reputation. He knew the men and would not trust them."[43] While he futilely

41. Jessie Benton Frémont to George W. Childs, February 8, 1862, in Herr and Spence, eds., *Letters,* 314–5. For a full evaluation of the novel, see Herr, *Frémont,* 353–5. It was not published until late 1862, after Frémont had resigned and appeared to have little chance of a new assignment. See Herr, *Frémont,* 366–7.

42. Jessie Benton Frémont to Frederick Billings, February 8, 1862, Jessie Benton Frémont to Julian, May 1, 1862, in Herr and Spence, eds., *Letters,* 316–9, 319–22.

43. Jessie Benton Frémont to Julian, January 16, 1864, in ibid., 361–3.

sought another command, the Frémonts now remained in the East waiting for the opportunity to reestablish John's career and play a role in the rapidly accelerating abolition drive.

Jessie and John Frémont spent much of 1863 in New York brooding over what they regarded as their shabby treatment by the Lincoln government. Both hoped John might receive another command, but when that failed to materialize, Jessie lamented that her husband had been reduced to teaching his daughter to ride in Central Park: "Isn't it a shame that such men have no better use of their time than to train a girl to ride?" The rebuff by the administration led her to dismiss Lincoln's Emancipation Proclamation of January 1, 1863, as too little and too late; she charged that his alliance with the Blairs was indicative of a surrender of abolition principle: "Never could the rebels have had such success had not our own political chiefs helped them."[44] As long as he continued to deny her husband the place he deserved, she would refuse to recognize the momentous step the president's Proclamation represented. By the end of the year, with no appointment forthcoming, she concluded bitterly: "I am hoping great things for the country from the growing knowledge of the President as he really is—a sly slimy nature." She cherished the friendship, support, and writings of abolitionist friends such as Harriet Beecher Stowe, Wendell Phillips, and John Greenleaf Whittier, yet appeared frustrated that she and her husband could not bring their abolitionist goals to fruition more quickly than the bungling, inept, and hostile administration permitted.[45]

During these months of 1863 and early 1864, while John played no role in the political and military events, Jessie busied herself in the fund-raising efforts of the Sanitary Commission. Her major concern was a fair in New York in April 1864 which raised thousands of dollars for war relief. During the summer months she spent much of her time in the cool breezes of Nahant on the Massachusetts coast, where she found friendly encouragement for her abolitionist beliefs from such kindred spirits as Whittier and her neighbor, Henry Wadsworth Longfellow, and others who visited at her shore retreat.[46] There, she could also play a role in the developing movement

---

44. Jessie Benton Frémont to Thomas Star King, early 1863, February 27, 1863, Jessie Benton Frémont to Julian, March 3, 1863, in ibid., 338–41, 343–8, 348–50.

45. Jessie Benton Frémont to Thomas S. King, October 16, 1863, Jessie Benton Frémont to Whittier, February 14, 1864, in ibid., 355–6, 370–2. See also Herr, *Frémont*, 368.

46. Jessie Benton Frémont to Whittier, February 14, 1864, in Herr and Spence, eds., *Letters*, 370–2; Herr, *Frémont*, 370–2.

to nominate her husband to challenge Lincoln in the presidential election of 1864.

As the war lengthened and the bloodshed increased, with no apparent end in sight, an unusual assortment of dissidents—most frustrated by the lack of both Union war progress and the completion of emancipation— began to urge Frémont to run. The movement occurred after a more serious challenge from Treasury Secretary Chase had been abandoned earlier in the year. Meeting in Cleveland in late May, approximately four hundred delegates chose the general on a third-party ticket and promised a quick end to both the war and slavery, as well as the unconstitutional powers seized by Lincoln in waging war.[47] The movement had little support beyond fringe elements in scattered parts of the North. The only prominent northerners to join in support were Wendell Phillips and Elizabeth Cady Stanton, while most Republicans rallied without enthusiasm behind Lincoln's renomination in Baltimore nine days later. Jessie did not record her immediate reaction, while John readily accepted the nomination because the Lincoln war effort showed "the abuses of a military dictation without its unity of action and vigor of execution."[48] But it was clear to all that Jessie wholeheartedly endorsed the movement as a means of completing the destruction of slavery and vindicating her husband's honor against the perfidy of the administration.

Outwardly, the Lincoln campaign showed little concern over the Frémont challenge, but as war news remained bad through July and early August, it worried that Frémont would further aid the challenge of the Democrats under George McClellan by siphoning off potential Republican votes. Attacks on her husband's candidacy from Garrison and Greeley and other prominent Republicans enraged Jessie, and she insisted to Whittier that John would withdraw only if Lincoln were dropped from the Republican ticket. Claiming that the Richmond government sought the president's reelection "as their most speedy and easy means of independence," she concluded that "someone else must be put in his place. It must be someone firm against slavery." Only for such a candidate would John withdraw "and give his most active support."[49] Battlefield events intervened, however, and quickly ended any speculation of a Lincoln withdrawal, and with the fall of Atlanta in early

47. The Frémont movement is described in Bartlett, *Frémont*, 95–104.

48. *New York Tribune*, June 6, 1864; Bartlett, *Frémont*, 104; Nevins, *Frémont*, 2:514.

49. Julian, Journal, in Clarke, ed., "George W. Julian's Journal: The Assassination of Lincoln," 330; Jessie Benton Frémont to Whittier, August 22, 1864, in Herr and Spence, eds., *Letters*, 382–3.

September there only remained the task of negotiating the terms of Frémont's withdrawal. Whittier was instrumental in convincing Jessie that "there is a time to act and a time to stand aside." John's withdrawal was followed by Lincoln's dismissal of their key antagonist, Montgomery Blair, from the cabinet, although the Frémonts never admitted to being a part of such a quid pro quo. In bowing out of the race, John was highly critical of Lincoln but urged his election as preferable to McClellan's. Jessie later bitterly recalled how Lincoln's "cruel death silenced much truth" about the president's actual role, as "he was made to appear incapable of error." In contrast, Republicans had abandoned her husband: "The General was shamefully betrayed by pretended radical and anti Lincoln men who deserted him in time of greatest need, after encouraging him to stand in the breach."[50] Jessie's anger, however, could not obscure the fact that she and her husband had been important elements in the inexorable drive toward emancipation. Their dedicated insistence that the war destroy slavery as well as preserve the Union had added a strong and influential voice in persuading the president.

The remaining decades of their lives fall outside of an account of antislavery politics. Initially, Jessie remained in relative seclusion at an elaborate estate on the Hudson near Tarytown, while John's financial undertakings mostly resulted in disaster and brought eventual financial ruin for the couple. Neither played a role in the politics of Reconstruction or in the drive for political and economic rights for the former slaves, although John served briefly and unsuccessfully as territorial governor of Arizona from 1878 to 1881. No longer in positions of influence, they withdrew to their personal concerns much as they had between 1857 and 1860. Jessie refused participation in the women's suffrage movement. As their financial plight deepened after the panic of the 1870s, she turned to writing and especially to John's memoirs, which she hoped would reestablish their financial stability and restore his flagging reputation; in neither was she successful.[51] Following John's death in a New York boardinghouse in 1890, Congress granted Jessie a small widow's pension, and with further aid from friends, she continued her work on his memoirs in Los Angeles. Her death at seventy-eight in 1902

50. Jessie Benton Frémont to Samuel T. Pickard, May 28, 1893, in Herr and Spence, eds., *Letters*, 448–50; Julian, Journal, in Clarke, ed., "George W. Julian's Journal: The Assassination of Lincoln," 330. See Tap, *Over Lincoln's Shoulder*, 219–20.

51. For his memoirs (which Jessie wrote), see John C. Frémont, *Memoirs of My Life* (Chicago: Belford, Clarke, and Co.), 1887. For an account of John's remaining years from the end of the Civil War until his death, see Chaffin, *Pathfinder*, 479–87, 495–7.

ended a more than thirty-five year period of relative obscurity. Yet for Jessie Benton Frémont, the quarter century between 1840 and 1865 had been a time of exciting, personal struggle and a genuine reform crusade. She had entered antislavery politics with hesitation and some reluctance at first, only to embrace abolitionism with abandon during the war. Slow to become a part of the political antislavery movement, she never considered joining the early third-party drives. Only with her husband a candidate for president in 1856 did she assume a role. But it was a role unmatched by any American woman before her and none in the remaining decades of the century. With emancipation achieved and her husband relegated to a secondary role, however, she chose to remain aloof from the continuing issues that freedom had brought. Shortly after John's death, she thanked Whittier for sending her his latest poem, for his "warming, softening influence," and for his support as a co-worker in the political struggle against slavery.[52]

52. Jessie Benton Frémont to Whittier, February 8, 1891, in Herr and Spence, eds., *Letters,* 540–1.

TWELVE

CRUSADERS IN ANTISLAVERY POLITICS

A Shared Commitment

THE TIMING OF a decision to join the political antislavery movement is the yardstick used in determining the sequence of the individuals in this study. Also included are the achievements of each, the duration of their involvement, and the risks they took in becoming a part of the movement. The latter is a subjective question, but, combined with when they entered and how long they were a part of antislavery politics (and their role in it), the question helps us assess where each one fits in the spectrum of leadership. Together, these factors are a more reliable standard than the more elusive issue of degree of commitment. How fully or to what degree an individual supported the political attack on slavery is a more subjective question and raises problems not easily resolved. At the same time, placing them in the antislavery spectrum according to the date of entry is not meant as a value judgment. Those who helped form the Liberty party in 1840, such as Alvan Stewart and John Greenleaf Whittier, may not have been any more committed than those who waited for the Republican party to form, such as Benjamin Wade and Jessie Benton Frémont. For them, a commitment to halting the spread of slavery and removing federal government support of the institution through the two-party system was as meaningful and difficult a decision and involved as many personal risks as seeking its total abolition through a third party.

Those who sought equality for African Americans through the right to vote or to join Union armies along with emancipation were less tied to the nineteenth-century racial stereotypes but perhaps no more dedicated than those who were unable to rise above the views of most of their fellow white

Americans. As a black man, Charles Langston devoted full attention to racial equality, while all of the others except one agreed with him but saw the issue as less pressing than emancipation. David Wilmot alone appeared unconcerned with the rights of blacks, instead focusing on the interests of his white constituents. Nonetheless, all eleven individuals studied represent a remarkable willingness to challenge the status quo and to seek a political end to slavery.

All of those studied shared certain common traits and characteristics even as they differed significantly. In addition to a general belief in the political process, specific issues united them, such as their common revulsion at the enactment by Congress of the Fugitive Slave Act of 1850 and Abraham Lincoln's revoking of John C. Frémont's order to free the slaves in his Missouri command in 1861. No act galvanized and united those opposed to slavery more than the Fugitive Slave Act, which denied traditional legal rights to those accused and obligated northerners to assist in the return of alleged runaways. It was a defining moment and no issue could have been better calculated to create a common drive against slavery and its defenders, whether Henry Clay, Daniel Webster, or someone more extreme. Only slightly less alarming was the president's apparent effort to slow the process of emancipation during the war. Whatever the roadblock, all were united in their overall feeling of hostility to the Slave Power, which united slaveholders with northern allies in defense of what the reformers believed to be an immoral institution.

Many faced a personal trial by fire in the hostility of a northern anti-abolitionist mob. Having taken a bold defense of the rights of fugitives or their own right to publish or organize, Stewart, Whittier, Langston, Sherman Booth, Jane Swisshelm, and Owen Lovejoy knew the fury of angry rioters bent on denying equal rights. Those who did not directly face this danger, including George Julian, Wilmot, the Wade brothers, and Frémont, were no less concerned over civil liberties or the plight of escaping slaves.

Some came to their antislavery concern as a result of a Christian calling or theology, often from an evangelical Protestant background which urged its members into a concern for those in bondage. Stewart, Whittier, Langston, Lovejoy, Julian, and Swisshelm shared this background. Others had a more secular, humanitarian zeal and devotion to resist slavery. Booth, the Wades, Wilmot, and Frémont appeared much more affected by a broader, secular appeal.

The issue of slavery's constitutionality found varied responses. Alvan Stewart believed that the Constitution was an antislavery document in part, he said, because slaves were protected under the due process clause of the Fifth Amendment. Whittier and Swisshelm agreed on slavery's unconstitutionality but never developed their arguments systematically. All took issue with the Garrisonian stance, endorsed by slavery's apologists, that the fundamental law was a proslavery document which precluded any governmental challenge. And, while many were unwilling to use the Constitution to attack slavery, all could agree that it did not guarantee slavery's right to expand, its existence in the nation's capital, or the obligation of federal officials to assist in the return of fugitives. All agreed that the First Amendment protected their right to speak, write, organize, and petition their government over slavery. While Stewart, Whittier, and Swisshelm would go further, all could agree that the federal government must contain slavery and divorce itself from any obligation to protect the South's peculiar institution.

The eleven came from a wide variety of positions and continued to vary greatly in their reactions and roles as the war ended. For the most part, those who initially joined the Liberty party in 1840 or shortly thereafter remained somewhat marginalized as the Republican party formulated its Reconstruction policies. Conversely, those who waited for the formation of the Free Soil and Republican parties occupied positions of greater influence as the war ended. The three who joined the movement earliest, Alvan Stewart, John Greenleaf Whittier, and Charles Langston, took positions which left them out of the mainstream of Republican thinking and policy-making during Reconstruction. Stewart, who died in 1849, had already broken with his Liberty colleagues and would most certainly have been unable to support Republican positions before, during, or after the war. Whittier, who lived into the 1890s, had withdrawn from an active Republican role by the late 1850s, disturbed by the escalation in sectional violence and the threat of civil war. He found the poetry of his New England past and childhood a safe haven from the turmoil of politics, in which he had never been fully comfortable. Langston moved from Ohio to Kansas during the war, and there remained active in seeking suffrage and jury rights for African Americans. He also sought educational opportunities for Kansas blacks even as he worked as a grocer and farmer. Kansas Republicans denied him the political equality he sought for himself and others of his race, and he eventually left the party in frustration.

Similarly, those who came to antislavery politics slightly later, Owen Lovejoy, Edward Wade, Sherman Booth, and Jane Swisshelm, enjoyed mixed success as Republican leaders in later years. Lovejoy died near the end of the war, and Wade the year after it ended; thus we are forced to speculate on what role they might have played had they lived longer. Lovejoy, a critic of President Lincoln, was perhaps closest to Benjamin Wade and George Julian in philosophy and temperament, and most likely would have agreed with them in insisting on full equality for the freed population, although he preferred punishing individual Confederate leaders rather than the seceded states in general. Edward Wade withdrew from active politics in 1861 due to poor health, but probably would have been in accord with brother Benjamin had he still been in politics. Sherman Booth is more problematic. Struggling for an identity until the fugitive question thrust him into the spotlight in 1854, personal scandal took away whatever influence he might have retained as a Wisconsin Republican during and after the war. Although he lived into the early twentieth century, few remembered him after the war. Jane Swisshelm's career took a surprising twist during the Civil War, as she became a central part of the Minnesota drive to punish the Lakota for attacking white settlers, even urging the president to pardon no Indian convicted of complicity in the violence. While retaining her humanitarian concern for the freed population in the early months of Reconstruction, she returned to her Pennsylvania roots and lived her remaining years in relative obscurity. While she remained active, however, few exceeded her commitment to the causes she pursued.

The final group of four, George Julian, David Wilmot, Benjamin Wade, and Jessie Frémont, came to antislavery politics later in the period and were more central to Republican ideology and policy-making during Reconstruction years. To one degree or another, each had enjoyed political influence in either the Democratic or Whig party before bolting. At the same time variations in their lives make a common assessment impossible. Julian, an Indiana Whig before becoming a prominent Free Soil congressman, never hesitated in switching parties and, after the war, left the Republicans to become first a Liberal Republican and finally a Democrat. Yet as a member of the Committee on the Conduct of the War, he was exceeded in his dedication to Radical causes only by Wade. Wilmot, a Pennsylvania Democrat before joining the Free Soil movement, enjoyed a brief Senate career during the war and witnessed the enactment of his Proviso into law. Appointed a Pennsylvania judge, he had minor influence in Republican circles after the war. Most significant, longtime Ohio Whig Benjamin Wade came within one Senate vote of becoming president in 1868. At the same time, his insistence on black suffrage led to his being denied reelection to the Senate in 1869, cutting short his role in national politics. Jessie Frémont, the last of this group to enter antislavery politics, did so in 1856 with the nomination of her husband for president after a background in her father's Democratic party. Deeply committed to both John's career and to emancipation, she played a central role until her husband's military and political efforts ended during the war. Denied a career of her own by her gender, she nonetheless had a significant impact through her husband. Whether remaining active or not, all of these political abolitionists had enjoyed a degree of influence that few would have predicted for them in 1840.

Jane Swisshelm's insensitivity to the rights of the Minnesota Lakota points out an inconsistency on human rights that is sometimes evident among abolitionists in general and political antislavery leaders in particular. She also attacked the Roman Catholic Church of Pittsburgh for its alleged ties with slavery and its desire for public monies to help support parochial schools. Owen Lovejoy's brother Elijah was guilty of intense anti-Catholicism even as he attacked slavery, a bias which Owen shared, although far less blatantly. Most of those in this study revealed little affinity for the Know-Nothing movement of the 1850s in its anti-Irish, anti-Catholic leanings, and many campaigned actively against it. But if they did not reflect the religious and ethnic biases of many of their fellow Protestant Americans, they were at times slow to move beyond their racial feelings to champion equal rights for African Americans. David Wilmot never did rise above his concern for his white constituents. Even the most radical Republicans, such as George Julian and Benjamin Wade, accepted civil rights with some reservations. All put the attack on slavery on a higher plain than women's rights or at least believed the issues should be kept separate, realizing that seeking women's suffrage could detract from the immediate goal of the slave's emancipation. Neither Jane Swisshelm nor Jessie Frémont was an active women's rights advocate, although they like some of their male counterparts believed it a worthy goal. So too were some, on occasion, willing to sacrifice antislavery principle to forward more immediate goals. All of the Liberty people except Stewart temporarily backed away from their desire for immediate abolition to accept the Free Soil plank of preventing the expansion of slavery. They thus all endorsed Joshua Leavitt's belief that as the abolitionist party was absorbed into a movement which argued only for containing slavery, "The Liberty party is not dead, but translated." The eleven in this study were therefore products of their times even as they were in advance of most on the issues of human rights.

What most united the eleven was their acceptance of the political process as the most desirable and effective way to bring change and the eventual abolition of slavery. They might have disagreed on what other reforms were desirable and how politicians should attack slavery, but they all agreed that the

Garrisonian approach of avoiding politics had been counterproductive. In 1840, only a small minority of abolitionists was willing to look to third-party politics as a solution to Slave Power dominance. As the 1840s evolved, with the annexation of Texas and a war against Mexico which they feared might add territories for slavery's expansion, a growing number reached the conclusion that the political process held out the greatest prospect to block slaveholders and their northern allies. As the abolitionist Liberty party was swallowed up by the containment-oriented Free Soilers, more northerners broke with Democrats and Whigs to voice their political resistance to slavery. Finally, with the enactment of the Compromise measures of 1850 and the Kansas-Nebraska Act of 1854, the demise of the Whigs followed and the Republicans, committed to halting the spread of slavery, emerged as a part of the two-party system. When Republicans won the presidency in 1860, the achievement of the goal of the political antislavery movement appeared imminent.

There are clearly limitations and potential pitfalls in a collective biographical approach. Can the eleven in this study be considered representative of the many who came to advocate a political attack on slavery? Those studied were not usually the most prominent and represented a wide variety of approaches. They did not usually agree with each other on specific tactics any more than those in the larger abolition movement did. Yet as the attack on slavery became more political in the 1840s and 1850s, these eleven men and women represent a remarkable degree of consensus and they emerge as representative of the larger group of adherents. They came from a variety of backgrounds and arrived at a decision to join antislavery politics at different times, and their accomplishments in achieving antislavery goals varied. They took different kinds of risks in advocating emancipation. They were part of a society which preferred the status quo, but, together, they were crusaders in antislavery politics who came to represent the wave of the future as the nation moved toward freedom for those enslaved and at least a measure of equality. As such, they collectively represented the future of American society.

The attack on slavery through the political process evolved gradually from tiny beginnings in 1840 to culmination in 1865. Reformers attempted a variety of approaches until bloody civil war made their common goal a reality. Whether helping to found the process in the Liberty party or joining only when the Republicans formed, those who led the nation to emancipation united in a belief that freeing the slaves could only be achieved through the political process. In this shared commitment, they showed no taint of compromise.

BIBLIOGRAPHY

GENERAL

American National Biography. Edited by John A. Garraty and Mark Carnes. 24 vols. New York: Oxford Univ. Press, 1999.

Blue, Frederick J. *The Free Soilers: Third-Party Politics, 1848–54.* Urbana: Univ. of Illinois Press, 1973.

———. *Salmon P. Chase: A Life in Politics.* Kent, Ohio: Kent State Univ. Press, 1987.

Davis, Hugh. *Joshua Leavitt, Evangelical Abolitionist.* Baton Rouge: Louisiana State Univ. Press, 1990.

Dumond, Dwight, ed. *Letters of James Gillespie Birney, 1831–1857.* 2 vols. 1938. Reprint, Gloucester, Mass: Peter Smith, 1966.

Filler, Louis. *The Crusade Against Slavery, 1830–1860.* New York: Harper and Row, 1960.

Gara, Larry. "Slavery and the Slave Power: A Crucial Distinction." *Civil War History* 15 (March 1969): 5–18.

Hamilton, Holman. *Prologue to Conflict: The Crisis and Compromise of 1850.* Lexington: Univ. of Kentucky Press, 1964.

Harrold, Stanley. *Gamaliel Bailey and Antislavery Union.* Kent, Ohio: Kent State Univ. Press, 1986.

Jeffrey, Julie Roy. *The Great Silent Army of Abolitionism: Ordinary Women in the Antislavery Movement.* Chapel Hill: Univ. of North Carolina Press, 1998.

Johnson, Donald Bruce, and Kirk H. Porter, eds. *National Party Platforms, 1840–1972.* 5th ed. Urbana: Univ. of Illinois Press, 1973.

Johnson, Reinhard O. "The Liberty Party in Massachusetts, 1840–1848: Antislavery Third Party Politics in the Bay State." *Civil War History* 28 (September 1982): 237–65.

Kraditor, Aileen. *Means and Ends in American Abolitionism; Garrison and His Critics on Strategy and Tactics, 1834–1850.* New York: Pantheon, 1969.

Kraut, Alan M., ed. *Crusaders and Compromisers: Essays on the Relationship of the Antislavery Struggle to the Antebellum Party System.* Westport, Conn.: Greenwood, 1983.

Liberator (Boston), 1831–1860.

National Era (Washington), 1847–1860.

Newman, Richard S. *The Transformation of American Abolitionism: Fighting Slavery in the Early Republic.* Chapel Hill: Univ. of North Carolina Press, 2002.

New York Times, 1851–1865.

New York Tribune, 1841–1865.

Pease, Jane, and William Pease. *Bound With Them in Chains: A Biographical History of the Antislavery Movement.* Westport, Conn.: Greenwood, 1962.

The Philanthropist (Cincinnati), 1839, 1843.

Richards, Leonard L. *The Slave Power: The Free North and Southern Domination, 1780–1860.* Baton Rouge: Louisiana State Univ. Press, 2000.

Sewell, Richard H. *Ballots for Freedom: Antislavery Politics in the United States, 1837–1860.* New York: Oxford Univ. Press, 1976.

Smith, Theodore C. *The Liberty and Free Soil Parties in the Northwest.* Cambridge, Mass.: Harvard Univ. Press, 1897.

Stauffer, John. *The Black Hearts of Men: Radical Abolitionists and the Transformation of Race.* Cambridge, Mass.: Harvard Univ. Press, 2001.

Volpe, Vernon. *Forlorn Hope of Freedom: The Liberty Party in the Old Northwest, 1838–1848.* Kent, Ohio: Kent State Univ. Press, 1990.

ALVAN STEWART

Beardsley, Levi. *Reminiscences; Personal and Other Incidents; Early Settlement of Otsego County, etc.* New York: C. Vinten, 1852.

Douglass, Frederick. *The Life and Times of Frederick Douglass.* 1892. Rev. ed., New York: Collier Books, 1962.

Ernst, Daniel. "Legal Positivism, Abolitionist Litigation, and the New Jersey Slave Case of 1845." *Law and History Review* 4 (1986): 339–65.

Friedman, Lawrence. "The Gerrit Smith Circle: Abolitionism in the Burned-Over District." *Civil War History* 26 (March 1980): 18–38.

Friend of Man (Utica, N.Y.), 1836–1842.

Harlow, Ralph. *Gerrit Smith: Philanthropist and Reformer.* New York: Holt, 1939.

Lovejoy, Joseph C., and Owen Lovejoy. *Memoir of the Rev. Elijah P. Lovejoy,* with an introduction by John Quincy Adams. New York: J. S. Taylor, 1838. 362–6.

Marsh, Luther R., ed. *Writings and Speeches of Alvan Stewart on Slavery.* New York: A. B. Burdick, 1860.

Richards, Leonard. *Gentlemen of Property and Standing: Anti-Abolition Mobs in Jacksonian America.* New York: Oxford Univ. Press, 1970.

Sernett, Milton C. *Abolition's Axe: Beriah Green, Oneida Institute and the Black Freedom Struggle*. Syracuse, N.Y.: Syracuse Univ. Press, 1986.

———. "Alvan Stewart." *American National Biography*. Edited by John Garraty and Mark Carnes. 20:742–3. New York: Oxford Univ. Press, 1999.

———. *North Star Country: Upstate New York and the Crusade for African American Freedom*. Syracuse, N.Y.: Syracuse Univ. Press, 2002.

Sorin, Gerald. *The New York Abolitionists: A Case Study of Political Radicalism*. Westport, Conn.: Greenwood, 1971.

Spooner, Lysander. *The Unconstitutionality of Slavery*. Boston: B. Marsh, 1860.

Stewart, Alvan. Correspondence. New York State Historical Association Library, Cooperstown, N.Y.

———. *A Legal Argument Before the Supreme Court of the State of New Jersey at the May Term, 1845 at Trenton for the Deliverance of Four Thousand Persons from Bondage*. New York: Finch and Weed, 1845.

———. Miscellaneous Papers, New-York Historical Society, New York City.

Strong, Douglas M. *Perfectionist Politics: Abolitionism and the Religious Tensions of American Democracy*. Syracuse, N.Y.: Syracuse Univ. Press, 1999.

Ten Broek, Jacobus. *Equal Justice Under the Law*. New York: Collier, 1965.

Utica Observer Dispatch (Utica, N.Y.), 1929.

Wiecek, William M. *The Sources of Antislavery Constitutionalism in America, 1760–1848*. Ithaca, N.Y.: Cornell Univ. Press, 1977.

Wright, Elizur. Papers. Boston Public Library.

JOHN GREENLEAF WHITTIER

Atlantic Monthly, 1862–1863.

Bennett, Whitman. *Whittier, Bard of Freedom*. 1941. Reprint, Port Washington, N.Y.: Kennikat, 1972.

Boston Evening Transcript, 1861.

Cluff, Randall. "John Greenleaf Whittier." In *American National Biography*, edited by John Garraty and Mark Carnes. 23:320–2. New York: Oxford Univ. Press, 1999.

Haverhill (Mass.) Gazette, 1833–1836.

Holmes, J. Welfred. "Whittier and Sumner: A Political Friendship." *New England Quarterly* 30 (1957): 58–72.

Jarvis, Charles A. "Admission to Abolition: The Case of John Greenleaf Whittier." *Journal of the Early Republic* 4 (summer 1984): 161–76.

Johnson, Reinhard O. "The Liberty Party in Massachusetts, 1840–1848: Antislavery Third Party Politics in the Bay State." *Civil War History* 28 (1982): 237–65.

Leary, Lewis. *John Greenleaf Whittier*. New York: Twayne, 1961.

Middlesex Standard (Lowell, Mass.), 1844.

Mordell, Albert. *Quaker Militant: John Greenleaf Whittier*. 1933. Reprint, Port Washington, N.Y.: Kennikat, 1969.

National Era (Washington), 1847–1860.

Pennsylvania Freeman (Philadelphia), 1838–1839.

Pickard, John B. *John Greenleaf Whittier: An Introduction and Interpretation*. New York: Holt, Rinehart and Winston, 1961.

————, ed. *The Letters of John Greenleaf Whittier*. 3 vols. Cambridge, Mass.: Harvard Univ. Press, 1975.

Pollard, John A. *John Greenleaf Whittier: Friend of Man*. Boston: Houghton Mifflin, 1949.

Summer, Charles. Papers. Harvard University.

Taylor, Anne-Marie. *Young Charles Sumner and the Legacy of the American Enlightenment, 1811–1851*. Amherst: Univ. of Massachusetts Press, 2001.

Wagenknecht, Edward. *John Greenleaf Whittier: A Portrait of Paradox*. New York: Oxford Univ. Press, 1967.

Whittier, John Greenleaf. *Anti-Slavery Poems: Songs of Labor and Reform*. Boston: Houghton Mifflin, 1892.

————. "Autobiography." May 1882. Haverhill, Mass: The Trustees of the John Greenleaf Whittier Homestead, 1957.

————. *The Writings of John Greenleaf Whittier*, Riverside Edition. Boston: Houghton, Mifflin, 1900.

Woodwell, Roland. *John Greenleaf Whittier: A Biography*. Haverhill, Mass.: The Trustees of the John Greenleaf Whittier Homestead, 1985.

CHARLES HENRY LANGSTON

Anti-Slavery Bugle (Salem, Ohio), 1847–1860.

Baumann, Roland M. "The 1858 Oberlin-Wellington Rescue: A Reappraisal." Oberlin, Ohio: Oberlin College, 2003.

Bell, Howard H. "National Negro Conventions of the Middle 1840's: Moral Suasion vs. Political Action." *Journal of Negro History* 42 (October 1957): 247–60.

Berwanger, Eugene H. "Hardin and Langston: Western Black Spokesmen of the Reconstruction Era." *Journal of Negro History* 64 (1979): 101–15.

Brandt, Nat. *The Town That Started the Civil War*. Syracuse, N.Y.: Syracuse Univ. Press, 1990.

Chase, Salmon P. Papers. Library of Congress.

Cheek, William. "John Mercer Langston, Black Protest Leader and Abolitionist." *Civil War History* 16 (June 1970): 101–20.

Cheek, William, and Aimee Lee Cheek. *John Mercer Langston and the Fight for Black Freedom, 1829–1865*. Urbana: Univ. of Illinois Press, 1989.

Cleveland Morning Leader, 1858–1859.

Cleveland Plain Dealer, 1858–1859.

Cleveland True Democrat, 1850.

Dann, Martin E., ed. *The Black Press, 1827–1890: The Quest for National Identity*. New York: Capricorn, 1971.

Foner, Philip S., and George E. Walker, eds. *Proceedings of the Black State Conventions, 1840–1865.* 3 vols. Philadelphia: Temple Univ. Press, 1979.

Gerber, David A. *Black Ohio and the Color Line, 1860–1915.* Urbana: Univ. of Illinois Press, 1976.

Hickok, Charles Thomas. *The Negro in Ohio, 1802–1870.* 1896. Reprint, New York: AMS Press, 1975.

Hughes, Langston. *The Big Sea.* New York: Hill and Wang, 1940.

Langston, John Mercer. *From the Virginia Plantation to the National Capitol.* Hartford: American Publishing Co., 1894. Reprint, Johnson Reprint Corp., 1968.

———. "The Oberlin-Wellington Rescue." *The Anglo-African Magazine* 1 (July 1859): 209–16.

Lubet, Steven. "Slavery on Trial: The Case of the Oberlin Rescue." *Alabama Law Review* 54 (spring 2003): 785–829.

McCormick, Robert, and Frederick J. Blue. "Norton S. Townshend: A Reformer for All Seasons." In *The Pursuit of Public Power: Political Culture in Ohio, 1787–1861,* edited by Jeffrey Brown and Andrew Cayton, 144–54. Kent, Ohio: Kent State Univ. Press, 1994.

Middleton, Steven. *The Black Laws in the Old Northwest: A Documentary History.* Westport, Conn.: Greenwood Press, 1993.

North Star (Rochester, N.Y.), 1848–1849.

Ohio State Journal (Columbus), 1850.

Proceedings of the Colored National Convention, Held in Rochester, July 6th, 7th, and 8th, 1853. Rochester, 1853.

Proceedings of the State Convention . . . Columbus, Jan., 1857. Columbus, 1857.

Quillin, Frank U. *The Color Line in Ohio.* Ann Arbor: G. Wahr, 1913.

Report of the Proceedings of the Colored National Convention . . . Cleveland, Sept. 1848. Rochester, 1848.

Russell, Thaddeus. "Charles Henry Langston." In *American National Biography,* edited by John Garraty and Mark Carnes, 13:163–4. New York: Oxford Univ. Press, 1999.

Sheridan, Richard B. "Charles Henry Langston and the African American Struggle in Kansas." *Kansas History* 22 (winter 1999–2000): 268–83.

Shipherd, Jacob R. *History of the Oberlin-Wellington Rescue.* Boston, 1859. Reprint, New York: Da Capo Press, 1972.

Smith, J. V., ed. *Report of the Debates and Proceedings of the Convention for the Revision of the Constitution of the State of Ohio.* 2 vols. Columbus: S. Medary, 1851.

OWEN LOVEJOY

Basler, Roy P., ed. *The Collected Works of Abraham Lincoln,* vol. 7. New Brunswick: Rutgers Univ. Press, 1953.

Blue, Frederick J. "Owen Lovejoy." In *American National Biography,* edited by John Garraty and Mark Carnes, 14:6–7. New York: Oxford Univ. Press, 1999.

Bohman, George. "Owen Lovejoy on 'The Barbarism of Slavery,' April 6, 1860." *Anti-Slavery and Disunion, 1858–1861: Studies in the Rhetoric of Compromise and Conflict*. New York: Harper and Row, 1963. 114–32.

Boston Courier, 1860.

Bradsby, H. C., ed. *History of Bureau County, Illinois*. Chicago: World Publishing Co., 1885.

Bureau County Republican (Princeton, Ill.), 1858–1864.

Chicago Tribune, 1874.

Congressional Globe, 35th–38th Cong., 1857–1865.

Dillon, Merton. *Elijah P. Lovejoy, Abolitionist Editor*. Urbana: Univ. of Illinois Press, 1961.

Free West (Chicago), 1855–1858.

Genius of Liberty (Lowell, Ill.), 1841.

Haberkorn, Ruth. "Owen Lovejoy in Princeton, Illinois." *Journal of the Illinois State Historical Society* 36 (1943): 284–315.

Julian, George W. "The First Republican National Convention." *American Historical Review* 4 (January 1899): 314–6.

Lincoln, Abraham. Papers. Library of Congress.

Lovejoy, Joseph C., and Owen Lovejoy. *Memoir of the Rev. Elijah P. Lovejoy*, with an introduction by John Quincy Adams. New York: James S. Taylor, 1838. Reprint, New York: Arno Press, 1969.

Lovejoy, Owen. Papers. Bureau County Historical Society (Illinois).

———. Papers. William Clements Library, Univ. of Michigan.

Magdol, Edward. *Owen Lovejoy: Abolitionist in Congress*. New Brunswick: Rutgers Univ. Press, 1967.

———. "Owen Lovejoy's Role in the Campaign of 1858." *Journal of the Illinois State Historical Society* 51 (1958): 403–16.

Peterson, Svend. *A Statistical History of the American Presidential Elections*. New York: Frederick Ungar, 1963.

Pierson, Michael D. *Free Hearts and Free Homes: Gender and American Antislavery Politics*. Chapel Hill and London: Univ. of North Carolina Press, 2003.

Stampp, Kenneth M. *And the War Came: The North and the Secession Crisis, 1860–61*. Baton Rouge: Louisiana State Univ. Press, 1950.

Vorenberg, Michael. *Final Freedom: The Civil War, the Abolition of Slavery and the Thirteenth Amendment*. Cambridge, U.K.: Cambridge Univ. Press, 2001.

Wesley, Charles H. "The Participation of Negroes in Anti-Slavery Political Parties." *Journal of Negro History* 29 (1944): 32–72.

Western Citizen (Chicago), 1843–1854.

SHERMAN M. BOOTH

Agnew, Dwight, et al., eds. *Dictionary of Wisconsin Biography*. Madison: State Historical Society of Wisconsin, 1960.

American Freeman (Milwaukee), 1848.

Booth, Sherman. Papers. State Historical Society of Wisconsin.

———. "Reminiscences of Early Struggles in Wisconsin Politics and Press." *Wisconsin Press Association* 44 (1897): 105–19.

Butler, Diane S. "The Public Life and Private Affairs of Sherman M. Booth." *Wisconsin Magazine of History* 82 (spring 1999): 166–97.

Current, Richard N. *The Civil War Era, 1848–1873.* Vol. 2 of *The History of Wisconsin.* Madison: State Historical Society of Wisconsin, 1976.

Jones, Howard. *Mutiny on the* Amistad: *The Saga of a Slave Revolt and Its Impact on American Abolition Law and Diplomacy.* New York: Oxford Univ. Press, 1987.

McManus, Michael J. "Freedom and Liberty First and the Union Afterwards: States Rights and the Wisconsin Republican Party, 1854–1861." In *Union and Emancipation: Essays on Politics and Race in the Civil War Era,* edited by David W. Blight and Brooks D. Simpson, 29–56. Kent, Ohio: Kent State Univ. Press, 1997.

———. *Political Abolitionism in Wisconsin, 1840–1861.* Kent, Ohio: Kent State Univ. Press, 1998.

———. "Wisconsin Republicans and Negro Suffrage: Attitudes and Behavior, 1857." *Civil War History* 25 (1979): 36–54.

Milwaukee Sentinel, 1894, 1897.

Ranney, Joseph A. " 'Suffering the Agonies of Their Righteousness': The Rise and Fall of the States Rights Movement in Wisconsin, 1854–1861." *Wisconsin Magazine of History* 75 (winter 1991–1992): 83–116.

Swift, David E. *Black Prophets of Justice: Activist Clergy Before the Civil War.* Baton Rouge: Louisiana State Univ. Press, 1989.

Thomson, Alexander M. *A Political History of Wisconsin.* Milwaukee: C. N. Casper Co., 1902.

Trefousse, Hans L. *Carl Schurz: A Biography.* Knoxville: Univ. of Tennessee Press, 1982.

Wisconsin Free Democrat (Milwaukee), 1848–1860.

Wisconsin Freeman (Milwaukee), 1848.

Wisconsin Supreme Court. *Wisconsin Reports: Reports of the Cases Argued and Determined in the Supreme Court of the State of Wisconsin, 1854 and 1855.* N.p.: n.d.

Yale, Class of 1841. *Semi-Centennial of the Historical and Biographical Record of the Class of 1841 in Yale University.* New Haven, Conn.: Tuttle, Morehouse and Taylor, 1892. 46–53.

JANE SWISSHELM

Dyer, Thomas G. *Secret Yankees: The Union Circle in Confederate Atlanta.* Baltimore: Johns Hopkins Univ. Press, 1999.

Folwell, William W. *A History of Minnesota,* vol. 2. St. Paul: Minnesota Historical Society, 1924.

Hoffert, Sylvia. "Gender and Vigilantism on the Minnesota Frontier: Jane Grey Swisshelm and the U.S.-Dakota Conflict of 1862." *Western Historical Quarterly* 29 (1998): 343–62.

―――. "Jane Grey Swisshelm and the Negotiation of Gender Roles on the Minnesota Frontier." *Frontiers* 18 (1997): 17–39.

―――. "Theoretical Issues: Jane Grey Swisshelm, Elizabeth Keckley, and the Significance of Race Consciousness in American Women's Lives." *Journal of Women's History* 13 (2001): 8–32.

Larsen, Arthur J., ed. *Crusader and Feminist: Letters of Jane Grey Swissholm, 1858–1865.* St. Paul: Minnesota Historical Society, 1934.

Pierson, Michael D. "Between Antislavery and Abolition: The Politics and Rhetoric of Jane Grey Swisshelm." *Pennsylvania History* 60 (July 1993): 305–21.

―――. *Free Hearts and Free Homes: Gender and American Antislavery Politics.* Chapel Hill and London: Univ. of North Carolina Press, 2003.

―――. "Gender and Party Ideologies: The Constitutional Thought of Women and Men in American Anti-Slavery Politics." *Slavery and Abolition* 19 (December 1998): 46–67.

Pittsburgh Saturday Visiter, 1848–1854.

Ritchie, Donald A. *Press Gallery: Congress and the Washington Correspondents.* Cambridge, Mass.: Harvard Univ. Press, 1991.

St. Cloud (Minn.) Democrat, 1858–1862.

St. Cloud (Minn.) Visiter, 1857–1858.

Shippee, Lester. "Jane Grey Swisshelm, Agitator." *Mississippi Valley Historical Review* 7 (December 1920): 206–27.

Sigerman, Harriet. "Jane Grey Cannon Swisshelm." In *American National Biography,* edited by John Garraty and Mark Carnes, 21:217–8. New York: Oxford Univ. Press, 1999.

Stearns, Bertha-Monica. "Reform Periodicals and Female Reformers, 1830–1860." *American Historical Review* 37 (July 1932): 678–99.

Swisshelm, Jane Grey. *Half a Century.* 1880. Reprint, New York: Sourcebook Press, 1970.

―――. *Letters to Country Girls.* New York: J. C. Riker, 1853.

Walker, Peter. *Moral Choices: Memory, Desire and Imagination in Nineteenth-Century American Abolition.* Baton Rouge: Louisiana State Univ. Press, 1978.

GEORGE WASHINGTON JULIAN

Blue, Frederick J. "George Washington Julian." In *American National Biography,* edited by John Garraty and Mark Carnes, 10:315–6. New York: Oxford Univ. Press, 1999.

Clarke, Grace Julian. *George W. Julian.* Indianapolis: Indiana Historical Commission, 1923.

———, ed. "George W. Julian's Journal: The Assassination of Lincoln." *Indiana Quarterly Magazine of History* 11 (1915): 324–37.

———, ed. "Home Letters of George W. Julian, 1850–1851." *Indiana Magazine of History* 29 (1933): 130–63.

Congressional Globe, 31st Cong., 1849–1851; 37th–41st Cong., 1861–1871.

Giddings-Julian Papers. Library of Congress

Julian, George W. "The First Republican National Convention." *American Historical Review* 4 (January 1899): 313–22.

———. *The Life of Joshua Giddings*. Chicago: A. C. McClurg, 1892.

———. *Political Recollections, 1840–1872*. Chicago: Jansen, McClurg and Co., 1884.

———. *Speeches on Political Questions*. 1872. Reprint, Westport, Conn.: Negro Univs. Press, 1970.

Riddleberger, Patrick W. *George Washington Julian, Radical Republican*. Indianapolis: Indiana Historical Bureau, 1966.

Tap, Bruce. *Over Lincoln's Shoulder: The Committee on the Conduct of the War*. Lawrence: Univ. Press of Kansas, 1998.

DAVID WILMOT

Basler, Roy P., ed. *The Collected Works of Abraham Lincoln*, vol. 2. New Brunswick: Rutgers Univ. Press, 1953.

Blue, Frederick J. "David Wilmot." In *American National Biography*, edited by John Garraty and Mark Carnes, 23:553–4. New York: Oxford Univ. Press, 1999.

Bradford Reporter (Towanda, Pa.), 1844–1863.

Congressional Globe, 29th–31st Cong., 1845–1851; 36th–37th Cong., 1859–1863.

Craft, David. *History of Bradford County, Pennsylvania*. Philadelphia: L. H. Everts, 1878.

Earle, Jonathan H. "The Undaunted Democracy: Jacksonian Antislavery and Free Soil, 1828–1848." Ph.D. diss., Princeton University, 1996.

Foner, Eric. "The Wilmot Proviso Revisited." *Journal of American History* 56 (1969): 262–79.

Gardiner, O. C. *The Great Issue; or, the Three Presidential Candidates*. New York: W. C. Bryant and Co., 1848.

Going, Charles B. *David Wilmot, Free-Soiler: A Biography of the Great Advocate of the Wilmot Proviso*. New York: D. Appleton, 1924.

Ilesevich, Robert D. *Galusha A. Grow, The People's Candidate*. Pittsburgh: Univ. of Pittsburgh Press, 1988.

Morrison, Chaplain W. *Democratic Politics and Sectionalism: The Wilmot Proviso Controversy*. Chapel Hill: Univ. of North Carolina Press, 1967.

Persinger, Clark E. "'The Bargain of 1844' as the Origin of the Wilmot Proviso." In American Historical Association, *Annual Report of the American Historical Association, 1911* (1913): 187–95.

Potter, David. *Lincoln and His Party in the Secession Crisis.* New Haven: Yale Univ. Press, 1942.

Quaife, Milo M., ed. *The Diary of James K. Polk, 1845–1849.* 4 vols. Chicago: A. C. McClurg, 1910.

Stenberg, Richard. "The Motivation of the Wilmot Proviso." *Mississippi Valley Historical Review* 19 (March 1932): 535–41.

BENJAMIN AND EDWARD WADE

Ashtabula (Ohio) Sentinel, 1836–1860.

Biographical Directory of the American Congress, 1774–1996. Comp. by James L. Harrison. Alexandria, Va.: C. Q. Staff Directories, 1997.

Chandler, Zachariah. Papers. Library of Congress.

Chase, Salmon P. Papers. Historical Society of Pennsylvania.

Congressional Globe, 32nd–40th Cong., 1851–1869.

Giddings-Julian Papers. Library of Congress.

Riddle, Albert G. *The Life of Benjamin F. Wade.* Cleveland: William W. Williams, 1886.

———. *Recollections of War Times: Reminiscences of Men and Events in Washington, 1860–1865.* New York: G. P. Putnam's Sons, 1895.

Stewart, James B. *Joshua R. Giddings and the Tactics of Radical Politics.* Cleveland: Case Western Reserve Univ. Press, 1970.

Tap, Bruce. *Over Lincoln's Shoulder: The Committee on the Conduct of the War.* Lawrence: Univ. Press of Kansas, 1998.

Trefousse, Hans L. "Benjamin Franklin Wade." In *American National Biography,* edited by John Garraty and Mark Carnes, 22:431–2. New York: Oxford Univ. Press, 1999.

———. *Benjamin Franklin Wade: Radical Republican from Ohio.* New York: Twayne, 1963.

———. "Ben Wade and the Negro." *Ohio Historical Quarterly* 68 (1959): 161–76.

Van Tassel, David, and John Grabowski, eds. *The Encyclopedia of Cleveland History.* Bloomington: Indiana Univ. Press, 1987.

Volpe, Vernon. "Benjamin Wade's Strange Defeat." *Ohio History* 97 (1988): 122–32.

Wade, Benjamin. Papers. Library of Congress.

Whittlesey, Elisha. Papers. Western Reserve Historical Society.

Williams, William W. *History of Ashtabula County, Ohio.* Philadelphia: Williams Bros., 1878.

Wilson, Henry. *History of the Rise and Fall of the Slave Power,* vol. 2. Boston: J. R. Osgood, 1877.

JESSIE BENTON FRÉMONT

Bartlett, Ruhl J. *John C. Frémont and the Republican Party.* 1930. Reprint, New York: Da Capo Press, 1970.

Bigelow, John. *Memoir of the Life and Public Services of John Charles Frémont.* New York: Derby and Jackson, 1856.

Chaffin, Tom. *Pathfinder: John Charles Frémont and the Course of American Empire.* New York: Hill and Wang, 2002.

Clapp, Margaret. *Forgotten First Citizen: John Bigelow.* 1947. Reprint, New York: Greenwood, 1968.

Frémont, Jessie Benton. "Great Events During the Life of Major General John C. Frémont, United States Army, and of Jessie Benton Frémont." Unpublished manuscript, 1891.

———. *The Story of the Guard: A Chronicle of the War.* Boston: Ticknor and Fields, 1863.

———. *A Year of American Travel.* New York: Harper and Bros., 1878.

Frémont, John C. *Memoirs of My Life.* Chicago: Belford, Clarke, and Co., 1887.

———. *Report of the Exploring Expedition to the Rocky Mountains in the Year 1842, and to Oregon and North California in the Years 1843–'44.* Washington, D.C.: Gales and Seaton, Printers, 1845.

Gerteis, Louis S. *Civil War St. Louis.* Lawrence: Univ. Press of Kansas, 2001.

Gienapp, William E. *The Origins of the Republican Party, 1852–1856.* New York: Oxford Univ. Press, 1987.

Herr, Pamela. "Jessie Benton Frémont." In *American National Biography,* edited by John Garraty and Mark Carnes, 8:458–9. New York: Oxford Univ. Press, 1999.

———. *Jessie Benton Frémont: A Biography.* New York: F. Watts, 1987.

———. "Permutations of a Marriage: John Charles and Jessie Benton Frémont's Civil War Alliance." In *The Intimate Strategies of the Civil War: Military Commanders and Their Wives,* edited by Carol K. Blaser and Lesley Gordon, 199–224. New York: Oxford Univ. Press, 2001.

Herr, Pamela, and Mary Lee Spence, eds. *The Letters of Jessie Benton Frémont.* Urbana: Univ. of Illinois Press, 1993.

Nevins, Allan. *Frémont in the Civil War.* Vol. 2 of *Frémont, Pathmarker of the West.* New York: Frederick Ungar, 1962.

Nicolay, John G., and John Hay. *Abraham Lincoln: A History,* vol. 4. New York: Century Co., 1890.

Quaife, Milo M., ed. *The Diary of James K. Polk, 1845–1849.* 4 vols. Chicago: A. C. McClurg, 1910.

"Report of the Joint Committee on the Conduct of the War." Part 3: "Department of the West." *Senate Executive Documents,* 37th Cong., 3rd sess., document 108, 6.

Rolle, Andrew. *John Charles Frémont: Character as Destiny.* Norman: Univ. of Oklahoma Press, 1991.

Tap, Bruce. *Over Lincoln's Shoulder: The Committee on the Conduct of the War.* Lawrence: Univ. Press of Kansas, 1998.

War of the Rebellion; A Compilation of the Official Records of the Union and Confederate Armies, vol. 3. Washington, D.C., 1880–1901, 1st Series.

Volpe, Vernon. "The Frémonts and Emancipation in Missouri." *The Historian* 56 (1994): 339–54.

———. "The Origins of the Frémont Expeditions: John J. Abert and the Exploration of the Trans-Mississippi West." *The Historian* 62 (2000): 244–63.

Whittier, John Greenleaf. *Anti-Slavery Poems: Songs of Labor and Reform.* Boston: Houghton Mifflin, 1892.

ILLUSTRATION CREDITS

Alvan Stewart (chapter 2, page 15): From Luther Nash, ed., *Writings and Speeches of Alvan Stewart* (New York: A. B. Burdick, 1860).

John Greenleaf Whittier (chapter 3, page 37): Engraving by A. C. Warren of A. G. Hoit's 1846 painting. Courtesy of the Trustees of the Havershill Public Library, Special Collections Department.

Charles Langston (chapter 4, page 65): Detail from the 1859 photograph "Wellington Rescuers," by J. M. Green. Oberlin College Archives, Oberlin, Ohio.

Owen Lovejoy (chapter 5, page 90): Courtesy of the Lovejoy Society.

Sherman M. Booth (chapter 6, page 117): Wisconsin Historical Society. Image number WHi-6269. Used by permission.

Jane Swisshelm (chapter 7, page 138): "Jane Grey Swisshelm in 1852." Detail of a photo by Eugene S. Hill. Minnesota Historical Society MHS Locator #por/11054/r2. Negative #82257.

George Washington Julian (chapter 8, page 161): Photograph by Indiana Historical Society, C3702. Used by permission.

David Wilmot (chapter 9, page 184): From *David Wilmot: Free Soiler,* by Charles Buxton Going (New York: D. Appleton and Company, 1924).

Benjamin Wade (chapter 10, page 213): Cincinnati Museum Center, Cincinnati Historical Society. Used by permission. No picture of Edward Wade exists.

Jessie Benton Frémont (chapter 11, page 238): Portrait by T. Buchanan Read, 1856. Courtesy of the Southwest Museum, Los Angeles. Photo Number N30665.

INDEX

Calhoun, John C., 51, 194, 202
Calhoun, Thomas, 156
Cameron, Simon, 208–9
Cannon, Jane Grey. *See* Swisshelm, Jane
  Grey
Cannon, Mary Scott, 139, 141
Cannon, Thomas, 139
Cannon, William, 139
Capital punishment, 44, 138, 142, 163, 254
Carrington, Henry B., 87
Carson, Kit, 242
Cass, Lewis, 164, 195, 196, 197, 198, 219
Catholic Church. *See* Anti-Catholicism
Chandler, Zachariah, 228, 229
Channing, William Ellery, 9, 161, 163
Chapman, Maria Weston, 48
Chase, Salmon P.: and motivation for anti-
  slavery politics, 19; in Liberty party, 30,
  34, 99, 100, 121, 122; and presidential
  election of 1864, 61, 177, 262; in Free Soil
  party, 70–71, 245; and racial equality,
  70–73, 76–78; in Congress, 72, 166, 220,
  228, 245; as governor of Ohio, 76–78,
  225, 226; and presidential election of
  1860, 77, 87, 174, 226–27; and Price
  case, 84, 226; and Booth on third-party
  politics, 123, 124; in Lincoln's cabinet,
  177, 229, 259; as Supreme Court chief
  justice, 178; and Washington Peace Conference, 209; and Kansas-Nebraska Act,
  221; and Republican party, 223; and presidential election of 1856, 247, 248; and
  Frémont's emancipation order during Civil
  War, 259
Child, Lydia Maria, 250, 251
Christian Freeman, 119, 120
Churches. *See* Religion; and specific
  churches
Cinque, Joseph, 119–20
Civil rights for blacks: and Langston, 6, 66–
  78, 83–88, 120, 267; and Swisshelm, 9,
  158; and antislavery politics generally, 14,
  265–69; and Whittier, 46, 62–63; and
  Free Soil party, 54–55, 68, 101, 102; and
  Lovejoy, 116; and Booth, 121, 130, 132;
  and Wisconsin personal liberty law, 130,

132; and Julian, 170; and Fourteenth
  Amendment, 181, 235; Benjamin Wade
  on, 231–32, 234–36, 268, 269; and Jessie
  Benton Frémont, 254. *See also* Black
  troops in Civil War; Voting rights
Civil War: and Whittier, 5, 59–64; purpose
  of, 6, 87, 91, 112, 113, 175, 263; John C.
  Frémont in, 13, 60, 113, 174, 176, 228,
  229, 239, 254–60, 266; and Quakers, 59,
  256; McClellan in, 61, 176; and Lovejoy,
  91, 112–13, 115–16, 210, 229, 256,
  258–59; and Booth, 135–36; and Swisshelm, 157–60, 259; and Julian, 158, 174–
  79, 210, 229, 258–60; and Benjamin
  Wade, 175, 176, 177, 210, 227–32, 234,
  258–59; Union defeats in, 176, 228, 232,
  255; prisoners of war in, 177–78, 179;
  and Wilmot, 204, 210–11; end of, 234;
  and Jessie Benton Frémont, 254–62. *See
  also* Black troops in Civil War; Committee
  on the Conduct of the War
Clark, William, 240
Clay, Cassius M., 157, 171
Clay, Henry: and presidential election of
  1844, 11, 29, 50–51, 99, 163, 217; and
  National Republican party, 16, 40, 41;
  on third-party antislavery politics, 24; and
  Whig party, 24, 27, 47, 50–51, 96, 162,
  163, 218; Whittier's criticism of, 44; and
  Compromise of 1850, 55, 123–24, 166–
  67, 202–3, 219, 245; personality of, 166;
  and American System, 186; and Fugitive
  Slave Act, 266
Cleveland, Grover, 183
Cleveland Morning Leader, 80, 81
Cobb, Howell, 165, 169, 200–202, 235
Codding, Ichabod, 119, 120
Coffin, John, 39
Collins, James, 96
Colonization movement for blacks, 19, 41,
  43, 72–76, 92, 231
Committee on the Conduct of the War: and
  Julian, 9, 162, 175–78, 180, 228, 259,
  260, 268; and Benjamin Wade, 11, 175,
  176, 228, 229, 231, 234, 259; creation
  and purpose of, 175–76